Comics and Videogames

This book offers the first comprehensive study of the many interfaces shaping the relationship between comics and videogames. It combines in-depth conceptual reflection with a rich selection of paradigmatic case studies from contemporary media culture.

The editors have gathered a distinguished group of international scholars working at the interstices of comics studies and game studies to explore two interrelated areas of inquiry: The first part of the book focuses on hybrid medialities and experimental aesthetics "between" comics and videogames; the second part zooms in on how comics and videogames function as transmedia expansions within an increasingly convergent and participatory media culture. The individual chapters address synergies and intersections between comics and videogames via a diverse set of case studies ranging from independent and experimental projects via popular franchises from the corporate worlds of DC and Marvel to the more playful forms of media mix prominent in Japan.

Offering an innovative intervention into a number of salient issues in current media culture, *Comics and Videogames* will be of interest to scholars and students of comics studies, game studies, popular culture studies, transmedia studies, and visual culture studies.

Andreas Rauscher is a Senior Lecturer in the Department of Media Studies at the University of Siegen, Germany. He is the author of *Das Phänomen Star Trek* [*The Star Trek Phenomenon*] (2003), *Spielerische Fiktionen: Transmediale Genrekonzepte in Videospielen* [*Ludic Fictions: Transmedial Genre Concepts in Videogames*] (2012), and *Star Wars: 100 Seiten* [*Star Wars: 100 Pages*] (2019).

Daniel Stein is Professor of North American Literary and Cultural Studies at the University of Siegen, Germany. He is the author of *Music Is My Life: Louis Armstrong, Autobiography, and American Jazz* (2012), co-editor of *From Comic Strips to Graphic Novels* (2013/[2]2015), and one of the editors of *Anglia: Journal of English Philology*.

Jan-Noël Thon is Professor of Media Studies at the Norwegian University of Science and Technology (NTNU), Guest Professor of Media Studies at the University of Cologne, Germany, and Professorial Fellow at the University for the Creative Arts, UK. He has published widely in comics studies, game studies, and media studies.

Routledge Advances in Game Studies

Fans and Videogames
Histories, Fandom, Archives
Edited by Melanie Swalwell, Helen Stuckey and Angela Ndalianis

Identity and Play in Interactive Digital Media
Ergodic Ontogeny
Sara M. Cole

Videogames, Identity and Digital Subjectivity
Rob Gallagher

Evolutionary Psychology and Digital Games
Digital Hunter-Gatherers
Edited by Johannes Breuer, Daniel Pietschmann, Benny Liebold, and Benjamin P. Lange

The Playful Undead and Video Games
Critical Analyses of Zombies and Gameplay
Edited by Stephen J. Webley and Peter Zackariasson

Hybrid spaces
Crossing Boundaries in Game Design, Players Identities and Play Spaces
Edited by Adriana de Souza e Silva and Ragan Glover-Rijkse

Forms and Functions of Endings in Narrative Digital Games
Michelle Herte

Independent Videogames
Cultures, Networks, Techniques and Politics
Edited by Paolo Ruffino

Comics and Videogames
From Hybrid Medialities to Transmedia Expansions
Edited by Andreas Rauscher, Daniel Stein, and Jan-Noël Thon

Comics and Videogames

From Hybrid Medialities to Transmedia Expansions

Edited by
Andreas Rauscher, Daniel Stein, and Jan-Noël Thon

First published 2021
by Routledge
2 Park Square, Milton Park, Abingdon, Oxon OX14 4RN

and by Routledge
52 Vanderbilt Avenue, New York, NY 10017

Routledge is an imprint of the Taylor & Francis Group, an informa business

The Open Access publication of this book was assisted by generous funding from the Volkswagen Foundation (www.volkswagenstiftung.de/en).

British Library Cataloguing-in-Publication Data
A catalogue record for this book is available from the British Library

Library of Congress Cataloging-in-Publication Data
A catalog record has been requested for this book

ISBN: 9780367474195 (hbk)
ISBN: 9781003035466 (ebk)

Typeset in Sabon
by Newgen Publishing UK

Contents

Figures

Contributors

Hans-Joachim Backe is Associate Professor at the Center for Computer Games Research of the IT University of Copenhagen, Denmark. He holds an MA degree and a PhD in Comparative Literature from Saarland University, Saarbrücken, Germany. He was chairperson of the ICLA Research Committee on Comparative Literature in the Digital Age and is a member of both the German Association for Comics Studies (ComFor) and the Comics Studies Research Group in the German Society for Media Studies (GfM). He has published extensively on self-referentiality and discourses of alterity in videogames and comics, as well as on ecocriticism, narrative theory, and media theory. Website: www.hajobacke.com/.

Joleen Blom is a lecturer at the IT University of Copenhagen, Denmark, and a lecturer at Utrecht University, The Netherlands. She holds a BA degree in Japanese Studies, an MA degree in Media and Performance Studies, and a PhD in Game Studies. During her PhD, she contributed to the *Making Sense of Games* project for which she wrote her thesis on dynamic game characters, developing a transmedial approach to study their proliferation across popular cultural media, with special attention to the role of games and characters within the Japanese media mix.

Robert Alan Brookey is a Professor in the Department of Telecommunications at Ball State University in the US. His books have included *Hollywood Gamers: Digital Convergence in the Film and Video Game Industries* (2010) and *Playing to Win: Sports, Video Games, and the Culture of Play* (2015). His work has also appeared in *Games and Culture*, *Convergence*, and *Communication, Culture and Critique*, and he has served as the Editor for *Critical Studies in Media Communication*.

Nina Eckhoff-Heindl is a MSCA-Fellow in the program "a.r.t.e.s. EUmanities" at the a.r.t.e.s. Graduate School for the Humanities, University of Cologne, Germany (Horizon 2020: Marie Skłodowska-Curie grant No. 713600). Currently, she is a PhD student in art history at the University of Cologne, Germany, as well as the University of Zurich, Switzerland, with a project on aesthetic experience and the visual-tactile dimensions of comics.

Her research as well as her publications focus on modern and contemporary art, image theory, aesthetics, comics studies, disability studies, and Holocaust studies. Website: www.ninaheindl.com.

James Fleury is a Lecturer in Film and Media Studies at Washington University in St. Louis in the US. He received his PhD in Cinema and Media Studies from UCLA in 2019. He is the co-editor of the anthology *The Franchise Era: Managing Media in the Digital Economy* (with Bryan Hikari Hartzheim and Stephen Mamber, 2019). His publications have appeared in *Mediascape*, the *South Atlantic Review*, and the edited collections *James Bond and Popular Culture: Essays on the Influence of the Fictional Superspy* (edited by Michele Brittany, 2014), *Film Reboots* (edited by Daniel Herbert and Constantine Verevis, forthcoming), and *Content Wars: Tech Empires vs. Media Empires* (edited by Denise Mann, forthcoming). Website: www.jamesfleury.net.

Tim Glaser is a PhD student and a Research Associate at the Chair of Media Studies at the Braunschweig University of Art, Germany. His research focuses on videogame culture, digital comics, platform capitalism, and speculative fiction. Recent publication: "oh no—this comic is literally me: Webcomics im Zeitalter ihrer memetischen Rezeption." ["oh no—this comic is literally me: Webcomics in the Age of Their Memetic Reception."] *CLOSURE: Kieler e-Journal für Comicforschung* 4.5 (2018): n.p. Website: www.timglaser.de.

Daniel Merlin Goodbrey is a Principal Lecturer in Narrative and Interaction Design at the University of Hertfordshire, UK. A prolific and innovative comics creator, Goodbrey has gained international recognition as a leading expert in the field of experimental digital comics. His hypercomic work received the International Clickburg Webcomic Award in Holland in 2006 and his smartphone app *A Duck Has an Adventure* was shortlisted in the 2012 New Media Writing Prize. Website: www.e-merl.com.

Nicolas Labarre is an Assistant Professor at University Bordeaux Montaigne, France, where he teaches US society and culture, comics, and videogames. He is the author of Heavy Metal, *l'autre* Métal Hurlant (2017), a transnational history of the *Heavy Metal* magazine, and of *Understanding Genres in Comics* (2020). He has published several articles on the topic of adaptation into comics.

Dominik Mieth is Professor of Game Design at the Mediadesign University of Applied Sciences in Munich, Germany. He has worked on a variety of different videogames as game designer and producer at developers like Coreplay GmbH, where he oversaw design and production of projects such as *Jagged Alliance: Back in Action* (2012). His academic interests include game design and development, narrative design for interactive narratives, and the history of videogames. His lectures cover game design and game development documentation, game rules and mechanics, interactive storytelling, and the history of game development.

Josefa Much is a Lecturer and Research Associate at the Chair of Media Research and Adult Education at the University of Magdeburg, Germany. She holds an MA degree in Media Literacy from the University of Magdeburg and is currently working on her PhD thesis, which deals with the presentation of biography in videogames and comics. Her research interests include game studies, media literacy, film studies, transmedia storytelling, biography studies, and new forms of interactive and audiovisual communication.

Carman Ng is a Postdoctoral Fellow affiliated with the University of Bremen and the Free University Berlin, Germany, with research sojourn experiences in the US (Fulbright) and Germany (Erasmus Mundus, DAAD). Her current research explores the intersections of game studies, transmedia studies, and affective sciences in order to theorize multimodal semiotics for social impact game designs that engage with empathy and mental health. She is interested in examining aesthetics and ideologies of popular media, including videogames, anime, comics, graphic novels, and media art. Outside academia, she has participated in the Hong Kong community theater as a performer, writer, and techie.

Andreas Rauscher is a Senior Lecturer in the Department of Media Studies at the University of Siegen, Germany, where he focuses on film and game studies. He was a Visiting Professor at the University of Mainz, the University of Kiel, and the University of Freiburg, and has also worked as a journalist and academic curator for the exhibition *Film and Games: Interactions* at the Frankfurt Film Museum (2015). He is the author of *Das Phänomen Star Trek* [*The Star Trek Phenomenon*] (2003), *Spielerische Fiktionen: Transmediale Genrekonzepte in Videospielen* [*Ludic Fictions: Transmedial Genre Concepts in Videogames*] (2012), and *Star Wars: 100 Seiten* [*Star Wars: 100 Pages*] (2019) as well as the co-editor of essay collections on *The Simpsons*, superhero movies, the Czechoslovakian Nová Vlna, and the *James Bond* film series. Website: www.andreas-rauscher.de/.

Daniel Stein is Professor of North American Literary and Cultural Studies at the University of Siegen, Germany. He is the author of *Music Is My Life: Louis Armstrong, Autobiography, and American Jazz* (2012) as well as the co-editor of *From Comic Strips to Graphic Novels* (with Jan-Noël Thon, 2013/^{2}2015) and *Nineteenth-Century Serial Narrative in Transnational Perspective, 1830s–1860s* (with Lisanna Wiele, 2019). His work has appeared in *Popular Music and Society*, *Southern Literary Journal*, *Journal of Graphic Novels and Comics*, and *Amerikastudien/*

American Studies. He co-edits *Anglia: Journal of English Philology* as well as the *Anglia* book series and has received the Heinz Maier-Leibnitz Prize in 2013 (German Research Foundation/Ministry of Education and Research).

Claudius Stemmler is a PhD student at the University of Siegen, Germany, where he currently receives a scholarship from the House of Young Talents graduate center. His PhD thesis presents an analysis of the oeuvre of Japanese videogame designer Hideo Kojima. Previously, he has contributed to edited collections on the *Call of Duty* videogame series and jazz singer Billie Holiday.

Jan-Noël Thon is Professor of Media Studies at the Norwegian University of Science and Technology (NTNU), Guest Professor of Media Studies at the University of Cologne, Germany, and Professorial Fellow at the University for the Creative Arts, UK. Recent books include *From Comic Strips to Graphic Novels* (co-edited with Daniel Stein, 2013/^{2}2015), *Storyworlds across Media* (co-edited with Marie-Laure Ryan, 2014), *Game Studies* (co-edited with Klaus Sachs-Hombach, 2015), *Transmedial Narratology and Contemporary Media Culture* (2016/^{2}2018), *Subjectivity across Media* (co-edited with Maike Sarah Reinerth, 2017), and *Comicanalyse* (co-authored with Stephan Packard, Andreas Rauscher, Véronique Sina, Lukas R. A. Wilde, and Janina Wildfeuer, 2019). Website: www.janthon.net.

Susana Tosca is Associate Professor in the Department of Communication and Humanities at Roskilde University, Denmark. Over the past twenty years, her research has combined aesthetic and media studies approaches to investigating the reception of digital media. She has published widely in the areas of hypertext, digital literature, computer games, and transmediality, including the books *Literatura Digital* (2004), *Understanding Video Games: The Essential Introduction* (with Simon Egenfeldt-Nielsen and Jonas Heide Smith, 2008/^{2}2013/^{3}2016/^{4}2020), and *Transmedial Worlds in Everyday Life: Networked Reception, Social Media and Fictional Worlds* (with Lisbeth Klastrup, 2019).

William Uricchio is Professor of Comparative Media Studies at MIT in the US as well as at Utrecht University in the Netherlands. He is Principal Investigator of the MIT Open Documentary Lab, which explores interactive and participatory reality-based storytelling. His work explores the frontiers of new media, at times using a historical lens (old media when they were new, such as nineteenth-century television) and at times by working with interactive and algorithmically generated media forms (interactive documentaries and games in particular). He has received numerous awards for his work, including Guggenheim, Humboldt, and Fulbright research fellowships, as well as the Berlin Prize.

Nan Zhang is a second-year graduate student in the Department of Telecommunications at Ball State University in the US. She worked as an Editorial Assistant for *Critical Studies in Media Communication*. Her research interests include social media, user-generated content, and cross-cultural consumer behavior.

Acknowledgments

This book emerges from the three-day symposium "Comics|Games: Aesthetic, Ludic, and Narrative Strategies," which took place from 5 to 7 November 2018 at Herrenhausen Palace in Hanover, Germany. We wish to thank all participants for their spirited contributions to a number of wide-ranging discussions, their consistently outstanding scholarship, and their willingness to build on the latter in developing the chapters presented on the following pages. Moreover, we are very grateful to the Volkswagen Foundation for generously funding not only the symposium itself but also the Open Access publication of the present volume.

1 Introduction

Comics and videogames

Andreas Rauscher, Daniel Stein, and Jan-Noël Thon

In recent years, comics studies and game studies have each developed from marginal subfields into two of the most dynamic and vital areas of current humanistic scholarship. Increasingly, this entails not only an expanding corpus of in-depth studies on comics and videogames as aesthetic forms (e.g., Carrier 2000; Ensslin 2014; Etter 2020; Groensteen 2007; Juul 2019; Kirkpatrick 2011), their narrative potentials (e.g., Domsch 2013; Kukkonen 2013; Mikkonen 2017; Murray 2017; Postema 2013; Thon 2016), and their phenomenological appeal (e.g., Aldama 2012; Anable 2018; Hague 2014; Isbister 2016; Keogh 2018; Packard 2006) but also the codification of knowledge via a growing number of wide-ranging edited collections (e.g., Deterding and Zagal 2018; Meskin and Cook 2012; Perron and Schröter 2016; Ruberg and Shaw 2017; Stein and Thon 2013; Williams and Lyons 2010), field-defining handbooks (e.g., Bramlet et al. 2016; Hatfield and Beaty 2020; Raessens and Goldstein 2005; Sachs-Hombach and Thon 2015; Smith and Duncan 2017; Wolf and Perron 2014), and introductory textbooks (e.g., Abel and Klein 2016; Beil et al. 2017; Duncan and Smith 2009; Egenfeldt-Nielsen et al. 2020; Newman 2013; Packard et al. 2019).

Despite the fact that comics and videogames have intersected frequently since the late 1970s and early 1980s, neither comics studies nor game studies have adequately addressed the various historical synergies between the two media or their increasing convergence in the current cultural landscape. Evidence of such synergies abounds: In 1979, Atari published a videogame based on DC's *Superman* comics; in 1982, a videogame developed by Parker Brothers based on Marvel's *Spider-Man* comics followed. Both videogames used abstract variations of stock scenes from the comic books and turned them into ludic standard situations for scrolling action games (Rauscher 2012, 2014). A few years later, a series of three adventure games—*Questprobe Featuring Hulk* (1984), *Questprobe Featuring Spider-Man* (1984), and *Questprobe Featuring Human Torch and Thing* (1985)—were published by Adventure International. In contrast to the earlier Atari action games that had focused on dexterity and capacity of reaction, these graphic adventures made an effort to adapt the narrative patterns of superhero comics. Instead of exercising skill-based movements, players had to collect clues and solve puzzles to free the superheroes' friends and battle their foes. Moreover, comic tie-ins accompanied these videogames in an early example of transmediality until Adventure International's bankruptcy in 1985.

Videogames produced for the Atari home consoles like *Yar's Revenge* (1982) and *Centipede* (1983) were accompanied by comics that were included in the videogame boxes and written by popular comics authors such as Gerry Conway and Roy Thomas (see also the contribution by Labarre in the present volume). Comparable to the popular 1980s toy franchise *Masters of the Universe*, which featured comics as a special gimmick for every action figure, the comics accompanying these early videogames added background stories that helped "color" the gameplay. The images in the comics thus provided narrative and visual details to the videogames' storyworld that, due to limitations in processing power and graphic capacities, could not be represented within the videogames themselves. Often, these comics also integrated more extensive intermedial references. To take just one example: The 3D-comic *The Adventures of Lane Mastodon*, which accompanied the Infocom adventure *Leather Goddesses of Phobos* (1986), contained not just information necessary to completing the game (and thus acted as a form of copy protection) but also offered a wealth of references to the iconography of science-fiction B-pictures that further enriched the peculiar humor of the largely text-based videogame. By the early 1990s, stand-alone comics series based upon successful videogames such as *Double Dragon* (1991), *Indiana Jones and the Fate of Atlantis* (1991), or *Street Fighter* (1993) sold separately, while comic tie-ins have also increasingly been used to bridge the narrative gap between videogame sequels and to add detail to an expanding storyworld (see below).

Despite the fact that both videogames based on successful comics series and comics based on successful videogame franchises have been in production for several decades, the examination of their synergies and interactions remains largely uncharted territory in both comics studies and game studies (with the scope of existing studies focusing on comics and videogames [e.g., Backe 2012; Goodbrey 2015; Lippitz 2019] remaining considerably more limited than those focusing on comics and film [e.g., Burke 2015; Davis 2016; Gordon et al. 2007] or on videogames and film [e.g., Brookey 2010; Kallay 2013; Lenhardt and Rauscher 2015]). This is even more surprising since the two media forms' move from the margins to the mainstream of current media culture and the considerable rise in associated fan activities (Bolling and Smith 2014; Scott 2019; Tosca and Klastrup 2019) have made their complex interrelations ever more visible. Among the plethora of potentially productive avenues of inquiry that are thus opened up, we highlight two different, and arguably complementary, kinds of interrelations between comics and videogames. On the one hand, it is possible to frame the ways in which comics and videogames borrow, adapt, and transform a diverse range of aesthetic, ludic, and narrative strategies conventionally associated with the "other" medium in terms of *hybrid medialities*, which are realized in a broad range of examples such as *Comix Zone* (1995), *Homestuck* (2009–2016), *A Duck Has an Adventure* (2012), or *Framed* (2014) (see also the contributions by Backe, Eckhoff-Heindl, Goodbrey, Glaser, and Ng in the present volume).

On the other hand, both comics and videogames often function as *transmedia expansions* of existing media products, whether as adaptations of specific stories (e.g., Hassler-Forest and Nicklas 2015; Hutcheon and O'Flynn 2013; Parody 2011) or as more dispersed contributions to the kinds of transmedia franchises that have increasingly come to define our current media environments (e.g., Freeman and Gambarato 2018; Jenkins 2006; Johnson 2013). Parallel to the recent rise of superhero blockbusters based on intellectual property originating in the realm of comics (e.g., Burke 2015; McEniry et al. 2016; Yockey 2017), popular videogames from very different genres contribute to a variety of comics-based franchises from those built on Bill Willingham's *Fables* series (2002–2015) or Alan Moore's *Watchmen* series (1986) to DC's *Batman* comics or Marvel's *Spider-Man* comics (see also the contributions by Brookey and Zhang, Fleury, Mieth, and Uricchio in the present volume). Similarly, videogame–based franchises from *Metal Gear Solid* or *Persona 5* to *Tomb Raider* or *Warcraft* have included comics of various kinds amongst their more prominent installments (see also the contributions by Blom, Much, and Stemmler in the present volume). While it goes without saying that the centripetal force of hybrid medialities and the centrifugal force of transmedia expansions are not mutually exclusive, distinguishing between them may still be a helpful first step toward coming to terms with the complex synergies, interactions, and interrelations between comics and videogames.

From hybrid medialities to transmedia expansions

The notions of hybrid medialities and transmedia expansions both draw on a more fundamental conceptualization of comics and videogames as media. While it would go beyond the scope of this brief introduction to reconstruct the many different and partially contradictory conceptualizations of the term *medium* and the development of its different forms in any detail (e.g., Bolter and Grusin 1999; Manovich 2001; McLuhan 1964; Murray 2012; Ryan 2006; Schmidt 2000), we would still suggest that "newspapers," "novels," "photographic pictures," "films," or indeed "comics" and "videogames" may be best understood as *conventionally distinct media*, "which can be distinguished not only by way of the technological or material base and/or the semiotic system(s) they use but also by way of the 'social fact' that they are conventionally treated as distinct media" (Thon 2014, 335; see also Rajewsky 2010; Ryan 2006; Thon 2016; Wilde 2015; Wolf 1999). *Mediality* would then, at least in principle, refer not just to "transmedial notions of 'mediumness' " but also "to the set of prototypical properties that can be considered constitutive for a conventionally distinct medium" (Thon 2014, 335), even though "the dynamic processes shaping, modifying and transforming the conventions of this distinct medium" (Wilde 2015, 2) are often complex and may put the always already remediated mediality of a specific manifestation of what we might consider a comic or a videogame into sharp relief only if we attempt to differentiate it from another media form.

Scott McCloud, for example, notes that "the basic difference [between animation and comics] is that animation is sequential in time but not spatially juxtaposed as comics are" (1993, 7; see also, once more, Wilde 2015). While many action adventures and platformers do indeed appear much closer to animation than to traditional comics, one can also find more than a few videogames that do not just draw on stories told by comics but also (or primarily) work to evoke the combination of words and pictures in panels and panel sequences that defines comics' mediality. As mentioned above, an early example of this kind of hybrid mediality is the 1995 beat 'em up *Comix Zone*, which presents its game spaces much like a comics page, with several panels to be traversed by the protagonist as he fights the evil mutant Mortus. More recently, the 2014 puzzle game *Framed* tasks the player with (re)arranging different comics panels represented on the screen in order to allow the player-controlled character to escape from his relentless pursuers in the videogame's heavily noir-inspired storyworld. Evidently, both *Comix Zone* and *Framed* foreground their remediation of comics elements, but it is worth stressing that one can also find numerous less pronounced—but certainly no less important—examples of this kind of remediation, including the third-person shooter *Max Payne* (2001), which employs cutscenes that take the form of comics, and the first-person shooter *XIII* (2003), which is based on a successful comics series with the same title and uses a cel-shading technique that results in a graphic style reminiscent of "hand-drawn" comics, while also employing a panel-like structure to represent part of its gameplay.

While videogames can reproduce the verbal-pictorial form of comics quite easily, then, the situation is slightly more complicated when print comics attempt to remediate the interactivity and nonlinearity of videogames. While there are well-known examples such as Bryan Lee O'Malley's *Scott Pilgrim* series (2004–2010) that evoke videogame tropes, print comics that launch more ambitious attempts to integrate ludic elements tend to draw on the realm of nondigital games. The resulting processes of remediation are still quite diverse, however, ranging from the nonlinear narrative structure in comics such as *The Unwritten* #17 (Carey and Gross 2010) and *Adventure Time* #10 (North et al. 2012), both of which are clearly inspired by the *Choose Your Own Adventure* book series, to the integration of board game elements in Chris Ware's experimental "'Fairy Tale' Road Rage" (Ware 2000) and *Building Stories* (Ware 2012) (see also the contribution by Eckhoff-Heindl in the present volume). While not as common as videogames' remediation of comics' mediality, the fact that this integration of elements from nondigital games into print comics has recently even been taken up by an entry in Marvel's *Deadpool* franchise would indicate that it is anything but marginal. Indeed, *You Are Deadpool* (Ewing et al. 2018) not only includes a pair of *Deadpool*-branded dice and pencils that allow the reader/player to follow the many different "forking paths" that the comic's nonlinear narrative structure affords. It also employs even more pronounced forms of metareferentiality and metalepsis than the above-mentioned examples (which is, of course, very much on brand for the *Deadpool* franchise [e.g., Darowski 2009; Thon 2017; Wolf 2009]). Repeatedly switching between graphic styles, narrative frames, and ludic references, the comic's self-reflexive approach to its hybrid mediality is established early on, when Deadpool (the character) encourages the reader/player to build a dice from a punch-out-sheet, only to be killed by the scissors on the next page if the reader/player follows his instructions.

As instructive as these instances of print comics remediating elements of nondigital games are, we also find numerous and no less pertinent examples of webcomics remediating *video*game elements, which sometimes leads to a noteworthy blurring of the (conventionally drawn) line between the two media forms: Andrew Hussie's webcomics series *Homestuck*, for example, tells a story that focuses on a group of teenagers exploring the world of the upcoming videogame Sburb, which increasingly turns out to be closely integrated with the characters' actual world. *Homestuck* also uses a complex combination of static pictures, animations, and interactive segments that commonly include the remediation of videogame elements—from the initial prompt to the reader/player to name the protagonist via the various battle commands that the characters can execute during so-called strife to the obnoxiously complex and unintuitive inventory system of the Sylladex—not just on the level of the represented storyworld but also on that of its multimodal representation (see also Glaser's contribution in the present volume). Another example of this kind of hybrid mediality would be Daniel M. Goodbrey's *A Duck Has an Adventure*, which employs a simpler, but also decidedly more nonlinear narrative structure to tell the story of a duck making a number of consequential choices. While the focus here is primarily on the agency of the reader/player in deciding which course of action the duck should take, *A Duck Has an Adventure* also integrates a videogame-inspired scoring system that keeps track of the number of endings the reader/player has explored, the number of hats they have successfully made the duck collect, and other assorted achievements they have attained (see also the contribution by Goodbrey in the present volume).

As this necessarily brief discussion of salient examples should already have illustrated, there is a rich tradition of comics and videogames "borrowing" formal elements conventionally attributed to the "other" medium, and while these processes of remediation may only very rarely push a given work beyond the boundaries of what we would still recognize as a "comic" or a "videogame," they still create a continuum of what could be described as hybrid medialities (see also, again, Wilde 2015; and, for a critical perspective, the contribution by Backe in the present volume). As mentioned above, however, it is important to note that the centripetal force of hybrid medialities is not all there is to the comics-videogames nexus, as the two conventionally distinct media also play an important part within the more or less encompassing transmedia franchises that have increasingly come to define our current media culture. Again, the resulting processes of transmedia expansions can take very different forms (Ryan 2008, 2015; Thon 2015, 2019), from the largely redundant "retelling" of a story previously told in the "other" medium (as is the case in comics such as *Star Wars: The Force Unleashed* [Blackman et al. 2008] and videogames such as *DC Infinite Crisis* [2015]) via a carefully tuned expansion of previously established storyworlds (as is the case in comics such as the *Batman: Arkham City* series [2011] and videogames such as *The Wolf Among Us* [2013]) to the modification of such previously established storyworlds in various kinds of reboots and reimaginations (as is the case in comics such as the *Star Wars: Knights of the Old Republic* series [2006–2010] and videogames such as *LEGO Batman: The Videogame* [2008]). Accordingly, the chapters collected in the present volume aim to develop a more nuanced understanding of the theory, history, and current iterations of the synergies, interactions, and interrelations between comics and videogames by exploring both their potential to create hybrid medialities and their role in various kinds of transmedia expansions.

Part I: Hybrid medialities

In "Of Pac-Men and Star Raiders: Early mutual representations between comics and videogames (1981–1983)," Nicolas Labarre examines the moment in videogame history when the medium first attracted attention as an increasingly popular phenomenon beyond the realm of gaming culture. He suggests that, over a relatively short period of time in the early 1980s, comics not only recognized the possibilities of videogames but also discovered a number of synergies between the two media. According to Labarre, comics depicted videogames as a catalogue of icons, as potential yet incomplete narratives akin to toys, and as a new aesthetic that could impact future developments in comics storytelling and design. In addition, comics contributed to the formation of popular figures such as Pac-Man and Donkey Kong, which eventually became globally recognizable icons.

Carman Ng's "Interfacing comics and games: A socio-affective multimodal approach" combines notions of socio-semiotic multimodality with an empirical orientation and a profound interest in theories of affect. Ng applies digital annotation and gameplay analysis to determine how videogames instantiate the aesthetics of different forms of audiovisual narrative. In order to do so, she develops a multifaceted approach to multimodality that favors fine-grained analysis of intermedial and transmedial elements and concentrates on the affective dimensions of three types of interactive audiovisual narrative: the digital graphic novel *Metal Gear Solid 2: Bande Dessinée* (2008), which adapts Hideo Kojima's successful videogame *Metal*

Gear Solid 2: Sons of Liberty (2001), the comic-game hybrid *Gorogoa* (2017), and the gesture-based literary artwork *Breathing Room* (2014).

In "Game comics: Theory and design," Daniel Merlin Goodbrey further explores the hybridity that may result when the verbal-pictorial form of comics and the ludic qualities of videogames intersect. Taking Jesper Juul's (2005) classic game model as his starting point, Goodbrey argues that what he calls game comics combine key characteristics of videogames with key characteristics of comics in order to establish the basis for gameplay that highlights the productive interfaces between the two media forms. He tests this hypothesis by offering in-depth analyses of three game comic prototypes he designed as part of his own practice-as-research activities: the above-mentioned *A Duck Has an Adventure* as well as *Icarus Needs* (2013) and *Margaret Must Succeed* (2013).

Challenging the seemingly omnipresent notion of hybridity, Hans-Joachim Backe's "Game-comics and comic-games: Against the concept of hybrids" argues that the complex relations between videogames and comics invalidate any attempt to frame these two media as coherent cultural phenomena. Criticizing previous research for its reliance on a priori assumptions of hybridity that would require clearly delineated characteristics rather than prevalent notions of prototypical features and family resemblances, Backe questions the supposed hybridity of a wide range of examples. While he acknowledges the existence of a broadly conceived comics-videogames nexus, he concludes that diagnoses of hybrid medialities generally do not hold up to close analyses of individual artifacts.

Turning to analogue synergies between ludic forms and comics in "Building stories: The interplay of comics and games in Chris Ware's works," Nina Eckhoff-Heindl shows how game structures shape graphic novelist Chris Ware's artistic approach. Eckhoff-Heindl reads Ware's board game "'Fairy Tale' Road Rage" (Ware 2000) as a critical take on fairy-tale and educational games, suggesting that the narratives of loneliness and depression that dominate Ware's groundbreaking *Building Stories* (Ware 2012) are productively contrasted with the more playful board game. At the same time, *Building Stories* establishes a connection to board games through its materiality, size, and visual design, which readers must try to decode with the help of a manual that does not in fact prove to be very helpful, a potentially frustrating experience Eckhoff-Heindl identifies as a deconstruction of received knowledge about printed artifacts.

Tim Glaser's "*Homestuck* as a game: A webcomic between playful participation, digital technostalgia, and irritating inventory systems" explores the hybrid medialities that may or may not emerge from the comics-videogames nexus. Glaser discusses Andrew Hussie's webcomic *Homestuck* as a popular experiment and exercise in metareferential storytelling that offers playfully critical reflections on various elements of videogames, including their connection to fandom and participatory culture. Accordingly, Glaser reads *Homestuck* as an example of technostalgia that oscillates between an ironic distancing from and a serious investigation of adolescence in the age of online communication and digital computation—and that, in doing so, routinely implicates the readers/players in the act of storytelling.

In "*Metal Gear Solid* and its comics adaptations," Claudius Stemmler works against the grain of popular and scholarly inquiries into the interrelations between comics and videogames. Stemmler conducts a case study that looks at the adaptation of the well-known *Metal Gear Solid* stealth game series (1998–2015) into lesser-known comics formats, beginning with Konami's release of *Metal Gear Solid: Digital Graphic Novel* (2006) for the PlayStation Portable. His comparison of the videogames and their comics adaptations reveals a concerted effort to retain certain core elements of the former's aesthetics in the latter, while also modifying the stories being told in ways that privilege the affordances of comics in general and that of the digital graphic novel format in particular.

Part II: Transmedia expansions

Moving from the notion of hybrid medialities at the center of the chapters in the first part of the present volume to the notion of transmedia expansion that binds together those in the second part, Dominik Mieth's "Many Spider-Men are better than one: Referencing as a narrative strategy" examines how serial superhero characters such as Spider-Man have tried to reconcile an incessant need to update with the expectations of long-term fans and followers of the properties. Looking at Spider-Man comics, blockbuster movies, and videogames, Mieth discerns a paradigm shift from earlier adaptations that sought to stay more or less true to canonical, or at least specific, versions of the character to more recent expansions that display a greater interest in multiplication and diversification.

Robert Alan Brookey and Nan Zhang employ a critical political economy approach in "The not-so *Fantastic Four* franchise: A critical history of the comic, the films, and the Disney/Fox merger" to question the notion of transmedia expansion. Different from the many stories of success about the Marvel Cinematic Universe, the fate of the Fantastic Four was marred by several troubled film adaptations, in addition to getting caught in the Disney takeover of Twentieth Century Fox. Brookey and Zhang thus critically examine the "dubious division" between political economy approaches to popular franchises and treatments of fan culture as they reassess the role of intellectual property considerations in Disney's acquisition of Marvel. Instead of embracing an idealized view of participatory culture, they call for an increase in awareness of actual corporate practices among both scholars and fans.

Against the background of the crisis of the *Batman* brand that followed the release of Joel Schumacher's notorious *Batman and Robin* (1997), James Fleury's "The road to *Arkham Asylum*: *Batman: Dark Tomorrow* and transitional transmedia" zooms in on a part of the franchise's transmedia history that, in contrast to its more successful adaptations, has not yet garnered major scholarly attention. Fleury's case study of one of the lesser-known *Batman* videogames, *Batman: Dark Tomorrow* (2003), allows him to reconstruct a rarely explored aspect of the multiplicity of the many Batmen that are subsumed under the *Batman* brand and to highlight how *Batman: Dark Tomorrow* facilitated the emergence of the *Arkhamverse* transmedia franchise despite its limited multiplatform storytelling and less-than-stellar reception.

The rules associated with superhero storyworlds and the continuity "bibles" commonly employed to manage them inform William Uricchio's "When rules collide: Definitional strategies for superheroes across comic books and games." Uricchio shares Brookey and Zhang's interest in the commercial concerns behind transmedia franchises like *Batman* and *Spider-Man* when he argues that the diegetic rules of the comics' storyworlds and the financial rules that determine the fate of a franchise and limit its storytelling options often collide. Adding a third element—what he calls emerging media technologies, story-generating technologies in particular—to this equation, Uricchio ponders the potential of comics "bibles" and videogame rules for the development of algorithmically-generated stories.

In "The manifestations of game characters in a media mix strategy," Joleen Blom aims to complicate established notions of media convergence by complementing Western theories of transmedia characters in transmedia franchises with Japanese theories of *kyara* in what is more commonly called the media mix in Japanese media culture. Using the highly successful *Persona 5* franchise as a case study, Blom argues that, while the main characters do connect different parts of the franchise, including videogames and manga, they do not create coherence but rather proliferate—countering the emphasis on identity, continuity, and consistency that appears to be at the heart of many, if certainly not all, Western theories of transmedia characters and transmedia storytelling.

Josefa Much's "Creating Lara Croft: The meaning of the comic books for the *Tomb Raider* franchise" examines the productive tensions that tend to occur whenever videogame versions of Lara Croft are revisited and revised in comics spin-offs by different licensees. Much reconstructs in meticulous detail how the *Tomb Raider* videogame series (1996–) has become a salient point of reference for comics adaptations and expansions that may have their origins in videogames but still regularly take on "a life of their own." As Much shows, this leads to complex interactions not just between videogames and comics but also between officially licensed products and a broad variety of fan productions that add ever more interesting aspects to the official versions of Lara Croft.

In the concluding chapter of the present volume, "Beyond immersion: *Gin Tama* and palimpsestuous reception," Susana Tosca discusses the mix of genres and styles as well as the penchant for intertextuality, metareferentiality, and metalepsis that are the hallmarks of the manga series *Gin Tama* (2003–), the anime series of the same title (2006–2018), and other entries in the transmedia franchise. Not limiting her analysis to *Gin Tama*'s substantial reflection on videogame tropes, Tosca explores the broader question whether fragmentation and immersion can coexist. Rather than maintaining this supposed opposition, she proposes the concept of "palimpsestuous reception" in order to more precisely describe how the various ways in which *Gin Tama* encourages its recipients to keep track of its myriad metareferential transgressions can itself lead to highly immersive processes of (re)interpretation and (re)appropriation.

Works cited

Abel, Julia, and Christian Klein, eds. 2016. *Comics und Graphic Novels: Eine Einführung*. Stuttgart: Metzler.

Aldama, Frederick Luis. 2012. *Your Brain on Latino Comics: From Gus Arriola to Los Bros Hernandez*. Austin: University of Texas Press.

Anable, Aubrey. 2018. *Playing with Feelings: Video Games and Affect*. Minneapolis: University of Minnesota Press.

Backe, Hans-Joachim. 2012. "Vom Yellow Kid zu Super Mario: Zum Verhältnis von Comics und Computerspielen." In *Comics Intermedial*, edited by Christian Bachmann, Véronique Sina, and Lars Banhold, 147–157. Essen: Ch. A. Bachmann Verlag.

Batman and Robin. 1997. Dir. Joel Schumacher. USA: Warner Bros. Pictures.

Batman: Dark Tomorrow. 2003. Developed by Hot Gen. Published by Kemco. GameCube.

Beil, Benjamin, Thomas Hensel, and Andreas Rauscher, eds. 2017. *Game Studies*. New York: Springer.

Blackman, Haden, Brian Ching, Bong Dazo, and Wayne Nichols. 2008. *Star Wars: The Force Unleashed*. Milwaukie: Dark Horse Comics.

Bolling, Ben, and Matthew J. Smith, eds. 2014. *It Happens at Comic-Con: Ethnographic Essays on a Pop Culture Phenomenon*. Jefferson: McFarland.

Bolter, Jay David, and Richard Grusin. 1999. *Remediation: Understanding New Media*. Cambridge, MA: MIT Press.

Bramlett, Frank, Roy Cook, and Aaron Meskin, eds. 2016. *The Routledge Companion to Comics*. New York: Routledge.

Breathing Room. 2014. Designed by Erik Loyer. Unpublished. Mac OS X.

Brookey, Robert A. 2010. *Hollywood Gamers: Digital Convergence in the Film and Video Game Industries*. Bloomington: Indiana University Press.

Burke, Liam. 2015. *The Comic Book Film Adaptation: Exploring Modern Hollywood's Leading Genre*. Jackson: University Press of Mississippi.

Carey, Mike, and Peter Gross. 2010. *The Unwritten #17: The Many Lives of Lizzie Hexam: A Choose-a-Story Adventure*. New York: Vertigo.

Carrier, David. 2000. *The Aesthetics of Comics*. University Park: Pennsylvania State University Press.

Centipede. 1983. Developed and published by Atari. Atari 2600.

Comix Zone. 1995. Developed and published by Sega. Sega Genesis.

Darowski, Joseph J. 2009. "When You Know You're Just a Comic Book Character: Deadpool." In *X-Men and Philosophy: Astonishing Insight and Uncanny Argument in the Mutant X-Verse*, edited by Rebecca Housel and J. Jeremy Wisnewski, 107–121. Hoboken: Wiley.

Davis, Blair. 2016. *Movie Comics: Page to Screen/Screen to Page*. New Brunswick: Rutgers University Press.
DC Infinite Crisis. 2015. Developed by Turbine. Published by Warner Bros. Interactive Entertainment. Windows.
Deterding, Sebastian, and José P. Zagal, eds. 2018. *Role-Playing Game Studies: Transmedia Foundations*. New York: Routledge.
Domsch, Sebastian. 2013. *Storyplaying: Agency and Narrative in Video Games*. Berlin: De Gruyter.
A Duck Has an Adventure. 2012. Developed by Daniel M. Goodbrey. Published by E-merl.com. Android.
Duncan, Randy, and Matthew J. Smith. 2009. *The Power of Comics: History, Form and Culture*. New York: Continuum.
Egenfeldt-Nielsen, Simon, Jonas Heide Smith, and Susana Tosca. 2020. *Understanding Video Games: The Essential Introduction*. 4th edition. New York: Routledge.
Ensslin, Astrid. 2014. *Literary Gaming*. Cambridge, MA: MIT Press.
Etter, Lukas. 2020. *Distinctive Styles and Authorship in Alternative Comics*. Berlin: De Gruyter.
Ewing, Al, Salva Espin, and Paco Diaz. 2018. *You Are Deadpool*. New York: Marvel Comics.
Framed. 2014. Developed and published by Loveshack Games. iOS.
Freeman, Matthew, and Renira Rampazzo Gambarato, eds. 2018. *The Routledge Companion to Transmedia Studies*. New York: Routledge.
Goodbrey, Daniel M. 2015. "Game Comics: An Analysis of an Emergent Hybrid Form." *Journal of Graphic Novels and Comics* 6 (1): 3–14.
Gordon, Ian, Mark Jancovich, and Matthew P. Allister, eds. 2007. *Film and Comic Books*. Jackson: University Press of Mississippi.
Gorogoa. 2017. Developed by Jason Roberts. Published by Annapurna Interactive. Windows.
Groensteen, Thierry. 2007. *The System of Comics*. Jackson: University Press of Mississippi,
Hague, Ian. 2014. *Comics and the Senses: A Multisensory Approach to Comics and Graphic Novels*. New York: Routledge.
Hassler-Forest, Dan, and Pascal Nicklas, eds. 2015. *The Politics of Adaptation: Media Convergence and Ideology*. Basingstoke: Palgrave Macmillan.
Hatfield, Charles, and Bart Beaty, eds. 2020. *Comics Studies: A Guidebook*. New Brunswick: Rutgers University Press.
Hutcheon, Linda, and Siobhan O'Flynn. 2013. *A Theory of Adaptation*. 2nd edition. Abingdon: Routledge.
Icarus Needs. 2013. Developed by Daniel M. Goodbrey. Published by Kongregate. Browser. www.kongregate.com/games/Stillmerlin/icarus-needs (accessed 31 January 2020).
Isbister, Katherine. 2016. *How Games Move Us: Emotion by Design*. Cambridge, MA: MIT Press.
Jenkins, Henry. 2006. *Convergence Culture: Where Old and New Media Collide*. New York: New York University Press.
Johnson, Derek. 2013. *Media Franchising: Creative License and Collaboration in the Culture Industries*. New York: New York University Press.
Juul, Jesper. 2005. *Half-Real: Video Games between Real Rules and Fictional Worlds*. Cambridge, MA: MIT Press.

Juul, Jesper. 2019. *Handmade Pixels: Independent Video Games and the Quest for Authenticity*. Cambridge, MA: MIT Press.

Kallay, Jasmina. 2013. *Gaming Film: How Games Are Reshaping Contemporary Cinema*. Basingstoke: Palgrave Macmillian.

Keogh, Brendan. 2018. *A Play of Bodies: How We Perceive Videogames*. Cambridge, MA: MIT Press.

Kirkpatrick, Graeme. 2011. *Aesthetic Theory and the Video Game*. Manchester: Manchester University Press.

Kukkonen, Karin. 2013. *Contemporary Comics Storytelling*. Lincoln: University of Nebraska Press.

The Leather Goddesses of Phobos. 1986. Developed and published by Infocom. C64.

LEGO Batman: The Videogame. 2008. Developed by Traveller's Tales. Published by Warner Bros. Interactive. Windows.

Lenhardt, Eva, and Andreas Rauscher, eds. 2015. *Film and Games: Interactions*. Berlin: Bertz.

Lippitz, Armin. 2019. "Lost in the Static? Comics in Video Games." In *Intermedia Games—Games Inter Media: Video Games and Intermediality*, edited by Michael Fuchs and Jeff Thoss, 115–132. New York: Bloomsbury.

Manovich, Lev. 2001. *The Language of New Media*. Cambridge, MA: MIT Press.

Margaret Must Succeed. 2013. Developed by Daniel M. Goodbrey. Unpublished. Android.

Max Payne. 2001. Developed by Remedy. Published by Rockstar Games/Gathering of Developers. Windows.

McCloud, Scott. 1993. *Understanding Comics*. New York: Harper Collins.

McEniry, Matthew J., Robert Moses Peaslee, and Robert G. Weiner, eds. 2016. *Marvel Comics into Film: Essays on Adaptation since the 1940s*. Jefferson: McFarland.

McLuhan, Marshal. 1964. *Understanding Media: The Extensions of Man*. New York: McGraw-Hill.

Meskin, Aaron, and Roy T. Cook, eds. 2012. *The Art of Comics: A Philosophical Approach*. Malden: Wiley-Blackwell.

Metal Gear Solid: Digital Graphic Novel. 2006. Developed by Kojima Productions. Published by Konami. PlayStation Portable.

Metal Gear Solid 2: Bande Dessinée. 2008. Developed by Kojima Productions. Published by Konami. DVD.

Metal Gear Solid 2: Sons of Liberty. 2001. Developed and published by Konami. PlayStation 2.

Mikkonen, Kai. 2017. *The Narratology of Comic Art*. New York: Routledge.

Murray, Janet H. 2012. *Inventing the Medium: Principles of Interaction Design as Cultural Practice*. Cambridge, MA: MIT Press.

Murray, Janet H. 2017. *Hamlet on the Holodeck: The Future of Narrative in Cyberspace*. 2nd edition. Cambridge, MA: MIT Press.

Newman, James A. 2013. *Videogames*. 2nd edition. Abingdon: Routledge.

North, Ryan, Shelli Paroline, and Braden Lamb. 2012. *Adventure Time* #10: *Choose Your Own Adventure Time*. Los Angeles: KaBoom!

Packard, Stephan. 2006. *Anatomie des Comics: Psychosemiotische Medienanalyse*. Göttingen: Wallstein Verlag.

Packard, Stephan, Andreas Rauscher, Véronique Sina, Jan-Noël Thon, Lukas R. A. Wilde, and Janina Wildfeuer. 2019. *Comicanalyse: Eine Einführung*. Stuttgart: Metzler.

Parody, Claire. 2011. "Franchising/Adaptation." *Adaptation* 4 (2): 210–218.

Perron, Bernard, and Felix Schröter, eds. 2016. *Video Games and the Mind: Essays on Cognition, Affect and Emotions*. Jefferson: McFarland.

Postema, Barbara. 2013. *Narrative Structure in Comics: Making Sense of Fragments*. Rochester: RIT Press.

Questprobe Featuring Hulk. 1984. Developed and published by Adventure International. ZX Spectrum.

Questprobe Featuring Human Torch and Thing. 1985. Developed and published by Adventure International. ZX Spectrum.

Questprobe Featuring Spider-Man. 1984. Developed and published by Adventure International. ZX Spectrum.

Raessens, Joost, and Jeffrey Goldstein, eds. 2005. *Handbook of Computer Game Studies*. Cambridge, MA: MIT Press.

Rajewsky, Irina O. 2010. "Border Talks: The Problematic Status of Media Borders in the Current Debate about Intermediality." In *Media Borders, Multimodality and Intermediality*, edited by Lars Elleström, 51–68. Basingstoke: Palgrave Macmillan.

Rauscher, Andreas. 2012. *Spielerische Fiktionen: Transmediale Genrekonzepte in Videospielen*. Marburg: Schüren.

Rauscher, Andreas. 2014. "Game Genre." In *The Johns Hopkins Guide to Digital Media*, edited by Marie-Laure Ryan, Lori Emerson, and Benjamin J. Robertson, 203–206. Baltimore: Johns Hopkins University Press.

Ruberg, Bonnie, and Adrienne Shaw, eds. 2017. *Queer Game Studies*. Minneapolis: University of Minnesota Press.

Ryan, Marie-Laure. 2006. *Avatars of Story*. Minneapolis: University of Minnesota Press.

Ryan, Marie-Laure. 2008. "Transfictionality across Media." In *Theorizing Narrativity*, edited by John Pier and José Angel Garcia Landa, 385–417. Berlin: De Gruyter.

Ryan, Marie-Laure. 2015. "Transmedia Storytelling: Industry Buzzword or New Narrative Experience?" *Storyworlds: A Journal of Narrative Studies* 7 (2): 1–19.

Sachs-Hombach, Klaus, and Jan-Noël Thon, eds. 2015. *Game Studies: Aktuelle Ansätze der Computerspielforschung*. Cologne: Herbert von Halem.

Schmidt, Siegfried J. 2000. *Kalte Faszination: Medien, Kultur, Wissenschaft in der Mediengesellschaft*. Weilerswist: Velbrück.

Scott, Suzanne. 2019. *Fake Geek Girls: Fandom, Gender, and the Convergence Culture Industry*. New York: New York University Press.

Smith, Matthew J., and Randy Duncan, eds. 2017. *The Secret Origins of Comics Studies*. New York: Routledge.

Spider-Man. 1982. Developed and published by Parker Brothers. Atari 2600.

Stein, Daniel, and Jan-Noël Thon, eds. 2013. *From Comic Strips to Graphic Novels: Contributions to the Theory and History of Graphic Narrative*. Berlin: De Gruyter.

Superman. 1979. Developed and published by Atari. Atari 2600.

Thon, Jan-Noël. 2014. "Mediality." In *The Johns Hopkins Guide to Digital Media*, edited by Marie-Laure Ryan, Lori Emerson, and Benjamin J. Robertson, 334–337. Baltimore: Johns Hopkins University Press.

Thon, Jan-Noël. 2015. "Converging Worlds: From Transmedial Storyworlds to Transmedial Universes." *Storyworlds: A Journal of Narrative Studies* 7 (2): 21–53.

Thon, Jan-Noël. 2016. *Transmedial Narratology and Contemporary Media Culture*. Lincoln: University of Nebraska Press.

Thon, Jan-Noël. 2017. "Transmedial Narratology Revisited: On the Intersubjective Construction of Storyworlds and the Problem of Representational Correspondence in Films, Comics, and Video Games." *Narrative* 25 (3): 286–320.

Thon, Jan-Noël. 2019. "Transmedia Characters: Theory and Analysis." *Frontiers of Narrative Studies* 5 (2): 176–199.

Tosca, Susana, and Lisbeth Klastrup. 2019. *Transmedial Worlds in Everyday Life: Networked Reception, Social Media and Fictional Worlds*. New York: Routledge.

Ware, Chris. 2000. "'Fairy Tale' Road Rage." In *Little Lit: Folklore and Fairy Tale Funnies*, edited by Art Spiegelman and Françoise Mouly, endpapers. New York: RAW Junior.

Ware, Chris. 2012. *Building Stories*. New York: Pantheon.

Wilde, Lukas R. A. 2015. "Distinguishing Mediality: The Problem of Identifying Forms and Functions of Digital Comics." *Networking Knowledge* 8 (4): 1–15. https://ojs.meccsa.org.uk/index.php/netknow/article/view/386 (accessed 31 January 2020).

Williams, Paul, and James Lyons, eds. 2010. *The Rise of the American Comics Artist: Creators and Contexts*. Jackson: University Press of Mississippi.

Wolf, Mark J. P., and Bernard Perron, eds. 2014. *The Routledge Companion to Video Game Studies*. New York: Routledge.

Wolf, Werner. 1999. *The Musicalization of Fiction: A Study in the Theory and History of Intermediality*. Amsterdam: Rodopi.

Wolf, Werner. 2009. "Metareference across Media: The Concept, Its Transmedial Potentials and Problems, Main Forms and Functions." In *Metareference across Media: Theory and Case Studies*, edited by Werner Wolf in collaboration with Katharina Bantleon and Jeff Thoss, 1–85. Amsterdam: Rodopi.

The Wolf Among Us. 2013. Developed and published by Telltale Games. Windows.

XIII. 2003. Developed and published by Ubisoft. Windows.

Yar's Revenge. 1982. Developed and published by Atari. Atari 2600.

Yockey, Matt, ed. 2017. *Make Ours Marvel: Media Convergence and a Comics Universe*. Austin: University of Texas Press.

Part I

Hybrid medialities

2 Of Pac-Men and Star Raiders

Early mutual representations between comics and videogames (1981–1983)

Nicolas Labarre

In the late 1970s and early 1980s, the increasingly visible success of videogames across their various incarnations triggered a self-reinforcing feedback loop: Other media took notice of the phenomenon and started to discuss these games as a set of distinct and novel cultural practices, which in turn helped give shape to these practices. While the various forms of videogames had hitherto been inscribed in the history of other media and cultural practices—such as stereoscopes, penny arcade machines, TV extensions, or toys (Huhtamo 2005, 2012; Newman 2017)—they became recognized as a new cultural form and a new medium. In *Atari Age*, Michael Newman points out that by 1982/1983, "the flexibility of [the] meanings [of videogames] was closed off" (2017, 2), as opposed to a period of emergence during which they were "without a fixed meaning, without a clear identity" (2017, 8). In that period, *video*games appeared to have morphed into *videogames*.

In addition to the well-known cycle of videogame-themed movies that appeared from July 1982 to June 1983 (*Tron* [1982], *Joysticks* [1983], *WarGames* [1983]), the content of popular magazines, especially when full-text indexes are available, confirms Newman's dating of the phenomenon. To cite a few examples: *Time Magazine* used its first videogame covers in January and then in October 1982; *Playboy*, which had advertised videogames sporadically until 1981, contained no less than three different ads in December of that year, along with a videogame illustration for an unrelated short story; the *National Lampoon* published its only videogame cover story in November 1981. Though these magazines had carried ads for videogames before, notably during an advertising blitz for the Atari 2600 in late 1978, this marked a significant and sudden spike in interest, which was replicated across numerous publications, including comic books, the subject of this chapter.

As indicated above, these mentions in other media do not merely attest to the popularity of games: They also helped frame them, as well as the cultural practices with which they were now associated. In particular, these representations and remediations (Bolter and Grusin 1999) allow us to examine the ways in which the aesthetics and mechanisms of videogames were becoming understood at the time. While gaming magazines were inventing and codifying gaming culture from the *inside* (Kirkpatrick 2015), the boundary setting process was also happening from the *outside*, in other media. Comics[1] are an especially fertile ground for such a study, for they had virtually no interaction with videogames at all until the early 1980s, only to become closely associated with them from this point onwards. This suggests the existence of a sustained and efficient process of domestication through remediation over a limited time span. The following study aims at charting this process and its modalities.

As befits a cultural object whose status was still in flux, videogames were depicted in comics in at least three different ways: as a catalogue of icons, as potential yet incomplete narratives akin to toys, and finally as a possible new aesthetic to be embraced, with various possible combinations between these approaches. I will focus in turn on these three different remediation strategies, using a corpus of comics mostly published between 1981 and 1983.[2]

Videogames as untethered icons, using icons without remediation

Archie offers a good starting point for any study of social and cultural changes as represented in comics. The mostly nonfantastic—"realistic" would hardly be an appropriate description—adventures of Archie and the other Riverdale teenagers have been published continuously since the mid-1950s, and they offer a partial, mildly conservative but extensive chronicle of social and cultural evolutions in the second half of the twentieth century (Beaty 2015; Miller 2018).

Unsurprisingly, *Archie* comics feature video and electronic games as early as 1980. One of the earliest examples is the one-page story "Game Blame" (Gladir et al. 1980), whose twist relies on the fact that *Pong* exists as a console *and* an arcade game. After 1981, videogames are featured regularly on covers and in stories, which typically depict them as a social practice, with little attempts at remediating the games themselves. A typical story is entitled "Video Vengeance" (Doyle et al. 1982), during which Veronica convinces her father to buy all of Riverdale's ubiquitous arcade machines, described as "silly" and "miserable machine-merchants of mindless militaristic mayhem" (Doyle et al. 1982, n.p.), as they have been distracting the boys from their romance. As usual, the story ends with a minor twist: Veronica's father and his butler are captivated by the confiscated games. The games themselves ("Pac-O-M...," "Space War," "Monster Muncher," "Lunar Launch," and "Bomb Away") are only glimpsed in the final panel. A story like "The Ace of Space" (Gladir et al. 1983) is at once entirely about videogames—as Jughead unwittingly repels an alien invasion by impressing them with their skills at "Space Invader" [*sic*]—and devoid of any representation of what happens on the screen.

The games themselves make a rare appearance on the cover of *Everything's Archie* #106 (Goldwater 1983), as Archie dreams that he is being pursued and attacked by a green Pac-Man, two ghosts, two spaceships from *Omega Race* (1981), and Donkey Kong. Given *Archie*'s enduring connection to popular music, the title and the theme of the cover likely refer to *Pac Man Fever,* a 1981 LP that had gone on to sell one million copies (Donovan 2010, 88–89), and the composition may contain a critical allusion to Goya's *The Sleep of Reason* (1797–1799). The representation eschews any technical approach—there is no pixel, no joystick, no machine—and treats videogames as a collection of iconic characters. This reduction of the games to a flat surface is made even more conspicuous by the fact that this cover does not announce any story within the issue.

This image points to a strategy often found in the drawn ads of the period, and to some extent, in the packaging of videogames: using characters or situations from the games as icons untethered to a specific medium. As characters like Pac-Man or Donkey Kong proliferated across media, they became part of a global lexicon of popular icons with little connection to their point of origin: The animated television cartoons in which Pac-Man rubbed elbows with the Smurfs in an entirely compatible visual style serves as proper example of this intermedial syncretism. Nick Montfort and Ian Bogost point to the release of the Atari 2600 version of *Pac-Man* (1982) as a key moment of "cross-media consolidation" (2009, 78), which is consistent with the aforementioned examples as well as with Michael Newman's chronology. The cover to *Everything's Archie* #106 suggests that this consolidation was also taking place in media that had been hitherto little preoccupied with videogames, and in the absence of a direct commercial incentive.

As indicated above, this strategy was on full display in many of the videogame ads present in comic books, with drawn, cartoony representations eclipsing the more abstract forms of representations to be found in the actual games. The pixelated point of origin became in this case barely more than a historical accident, likely to be entirely erased if the property became successful enough. Indeed, there is little difference in composition or in representational strategies between these indigenous videogame characters, such as Frogger or Mario, and those adapted from other visual media, in the context of the adaptation boom of the early 1980s (Aldred 2012; Blanchet 2010). Although these ads were typically for console games, their scope also included arcade games through the numerous coin-op conversions. They thus represented a vast segment of videogame culture—with the exception of computer games—and positioned the most successful characters as reusable icons, untethered to a specific medium.[3]

Remediation as a narrative supplement

A second paradigm emphasized the similarities between videogames and toys. In this conception, comics could be used to supplement videogames and to provide them with a narrative, which they were unable to sustain on their own. To a certain extent, this conception echoed Caillois's assertion that games can have either rules or fiction.[4] In her work on early comics adaptations, Jessica Aldred notes that the manuals were called upon to "fill in" the narrative (2012, 92), and this is precisely what seems to be happening here, whether the comics were sold alongside the cartridges or not.

One of the most striking cases in point, which corresponds with some notable variations to Aldred's observations, is the series of mini-comics produced by DC Comics for Atari[5] in 1982/1983, which were all packaged with high-profile games: five volumes of *Atari Force*, three of *Swordquest*, one of *Centipede*, and one of *Yar's Revenge*. Most of these were scripted by Gerry Conway and adaptation specialist Roy Thomas, whose work ranged from popular fiction to classics to Hollywood movies, with illustrations by such experienced pencillers as Ross Andru and Gil Kane. Tim Lapetino, in the recent *Art of Atari*, and Raiford Guins, in *Games After*, have both argued that Atari possessed a distinct graphic culture, but *Atari Force* displays little of that culture and appears as a generic well-crafted series from that period (Guins 2014; Lapetino 2016).

The Atari Force mini-comics were all inserted into science-fiction-themed cartridges between March 1982 and January 1983: *Defender* (1982), *Berzerk* (1982), *Star Raiders* (1982), *Phoenix* (1982), and *Galaxian* (1983), though there were initially plans to package them with other types of games (Helfer 1982). Accordingly, they tell the story of a science-fiction super team whose adventures mirror the themes and setups of the games to a certain extent. The *Star Raiders* and *Galaxian* comics, in particular, take pains to integrate familiar representations in the comics narrative, while weaving them into an overarching storyline with recurring heroes and a villain, the Lovecraftian Dark Destroyer. This strategy could be described as *a posteriori* transmedia storytelling, in that a fictional universe was superimposed on existing playable moments to supply them with a continuity. The universe is not only constructed after the fact, from hitherto unrelated scenarios (*Star Raiders* was an Atari game, but the others were arcade conversions from various companies), but it is also secondary to the playable moments themselves. The process is to a large extent the mirror image of the reduction of characters to function which Aldred identifies.

This is perhaps best demonstrated by the fate of the *Liberator* mini-comic (20 pages, as opposed to 52 for the other issues). It was created to promote that fairly obscure coin-op (which featured the Atari Force), and it contained a detailed account of its gameplay, down to strategy tips and a presentation of the enemies. That version was used as a supplement in regular comic books, *New Teen Titans* #27 (Giordano et al. 1983b) and *DC Comics Presents* #53 (Giordano et al. 1983a). However, the very same comic was also used at about the same time to accompany *Phoenix*, another shoot 'em up. Only a few mentions of the *Phoenix* name had to be changed for the effort to fit, and the numerous traces of the original story, such as the names of the enemies (the Malaglon), do not hinder this reassignment. An example of an ambitious crossmedia synergy was thus turned into a minimal narrative supplement.

This approach to videogames as playable proto-narratives is reminiscent of the strategy pursued by toy-makers after the success of Kenner's licensed *Star Wars* toys. Indeed, the idea of using comics as a narrative supplement was likely an attempt at replicating a strategy implemented by Mattel in 1981, which had started shipping the first *Masters of the Universe* figures with narrative booklets written by Don Glut and illustrated by Marvel regular Alfredo Alcala. The series started with illustrated stories, which were quickly followed by actual mini-comics.[6] While the continuity of these inserts was superseded by the 1983 animated cartoon, they served as a prototype for this form of *a posteriori* transmedia continuity, which would become a staple for toy lines throughout the 1980s and very often involved either DC Comics or Marvel (*GI Joe*, *Transformers*, etc.) (Bainbridge 2010). It is difficult to ascertain whether Atari directly imitated Mattel, but the *Masters of the Universe* line was an instant success, and as such highly visible. Furthermore, by 1982, the production of these mini-comics had switched to DC Comics, Atari's ally and sister company. Finally, *Atari Age* describes the Atari mini-comics as having been rushed into production, which would fit with the timeline (Helfer 1982). Whether through inspiration or imitation, this strategy aligned videogames with toys, user-oriented rather than story-oriented media texts that could be repurposed in the context of a transmedia project thanks to the cheap narrative form of the comics.[7]

The non-*Atari Force* mini-comics present variations on these strategies, leaning more toward game instructions (*Yar's Revenge* [1982]) or pure narrative (*Centipede* [1983]), but they do not display the same level of ambition or the same attempt at creating a shared universe. The three *Swordquest* minis would warrant a more thorough study, especially in light of their recent nostalgic reexamination in comics (Bowers et al. 2018), but unlike *Atari Force* or *Star Raiders*, they contain little to no attempt at specific remediation. They appear as a supplement to the games, providing them with a fully realized graphic representation but also with clues to solving the various puzzles. Thus, they function like the supplementary material or "feelies" to be found in many games of the time (Kocurek 2013), from maps to bestiaries.

As Atari ran into financial difficulties in late 1982, plans to package mini-comics with other cartridges did not materialize, and while *Atari Force* received its own ongoing comic book series, it retained very little videogame inspiration beyond its name.[8] However, Atari and DC Comics partnered on a second and slightly different attempt to provide *Star Raiders*, one of their flagship titles, with a narrative in 1983.[9] This took the form of a graphic novel, illustrated by José Luis García-López, who became the main artist on *Atari Force* the following year. As indicated by the promotional copy in *Atari Age*, the graphic novel intended to account for the gameplay—a very early use of the word—of *Star Raiders* and not merely its narrative: "Writer Elliot S. Maggin and artist Jose Luis Garcia Lopez have taken the gameplay of **Star Raiders** and expanded it into a deluxe 62-page epic, full of action, adventure, and breathtaking graphics" (Atari Clubs 1983, n.p, original emphasis). This "expansion" is again an explicit reversal of Aldred's "reduction to function," and it underlines the difference between such a project and the use of videogames as pre-remediated icons, described previously. The story also plays into the transmedia universe set-up in the mini-comics by alluding to what happened in the story packaged with the *Star Raider* cartridge (more precisely, it explains away this story, before reintroducing the "real" enemies).

The graphic novel is inspired by contemporary space adventure comics and by *Star Wars*, but it also attempts to recreate the interface of the game. This is most notable in the opening splash page, which overlays the pixelated Atari 2600 display on an elaborate space scene, inspired by Chris Foss paintings, and frames all of this into a command panel that looks very similar to an arcade cabinet. To show the pixels is unusual—games were redrawn using geometric displays in the *Atari Force* mini-comics, for instance—since it identifies videogames as a technologically constrained visual enunciation, which sets them clearly apart from toys. The result of this assemblage is visually similar to that of the overlays used in early videogames such as *Space Invaders* to add an evocative background to the game beyond the technological means of 1978.[10] In doing so, the authors of the *Star Raiders* graphic novel emphasize the lacunary nature of the games, implying that comics can provide them with texture as well as fiction, but they also point to the specificity of videogames at a time when Atari had foregone its mini-comics strategy.

Beyond dedicated adaptations or supplements, publishers also used comics in videogame advertising. In addition to obvious candidates like *Spider-Man* (1982) or *Popeye* (1983), games such as *Solar Fox* (1983), *Battlezone* (1983), *Joust* (1983), *Mario Bros.* (1983), or *Moon Patrol* (1983) were all promoted through one-page comics, in comic books, but also in dedicated videogame magazines. These stories further affirm the usefulness of comics as a narrative form, used to frame the playable moments in the games themselves. In *The Formation of Gaming Culture*, Graeme Kirkpatrick argues that "a cultural practice judges its product by comparing them to each other and not with reference to things outside its domain" (2015, 65). Between 1981 and 1983, the recurrent use of comics and illustrations by game publishers suggests that even within this nascent field, actors felt the need to reference and use a better-established cultural field.

The perceived incompleteness of videogames was also on display, though in a different configuration, when they appeared in continuing comic book series, removed from a direct promotional purpose. A common storyline, found in *Weird War Tales* #102 (Wein and Barr 1981), *Wonder Woman* #294–296[11] (Giordano et al. 1982a, 1982b; Giordano and Wolfman 1982), and *Thor* #328 (Gruenwald et al. 1983), features videogames coming to life or becoming the locus for a "real" fight; as a matter of fact, a similar storyline also featured in the ABC *Spider-Man and His Amazing Friends* animated cartoon in 1981 (Newman 2017, 178–180). The *Thor* story is perhaps the simplest of these three and, as a result, the most easily legible. During an electronics show, an industrial spy disguised as the main character for the *Megatak* videogame is caught in a short-circuit and "sucked into the very machine he has sought to plunder" (Gruenwald et al. 1983, 11). While the game is being demoed, he emerges from the screen and unleashes Pac-Men and flying saucers on the crowd, until Thor and Sif intervene to stop him. The multiplying Pac-Men in the story owe a lot to the iconic use I have outlined above, but the story also reads as a discourse on comics against videogames. Before the spy is absorbed into the game, he is pictured in three successive positions in red, green, and blue dots, in a transparent nod to print technology, and a caption ominously indicates: "What happens next is no game" (Gruenwald et al. 1983, 11). Later in the story, when the videogame villain has been vanquished, another caption announces: "Gregory Nettles, briefly a super-man named Megatak […] collapses, now a mere industrial spy in a silly costume" (Gruenwald et al. 1983, 21). Throughout the story, Alan Kupperberg (pencil) and Vince Coletta (ink) contrast the dynamism of a graphic representation that quotes a lot from Jack Kirby, the paradigmatic superhero artist (in the poses, the character design, the abundant use of the distinctive "Kirby crackle"), with the flat graphics and the interchangeable characters of the videogames. A *Thor* story is "no game," indeed, and though there may be something tongue-in-cheek about the description of the villain's "silly costume," videogames end up defeated and even exposed as a mere distraction since the major reveal of the episode hinges on Thor's sentimental life.

Though the editors of the *Wonder Woman* story reference *Tron* in the letter column (Giordano and Wolfman 1983, n.p.), the celebration of the potential aesthetics of videogames to be found in that film is not replicated in the comics.

Remediation as engagement

While the aforementioned superhero comics served as an implicit cultural commentary, other comics publications offered a more overt cultural and aesthetic engagement with the form. John Holmstrom, working in magazines such as *Heavy Metal* and *Video Games*, produced a substantial body of work to that effect.

John Holmstrom was a key punk artist: He illustrated two of the early Ramones albums and was the founder of *PUNK* in 1976, then a contributor to its spiritual sibling, the *East Village Eye* (1979–1987) (Kelly 2016). In October 1981, he inaugurated a regular illustrated videogame column in *Heavy Metal*, which had at the time developed a keen interest in the popular avant-garde, from Blondie to H. R. Giger to Françoise Mouly and Art Spiegelman's *RAW* (Labarre 2017). Holmstrom's column became a regular feature in July 1982, always with accompanying illustrations. At about the same time, in August 1982, he became a contributing editor to *Video Games*, yet another New York–based publication, edited by Steve Bloom, along with transplants from both *PUNK* and *Heavy Metal*.

Most of Holmstrom's chronicles are game or system reviews, accompanied by redrawn graphic elements. In his *Robotron* review (Holmstrom 1982b), for instance, the handwritten text surrounds a large panel in which all the main characters are redrawn in a hybrid style, which combines their original design with Holmstrom's energetic angular rendition. On other occasions, the system is more elaborate, as in his full-page article "Joey Ramone Reviews Imagic" (Holmstrom 1982a), in which views of the system, diagrams, and recreations of the graphic elements coexist with stylized depictions of the players themselves. The page offers a fine demonstration of Holmstrom's idiosyncratic, adjustable but careful examination of the medium. His is a polyphonic approach that encompasses cultural permutations and stresses the phatic and embodied dimension of videogame playing.

The most accomplished example of this polyphony appears in "Three Days in Heaven," an illustrated report of Holmstrom's visit to the 1982 AMOA (Amusement and Music Operators Association), published in the sixth issue of *Video Games* (Holmstrom 1983). After a *Mad*-inspired yet carefully documented splash page, Holmstrom redraws game screens or marquees, uses collage to suggest the specific technology of *Astron Belt*, the first laser-disc game, and concludes the piece with a personal and amusing anecdote.

Unlike the other examples cited in this chapter, there is very little at stake commercially for Holmstrom in these columns. They are in effect fan creations that display a user-oriented form of remediation, as opposed to the more policed intermedial circulations found in official adaptations, extensions, or advertisements. Holmstrom appeared intent to represent and help create a crossover culture encompassing comics, heavy metal, and videogames; this combination, which was well-suited to *Heavy Metal*, appears to have been a specifically New Yorker phenomenon. While the short-lived magazine *Vidiot* (1982–1983) was betting on the compatibility of pop music and videogames in its full-page photos of pop stars playing arcade games, Holmstrom was adding comics to the cultural mix. Beyond Holmstrom's work, *Video Games* highlighted this crossover potential: It included a serialized comics story,[12] referenced the appearance of videogames in syndicated comic strips, and generally chronicled every form of hybridization between comics and videogames. This distinct crossover culture was thus sufficiently formed to generate or sustain its own publishing institution, at least for a while. The magazine lasted for 18 issues, and Holmstrom as well as the other comic's authors left the title after #16.

Conclusion

In the early 1980s, comics were used to come to terms with videogames through a variety of remediation strategies, from minimal engagement (videogames as brands, comics as "feelies") to more sustained examinations of the articulations between the two media. None of the approaches outlined in this chapter is inherently superior to the other, and, as a matter of fact, variations of these various strategies are still in use today, from Marvel-produced *Halo* tie-ins to one-page animated GIF comics of *Megaman*. These multiple attempts at overcoming the resisting difference between the two media provided consumers with multiple channels of engagement, braiding the two media, intertwining the two sets of cultural practices, and, in doing so, creating and refining the social and aesthetic position of videogames as a new medium.

Notes

1 I am deliberately using "comics" rather than "comic books"—a specific publishing format—so as not exclude from this study the comics pages published in magazines.
2 This corpus was constructed using contemporary sources (references in *Atari Age* or *Video Games*, for instance), fan forums (www.atariage.com; accessed 31 January 2020), extensive readings of magazines containing comics (*Heavy Metal*, *Video Games*), and especially the indexation of stories and covers in the *Grand Comic Book Database* (www.comics.org; accessed 31 January 2020).
3 Noticeably, many of the ads published in comic books were bought by Parker Brothers, which joined the videogame market in 1982 on the back of coin-op conversions and games licensed from various media properties (Montfort and Bogost 2009). The visual strategies of the ads thus echoed the underlying industrial convergence.
4 Of course, that assertion has been strongly challenged by games theorists, notably by Jesper Juul (2005).
5 Though the two companies existed as separate entities, they were both part of the Warner conglomerate.
6 The mini-comics can be read at www.he-man.org/publishing/subsection.php?id=52&subid=20 (accessed 31 January 2020).
7 Montfort and Bogost suggest that while Atari was pushing back against the toy paradigm in their advertisement, videogames were considered as toys by the industry at large in the late 1970s and early 1980s (Montfort and Bogost 2009, 119). Later, Nintendo's NES was famously positioned as a toy in the American market to avoid the stigma of the North-American videogame crash (Donovan 2010, 165–178).
8 Fittingly, the first issue contained ads for videogames but also for *Masters of the Universe* toys. The series was to be part of a broader line, Atari Comics, which did not materialize.
9 The collection also includes an adaptation of *Warlord*, another Atari game, but the game and the comics share very little beyond their title.

10 It is perhaps more than a coincidence that some of these overlays had been created by comics artists. For instance, Frank Brunner, who had worked for all the major comics publishers in the 1970s, designed the overlay for *Warriors* (1979) (Skelly 2012, 148–150).

11 This narrative arc was scripted by Roy Thomas around the same time as he was contributing to the *Atari Force* mini-comics.

12 "Zydroid Legion" by Matt Howarth and Lou Stathis, two *Heavy Metal* contributors, who used the already familiar trope of videogames as preparation for an actual science-fiction war.

Works cited

Aldred, Jessica. 2012. "A Question of Character: Transmediation, Abstraction and Identification in Early Games Licensed from Movies." In *Before the Crash: Early Video Game History*, edited by Mark J. P. Wolf, 90–104. Detroit: Wayne State University Press.

Atari Clubs. 1983. "Star Raiders." *Atari Age* 2 (2): 30–31.

Bainbridge, Jason. 2010. "Fully Articulated: The Rise of the Action Figure and the Changing Face of 'Children's' Entertainment." *Continuum* 24 (6): 829–842.

Battlezone. 1983. Developed and published by Atari. Atari 2600.

Beaty, Bart. 2015. *Twelve-Cent Archie*. New Brunswick: Rutgers University Press.

Berzerk. 1982. Developed and published by Atari. Atari 2600.

Blanchet, Alexis. 2010. *Des pixels à Hollywood: Cinéma et jeu vidéo, une histoire économique et culturelle*. Châtillon: Pix'n love.

Bolter, J. David, and Richard Grusin. 1999. *Remediation: Understanding New Media*. Cambridge, MA: MIT Press.

Bowers, Chad, Chris Sims, and Ghostwriter X. 2018. *Swordquest: Real World* Vol. 1. Mt. Laurel: Dynamite Entertainment.

Centipede. 1983. Developed and published by Atari. Atari 2600.

Defender. 1982. Developed and published by Atari. Atari 2600.

Donovan, Tristan. 2010. *Replay: The History of Video Games*. East Sussex: Yellow Ant.

Doyle, Frank, Dan DeCarlo, and Jim DeCarlo. 1982. "Video Vengeance." *Archie's Girls Betty and Veronica* #320, n.p. Pelham: Archie Comics Publications, Inc.

Galaxian. 1983. Developed and published by Atari. Atari 2600.

Giordano, Dick, and Marv Wolfman, eds. 1982. *Wonder Woman* Vol. 1 #295. New York: DC Comics.

Giordano, Dick, and Marv Wolfman. 1983. *Wonder Woman* Vol. 1 #302. New York: DC Comics.

Giordano, Dick, Julius Schwartz, and E. Nelson Bridwell, eds. 1983a. *DC Comics Presents* Vol. 1 #53: *Superman in the House of Mystery*. New York: DC Comics.

Giordano, Dick, Len Wein, and Nicola Cuti. 1983b. *New Teen Titans* Vol. 1 #27. New York: DC Comics.

Giordano, Dick, Len Wein, and Carl Gafford, eds. 1982a. *Wonder Woman* Vol. 1 #294. New York: DC Comics.

Giordano, Dick, Marv Wolfman, and Ernie Colon, eds. 1982b. *Wonder Woman* Vol. 1 #296. New York: DC Comics.

Gladir, George, Dan DeCarlo, and Jim DeCarlo. 1983. "The Ace of Space." *Jughead* #329, n.p. Pelham: Archie Comics Publications, Inc.

Gladir, George, Dick Malmgren, and Jon D'Agostino. 1980. "Game Blame." *Betty and Me* #110, n.p. Pelham: Archie Comics Publications, Inc.

Goldwater, Richard, ed. 1983. *Everything's Archie* #106. Pelham: Archie Comics Publications, Inc.

Gruenwald, Mark, Michael Carlin, and Jim Shooter, eds. 1983. *Thor* Vol. 1 #328. New York: Marvel Comics.

Guins, Raiford. 2014. *Game After: A Cultural Study of Video Game Afterlife.* Cambridge, MA: MIT Press.

Helfer, Andrew. 1982. "The Making of Atari Force." *Atari Age* 1 (4): 8–9.

Holmstrom, John. 1982a. "Joey Ramone Reviews Imagic." *Heavy Metal,* April 1982.

Holmstrom, John. 1982b. "Dossier: *Robotron: 2048.*" *Heavy Metal,* December 1982.

Holmstrom, John. 1983. "Three Days in Heaven." *Video Games* 6: n.p.

Huhtamo, Erkki. 2005. "Slots of Fun, Slots of Trouble: Toward an Archaeology of Electronic Gaming." In *Handbook of Computer Game Studies*, edited by Joost Raessens and Jeffrey Goldstein, 1–21. Cambridge, MA: MIT Press.

Huhtamo, Erkki. 2012. "What's Victoria Got to Do with It? Toward an Archeology of Domestic Video Gaming." In *Before the Crash: Early Video Game History*, edited by Mark J. P. Wolf, 30–52. Detroit: Wayne State University Press.

Joust. 1983. Developed by Williams Electronics. Published by Atari. Atari 2600.

Joysticks. 1983. Dir. Greydon Clark. USA: Citadel Films.

Juul, Jesper. 2005. *Half-Real: Video Games between Real Rules and Fictional Worlds.* Cambridge, MA: MIT Press.

Kelly, John. 2016. "Another Look at the East Village Eye." *The Comics Journal*, 15 February. www.tcj.com/another-look-at-the-east-village-eye/ (accessed 31 January 2020).

Kirkpatrick, Graeme. 2015. *The Formation of Gaming Culture: UK Gaming Magazines, 1981–1995.* New York: Palgrave Macmillan.

Kocurek, Carly A. 2013. "The Treachery of Pixels: Reconsidering Feelies in an Era of Digital Play." *Journal of Gaming and Virtual Worlds* 5 (3): 295–306.

Labarre, Nicolas. 2017. Heavy Metal, *l'autre* Métal Hurlant. Bordeaux: Presses universitaires de Bordeaux.

Lapetino, Tim. 2016. *Art of Atari.* Mt. Laurel: Dynamite Entertainment.

Mario Bros. 1983. Developed by Nintendo. Published by Atari. Atari 2600.

Miller, Nicholas E. 2018. "'Now That It's Just Us Girls': Transmedial Feminisms from *Archie* to *Riverdale.*" *Feminist Media Histories* 4 (3): 205–226.

Montfort, Nick, and Ian Bogost. 2009. *Racing the Beam: The Atari Video Computer System.* Cambridge, MA: MIT Press.

Moon Patrol. 1983. Developed by Irem Corp. Published by Atari. Atari 2600.

Newman, Michael Z. 2017. *Atari Age: The Emergence of Video Games in America.* Cambridge, MA: MIT Press.

Omega Race. 1981. Developed and published by Midway. Arcade.

Pac-Man. 1982. Developed and published by Atari. Atari 2600.

Phoenix. 1982. Developed and published by Atari. Atari 2600.

Popeye. 1983. Developed by Parker Brothers. Published by Atari. Atari 2600.

Skelly, Tim. 2012. "The Rise and Fall of Cinematronics." In *Before the Crash: Early Video Game History*, edited by Mark J. P. Wolf, 138–167. Detroit: Wayne State University Press.
Solar Fox. 1983. Developed by Midway. Published by CBS Electronics. Atari 2600.
Space Invaders. 1978. Developed and published by Taito. Arcade.
Spider-Man. 1982. Developed by Parker Brothers. Published by Atari. Atari 2600.
Star Raiders. 1982. Developed and published by Atari. Atari 2600.
Tron. 1982. Dir. Steven Lisberger. USA: Buena Vista Pictures Distribution.
WarGames. 1983. Dir. John Badham. USA: MGM/United Artists.
Warriors. 1979. Developed by Tim Skelly. Published by Vectorbeam. Arcade.
Wein, Len, and Mike W. Barr, eds. 1981. *Weird War Tales* Vol. 1 #102. New York: DC Comics.
Yar's Revenge. 1982. Developed and published by Atari. Atari 2600.

3 Interfacing comics and games

A socio-affective multimodal approach

Carman Ng

Once deemed mere pastimes, digital games and comics have evolved into significant sources of narrative deepening, aesthetic experimentation, and revenue in this cultural moment of transmedial storytelling and franchises. Each has become the subject of increasing academic interest, inspiring an expanding body of literature and research methods. Digital game criticism broadly involves three trajectories: formalist approaches that examine the aesthetics and forms of games, social approaches that consider cultural and historical aspects of the medium, and approaches that integrate practice and design (Jagoda 2017). The reconsideration of comics and graphic novels as complex artifacts has motivated, for instance, investigations of their role as critical discourses regarding identities and politics (Bramlett 2012); cognition and visual literacy (Cohn 2013b); the genealogy of comics as ethical engagement with history, war, and trauma (Chute 2016); interactions with documentaries as carriers of narrative, performativity, and witnessing (Mickwitz 2016); and the medium's potential contributions to memory studies (Ahmed and Crucifix 2018). Against this backdrop, we find digital games characterized as hybrid forms, such as *Framed* (2014) and *XIII* (2003), which play with the structures and stylistic conventions of comics, creating distinct gameplay experiences indicative of changing media technologies and landscapes, as well as aesthetic experimentation practices.[1]

Examining such "in-between" media creates a multilayered challenge. For games and comics as emergent media forms, analytical literature, approaches, and tools geared to dissect their materiality on a foundational basis are still emerging.[2] Attempts at critical inquiries appear to be commonly restricted by research foci and the vocabulary of particular disciplines, or by degrees of interdisciplinarity at the potential expense of maintaining analytical control. In this context, "hybridity" has become a default descriptor in research and design that is devoid of distinct elements. A notion transposed from biology to the humanities, social sciences, and media studies, hybridity concerns new forms of media and aesthetics resulting from interweaving media logics and technologies. For instance, films such as *The Matrix* trilogy (1999–2003) or comics adaptations like *Sin City* (2005) and *300* (2007) signal a change in global visual culture since the late 1990s. Shot on digital backlit sets, they blend the medial logics of illustration and filmmaking, as well as architectural design, for a new visual aesthetics of continuity. This aesthetics explores juxtaposition and integration of varied visual media within the same frame in ways that are unlike live-action cinematography or computer-generated imagery (Manovich 2007). Approaching this phenomenon from a political science perspective, Andrew Chadwick (2017) examines hybridity as a constant in all contemporary media systems, where political communication and power are increasingly defined by the effective blending of older and newer media logics by sign users and organizations.

This sketch already suggests the conceptual and sociopolitical heft of hybridity. Yet it has shifted from a necessary heuristic into a banal assumption (Kraidy 2015). While isolating "permissible" design units may risk promoting a normative understanding of medium specificity that, in relatively radical forms, resembles purism, it remains constructive to gain a deeper understanding of what combinations of semiotic resources constitute hybridity, and from what aspects we can appropriately investigate such hybridization processes. Artifacts connecting games and comics involve and implicate three dimensions, namely aesthetic, ludic, and narrative. Expounding these dynamics requires a methodological intervention anchored in the empirical inquiry of multimodal complexities and meaning-making mechanisms of media. This chapter therefore first outlines the socio-semiotic theory of multimodality and processes of digital annotation, focused on delineating layers and combinations of semiotic resources for systematic analyses. Second, I examine three interactive audiovisual media to illustrate development foci in particular moments of the continuous convergence between games and comics. This provides the basis to discuss four facets of "movement" that I consider significant to examining such convergence: (1) on medium, (a) the animation of semiotic resources that transpose meaning-making functions across media; (b) the kinetic aspect of player enactment; (2) on sociocultural context, (c) a heightened focus on embodiment in interface design; and (d) shifts in societal discourses on the role of digital games and comics. Orienting this analysis toward the perspective of media ecology, my last section posits an interdisciplinary approach of intersecting affective sciences, multimodality, and media user experiments to account for patterns among meaning making, affects, and perception for a critical evaluation of what hybridity entails and of its relevance to the study of any emergent media.

Multimodality

Multimodality examines how diverse media artifacts, interactions, and performances combine expressive resources for communication, including visual, linguistic, sonic, haptic elements, and more. Research of the field aims at a foundational understanding of how an expanding range of phenomena convey meaning, enabling productive, empirical collaborations across disciplines. These encompass inquiries in reception and perception studies, psychology, cognitive science, and growing work in empirical comics research (Dunst et al. 2018). In investigating (hybrid) media, it is necessary to identify the meaning-making mechanisms involved as they manifest in the combinations of semiotic resources and the ways of engagement within specific medial and technological constraints. Examining how adaptation and crossmedia experimentations transfect such mechanisms is integral to any meaningful discussion of hybridity. For this endeavor, data-driven approaches of multimodality introduce analytical rigor, with emphasis on artifact-guided interpretation, discourse, and the provision of the analytical concept "canvas" (Bateman et al. 2017a). To articulate complex intersemiotic relations, the concept of canvas, or multimodal slices, ensures that one selects and analyzes meaning-making units and aspects appropriate to particular research questions. Regarding comics, the canvas as a perceptual unit refers to any comics-resembling organizations, such as pages, double-page spreads, panels, and any panel-binding visual resources (see Figure 3.1). In this analysis, the selected canvases are the gameplay interface/screen and the medium-specified range of player enactment possibilities.

As detailed in a recent article on comics studies and digital humanities scholarship analyzing comics from the 1930s through the early 2010s (Bateman et al. 2017a), page layout and the organization of panels as well as visual materials fundamentally shape the interpretation processes of comics and graphic novels. Yet page composition receives inadequate analytical attention, even as psychological studies affirm that panel layouts notably affect reading paths (Cohn 2013a). A linguistics-inflected multimodal

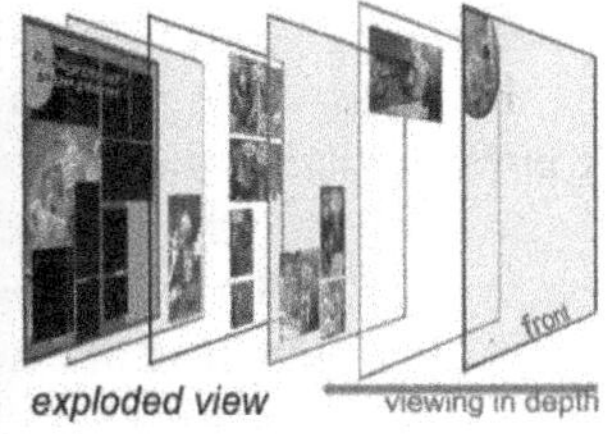

Figure 3.1 Exploded view of *Batwoman* Vol. 2: *To Drown the World* (Williams and Blackman 2013, 54–55; see also Bateman et al. 2017a, 478).

approach examines organization patterns of meaning-making units. These foci motivate an open, multilevel, annotation scheme complementary to extant ones inclined toward geometric descriptions (which are limited for interpretive analyses) and further empirical, corpus-based inquiries. Additionally, this provides access to understanding the diachronic development of comics and graphic novels, a dimension likewise relevant in the present task of researching hybrid media forms.

The theory and methodologies of multimodality are increasingly taken up in media and communication studies, including inquiries into the rhetoric of digital games (Hawreliak 2018, 2019) and ludonarrative models for game analyses (Toh 2019), experimental literature (Gibbons 2012), and the narratology of comic art (Mikkonen 2017).[3] From a disciplinary perspective, multimodal analyses have been applied to, among others, film (Bateman and Schmidt 2012), interactions (Norris 2004), movement in space (McMurtrie 2016), and digital platforms (Jewitt 2014). A framework considering multimodal discourse semantics will facilitate further research involving larger data sets, degrees of computer-assisted automatic analyses, and current convergences among media and neuroscience studies on the role of semiotic mode organization in guiding interpretations. Concerning the visual narratives of comics and graphic novels, there is a need to explore additional annotations for intra-panel and panel-linking operations, to articulate the discursive dimensions of meaning making involved. This chapter addresses this need.

Analyses and discussion

In this section, I explore three types of interactive audiovisual media: the digital graphic novel, gestural media, and the comics game. They are, respectively, *Metal Gear Solid 2: Bande Dessinée* (2008),[4] *Breathing Room* (2014), and *Gorogoa* (2017). The aim is to identify commonalities and contrasts among these selected artifacts as indicators of shifting foci in the technological and aesthetic intersections between games and comics. *Metal Gear Solid 2: Bande Dessinée* forms part of a war-themed, Japanese stealth videogame franchise of the same title (1998–2015), globally recognized for subversive gameplay, narrative complexity, and a critical stance toward the military-entertainment complex (Noon and Dyer-Witheford 2010).[5] Adapted from the second installment *Metal Gear Solid 2: Sons of Liberty* (2001), the digital graphic novel, along with the one based on its prequel *Metal Gear Solid* (1998), construes the first medial transposition of its kind: from games to graphic novels, then interactive and animated versions. *Breathing Room* was a gesture-driven comic exhibited at the 2014 Conference of the Modern Language Association, which focused on the 25-year history of experimental literary art. The most recent among the selected media, *Gorogoa*, is an independent digital game playable on PC, console, and mobile systems.

Through puzzle-solving, it explores the protagonist's childhood encounter with a mythical beast and the lifelong ramifications.

As a potential result of an unquestioned embrace of medial hybridity, few studies demonstrate in detail how alleged features, such as animation in comics, communicate and shape the medium experience. To address this research gap, transcription is a productive start. Figure 3.2 provides a snapshot of the process, applied to analyzing the *development* stage of *Metal Gear Solid 2: Bande Dessinée* (shots 12–19, totaled 50 seconds).[6] Based on shots as the analytical units, the transcription sequentially tabulates the use of seven semiotic resources in relation to content, ranging from graphics, speech, intermedial features, to sound/music. In this narrative stage, we find the protagonist, Snake, infiltrate a US military tanker to capture photo evidence of a latest prototype Metal Gear Ray, an amphibious machine with nuclear capacity in secret development. Snake is, unknowingly, being photographed by the antagonist, Ocelot, and will be framed as the perpetrator for sinking the tanker.

The current analysis emphasizes *functional* motivations that anchor intermedial experimentations. I posit that using the panel as an analytical threshold contributes to examining animations of traditionally motionless features of comics, for it sheds light on two scales: content communicated in individual panels and content interpreted across panels. That is, the analysis examines intended interpretations shaped by the layout designs. The *Metal Gear Solid 2: Bande Dessinée* sequence stresses shifts in point of view. Three instances of *zoom-out* occur from shots 15–17, shifting from a contextualizing, level-angle shot stressing the enormity of Metal Gear, to two shots of increased shot sizes (close to medium) that denote Snake's perspective and then the fact that he is a subject of surveillance. The use of a *handheld* camera and the coupling of semiotic resources in shots 17 and 19 further support this discourse interpretation. With a frame-crossing speech bubble, characters' speech, changes in music, sound effect, and image brightness, the intermedial feature "insertion" in shot 19 communicates a layering of points of view via a visual overlay—a panel-within-panel presentation.

Across 12 chapters of the digital graphic novel, we find different combinations of intermedial features that modulate dramatization effects and pace (see Figure 3.3). Four intermedial features are identified, three of which concern the animation and interaction of panels; one involves the animation of onomatopoeia, i.e., word formations of sounds, such as "click" in imitation of camera shutters movements in photo-taking. Occurrences of these features reflect the narrative development of *Metal Gear Solid 2: Sons of Liberty*, widely deemed a significant postmodern videogame that critiques motifs of control, social engineering, artificial intelligence, and existentialism. Regularly presenting players with contradictory information, the gameplay experience is undergirded by uncertainty and unease. Thus, we find in the initial narrative stages limited instances of *panel flash* (n=3),

	#12-14: 0:04:07-0:04:09	#15: 0:04:13-0:04:18	#16: 0:04:19-0:04:37	#17: 0:04:38-0:04:41	#18: 0:04:42-0:04:48	#19: 0:04:49-0:04:57
Content	Parts of a gigantic machine (Metal Gear Ray) are shown, via 3 shots.	The Metal Gear Ray prototype is shown to be amid gathered marines.	Snake begins taking photos of the prototype, which is more advanced than the Rex model.	Snake is being observed by an unidentified character (Ocelot).	Ocelot takes photos of Snake.	Ocelot takes photos of Snake.
Graphics	N/A	Pop-up of speech bubble	Pop-up of speech bubble	The string-like tail of the speech bubble goes beyond the frame.	Onomatopoeia: KLICK (blue, comics-ish font)	Onomatopoeia: KLICK Adjustment of image clarity in inserted panel (POV)
Inter-Medial Features	N/A	N/A	N/A	N/A	Onomatopoeia	Insertion Onomatopoeia
Shot / Angle	Extreme close; Low	Extreme close; Level	Close; Above	Medium; Above	Medium; Low	Close; Above
Camerawork	Pan	Handheld; Zoom out	Zoom out	Zoom out (Fast)	Handheld	Dissolve (end)
Speech	N/A	Snake: "There it is. Metal Gear Ray..."	S: "Impressive. You should see how **sleek** this Metal Gear is, Otacon. It makes ol' Rexxy look like a dumpster with legs." O: "Yeah, yeah... Just make sure you remove the lens cap before shooting, okay?"	Ocelot: "Heh. Our boy is right on schedule."	Ocelot: "Smile for your adoring public, **hero.**"	Ocelot: "After I'm done with you, they'll all think you're **public enemy number one.**"
Sound /Music	SFX: Air effects	SFX: Thunder	SFX: Camera shutters	Ominous music	SFX: Camera shutters	SFX: Impact

Figure 3.2 Transcription of *Metal Gear Solid 2: Bande Dessinée* (narrative stage: development).

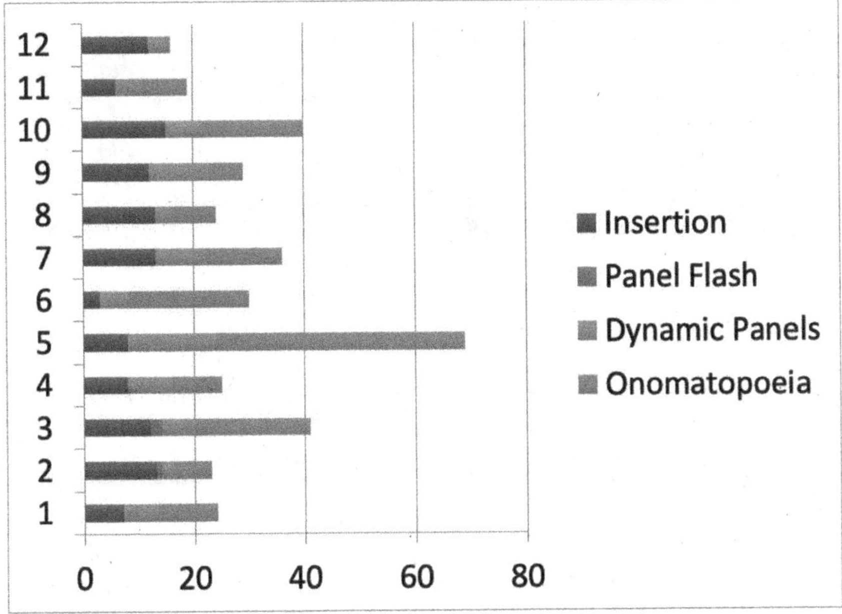

Figure 3.3 Intermedial features in *Metal Gear Solid 2: Bande Dessinée* (x-axis: number of instances; y-axis: chapters).

which communicate action sequences through fast successions of panels. Occurring in all chapters and concentrated in chapters 2, 7, and 10, *insertion* (n=122) highlights changes in perspectives or focuses on significant objects, by injecting panel(s) onto existing frames. *Dynamic panels* kinetically interact with one another, occurring in spikes in chapters 5, 7, and 9. While *Metal Gear Solid 2: Bande Dessinée* is approximately 14 minutes longer than the animated version of its prequel, the use of dynamic panels has increased fourth-fold (n=80). I propose that this is in part a technological and commercial decision. *Metal Gear Solid 2: Bande Dessinée* was released simultaneously with *Metal Gear Solid 4: Guns of the Patriots* (2008) and the *Metal Gear Solid 4 Database* (2008). At that historical moment, videogames and console systems were heavily evaluated by audiovisual aesthetics and processing power. Dynamic panels transpose what is conveyed in the organization of panels with higher technical finesse, offering optimal indicators of the pursued technological progress.

The analysis above points to an ability to construe complex semiotic operations in what are generally considered motion comics. More importantly, it indicates intentional animation, motivating particular forms of reading that align with the layout and thus designers' intended interpretations. In this regard, ludicity further complicates meaning communication

Figure 3.4 Dynamic layouts and time-lapse effects by dialing motion in *Breathing Room* © Erik Loyer.

and organization mechanisms through the procedural and interactive elements entailed in player action. *Framed* (2014) is, for instance, among the pioneering comics-games where panel manipulation shifts the narrative and gameplay outcomes.

My discussion turns to two media as illustrative of experimentations that play with the said principle with distinct aesthetic and immersive experiences. The first is *Breathing Room*. A prototype developed for the Leap Motion controller, *Breathing Room* intersects players' arm and hand gestures, audiovisual aesthetics, and algorithms to generate dynamic layouts, captions, and distinct experiences (see Figure 3.4). "Breathing," in the literal sense of the narrative, is the sound of breath triggered by player motion and accompanies changing visuals of a tree and the landscape. This interactive multimedia experience shows the possibility of using contemporary technologies for artistic and literary expressions. Experiencing *Breathing Room* involves an interplay of semiotic, procedural, and embodied elements, which, as we shall see below, is an aspect increasingly emphasized in the digital present.

Lastly, I turn to *Gorogoa*. The 2017 puzzle game originates from an attempted interactive graphic novel, from which the designer, Jason Roberts, experimented with concepts of comics panels, frames, and layout structure. Like *Framed*, *Gorogoa* proceeds from the manipulation of frames. Players explore, combine, and overlay frames within a two-by-two structure, thereby opening up subsequent scenes and puzzles of the narrative (see Figure 3.5). Yet its jigsaw puzzle mechanic and reliance on visual matching introduces an analogue quality to its narrative revelation and gameplay experience. A likewise productive metaphor in understanding the gameplay is, in my view, forming stacks and combinations of cards. By amplifying a specific nostalgic aura and aesthetics, *Gorogoa*'s puzzle-solving mechanics "stretch" the gameplay experience between a two-dimensional interface and a three-dimensional game world, crisscrossing between periods of the protagonist's lifetime (the narrative dimension), the audiovisual ensemble at localized gameplay moments and a creative process of

Figure 3.5 Capture from *Gorogoa* (2017).

producing hand-drawn graphics for over five years (the aesthetic dimension), and different forms of frame manipulation to realize gameplay (the ludic dimension).

With *Breathing Room* and *Gorogoa*, this chapter discusses ways of experimenting with frames and panels observed in recent multimodal artifacts that are technologically refined and gradually diverge from page-based comics conventions. Rather than an uncritical celebration of technology, my provocation is to re-contextualize our perception of digital games and gamified comics as interfaces. To evaluate the analytical possibilities of this perspective, we should take into account trajectories in motion in our current mediasphere.

Tracing trajectories

Motivating the diverse phenomena of the mediasphere are practices of transmedial storytelling and intermediality, embedded in wider sociocultural contexts where technological, economic, and social discourse factors shape media developments. Appreciating the multivalence of the comics and games nexus needs a joined understanding of the micro- and macro-level effects of such practices. The discussion thus far identifies how movement becomes manifest on the micro level. When content is transposed across media, shifts in the main meaning-making mechanisms change the (aesthetic) delivery and experiences of narratives. For instance, *Metal Gear Solid 2: Bande Dessinée* demonstrates how the animation of panels realizes inference patterns informed by the layout of a comics page. The forms of movement in *Breathing Room* and *Gorogoa* indicate an arising trajectory in the current media ecology, a fuller understanding of which requires a contextualizing perspective. I posit that such perspective specifically concerns notions of digital interfaces, where the assorted media and experiences within the comics and games nexus bear relevance.

Digitally mediated experiences and their development are anchored by two logics: immediacy and hypermediacy (Bolter and Grusin 1999). The former concerns transparency, the illusion that the user interacts with a technology, medium, and its content directly without mediation. This often takes the form of close reflection of the user's visual experience, as pursued in virtual reality interfaces. Second, hypermediacy refers to the use of multiple resources, such as linguistic texts, images, and videos, to enable user interaction. In other words, interfaces are intermediary, rhythmic, and multimodal, involving both algorithmic and interactive processes. Recent accounts further reveal inherent complexities in interfaces as zones of effects and processes (Galloway 2012) and organizations of "envelopes" that regulate users' perception, attention, and media use (Ash 2015), diverging from the industrial focus on instrumentality. To counter the risk of muddling all digital media as interfaces, the present approach emphasizes systematic dissection of analytical units, aspects, and their layered dynamics. These include, for example, gameplay mechanics, narrative, and representations. I provide a more detailed conceptualization of digital games as interfaces in earlier work (Ng 2017), which considers how digital gameplay creates edges, where traversals among proceduralism and semiotics, aesthetics and narratives, players and machines occur.

Both *Breathing Room* and *Gorogoa* emerge at a moment when the proliferation of digital media and interfaces capitalizes on (a) technologically-expanded possibilities for aesthetic experimentation and interaction; (b) an increasing overlap between the real and virtual worlds; and (c) a heightened focus on embodiment, observed across designs, visions, and discourses of human-technology interactions. Exemplars include electronic literature (E-lit) and interfaces for virtual and augmented reality experiences. E-lit, as texts of digital creation and consumption, harnesses fundamental properties of digital environments, such as their procedural and navigable aspects (Murray 2012). In so doing, they realize a multimodal complexity illustrating the distributed subjectivities characteristic of experiences in the digital present, involving bodies, machines, and networks, to name a few (Hayles 2008). Gaming devices and virtual reality headsets, such as Meta AR headsets, similarly facilitate experiences that are interactive, intuitive, and attuned to users' embodied actions (Gribetz 2016). Within such emerging technologies and contexts, research into digital games and comics necessitates a rigorous, empirical approach that identifies the meaning-making mechanisms as they manifest in the materialities involved. This vitally contributes to the refinement of theories and methods for understanding and problematizing important concepts revolving around media, including hybridity and embodiment, as this chapter attempts to illustrate. Next, I summarize an affect-driven approach in contribution to further research on comics and digital games.

Envisioning an affective multimodal approach

At the next frontier of conducting empirical multimodal research on comics and digital games, I contend that consolidating knowledge on how the materiality of media incubates both the use of semiotic modes *and* medium users' affects is crucial. Where meaning is bound by contexts and configurations of semiotic resources, it inheres an affective aspect. Affect and theories of affect have challenged the longstanding notion of emotions as universal categories, redirecting our focus to fluctuating, moment-to-moment bodily intensities that shape thought and behaviors, yet often beyond human observation (Massumi 2002; Stewart 2007). While recent work discusses intersections among digital games and emotions (Tettegah and Huang 2016), with inquiries into comics, cognition, and visual literacy, studies that aim to empirically expound dynamics among affect, meaning, and communicative logics of media are only nascent. To comprehend connections among the medial, semiotic, and affective aspects of meaning in experiencing shifting media forms, I propose a mixed-method research methodology that combines qualitative and quantitative data through "body-text assemblages." This involves cross-examining findings from multimodal analyses, interviews with medium users, and experiments with affect-sensing equipment, which registers users' affective states through, for instance, skin conductance and facial expressions. This introduces an analytical vector that guides us to appreciate the varied meaning-making strategies and interpretive possibilities of particular media, rather than medium-specific "aesthetics," which implies unwarranted oppositions among art, mass culture, and what is deemed valuable or inconsequential (Manovich 2001). The aim is to acquire an empirical understanding of the affective impact of comics and digital games as complex multimodal artifacts and experiences by identifying the relevant affect-semiotic-procedural patterns. This knowledge expectedly informs and enhances the design of future medial renditions resulting from the comics/games cross-pollination.

Conclusion

In this chapter, I have discussed socio-semiotic multimodality with an empirical orientation as a productive methodology to examine contemporary media that interconnect digital games and comics. Through exploring a digital graphic novel, a comic-game, and gestural literary media, this chapter has presented the analytical concept of "canvas" and digital annotation as a first step in conducting multimodal analysis, which aims to secure a foundation for studying the materiality of media. I propose to re-conceptualize digital games and gamified comics as interfaces that emerge from changes in medial complexity, designs of digital interfaces, and shifting social discourses on human-technology interactions. This conceptualization, combined with a fine-grained understanding of how meaning unfolds across semiotic modes and mechanics, can contribute to addressing several significant questions about design, media studies, and projections on how interactions between games and comics may foster new forms of media and experiences.

Among such questions, expounding just what "hybridity" means beyond a buzzword associated with the gamification of media is important. Not only does this affect the development of aesthetic and commercial practices of particular media, it gestures toward queries in the broader media ecology, the historical development of specific technologies, and social contexts.[7] One issue concerns increasing overlaps between "immaterial interfaces" and the real world, as evidenced by how digital games and their meaning-making logic via mechanics and interfaces have turned from metaphorical to instrumental social tools (Trammell and Sinnreich 2014). For instance, research has shown how digital interfaces shape economic subjectivity and contemporary indebtedness by modulating user affective states at thresholds of application processes for high-cost short-term credit loans (Ash et al. 2018). Building critical literacies about the sociopolitical impact of digital media and interfaces, in addition to their aesthetic influences on existent audiovisual narratives, is therefore vital. For such endeavors, various parties involved (including researchers, educators, designers, and medium users) will benefit from ways of re-framing that expand our understanding of how ramifications of digital games and interfaces extend into the sociopolitical realms.

For this purpose, this chapter has centered on the question of how to conceptualize and research forms of medial experimentation that arise from the comics and games nexus. Oriented to socio-semiotic multimodality for such re-framing, I illustrate transcription as a means to capture communicative dynamics among semiotic resources on an intra-panel level and cross-panel dynamics realized by layouts and animation. Knowledge of such dynamics fundamentally informs our grasp of the inclusion of ludic strategies and their diversifying effects on aesthetics, interpretation, experiences, and design. Research on digital games, comics, and the in-between artifacts, as explored in the present chapter, can benefit from linguistics-inflected approaches. Such approaches aim to render complex multimodal data and visual compositions analyzable across scales and thus make them open to further empirical validation. The socio-affective multimodal approach I have described provides one such example, indicating opportunities for mixed-method research initiatives that examine the communicative and affective effects of digital media through qualitative and quantitative data.

At the Game Developers Conference, Roberts (2018) articulated several aspects of the concept and entity of the "frame," which guides his design process of *Gorogoa*. For him, a frame is at once poignant, affectionate, a source of tension, and a curation practice. These evocative descriptions resonate with the analytical vocabulary and orientation of multimodality. In its socio-semiotic dimension, the field likewise considers aspects of meaning making, such as materiality, salience, framing, and semiotic labor, in relation to design, contexts, and power. This indicates an overlap in subjects of interest, and more importantly, complementarities among art, design, technology, and research. To harness such complementarities for future designs and experimentations, a just understanding of how media mean matters, with building the appropriate methodologies and systematic research practices as important aspects. Aligned with the underlying focus on empirical work of this chapter, it is crucial to emphasize that in any media encounters there remain elements that we are still pursuing to capture, articulate, and empirically examine. A critically playful attitude thus similarly contributes to the experience and research of such evolving media as digital games and comics. Akin to how ludic strategies mobilize interacting dynamics between aesthetic and narrative strategies, incorporating ludicity in research invites the necessary openness toward engaging with how media function and what they may develop to be. Instead of seeking fixed answers, this openness revolves around navigating what is ambiguous and yet to be known. At once critical and playful in contrast with the overused descriptor "hybridity," this curiosity potentially offers more analytical guidance and possibilities for inquiries into emerging forms of visual narratives, digital games, and artifacts. It opens up further questions about meaning, affect, and how trajectories of digital media and interfaces increasingly affect our ways of being in the mediatized historical present.

Notes

1 A recurrent motif on aesthetic experimentation concerns abstraction and nostalgia. The cell-shading visuality of *XIII* (2003), for instance, contributes to a visual experience distinct from current, digitally produced comics.

2 Materiality entails a historical dimension: Forms of meaning making (from drawing, language, and music to dance) arise from use, interpretations, designs, and conventions within particular communities of sign makers. Likewise, in transmedial artifacts and performances, historical factors extend across production and consumption. For example, the transmedia franchise based on *The LEGO Movie* (2014) adopts a cartoon aesthetic reminiscent of television series in the 1960s. Its divergence from the aesthetics of recent comic books or games on Batman (a character in the film series) is, within reason, seen as a commercial or artistic decision motivated by interacting contextual factors, for which historical components may play a role.

3 While the application of multimodality to game studies signals the analytical strength of the field, problematic notions such as the "procedural mode" and characterizing interactivity as a semiotic mode have surfaced (Chew and Mitchell 2019; Hawreliak 2018, 2019). These notions rightly observe the communicative capacities and effects of gameplay mechanics and interactivity, but they muddle a number of fundamental concepts, specifically semiotic modes and affordances. For detailed and accurate conceptual distinctions, see Bateman et al. 2017b.

4 Later re-released as part of *Metal Gear Solid: The Legacy Collection* (2013).

5 The progenitor title *Metal Gear* was released solely in Japan in 1987. The franchise has since developed to include 12 games, graphic novels (and their digital adaptations), novels, various merchandise, and a film adaptation in production.

6 My earlier work (Ng 2017, chapter 2) details both digital and manual multimodal annotation of digital games, with selected sequences and split screens from the videogame *Metal Gear Solid 4: Guns of the Patriots* (2008) as examples. For details on the software-assisted annotation of dynamic audiovisual media, as well as an overview of linguistics-inspired methods and tools, see Bateman et al. 2017b, chapter 5.

7 Hybridity in media is a function of technological development; it carries a historical dimension. An example would be the development of CD-ROMs, which enabled the integration of full-motion video into computer games. Constructive discussions of relations among medial logics and progress in technology and science can be found in, for example, foundational readings by Manovich (2001) and Murray (1998), as well as Thimm et al. (2017) on the relationship among media technologies, institutions, power, and social change.

Works cited

300. 2007. Dir. Zack Snyder. USA: Warner Bros. Pictures.

Ahmed, Maaheen, and Benoît Crucifix, eds. 2018. *Comics Memory: Archives and Styles*. New York: Palgrave Macmillan.

Ash, James. 2015. *The Interface Envelope: Gaming, Technology, Power*. New York: Bloomsbury.

Ash, James, Ben Anderson, Rachel Gordon, and Paul Langley. 2018. "Digital Interface Design and Power: Friction, Threshold, Transition." *Environment and Planning D: Society and Space* 36 (6): 1136–1153.

Bateman, John A., and Karl-Heinrich Schmidt. 2012. *Multimodal Film Analysis: How Films Mean*. New York: Routledge.

Bateman, John A., Francisco O. D. Veloso, Janina Wildfeuer, Felix HiuLaam Cheung, and Nancy Songdan Guo. 2017a. "An Open Multilevel Classification Scheme for the Visual Layout of Comics and Graphic Novels: Motivation and Design." *Digital Scholarship in the Humanities* 32 (3): 476–510.

Bateman, John A., Janina Wildfeuer, and Tuomo Hippala. 2017b. *Multimodality: Foundations, Research and Analysis: A Problem-Oriented Introduction*. Berlin: De Gruyter.

Bolter, J. David, and Richard Grusin. 1999. *Remediation: Understanding New Media*. Cambridge, MA: MIT Press.

Bramlett, Frank. 2012. *Linguistics and the Study of Comics*. New York: Palgrave Macmillan.

Breathing Room. 2014. Designed by Erik Loyer. Unpublished. Mac OS X.

Chadwick, Andrew. 2017. *The Hybrid Media System: Politics and Power*. 2nd edition. New York: Oxford University Press.

Chew, Evelyn, and Alex Mitchell. 2019. "Multimodality and Interactivity in 'Natively' Digital Life Stories." *Poetics Today* 40 (2): 319–353.

Chute, Hillary L. 2016. *Disaster Drawn: Visual Witness, Comics, and Documentary Form*. Cambridge, MA: Harvard University Press.

Cohn, Neil. 2013a. "Navigating Comics: An Empirical and Theoretical Approach to Strategies of Reading Comic Page Layout." *Frontiers in Psychology* 4: Article 186.

Cohn, Neil. 2013b. *The Visual Language of Comics: Introduction to the Structure and Cognition of Sequential Images*. London: Bloomsbury.

Dunst, Alexander, Jochen Laubrock, and Janina Wildfeuer, eds. 2018. *Empirical Comics Research: Digital, Multimodal, and Cognitive Methods*. New York: Routledge.

Framed. 2014. Developed and published by Loveshack Games. iOS.

Galloway, Alexander R. 2012. *The Interface Effect*. Cambridge: Polity.

Gibbons, Alison. 2012. *Multimodality, Cognition, and Experimental Literature*. New York: Routledge.

Gorogoa. 2017. Developed by Jason Roberts. Published by Annapurna Interactive. Windows.

Gribetz, Meron. 2016. "A Glimpse of the Future through an Augmented Reality Headset." *TED*, February. www.ted.com/talks/meron_gribetz_a_glimpse_of_the_future_through_an_augmented_reality_headset (accessed 31 January 2020).

Hawreliak, Jason. 2018. *Multimodal Semiotics and Rhetoric in Videogames*. New York: Routledge.

Hawreliak, Jason. 2019. "On the Procedural Mode." In *Approaches to Videogame Discourse: Lexis, Interaction, Textuality*, edited by Astrid Ensslin and Isabel Balteiro, 13–38. London: Bloomsbury.

Hayles, Katherine N. 2008. *Electronic Literature: New Horizons for the Literary*. Notre Dame, IN: University of Notre Dame Press.

Jagoda, Patrick. 2017. "Videogame Criticism and Games in the Twenty-First Century." *American Literary History* 29 (1): 205–218.

Jewitt, Carey, ed. 2014. *The Routledge Handbook of Multimodal Analysis*. New York: Routledge.

Kraidy, Marwan. 2015. "Hybridity." In *Keywords for Media Studies*, edited by Jonathan Gray and Laurie Ouellette, 90–93. New York: New York University Press.

The LEGO Movie. 2014. Dir. Phil Lord and Christopher Miller. USA: Warner Bros. Pictures.

Manovich, Lev. 2001. *The Language of New Media*. Cambridge, MA: MIT Press.

Manovich, Lev. 2007. "Understanding Hybrid Media." http://manovich.net/index.php/projects/understanding-hybrid-media (accessed 31 January 2020).

Massumi, Brian. 2002. *Parables of the Virtual: Movement, Affect, Sensation*. Durham: Duke University Press.

McMurtrie, Robert James. 2016. *The Semiotics of Movement in Space: A User's Perspective*. New York: Routledge.

Metal Gear. 1987. Developed and published by Konami. MSX2.

Metal Gear Solid. 1998. Developed and published by Konami. PlayStation.

Metal Gear Solid: The Legacy Collection. 2013. Developed by Kojima Productions. Published by Konami. PlayStation 3.

Metal Gear Solid 2: Bande Dessinée. 2008. Developed by Kojima Productions. Published by Konami. DVD.

Metal Gear Solid 2: Sons of Liberty. 2001. Developed and published by Konami. PlayStation 2.

Metal Gear Solid 4 Database. 2008. Developed by Kojima Productions. Published by Konami. PlayStation 3.

Metal Gear Solid 4: Guns of the Patriots. 2008. Developed by Kojima Productions. Published by Konami. PlayStation 3.

Mickwitz, Nina. 2016. *Documentary Comics: Graphic Truth-Telling in a Skeptical Age*. New York: Palgrave Macmillan.

Mikkonen, Kai. 2017. *The Narratology of Comic Art*. New York: Routledge.

Murray, Janet H. 1998. *Hamlet on the Holodeck: The Future of Narrative in Cyberspace*. New York: The Free Press.

Murray, Janet H. 2012. *Inventing the Medium: Principles of Interaction Design as Cultural Practice*. Cambridge, MA: MIT Press.

Ng, Carman. 2017. "War and Will: A Multisemiotic Analysis of *Metal Gear Solid 4*." PhD thesis, Hong Kong Polytechnic University, Hong Kong, China. http://ira.lib.polyu.edu.hk/handle/10397/73115 (accessed 31 January 2020).

Noon, Derek, and Nick Dyer-Witheford. 2010. "Sneaking Mission: Late Imperial America and *Metal Gear Solid*." In *Utopic Dreams and Apocalyptic Fantasies: Critical Approaches to Researching Video Game Play*, edited by Talmadge J. Wright, David G. Embrick, and András Lukás, 73–96. Plymouth, UK: Lexington Books.

Norris, Sigrid. 2004. *Analyzing Multimodal Interaction: A Methodological Framework*. New York: Routledge.

Roberts, Jason. 2018. "*Gorogoa*: The Design of a Cosmic Acrostic." Paper presented at the Game Developers Conference, 19–23 March. https://twvideo01.ubm-us.net/o1/vault/gdc2018/presentations/Roberts_Jason_Gorogoa_design_of.pdf (accessed 31 January 2020).

Sin City. 2005. Dir. Robert Rodriguez, Frank Miller, and Quentin Taratino. USA: Miramax.

Stewart, Kathleen. 2007. *Ordinary Affects*. Durham: Duke University Press.

Tettegah, Sharon, and Wenhao David Huang, eds. 2016. *Emotions, Technology, and Digital Games*. London: Elsevier.

Thimm, Caja, Mario Anastasiadis, and Jessica Einspänner-Pflock, eds. 2017. *Media Logic(s) Revisited: Modelling the Interplay between Media Institutions, Media Technology and Societal Change*. New York: Palgrave Macmillan.

Toh, Weimin. 2019. *A Multimodal Approach to Video Games and the Player Experience*. New York: Routledge.

Trammell, Aaron, and Aram Sinnreich. 2014. "Visualizing Game Studies: Materiality and Sociality from Chessboard to Circuit Board." *Journal of Games Criticism* 1 (1): n.p. http://gamescriticism.org/articles/trammellsinnreich-1-1 (accessed 31 January 2020).

Williams, J. H. III, and W. Haden Blackman. 2013. *Batwoman* Vol. 2: *To Drown the World*. New York: DC Comics.

XIII. 2003. Developed and published by Ubisoft. Windows.

4 Game comics

Theory and design

Daniel Merlin Goodbrey

Comics and videogames have a shared history of visual influence and narrative crossover. Today, portable display devices such as tablet computers and smartphones provide common platforms of consumption on which comics and videogames are equally at home. Within this context, this chapter explores the potential for hybridization between the form of comics and the ludic qualities of videogames. Such hybrids can be described as "game comics." A game comic is a type of hypercomic that exhibits some of the key characteristics of a game and uses some of the key characteristics of the form of comics as the basis for its gameplay. In seeking to analyze the operation of the game comics format, it is necessary to draw on a range of ideas from comics, game, and media theory.

This chapter begins with an examination of the different types of visual and narrative crossover that have developed between comics and videogames. It identifies the key characteristics of games and considers the potential interplay of these characteristics with those of the form of comics. This leads into an extended analysis of three game comic prototypes that were created as a practice-based inquiry into the potential of the format: the smartphone app *A Duck Has an Adventure* (2012), the browser game *Icarus Needs* (2013), and the unpublished work *Margaret Must Succeed* (2013). These three major case studies provide the basis for a critically grounded exploration and analysis of how the form of comics can be adapted via hybridization with the ludic qualities of the videogame.

Videogames and comics

Videogames have their origins in the middle of the twentieth century, with the game *Spacewar!* (1961) often cited as the first fully-fledged example of the form (Juul 2005, 3). As videogames have developed as a form, they have also developed a shared history of visual influence and narrative crossover with the form of comics. Popular videogame franchises such as *Sonic the Hedgehog* (1991), *Resident Evil* (1996), or *World of Warcraft* (2004) regularly receive their own comic book adaptations and transmedia crossovers. Similarly, the adventures of comic book characters like Batman and Spider-Man have been adapted across a multitude of successful games. Videogames and the videogame industry also serve as the backdrop for many widely read webcomic series, such as *Penny Arcade* (1998–) and *PVP* (1998–), with gaming at one time forming the single most popular genre in the emergent webcomic scene (Campbell 2006, 49).

The form of comics is at times used as a linking device within videogames themselves. In the third-person shooter *Max Payne* (2001) and the puzzle game *Angry Birds Space* (2012), rather than animated cut scenes between each level, the narrative is progressed using digital comics in page-like groupings of panels. In the case of *Angry Birds Space*, these groupings are built up on the screen one panel at a time using "panel delivery" techniques similar to those commonly found in other formats of digital comics (Goodbrey 2017, 68). Other games like *Comix Zone* (1995) and *Comic Jumper: The Adventures of Captain Smiley* (2010) adapt common visual tropes like panels, pages, and captions for use in the context of animated, side-scrolling beat 'em ups. This visual appropriation between comics and videogames has moved in both directions. Bryan Lee O'Malley's graphic novel series *Scott Pilgrim* (2004–2010) makes use of popular videogame tropes in its narrative, with its titular protagonist encountering save points, leveling up, and collecting coins from defeated enemies.

There have also been some videogames that use the form of comics more directly as part of their gameplay. For example, the superhero videogame *Redhawk* (1986) mixes the tropes of an adventure game with a dynamically updating comic strip. Similarly, there have been comic books that integrate aspects of gameplay into their narrative. The five-issue *2000 AD* spin-off series *Dice Man* (1986) combines comics with the game rules of the *Choose Your Own Adventure* book series. *Redhawk* and *Dice Man* are early examples of the hypercomics format. Hypercomics exhibit "a multicursal narrative structure" (Goodbrey 2017, 87) in which readers must make choices as to the path they take through the narrative. The nature of the hypercomic as a hybrid between the forms of comics and hypermedia makes it well suited to further hybridization with the ludic qualities of videogames.

Hybridizing comics and games

To examine the hybrid game comics format, it is important to first consider some of the fundamental concepts that underlie games and comics. Juul provides a useful analysis of a range of different definitions of games and from these identifies six key characteristics of the form. These are:

1. *Rules*: Games are rule-based.
2. *Variable, quantifiable outcome*: Games have variable, quantifiable outcomes.
3. *Valorization of outcome*: The different potential outcomes of the game are assigned different values, some positive and some negative.

4. *Player effort*: The player exerts effort in order to influence the outcome. (Games are challenging.)
5. *Player attached to outcome*: The player is emotionally attached to the outcome of the game in the sense that a player will be a winner and "happy" in case of a positive outcome, but a loser and "unhappy" in case of a negative outcome.
6. *Negotiable consequences*: The same game [set of rules] can be played with or without real-life consequences. (2005, 36)

While many games exhibit all six of these criteria, Juul's model also allows for tertiary cases that share most, but not all, of the key characteristics. In addition to the above, Juul offers a useful division of games into two major categories. Games of emergence are "the primordial game structure" (Juul 2005, 73) in which a game consists of a small number of rules that combine to create a large number of different variations of play. In contrast, games of progression are "the historically newer structure that entered the computer game through the adventure genre" (Juul 2005, 72). Now common to many modern videogames, players in games of progression must perform predefined sequences of actions in order to progress through the game.

Juul's approach to establishing and analyzing the characteristics of games inspired my own approach to creating a model of the key characteristics of the form of comics. In the study of comics there has been some debate as to the nature and relative importance of the various characteristics of the form (Groensteen 2007; Hatfield 2009; McCloud 1993; Miodrag 2013). Through a process of critical analysis and synthesis I developed a model consisting of seven key characteristics that can be summarized as follows:

1. *Space as time*. Comics use arrangements of images in space to represent arrangements of moments or events in time.
2. *Simultaneous juxtaposition of images*. Comics place images in spatial juxtaposition to each other, such that two or more images may be viewed simultaneously by the reader.
3. *Closure between images*. The reader of a comic derives time, meaning, and motion out of sequences of static, juxtaposed images through the process of closure.
4. *Spatial networks*. Sequences of images form part of a larger spatial network of narrative and aesthetic interrelations that exists between all the elements in a comic.
5. *Reader control of pacing*. The pace at which the reader absorbs the information in a comic is controlled by the reader and determined by the pace at which they read and navigate the comic.
6. *Tablodic images*. The images in a comic exhibit qualities of the tableau, in that they are deliberately composed, framed, and illustrated to represent key moments of narrative meaning.

7. *Word and image blending*. Although sometimes wordless, comics typically use a blend of words and images in spatial juxtaposition to convey meaning to the reader. (Goodbrey 2017, 162–163).

This model is intended to provide a conceptual division of the interconnected and overlapping processes that are in operation when a comic is read. It is not meant as an exhaustive list; not all comics will display all seven characteristics. Different formats of print and digital comic can place each characteristic into greater or lesser emphasis, and some examples will omit certain characteristics completely.

As a hybrid of the two forms, a game comic should exhibit some of the key characteristics of games and some of the key characteristics of the form of comics. Many of the earlier examples of direct crossover between comics and games fail to meet these criteria. Animated games like *Comix Zone* and *Comic Jumper* do not qualify because although they adopt certain visual tropes, they ignore or replace too many of the key characteristics of comics such as space as time, closure, and spatial networks. Similarly excluded are games like *Max Payne* or *Angry Birds Space*, where comics are used as a linking device; here the gameplay and comics sections are kept completely separate from each other, and there is no opportunity for true hybridization.

Most hypercomics can also be discounted as they do not display enough of the key characteristics of games outlined by Juul. *Redhawk* and *Dice Man* do meet the criteria of game comics, operating both as comics and as games of progression. But in both cases, the mechanics of gameplay and the characteristics of the form of comics remain relatively separate. In *Redhawk*, the play is focused chiefly on interaction with the text parser, while the comic strip is used to visualize the result of this interaction. In *Diceman*, the *Choose Your Own Adventure* structure of play has been grafted on to the spatial network of the comic, but interaction between the two systems is limited.

During the process of practice-based research involved in the creation of new game comic prototypes, my aim has been to achieve a more direct synthesis between comics and videogames. The resulting game comics are not just games that are also comics, but games that make specific use of some of the key characteristics of the form of comics in the mechanics of their gameplay. In considering possible areas of crossover that could be conducive to greater synthesis between comics and videogames, my starting point was the use of space within the two forms.

Murray asserts that for some players, "videogames are about exploring an infinitely expandable space" (1997, 129). Other media (Aarseth 2000) and game theorists (Zagal et al. 2008) similarly assert that spatiality is a defining element of the videogame. The exploration and manipulation of space in videogames can form a fundamental part of gameplay, with the unlocking of space serving as a key aspect of a game's reward structure (Gazzard 2011).

Similarly, comics are also an intrinsically spatial form. Arrangements of panels in space are used to represent the passage of fictional time, and these panels exist as part of a spatial network of interrelations. Spatiality therefore makes for a strong common thread around which to develop new game comics.

In creating the three prototypes discussed in this chapter, I elected to focus on making games of progression. As Gazzard asserts, "at the heart of this type of game lies the concept of exploration" (2013, 59). The exploration and unlocking of space therefore became a key element of gameplay during this practice-based inquiry. Juul (2005, 73) also notes that games of progression often harbor "storytelling ambitions" in their design. This makes the structure particularly sympathetic to the strengths of the form of comics, which is commonly used to convey narrative via the use of simultaneously juxtaposed tablodic images and word and image blending.

A Duck Has an Adventure

A Duck Has an Adventure is the first of the three prototypes created during my inquiry. The game is based on the structure of a branching narrative hypercomic. This structure takes its lead from the *Choose Your Own Adventure* book series, where the player must make choices for the central character that influence the direction of the narrative. As an initial attempt at creating a game comic, the intent behind the work was to create something that comics readers would view as a comic and videogame players would view as a videogame. The design of the comic builds on my existing body of work as a digital comics practitioner. As a result, this first prototype sits nearer the comics end of the game comics spectrum. *A Duck Has an Adventure* first went on sale as an app for Android smartphones and tablets in February 2012. Its original description on *Google Play* reads as follows: "A Duck has an Adventure is a unique hypercomic adventure game that challenges you to discover all the different possible lives one duck could live. From adventures on the high seas to the halls of academia and beyond, every choice you make builds a new pathway along which to explore" (Goodbrey 2012a, n.p.). The app received positive reviews and in March of 2012 peaked at number six in the top ten paid comics apps on *Google Play* (Goodbrey 2012b). Later that year in November, *A Duck Has an Adventure* was also selected as one of the seven shortlisted nominees in the *New Media Writing Prize* (2012). In May of 2013, a new version of *A Duck Has an Adventure* was launched that was designed to be played in a web browser. This version of the game was free to play, with revenue coming from adverts placed at the start of the game and on the hosting websites. It was made available via online game hosts such as *Kongregate, Armor Games*, and *Mochimedia*. This brought the work to the attention of a large gaming audience, and as of August 2016, the browser version of *A Duck Has an Adventure* has received over half a million plays on *Kongregate* alone. This has resulted in lots of direct feedback from gamers, as well as several pages of reviews and playthroughs on *YouTube* (YouTube 2020a).

In both browser and app versions, *A Duck Has an Adventure* was designed with casual gaming audiences in mind. To target this audience, the game comic incorporates what Juul describes as "juiciness" (2010, 45), an excess of positive feedback that rewards the player for their interaction. One way *A Duck Has an Adventure* achieves this is through its use of animated panel delivery; when panels are tapped or new panels appear, they react and move with a satisfyingly elastic springing motion. Pursuit of juiciness also means encouraging regular interaction between the reader and the screen. A standard digital comic might require the reader to only interact with the screen when clicking or swiping to turn the page. But rather than being based around a digital recreation of a page, *A Duck Has an Adventure* uses an infinite canvas approach (McCloud 2000, 222), treating the screen as a window onto a much larger network of panels.

To navigate this network, the reader must regularly tap the screen to shift the focus of the window and make new panels appear. This places an emphasis on the reader's control over the pacing of the comic and establishes a regular rhythm of interaction, helping to ensure that "moving the character and/or object through the game space becomes habitual" for the player (Gazzard 2013, 99). For this habitual process to work successfully, the player has to be able to consume the information in each panel quickly before tapping to bring up the next in sequence. To help achieve this, the tablodic images in *A Duck Has an Adventure* follow the principle identified by McCloud as "amplification through simplification" (1993, 30). Narrative is conveyed by a combination of tersely worded captions and simple, icon-like images that can be quickly consumed and understood by the reader.

Gazzard notes that in a videogame, it is "often the feeling of discovery that keeps players within the playworld" (2013, 8). This sense of discovery is enhanced in *A Duck Has an Adventure* via the addition of two common gaming tropes: collectable hats that the player can find through exploration and an achievement system that rewards continued progress through the narrative. A scoring system is also provided that indicates the current number of hats, achievements, and endings that the player has discovered, as well as the total number of each to be found in the game. These scores provide a metric by which the player can measure how much of the game they have completed. Seeking completeness then becomes a game in itself, as the player tries to uncover all of the possible narrative pathways in order to collect every hat, achievement, and ending.

The addition of this completeness metric is a marked departure from my previous hypercomic work. In a typical hypercomic such as *The Formalist* (Goodbrey 2005) or *Four Derangements* (Goodbrey 2009), the reader may at times experience a sense of tmesis. This is the feeling that in choosing one path from the many potential narrative pathways, they may have skipped over or missed something important (Peacock 2005). Both *The Formalist* and *Four Derangements* lack any indicators as to which paths have already been followed or how much of the comic might still remain unseen. In contrast, by quantifying the amount that has been seen and unseen, the tmesis in *A Duck Has an Adventure* is diminished and refocused to become an explicit problem for the player to solve.

Another way *A Duck Has an Adventure* differs from my previous hypercomic work is in how it makes use of the infinite canvas. In hypercomics like *Never Shoot the Chronopath* (Goodbrey 2007) and *Doodleflak* (Goodbrey 2002), the entire temporal map of the comic is laid out from the very beginning. With the whole spatial network of the comic already constructed on the screen before them, readers are free to zoom in and read the story at any point or zoom out to navigate between different sections of the narrative. However, in a game, this approach would be problematic. As Gazzard asserts, players "do not expect to have the full game world open to them; to do so would take away the exploratory and learning aspects of the game that the players need to keep playing" (2013, 103).

Accordingly, in *A Duck Has an Adventure*, players begin with only a single panel of the comic visible and then construct the temporal map themselves through their play. While *A Duck Has an Adventure* does offer the player the ability to zoom out and view the whole temporal map of the comic, in its initial design, this was not the case. The zooming feature was only added later in development as a result of player feedback. The portable nature of smartphone apps meant that early builds of *A Duck Has an Adventure* could easily be passed around amongst friends and colleagues in order to observe their interaction with the game. The qualitative feedback received through this process filled a similar role to playtesting in videogame design. Fullerton identifies playtesting as "the single most important activity a designer engages in," providing a vital way to "gain an insight into whether or not the game is achieving your player experience goals" (2008, 248).

The early feedback I received on *A Duck Has an Adventure* indeed proved invaluable, influencing several aspects of the game's design. The most common request amongst testers was for the addition of a zoomed out view of the comic's spatial network that would serve as a record of where they'd been and the choices they'd made in the game so far. Being able to see the current state of the whole temporal map aids not only in basic navigation, but also in identifying the unexplored pathways that are necessary to achieve full completion of the game. Using the map in this way "requires the player to memorize parts of it in order to remember another sequence of possible spatial events and [the map] becomes as much a part of the problem solving of the game as the navigation itself" (Gazzard 2013, 82).

In *A Duck Has an Adventure*, some of the final narrative paths needed to fully complete the game only become accessible once the player has visited the same event via two different pathways. Accordingly, the zoomed out view serves a vital function for those engaged in completeness-seeking gameplay.

The next section further considers this aspect of the game and examines it in contrast to the gameplay of the second of my game comic prototypes.

Icarus Needs

The second prototype, *Icarus Needs*, is influenced by both text-based interactive fiction games like *Zork* (1980) and graphic adventure games like *The Secret of Monkey Island* (1990). Montfort outlines some of the key characteristics of such games:

- A potential narrative, that is, a system that produces narrative during interaction;
- A simulation of an environment or world; and
- A structure of rules within which an outcome is sought, also known as a game. (2005, 23)

The narrative of *Icarus* concerns the plight of cartoonist Icarus Creeps, who has fallen asleep playing videogames and now finds himself stuck in a surreal, metafictional dream world. The intent with the game was to build on the lessons learned with *A Duck Has an Adventure* and to push toward something that felt more game-like in its nature. Given the success achieved by *A Duck Has an Adventure* as a browser game, *Icarus* was designed from the very beginning to take advantage of this distribution platform. It was released across multiple online game-hosting websites in July 2014. The game shared the success of its predecessor, receiving over half a million plays by August 2016 and generating similar amounts of player feedback via comment threads and *YouTube* (YouTube 2020b).

Montfort notes that a typical adventure game "simulates a world that the interactor is supposed to figure out" (2005, 21). He further asserts that much of the fun in an adventure game comes from the act of exploring the game world itself (Montfort 2005, 4). My goal with *Icarus* was to create a simulated world that the player could explore, interrogate, and solve via the form of comics. Unlike a normal comic, the narrative of *Icarus* is not laid out in advance for the reader to read through and absorb. Adventure games are not themselves narratives but "produce narratives when a person interacts with them" (Montfort 2005, 23). Accordingly in *Icarus*, the narrative is created via the player's exploration and interaction with the comics-mediated world presented in the game.

During the game the player has control over the character of Icarus Creeps and is able to move him around from panel to panel in order to interact with the other characters and objects found in the world. It is important to stress that this movement is achieved using only the characteristics of the form of comics. Readers always remain in control of the pace at which they absorb the information, and no animation is used at any point inside the panels of the comic. Instead, movements in time are represented through movements in space and rely on the readers' use of closure to interpret the changes in the juxtaposed images that form the comic's spatial network.

To keep *Icarus* accessible for the casual player, I tried to simplify the gameplay mechanics as much as possible. Icarus Creeps is limited to carrying a single object at a time, and the player only controls the character's movement, with environmental interactions being triggered automatically on entering the appropriate panel. By collecting certain objects and applying them in the correct situation, the player is able to solve simple puzzles and progress further through the game. These puzzles form a key element of the narrative that unfolds in *Icarus*. Montfort highlights their importance to the adventure game genre, stating that "the puzzles in a work of interactive fiction function to control the revelation of the narrative; they are part of an interactive process that generates narrative" (2005, 3).

The player in *Icarus* is engaged in two simultaneous processes; they are attempting to both appreciate the world of the narrative and solve it in order to successfully traverse the game. In traversing the game world, players may at times be lead in certain directions by elements of the environment they encounter. Near the start of *Icarus*, a sign on the wall points in the direction of "reality" in order to encourage players to make their way further down the corridor. Later in the game, a hot air balloon and the empty panel of sky above it suggest to players that they might take flight and explore the skies. However, it is important to stress that ultimately it is always up to the players to determine their own path through the world. This freedom of choice is a key element of videogames, which offer us "the empowered experience of navigating our own individual paths" (Gazzard 2013, 8).

Murray notes that the ability to navigate through virtual landscapes "can be pleasurable in itself, independent of the content of the spaces" (1997, 129). This pleasure in navigation is one aspect of player agency, which can be defined as "the satisfying power to take meaningful action and see the results of our decisions and choices" (Murray 1997, 126). In aiming to make *Icarus* a more game-like experience than *A Duck Has an Adventure*, I took advantage of the browser-based aspect of the design to give the player direct control over the game's protagonist via the arrow keys on the keyboard. With this control in place, the representation of the protagonist serves as an avatar for the player within the game. The agency of the player in *Icarus* is significantly enhanced by the presence of an avatar with which they can identify and which they can use to navigate the game world. When considered in comparison to the earlier *A Duck Has an Adventure*, this increased sense of player agency is one of the key factors that makes *Icarus* feel more game-like in its nature.

Another set of linked concepts that are important to consider when comparing the gameplay of *A Duck Has an Adventure* and *Icarus* is the pairing of "aporia and epiphany" (Aarseth 1997, 90). Aarseth describes aporia and epiphany as the "pair of master tropes [that] constitutes the dynamic of hypertext discourse: the dialectic between searching and finding typical of games in general" (1997, 91–92). In terms of gameplay, aporia can be thought of as either the puzzle or the pause the player takes in order to try to solve the puzzle, while epiphany is the realization of the solution that allows the player to progress onwards to the next area or puzzle within the game (Gazzard 2013, 103). In *A Duck Has an Adventure*, the majority of the aporia-epiphany loops in the gameplay come only toward the end of the game, as the player searches for the final hats, endings, and achievements needed in order to achieve a complete playthrough of the game. This play takes place primarily on the zoomed out view of the temporal map, which becomes of strategic use to the players as they attempt to spot unexplored branches or find new pathways to unlock.

In contrast, *Icarus* spreads the player's experience of aporia-epiphany loops much more evenly throughout the entire length of its gameplay. The player is presented with regular gates to progress that must be overcome through further exploration of the game world and the correct application of the items the player discovers. As the solution to each puzzle is reached, the moment of epiphany is accompanied by the reward of newly unlocked areas of space to explore and new puzzles to solve. In this manner, *Icarus* manages to deliver a significantly better-paced gameplay experience than *A Duck Has an Adventure*, again highlighting the latter of the two prototypes as the more consistently game-like in its nature.

Margaret Must Succeed

The first two prototypes are games of progression based in the exploration-driven adventure genre. With the third prototype, *Margaret Must Succeed*, my aim was to create a comic that drew tropes from a different genre of games. *Margaret Must Succeed* is a narrative puzzle game originally intended for release both as a browser game and Android App. Like *Icarus, Margaret Must Succeed* has a regular, game-like distribution of aporia-epiphany loops, but it removes the focus on exploration found in both *Icarus* and *A Duck Has an Adventure*. In a puzzle game, the puzzles may still act as gates to control the reveal of narrative, but for the player the focus is placed more on the puzzles as being "pleasurable in themselves. The suspense that accompanies an attempt to find a solution to a challenging puzzle, or the anxiety that develops from not finding one right away, is a significant part of what makes the puzzle so fascinating and engaging" (Danesi 2002, 226–227). There are already some examples of game comics that exhibit this focus on puzzle solving in their gameplay. *Strip 'Em All* (2013) is a browser-based puzzle game in which the player rearranges panel sequences and manipulates the visual and textual elements in panels to "reveal the inner nature of the characters" in each comic. *Storyteller* (2013) is a puzzle game intended for iOS, Mac, and PC in which the player builds "visual stories by placing characters and props into a comic-like sequence of frames" (Benmergui 2013a, n.p.). In both game comics, the mechanics of play revolve around the player repositioning elements of the spatial network to create new meaning and narrative sequence out of sequentially juxtaposed images.

Strip 'Em All and *Storyteller* demonstrate "the pleasure of transformation" (Murray 1997, 154) that Murray identifies as being inherent to digital media. She asserts that digital mediation leads to artifacts becoming "more plastic" and "more inviting to change" (Murray 1997, 154). Barber similarly describes how the use of panel delivery in a digital comic can result in the creation of a "malleable page" or page-like grouping of panels (2002, 63). Hybridization with the mechanics of puzzle games extends this malleability further, giving the players a greater sense of agency in their transformation of the panels and sequences in each comic. *Margaret Must Succeed* also shares this quality, with a central gameplay mechanic based on swapping around key panels in the spatial network to "swap fates" between the different characters in the game. Unlike *Storyteller* and *Strip 'Em All*, which rely on stand-alone stories to provide the basis for each puzzle, *Margaret Must Succeed* uses this mechanic to tell a single, ongoing narrative.

The game's story follows the journey of Margaret, a young woman who must cross the city on a mysterious errand. Her journey is shown in a line of comics panels across the middle of the screen. The lives of other people in the city are shown in lines of panels above or below Margaret's. Certain panels in each line are highlighted as being swappable. When swapped, they alter the panels around them, creating new sequences of events that may change the content of another swappable panel. Each screen of panels represents one puzzle within the game, which the player must solve by changing events so that Margaret is able to continue her journey and progress forward to the next screen and the next puzzle.

As the game progresses, the challenges facing Margaret transition from the mundane (a missed bus; an empty phone battery) to the extraordinary (armed police raids; terror attacks). Juul notes than in puzzle games there is often an expectation on the part of the player for each puzzle to have "one single, perfect solution" (2005, 112). Aspects of *Margaret Must Succeed*'s design deliberately play against this expectation. While each puzzle has only a single solution, in terms of the narrative, this solution is deliberately imperfect; by solving each new puzzle the player makes the world better for Margaret, but worse for everyone else around her. As Margaret's actions become increasingly malign, the narrative is intended to make the players question their own complicity in the chaos Margaret's success causes for the rest of the city.

Although the player's actions may generate multiple different narratives while attempting to solve each puzzle, only a single correct configuration allows the player to progress further through the game. This aligns with Juul's classification of games of progression as characteristically featuring "more ways to fail than to succeed" (2005, 73). Juul (2005, 97–101) asserts the need for successful progression-based puzzle games to initially assist the player in understanding the mechanics of play and then to escalate in difficulty as the game progresses. In *Margaret Must Succeed*, the first two puzzles feature limited options as to which panels can be swapped and additional written instructions that inform players of the basic mechanics of the game. As the game progresses, the puzzles increase in complexity, adding more parallel timelines that necessitate more swapping and re-swapping of panels to achieve each solution. In the more difficult puzzles, the complexity of the spatial network is increased by the potential to create multiple narrative sequences in which panels form new juxtapositional relationships that require new acts of closure to interpret.

Sustaining the escalation in difficulty in *Margaret Must Succeed* without over-taxing the player's ability to interpret the comic's spatial network proved challenging as development of the game continued. The designer of *Strip 'Em All*, Ola Hansson observes that developing "interesting stories for our game is not so hard, of course, what is hard is making those stories fun and challenging to play" (2013, n.p.). *Storyteller* creator Daniel Benmergui encountered similar problems in developing his game comic. Although the playable alpha version of *Storyteller* was complete enough to win the Independent Games Festival Innovation Award in 2012, Benmergui suspended development of the game before its final release (Benmergui 2013b). He attributes this decision to feeling "creatively numb," stating that time away from the game was needed to better resolve "a few important things" (Benmergui 2013b, n.p.) in the game's design.

The difficulties encountered by Hansson and Benmergui were mirrored in my own work on *Margaret Must Succeed*. More complex puzzles required more complex coding to implement. Additional work was also required to ensure that all possible panel combinations within the spatial network resulted in comics narratives that made sense when read in sequence. The creation of new, different and more complex puzzles proved increasingly hard, while the informal testing of existing puzzles amongst friends and colleagues pointed to other problems with the gameplay. Players reported some puzzle solutions as feeling too arbitrary and too easy to achieve through the trial-and-error swapping of panels. It was this combination of factors that eventually lead me to suspend development on *Margaret Must Succeed*.

While I may return to the game at a later stage, I decided that continuing to iterate on the design within my doctoral study would not be the best use of available time and resources. Despite the game comic being unfinished, my work on *Margaret Must Succeed* has provided useful insight into another approach to hybridizing the spatial qualities of comics and videogames. The problems encountered in completing the game also serve to highlight the difficulty of achieving a successful combination of narrative and gameplay within the game comics format. Creating content in a game comic requires competencies in both games design and comics creation; challenges that arise out of either discipline can destabilize the success of the project as a whole.

Conclusion

This chapter has provided an overview of some of the visual influences and narrative crossovers that exist between comics and videogames. Today, the digital mediation of comics has led to the two forms sharing the same platforms of consumption and distribution; it is in this context that the hybrid format of game comics has been examined. The chapter has identified game comics as a format of comics that exhibits some of the key characteristics of a game and uses some of the key characteristics of the form of comics in its gameplay. The creation of the three game comic prototypes detailed in the chapter has allowed for an analysis of the ways in which the spatial nature of the two forms can provide common ground for such hybridization to occur. These prototypes operate as games of progression, with narratives that are advanced through styles of gameplay focused on the construction, exploration, or manipulation of each comic's spatial network.

In most traditional comics formats, readers are in full control of the reading and navigation of the comics' spatial network. Game comics operate differently, with deliberate limits placed on the ways the reader can view and progresses through the network. The more agency readers feel in controlling their navigation of the spatial network within these limits, the more game-like the experience of reading the comic becomes. A regular dispersal of aporia-epiphany loops throughout the comic is another key factor in creating a more game-like experience for the reader. These loops might typically take the form of a series of gates that prevent the reader's progress, forcing them to pause to find a solution that then allows for further progression.

In the creation of game comics, designing and implementing these progression gates can at times be challenging due to the potential complexity of interrelations between the panels that form a comic's spatial network. Because of their nature as a hybrid format, successful game comics must achieve a balance between their operation as comics narratives and the provision of an engaging gameplay experience. This balance can be difficult to achieve, as it requires creators to draw on design skills from two distinct disciplines. Ultimately, the design of a successful game comic may require simplifying some characteristics of the form of comics or some elements of gameplay in order to create an effective working balance between the two.

Works cited

Aarseth, Espen J. 1997. *Cybertext: Perspectives on Ergodic Literature*. Baltimore: Johns Hopkins University Press.

Aarseth, Espen J. 2000. "Allegories of Space: The Question of Spatiality in Computer Games." In *Cybertext Yearbook 2000*, edited by Markku Eskelinen and Raine Koskimaa, 152–171. Jyväskylä: Research Centre for Contemporary Culture.

Angry Birds Space. 2012. Developed and published by Rovio Entertainment. iOS.

Barber, John. 2002. "The Phenomenon of Multiple Dialectics in Comics Layout." Master thesis, London College of Printing, UK.

Benmergui, Daniel. 2013a. "Storyteller: A Game about Building Stories." www.storyteller-game.com/p/about-storyteller.html (accessed 28 August 2016).

Benmergui, Daniel. 2013b. "Storyteller: Ernesto RPG – A Side Project." www.storyteller-game.com/2014/01/ernesto-rpg-side-project.html (accessed 28 August 2016).

Campbell, T. 2006. *A History of Webcomics*. San Antonio: Antarctic Press.

Comic Jumper: The Adventures of Captain Smiley. 2010. Developed by Twisted Pixel Games. Published by Microsoft Game Studios. Xbox 360.

Comix Zone. 1995. Developed and published by Sega. Sega Genesis.

Danesi, Marcel. 2002. *The Puzzle Instinct: The Meaning of Puzzles in Human Life*. Bloomington: Indiana University Press.

A Duck Has an Adventure. 2012. Developed by Daniel M. Goodbrey. Published by E-merl.com. Android.

A Duck Has an Adventure. 2013. Developed by Daniel M. Goodbrey. Published by Kongregate. Browser. www.kongregate.com/games/Stillmerlin/a-duck-has-an-adventure (accessed 17 August 2016).

Fullerton, Tracy. 2008. *Games Design Workshop: A Playcentric Approach to Creating Innovative Games*. 2nd edition. Burlington: Morgan Kaufmann Publishers.

Gazzard, Alison. 2011 "Unlocking the Gameworld: The Rewards of Space and Time in Videogames." *Game Studies: The International Journal of Computer Game Research* 1 (1): n.p. http://gamestudies.org/1101/articles/gazzard_alison (accessed 31 January 2020).

Gazzard, Alison. 2013. *Mazes in Videogames: Meaning, Metaphor and Design*. Jefferson: McFarland.

Goodbrey, Daniel M. 2002. *Doodleflak*. http://e-merl.com/flak.htm (accessed 18 November 2015).

Goodbrey, Daniel M. 2005. *The Formalist*. http://e-merl.com/form.htm (accessed 18 November 2015).

Goodbrey, Daniel M. 2007. *Never Shoot the Chronopath*. http://e-merl.com/chrono.htm (accessed 20 July 2015).

Goodbrey, Daniel M. 2009. *Four Derangements*. http://e-merl.com/derange.htm (accessed 20 July 2015).

Goodbrey, Daniel M. 2012a. "A Duck Has an Adventure – Android Apps on Google Play." https://play.google.com/store/apps/details?id=air.com.emerl.duckadv (accessed 17 August 2016).

Goodbrey, Daniel M. 2012b. Untitled tweet. *Twitter*, 10 March. https://twitter.com/merlism/status/178275459023380480 (accessed 31 January 2020).

Goodbrey, Daniel M. 2017. "The Impact of Digital Mediation and Hybridisation on the Form of Comics." PhD thesis, University of Hertfordshire, UK. http://e-merl.com/thesis/DMGthesis2017web.pdf (accessed 31 January 2020).

Groensteen, Thierry. 2007. *The System of Comics*. Jackson: University Press of Mississippi.

Hansson, Ola. 2013. "Games Blog." *Athletic Design*, 17 June. www.athleticdesign.se/reviews/blog.html (accessed 17 August 2016).

Hatfield, Charles. 2009. "An Art of Tensions." In *A Comic Studies Reader*, edited by Jeet Heer and Kent Worcester, 132–148. Jackson: University Press of Mississippi.

Icarus Needs. 2013. Developed by Daniel M. Goodbrey. Published by Kongregate. Browser. www.kongregate.com/games/Stillmerlin/icarus-needs (accessed 17 August 2016).

Juul, Jesper. 2005. *Half-Real: Between Real Rules and Fictional Worlds*. Cambridge, MA: MIT Press.

Juul, Jesper. 2010. *A Casual Revolution: Reinventing Video Games and Their Players*. Cambridge, MA: MIT Press.

Margaret Must Succeed. 2013. Developed by Daniel M. Goodbrey. Unpublished. Android.

Max Payne. 2001. Developed by Remedy. Published by Rockstar Games/Gathering of Developers. Windows.

McCloud, Scott. 1993. *Understanding Comics*. New York: Harper Perennial.

McCloud, Scott. 2000. *Reinventing Comics*. New York: Paradox Press.

Miodrag, Hannah. 2013. *Comics and Language*. Jackson: University Press of Mississippi.

Montfort, Nick. 2005. *Twisty Little Passages: An Approach to Interactive Fiction*. Cambridge, MA: MIT Press.

Murray, Janet H. 1997. *Hamlet on the Holodeck: The Future of Narrative in Cyberspace*. Cambridge, MA: MIT Press.

New Media Writing Prize. 2012 "New Media Writing Prize 2012 Shortlist." www.newmediawritingprize.co.uk/shortlist.html (accessed 5 August 2015).

Peacock, Alan. 2005. "Towards an Aesthetic of the Interactive." *Soundtoys*, 25 July. www.soundtoys.net/journals/towards-an-aesthetic-of (accessed 5 August 2015).

Redhawk. 1986. Developed by Silhouette Software. Published by Melbourne House. ZX Spectrum.

Resident Evil. 1996. Developed and published by Capcom. PlayStation.

The Secret of Monkey Island. 1990. Developed and published by Lucasfilm Games. PC.

Sonic the Hedgehog. 1991. Developed by Sonic Team. Published by Sega. Sega Genesis.

Spacewar! 1961. Developed by Steve Russell. Unpublished. PDP-1.

Storyteller. 2013. Developed by Daniel Benmergui. Unpublished [Alpha]. iOS.

Strip 'Em All. 2013. Developed by Ola Hannson. Published by Athletic Design. Browser. www.athleticarcade.com/stripemall/index.html (accessed 28 August 2016).

World of Warcraft. 2004. Developed and published by Blizzard Entertainment. 2004. PC.

YouTube. 2020a. Search results for "A Duck Has an Adventure." *YouTube*, 31 January. www.youtube.com/results?search_query=A+Duck+Has+an+Adventure&sm=3 (accessed 31 January 2020).

YouTube. 2020b. Search results for "Icarus Needs." *YouTube*, 31 January. www.youtube.com/results?search_query=Icarus+Needs&sm=12 (accessed 31 January 2020).

Zagal, José P., Clara Férnandez-Vara, and Michael Mateas. 2008. "Rounds, Levels and Waves: The Early Evolution of Gameplay Segmentation." *Games and Culture* 3 (2): 175–198.

Zork. 1980. Developed and published by Infocom. PDP-10.

5 Game-comics and comic-games

Against the concept of hybrids

Hans-Joachim Backe

Comics and digital games have been among the most important arenas of popular culture throughout the past decades and have influenced each other in diverse ways. Comics based on computer games have become commonplace just as much as games based on comics, running the gamut from collaborations of high-profile artists released by major publishers to mass-produced glorified promotional material and fan-created or underground works. Besides these spin-offs, tie-ins, fan fictions, and other forms of engagement traditionally identified as adaptations, we also find a variety of cases of interrelation, from simple references to complex blended forms, all of which frequently reflect explicitly upon their expressive specificities. In other words, they are spread across the whole range of intermediality, broadly defined by Werner Wolf as "any transgression of boundaries between conventionally distinct media" (2011, 3). To Wolf (drawing on Marie-Laure Ryan [2005]), a medium is "a conventionally and culturally distinct means of communication," characterized by "the use of one or more semiotic systems," and pragmatically relevant because "media make a difference as to what kind of content can be evoked, how these contents are presented, and how they are experienced" (Wolf 2011, 2).

How are we to make sense of the overwhelming diversity of connections between comics and digital games? How do we arrive at an understanding of them as "conventionally distinct media," and how does this characterization impact the way we discuss their interrelation? Given the complexities at play—including the fact that comics in their own right pose a challenge to intermediality (Kukkonen 2011)—it is not surprising that only little research on these issues exists. In the authoritative text on the subject, Daniel Merlin Goodbrey describes the phenomenon as a process of digitalization and hybridization of comics, at the center of which exists "a hybrid of the two forms, a game comic [which] must exhibit some of the key characteristics of games and some of the key characteristics of the form of comics" (2017, 126). Goodbrey's work is invaluable for the study of the encounter between games and comics, and it deserves all the recognition usually bestowed upon such groundbreaking efforts. At the heart of Goodbrey's argument are, however, a number of ideas that warrant additional consideration. In the following,

I will raise a number of general issues of conceptual categorization in the humanities. That I use Goodbrey's research as a starting point for this discussion is not meant as a critique of his work. On the contrary, without its daring exploration of two notoriously undefinable forms of expression and its willingness to confront definitional and systematic problems, the phenomena discussed here would be much more difficult to take into focus.

Already the question of how to refer to the phenomena under scrutiny is far from trivial. Goodbrey approaches the subject matter as a scholar and creator of comics, and accordingly, his vision of an idealized hybrid would be a "game comic" and not a "comic game." While the necessity to settle for one of the two possible orders of the two terms is a linguistic inevitability, it still implicitly characterizes the object as something that is rather a comic than a game. This finer point of nomenclature seems to me indicative of general challenges we encounter wherever we observe a coincidence of traits we associate with comics and games. As W. J. T. Mitchell famously observed with regard to the relationship of image and text, typography carries enormous meaning in such cases, as different spellings—divided by a slash, compounded into one word, or hyphenated—signify, respectively, "[r]upture, synthesis, relationship" (2012, 1). According to Mitchell's logic, Goodbrey is searching for the *synthesis* of a "comicgame" that would best express the field of *relationships* of the "comic-game." But in the course of this search, he is trying to circumnavigate the *ruptures* of "comic/game" aporias. How do we make sense of this phenomenon, then, and how should we speak about it? Should we distinguish between "comic-game" and "game-comic," between "comicgame" and "gamecomic"? What character can these categories have—can they be definitional, descriptive, or heuristic? In other words, are they one thing or a class of things, a continuum of related examples, or an umbrella term for very different phenomena? Are general approaches of adaptation, transmediality, or intermediality sufficient to analyze them, or do we need a more medium-specific vocabulary?

In the following, I will address many of these questions and propose a specific terminology and a set of categories meant to clear up some of the categorical murkiness inevitable in a large and complicated field as the one discussed here. The overall train of thought is that the metaphor of the hybrid is a commonsensical but ultimately detrimental way of characterizing the relation between games and comics because it glosses over essential differences and because it carries biologistic and genealogic connotations. After discussing the central problems with applying the concept of hybridity to game-comics and comic-games, particularly because of the conflation of set theory and prototype theory, I will show that these arise from general challenges of classifying complex cultural phenomena. After this theoretical overview, I will use examples to demonstrate that for categorization and analysis, the concept of hybrid is unnecessary on both the generic and the individual level. Over the course of my argument, it will become apparent that attributing a privileged degree of importance of comics or digital games for a group of examples or a particular example will always run the risk of over-emphasizing this dimension over other, equally important facets, while naturalizing and obscuring this heuristic act by resorting to a metaphor that insinuates biologic, hereditary clarity.

Hybridity and prototype theory

Research into the relationship between comics and games has been relatively limited. It speaks to the real-world relevance of the topic that practical guides for adaptation of games into comics (Goodman 2004) and manga (Cavallaro 2010) as well as for didactic uses of games and comics (Jost and Krommer 2011) are quite numerous. Some of these contain advanced theoretical (Vandermeersche 2011) and ethnographic (Jones 2018) research. Still, there are surprisingly few in-depth studies of individual examples (e.g., Corstorphine 2008) and even fewer systematic inquiries into particular aspects of the relationship between games and comics (e.g., Taylor 2004).

Within this research context, Goodbrey's aforementioned work stands out as the fundamental inquiry into the topic. His study connects theoretical considerations with his own practice as a comics artist and game designer, and he presents several prototypes of (not exclusively digital) games to demonstrate the artistic as well as academic breadth of the issue. He identifies four central challenges: digital technology, architectural spatiality, ludic structures, and audible soundtracks (Goodbrey 2017, 1). Especially the first and the last challenge are equally relevant for digital comics in general—a category that encompasses webcomics, eComics, and digitalized archives of existing comics (Wilde 2015, 2)—as well as for motion comics (Morton 2015). The architectural dimension refers to the spatiality generally attributed to digital narratives (Murray 1998), which Goodbrey primarily connects to hypertextual structures with their need for user navigation (Goodbrey 2017, 99). Goodbrey determines the ludic dimension based on Jesper Juul's classic game model, i.e., primarily on rules and a quantifiable outcome (Juul 2005, 36).

The four central challenges Goodbrey identifies interrelate with one another and influence, individually as well as together, other contemporary forms of culture in ways that make them appear less distinct than they are. For instance, the primate of spatiality to which Goodbrey refers is often taken as typical of digital games, but it is just as important for electronic literature and nonludic virtual environments (including their origins, amusement parks). Goodbrey resolves this problem through a hierarchical structure of the criteria: Digitality is to him the precondition of the whole phenomenon, whereas audible soundtracks are a surface phenomenon of secondary importance. Primarily, he engages with spatiality and ludic elements, and with the question of how they work independently as well as in conjunction. The basic nontraditional comics form in this respect is the hypercomic, "a comic with a multicursal narrative structure" (Goodbrey 2017, 87).

This multicursal structure is not dependent on digital technology; it can be created by distributing comics panels in a physical space, e.g., an art gallery. It does not need to have ludic goals or quantifiable outcomes, either, but can be completely based on choice (or randomness) and focused on storytelling, not success or failure. Goodbrey's narrower category of "game comics" is a special type of hypercomics: "A game comic is a type of hypercomic that exhibits some of the key characteristics of a game and uses some of the key characteristics of the form of comics as the basis for its gameplay" (2017, 123)—it is, Goodbrey stresses, "a hybrid of the two forms" (2017, 126).

There are two major issues with Goodbrey's definition. The first issue concerns his characterization of game comics as hybrids, while the second one is the combination of the idea of "key characteristics" with definitions that build on family resemblance or prototypical thinking.

Theoretical problems of concepts of hybridity

Hybridity is a well-established, widely-used concept, which beyond its home domain of biology has come to indicate a blend of otherwise rather distinct yet hard to define concepts.[1] Some applications of this conceptual metaphor have become indispensable in humanistic scholarship, such as referring to the clash between identity politics and ideas of national, ethnic, or other normalization strategies as cultural hybridity (Bhabha 2004). In other cases, especially outside of culture and media studies—think of the idea of new hybrid professions in economy (Colley and Guéry 2015)—it is often an unreflected shorthand formula. In media studies, it is a technical term introduced by Marshall McLuhan, even if a broad and affirmative one: To him, a media hybrid is something ubiquitous, namely "the interpenetration of one medium by another" (1964, 51). In other words, every encounter between two media produces a hybrid, a process McLuhan likens to a moment of fusion or fission in that it sets free immense energies: "The hybrid or the meeting of two media is a moment of truth and revelation from which new form is born" (1964, 55).

In this tradition, hybridity has become a rather indiscriminate figure of thought. What this results in is the recursive use of the concept: In media theory and, by extension, comics studies, phenomena tend to become (implicitly) characterized as hybrids of hybrids. Goodbrey speaks of "the hybrid hypercomic format" (2017, 26), just as he identifies gallery comics "as a hybrid format that combines the form of comics with the qualities typical to many examples of installation art" (2017, 98). He explicitly draws on Thon's observation that "digital media with their characteristically hybrid nature [...] do not obliterate the notion of conventionally distinct media" (2014, 336), and he refers to Thierry Smolderen (2014), Hannah Miodrag (2013), and Robert C. Harvey (2001), who all speak of the general hybridity of comics (Goodbrey 2017, 19)—as do other theorists, including Charles Hatfield (2009, 133) and Thierry Groensteen (2009, 7). The use of "hybrid" in this fashion is indeed widespread. Neil Cohn (2013, 88) characterizes storyboards as hybrids of comics and film, while Craig Smith (2015) sees motion comics as a hybrid of comics and animation. Drew Morton not only affirms that motion comics are a "truly equal hybrid of animation and the comic" (2015, 364), he attests to them the ability to further hybridize into "motion comic/motion book hybrids" (2015, 350).

The rhetoric of the hybrid has found prominent use with regard to digital games, as well. Espen Aarseth, one of the leading figures in the field of game studies, has characterized digital games as hybrids in more than one respect. A narrative digital game is, according to him, neither simply a game or a (hyper)text, but instead a "story-game hybrid" (Aarseth 2004, 50), negotiating the openness of play with the (multi)linearity of an authored narrative. Going even further, he outlines that a digital game is in general "a piece of software that does contain, among other things, a game" (Aarseth 2012, 130), similarly evoking the idea of a hybrid or container.

By this line of reasoning, game comics would be hybrids of, on the one side, hybrids (hypercomics) of hybrids (comics) of hybrids (digital media), and, on the other, hybrids (story-games) of hybrids (games in software artifacts).[2] This raises, at least to me, both the question of the usefulness of such a categorization as a hybrid of hybrids and of the general applicability of biologistic metaphors for categorizing complex cultural artifacts. Does our understanding of how these two forms coincide benefit from the label of a hybrid? If we wanted to operationalize this kind of thinking, would we not need to be able to distinguish categorically between different forms of hybridization, thus creating categories that would be rather clearly defined instead of indistinct hybrids?

Key characteristics of a family resemblance?

The second issue with considering game comics a hybrid form is the criteria for forming this categorization. Goodbrey delimits the concept very strictly. He eventually only identifies a small handful of (mostly older) examples that "meet the criteria of game comics, operating both as comics and as games of progression. But in both cases the mechanics of gameplay and the characteristics of the form of comics remain relatively separate" (Goodbrey 2017, 126). He arrives at this strictly delimited corpus of examples by setting explicitly formulated qualitative boundaries: "The resulting game comics are not just games that are also comics, but games that make specific use of some of the key characteristics of the form of comics in the mechanics of their gameplay" (Goodbrey 2017, 127). The seven key characteristics of comics he identifies (based on an extensive literature review of well-regarded definitions) are: space as time, simultaneous juxtaposition of images, closure between images, spatial networks, reader control of pacing, tablodic images, and word and image blending (Goodbrey 2017, 44). For digital games, Goodbrey adopts Juul's classic game model, which operates with six characteristics: rules, quantifiable outcome, valorization of outcome, player effort, player attachment to outcome, and negotiable consequences (Juul 2005, 36). The criteria themselves are not of primary importance here, but rather the way in which they are applied. Goodbrey admits, as mentioned, very few existing games into the category of game comics because he applies the seven comics characteristics and six game characteristics very stringently. At the same time, he stresses with regard to his definition of comics that the "resulting model is not intended as an exclusory summation of the form and as such it allows for the study of comic formats that do not demonstrate all seven characteristics" (Goodbrey 2017, 162).

There are two problems with this unequal treatment of game comics and comics in general. First, it implies that while game comics are supposed to be a finite and clearly delimited phenomenon, a much less strict delimitation is accepted for comics. By this logic, game comics are expected to be more prototypical of the form than non-game-related comics. Secondly, it calls into question the nature of the characteristics: When applied as a means of rigorous exclusion of most examples, they would seem to stand for necessary and sufficient conditions; when treated as nonexclusory, they describe family resemblances (in the Wittgensteinian sense).

Again, it is not Goodbrey who is at fault here; the definition of comics is notoriously difficult and contested. The viewpoint of comics as a hybrid of words and images has already been discussed, but approaches that try to identify comics as a distinct medium are similarly problematic:

> Despite the constitutive vagueness inherent in the fundamental question of how comics can be conceptualised as a medium, the fact remains that they are generally treated "as conventionally distinct means of communicating cultural content" and, hence, can be considered to be media that are "conventionally perceived as distinct," even though—or, rather, precisely because—their mediality is "not entirely predictable from semiotic type and technological support."
>
> (Thon and Wilde 2016, 234)

As a result, there are at least three distinct and not always compatible lines of argumentation for the existence of comics as a medium (Holbo 2014; Thon and Wilde 2016): semiotic-communicative formalism in the vein of Scott McCloud (1993), conventional-institutional historicism as practiced by Aaron Meskin (2014), and material-technological approaches such as Christian Bachmann's (2016). The two latter scholars trace the problems with defining comics to even more foundational media-ontological questions when they problematize the difference between an issue of a comic and one individual copy of the same issue (Meskin 2014) or the aesthetic dependence of comics on the specificities of their technical media (Elleström 2010, 30–33).

These different approaches "let 'comics' be ambiguous between *genus* (McCloud's medium) and *species* (Meskin's history)" (Holbo 2014, 4, original emphasis). And this pluralism makes it all but inevitable to err on the side of inclusivity when determining criteria for the form. Taking Neil Cohn's definition as an example,

> a "comic" can use any combination of writing and images: single images, sequential images, some writing, no writing, dominated by writing, etc. In fact, all permutations of these combinations appear in objects we call "comics." Ultimately, the definition of comics includes a network of ideas composed of their subject matter, format, readership, history, industry, the specific visual languages they use, and other cultural characteristics.
>
> (Cohn 2013, 2)

That Cohn's "network of ideas" echoes, intentionally or not, Wittgenstein's "complicated network of similarities" (Wittgenstein 1958, 32) is not surprising at all. Cohn's method operates, after all, not with hard criteria assumed to be shared by all members of a group, but with a much fuzzier set of parameters—i.e., aforementioned Wittgensteinian family resemblances.

Definitions of games are equally difficult and multifaceted (Arjoranta 2015; Stenros 2015), with family resemblance as a consensual middle ground (Arjoranta 2019), comparable to the definitional situation in comics studies. Taking Brenda Brathwaite and Ian Schreiber's definition as an example, the similarities to Cohn's argument are unmistakable:

> A game is an activity with rules. It is a form of play often but not always involving conflict, either with other players, with the game system itself, or with randomness/fate/luck. Most games have goals, but not all (for example, *The Sims* and *SimCity*). Most games have defined start and end points, but not all (for example, *World of Warcraft* and *Dungeons & Dragons*). Most games involve decision making on the part of the players, but not all (for example, *Candy Land* and *Chutes and Ladders*).
>
> (Brathwaite and Schreiber 2009, 28)

This approach seems almost inevitable given the wide range of phenomena discursivized as games and the ongoing diversification of digital games in particular. The publication of independent games like *Dear Esther* (2012) and *Proteus* (2013) has led to the emergence of the (sometimes pejoratively used) category of "walking simulator" for artifacts that use the formal language of first-person shooter games yet remove both combat elements and ludic goals. The question of whether or not walking simulators are games continues to be debated, especially among fans. Yet the existence of a shared identity is not only doubtful for (digital) games in general. Even within a series of digital games, we might not find any shared "gameness": The top-down action-adventure *Castle Wolfenstein* (1981), the original first-person shooter *Wolfenstein 3D* (1992), its most recent sequel *Wolfenstein II: The*

New Colossus (2017), and its promotional browser game *Du Hast Strife* (2016) share virtually no common elements.

Even Juul's model, chosen by Goodbrey for its strong claims and clear categories, emerges as less than rigid upon closer inspection. Juul's model only claims to encompass "the way games have traditionally been constructed" (Juul 2005, 23), which means that it is "no longer all there is to games. With the appearance of role-playing games, where a game can have rules interpreted by a game master, and with the appearance of video games, the game model is being modified in many ways" (Juul 2005, 53). While the "vast majority of things called 'games' are found in the intersection of the six features of the game model" (Juul 2005, 52), Juul includes a wide range of "borderline cases"—otherwise, the vast majority of digital games would not qualify as "games."

Prototype theory and knowledge organization

By formulating a definition for a core concept of games while allowing for a grey area of borderline phenomena, Juul uses prototype theory in all but name. Other game scholars, particularly those working on the Game Ontology Project throughout the late 2000s, explicitly identified prototype theory as ideally suited for the discussion of digital games (Zagal et al. 2008). Prototype theory is a systematized and empirically validated version of Wittgenstein's family resemblance, developed by Eleanor Rosch in the 1970s through a series of anthropological experiments (Andersen et al. 1996, 351–353). Historically speaking, it is a reaction against linguistic and cognitive formalism, which its proponents see as "an attempt to impose formal syntax and formal semantics on the study of language and human reason in a particular way, which, as we have seen, is empirically inadequate" (Lakoff 1987, 219). Against that rigid logocentrism, prototype theory formulates the "idea that members of a category may be related to one another without all members having any properties in common that define the category" (Lakoff 1987, 12).

This way of forming categories is exactly what we find in much of game studies and comics studies, with prominent examples quoted above. A widespread methodical mistake—found in Goodbrey's as well as Juul's arguments—is a combination of prototype theory and thinking in key characteristics as they are used in set theory. As Rosch's experiments show, a category of objects is cognitively constructed not based on "some set of defining features, but a sufficient degree of resemblance to each other" (Hampton 2006, 80). Dissimilarity is, however, as important for categorization as similarity. Attempting to rely on similarity alone "would fail for the very same reasons that necessary and sufficient conditions fail. Categories may exist where different pairs of members have different things in common, and some members may even have some of these things in common with members of other categories" (Andersen et al. 1996, 351). While it is true that from this process a prototype emerges, this does not mean that some examples are absolute prototypes of a category: "[T]he prototype should better be considered as a more abstract, generic concept, that was constituted from the different ways in which the category members resembled each other, and differed from non-members" (Hampton 2006, 80).

That scholars nonetheless mix prototype theory with more traditional methods of knowledge organization seems to be rooted in a fear of anti-theoretical iconoclasm. It might not be immediately apparent how much of a provocation to traditions of categorization prototype theory entails. As linguists and philosophers regularly point out, prototype theory has a strong anti-definitionist implication in that it is based not on an epistemological but on an ontological assumption about the undefinability of objects and object classes by traditional means—it does not proclaim that no generally shared traits can be found, but that they do not exist. This is felt by (especially analytic) philosophers to be an imposition of psychologist epistemologies and to stand in the way of precise scholarly discourse (Adajian 2005, 234), and their critiques of prototype theory go very far in presenting it as unscientific.

Much of the philosophical criticism is based on the same subconscious combination or conflation of prototype theory and traditional categorization methods we can observe in applications of the concept. One of the most vocal critics, Thomas Adajian, observes that

> because the prototypes of complex concepts are usually not a function of their constituent concepts' prototypes, [prototype theory] lacks an adequate account of conceptual combination. Standard example: the prototype associated with the concept PET FISH is goldfish. The prototype associated with PET is cats and dogs, and the prototype associated with the concept FISH is something more like a trout. So it is hard to see how PET FISH could be a function of the prototypes associated with its component concepts.
>
> (Adajian 2005, 234)

Adajian's criticism might seem reasonable, but it stems from expecting prototype theory to adhere to traditional paradigms of categorization. He approaches the formulation of prototypes in terms of set theory and statistics, assuming that a composite concept must be a subset of its component concepts, and that it must necessarily be a combination of the most common specimen. In other words, he misinterprets prototypes for reified objects instead of generic concepts derived from complex networks of (dis)-similarity. The concept of "pet fish" is not the intersection of "pet" and "fish" (which would be set theory), and neither is it based on the most common house animals and their shared traits (which would be a statistical approach). It is an original concept that draws on the two related (yet not hierarchically superior) concepts, not by recombination, but by its own set of (dis) similarities.[3]

To fully understand the critiques of prototype theory and the problems resulting from combining it with other forms of categorization, we need to take one further step back and consider knowledge organization in itself. In the most general terms, distrust against prototype theory stems from the distinction between conceptual classification and systematic classification. The former is "the process of distinguishing and distribution kinds of 'things' into different groups" (Hjørland 2017, n.p.)—a quotidian task every human being performs countless times a day. The latter is based on this yet strives to establish a classification system, essentially making systematic classification the academic specialization of the everyday practice of conceptual classification. Systematic classification has, in the Aristotelian tradition, been based on the notion that an entity either is or is not a member of a particular class, the basis of mathematical set theory. If only one aspect is considered in distinguishing a higher-order "concept (*genus*) into several extensions corresponding to as many concepts of lower generality (*species*)" (Marradi 1990, 129, original emphasis), the result is a classification scheme; if several aspects are considered simultaneously, the result is a typology; and if several aspects are considered in succession, the result is a taxonomy.

Birger Hjørland identifies four approaches to classification in the *Encyclopedia of Knowledge Organization* (2017): rationalism, where subjects can be constructed logically based on fundamental attributes, as is possible for mathematical objects; empiricism, where groups are formed based on statistically derived common properties of elements, as practiced in Mendelian biology; historicism, where groups are formed based on common genealogy, dominant in contemporary biology; and pragmaticism, where groups are formed based on critical reflection of the purpose of the classification, acknowledging the value-laden and inevitably reductive nature of all classification. The different approaches have their distinct limitations. As Hjørland discusses, rationalism only is applicable to logical or synthetic concepts, not the contradicting complexity of real-world objects. Historicism implies a natural order and thus depends on actual genetic relations because it otherwise runs the risk of establishing revisionist "grand récits" that (intentionally or not) mistake an ideology for natural order. Empiricism produces blunt distinctions because "similarity" can be ambiguous beyond the capabilities of statistical criteria: If a black square, a white square, and a black triangle are to be categorized based on their similarity, the precedence of color or shape is not given a priori or deducible from the objects themselves, but is based on the purpose of the categorization. Thus, the categorization of such objects is inherently pragmatist. It follows that pragmatism is the only adequate approach to classification of complex cultural products, and that these classifications depend on an acute awareness of their purpose and application.

Based on this, both the misrepresentation of prototype theory by rationalist, empiricist, and historicist scholars as well as its subversion by methods from these areas become explicable. The significant departure from philosophical traditions as well as the difference in subject matter create hurdles that are not immediately apparent and that produce either resistance or confusion.[4] Prototype theory is not applicable to every domain but lends itself to pragmatic categorization especially with regard to natural language, complex social or artistic concepts, as well as other domains characterized by four general traits: vagueness (fuzziness of borders and uncertainty about exact categorization criteria), typicality (differing degrees to which examples represent the concept), genericity (traits identified as typical of a class of objects are not found in all members), and opacity (categorization based on implicit, tacit rules instead of explicit, formalized ones) (Hampton 2006, 84). It is, in other words, the systematic classification method that is closest to simple conceptual classification, which makes it simultaneously commensurate for the analysis of domains with the highest complexity and less rigid and formalized than traditional methods.

Examples and discussion

To sum up my (admittedly long-winded) theoretical argument: Soft definitions based on family resemblance or prototype theory are incompatible with "key element" arguments. If both comics and digital games are defined based on prototypicality, there can be no universally identifiable key components or traits. If those existed, we would be able to define games unequivocally (necessary and sufficient criteria). By a similar token, treating game-comics and comic-games as hybrids implies a certain degree of media essentialism by assuming that they are "distinct" or "conventionally considered distinct" media with some core properties.

After demonstrating the pitfalls of this line of reasoning on a theoretical basis, I want to use a variety of examples to illustrate its practical implications, as well as alternatives. I will break down the discussion into two segments: First, I will deal with the use of "hybrid" for the field of game-comics and comic-games; second, I move on to a narrower use of the term for a specific type of example, much like Goodbrey does.

Game-comics and comic-games as a hybrid genre?

As a figure of speech, every example that bears traces of digital games and comics might be referred to as a hybrid, in the sense that its analysis would tend to draw on knowledge and methods from the study of both forms. Obviously, even a less strict use of a concept cannot be all-encompassing, so that it makes sense to identify two closely related concepts that serve as conceptual borders: animation and hypertext.

Comics are static texts that do not necessarily have to originate in a print medium but can be reproduced in print without any loss because they only insinuate movement. Animation, on the other hand, "is not a making move of what lies beneath the surface, but a making move that is evident in and through the movement of surfaces" (Malpas 2014, 74). Whereas comics are fundamentally an arrangement of individual, distinct images, "animation is based not in the image as such, but in the movement between otherwise static images" (Malpas 2014, 75). As the discussion surrounding motion comics shows (Morton 2015; Smith 2015), the addition of movement (and sound) to comics images calls into question the categorization of an object as a comic, so that it seems reasonable to consider digital games that have strong and obvious ties to animated film (and not comics) as a separate matter. One canonical game example would be the arcade classic *Dragon's Lair* (1983), which prominently uses animation created by Don Bluth's studio. At the other end of the spectrum, the two comic book series (Johnston and Shy 2010; Johnston and Templesmith 2013) based on the game franchise *Dead Space* (2008–2013) would be more immediately relevant than the two animated feature films based on the games, *Dead Space: Downfall* (2008) and *Dead Space: Aftermath* (2011)—even though the latter were written by the game's story author Antony Johnston. In a study of digital games and graphic arts, visual storytelling, animation, or franchised storytelling, these examples should be centrally included. When discussing the interrelation of digital games and comics, however, phenomena that are unquestionably animated films would be considered peripheral.

According to this logic, it is heuristically beneficial not to equate hypertexts with digital games. Because the latter often present multilinear narratives, the distinction is sometimes blurred, but the brief reminder that hypertextual structures underlie all websites illustrates the need for upholding the distinction: Shopping on Amazon or navigating through *YouTube* is not the same as playing games, not even in a less prototypical sense. For the digital version of Jason Shiga's *Meanwhile* (2013) or the award-winning issue #17 of *The Unwritten* (Carey and Gross 2010) with its nonlinear structure, the context of games might be less meaningful than that of experimental hypertext narratives. This becomes more apparent when comparing them with an actual game book containing not only plot-level decision-making but diverse ludic challenges and fail states like *Sherlock Holmes & Moriarty associés* (CED and Boultanox 2015), or pen-and-paper role-playing games illustrated and distributed in the format of comics like *Rolled and Told* (Thomas 2019).

Both distinctions are, however, hard to uphold. Nearly every digital game animates the on-screen representation of characters and objects to convey their movement when they are used as game objects. At the same time, many nonprototypical digital games and even whole genres are little more than hypertexts. The visual novel, a game genre particularly popular in Japan, "consists largely of text [and] elements that do not appear on the computer screen at all" (Cavallaro 2010, 11), with little to no ludic elements, yet is nonetheless produced and distributed as digital games. A categorical delimitation of comic-games and game-comics as a genre of its own will therefore have to remain very tentative.

Using the terminology of hybrids for more particular groups of examples within this larger field is similarly problematic, not the least because what we encounter there can often be productively framed in the more specific and well-established terms of intermedia or transmedia research. For example, Irina Rajewsky's (2005) distinction between media combination, media transposition, and intermedia references is directly applicable to specimens from the game-comic and comic-game continuum.

Intermedia references are most obvious in games that cite a well-known comics series without actually adapting any specifics of the referenced work, e.g., *Corto Maltese: Secrets of Venice* (2014). *Max Payne* (2001) contains references to a fictional comic strip to thematize the discourse of comics collectors and consequence-less cartoon violence. Comic books have their characters play and discuss digital games as a means of characterization, e.g., in *Runaways* #1 (Vaughan and Alphona 2003), or as a metaphorical counterpoint to the main narrative, as in *Top 10* #8 (Moore and Ha 2000). Some examples, notably *Scott Pilgrim's Precious Little Life* (O'Malley 2004), take a more systemic approach and refer less to individual digital games than to digital games and nerd culture as a whole.

Media combination is prototypically found in *Max Payne*, which integrates complete comics sequences within the mixed-media arrangement of the software to replace or complement narrative passages executed as live action or animated cutscenes. The opposite case, the inclusion of digital games in comics, is obviously more complicated, especially when dealing with print comics. However, some major publications, e.g., the Italian *Topolino* (1932–), have distributed physical media like CD-ROMs or provided internet portals with games since the 1990s.

Media transposition, Rajewsky's term for different kinds of adaptation, is especially wide-spread and generally encompasses some elements of intermedia reference and media combination. Successful game series like *Tomb Raider* (1996–) have been adapted by major publishing houses and have inspired countless fan-made adaptations. *World of Warcraft* (2004) fan comics are hosted and moderated exclusively by game publisher Blizzard (Jones 2018, 131–171). Blizzard's somewhat restrictive regulations of content have led creators to experiment formally and treat much wider topics than those found in the game, which is why "*WoW* fan-comics can potentially represent a plethora of game genres" (Jones 2018, 133). Digital games not only adapt the iconography and narrative of comics but often strive to translate their characteristics into gameplay. The game *Batman: Arkham Asylum* (2009) is a very liberal adaptation of the plot of its source material (Morrison and McKean 2004), but it includes gadgets, investigation, and unarmed combat that together implement a gameplay commensurate to the myth, iconography, and narrative conventions of the "system Batman" (Brooker 2012). Even more system-oriented adaptations, such as *X-Men Legends II: Rise of Apocalypse* (2005), may be based on a limited run of issues, yet they constantly reference the much greater context of their narrative universes, even in explicit form such as trivia challenges about the history of the X-Men. From there, it is only a small step to *Freedom Force* (2002) or *City of Heroes* (2004), which use the genre of superhero comics and its conventions without direct genetic relations to any existing comics.

A comparable systemic adaptation of style instead of content can be observed, as well: *XIII* (2003), the digital game based on William Vance und Jean Van Hamme's comics series of the same name (1984–2009), evokes its comic book roots by using flat colors and strong outlines for its game world, as well as comics panels and sound words as part of the interface—none of which is typical of Vance and Van Hamme's books but is doubtlessly meant to evoke a certain "comicness." Again, there is an even more system-oriented transposition to be found, which might be called a pastiche in Genette's (1997, 78) use of the term (i.e., a nonsatirical imitation of style). Some digital games evoke the aesthetics of comics without having any content that originates in comic books or making any explicit reference to comics or their culture. *Borderlands* (2009) is a particularly successful example of using three-dimensional graphics with textures and post-processing that evoke drawings.

Particular examples as hybrids in a narrow sense?

The previous section has demonstrated that examples that bear traits of or refer to comics and digital games are too diverse to be classified, altogether, as one hybrid genre or type, but that they can be productively categorized and thus functionally distinguished through established concepts of intermediality. Goodbrey's idea of hybrids is, however, formulated as a narrower category. To qualify, an example needs to exhibit "some of the key characteristics of a game and use [...] some of the key characteristics of the form of comics as the basis for its gameplay" (Goodbrey 2017, 123). Goodbrey employs this as an artistic constraint in the creation of comics, and his research operates with several prototypes by which he approximates the ideal formulated in this definition of game-comic hybrids. The final prototype, which comes closest to the envisioned goals, is *The Empty Kingdom* (2014). Animation is kept minimal, sound is used mostly to increase the usability of the software, panel structures are formative for the overall aesthetic, and there is certainly some gameplay (including world navigation, light puzzle solving, basic inventory management, and item use). It is easy to see why the result satisfies Goodbrey's definition, but if we want to identify *The Empty Kingdom* as a hybrid of digital games and comics, then it is one of very atypical forms of both: a silent comic walking simulator, so to speak.

This is not necessarily a problem when keeping prototype theory in mind, as there the question anyway is not "Is this a game?" or "Is this a comic?" but "How (a)typical a game or a comic is this, and how does it adhere to or depart from our prototypical understanding?" It calls into question, in yet another way, the usefulness of the metaphor of hybrids for analytical purposes. Taking the idea of Goodbrey's ideal hybrid literally, it would mean that the artifact in question would have all the "necessary properties" of a comic and a digital game. Given that "digital games" is, as shown before, an inevitably inclusive and wide concept, including many forms that even by Juul's standards are not games in the narrow sense, this raises a logical conundrum. Speaking of hybrids implies, in an epistemological irony central to Bruno Latour's theories (Blok and Jensen 2012), the idea of distinct, pure forms that in turn hybridize. If we process artifacts that merely use navigational, distributional, techno-infrastructural, or other peripheral factors associated with "digital games proper" as "digital games," then any hybrid—i.e., any phenomenon considered a candidate for this hybridization between "digital games" and "comics"—already bears enough resemblance to a "digital game proper" to be a "digital game" and not a hybrid with anything else. The other way around: What would a nonhybrid "digital game" look like? What would its "purity" manifest in?

In terms of analytical process, one dimension of an artifact will always be foregrounded by studying it in relative isolation—which is what focusing on the traditions of comics in analyzing a digital game (and vice versa) amounts to. There is, however, nothing that would essentially, ontologically make a "game comic hybrid" any different from any other digital game, especially when following through on the logic of hybridization. Simply put: Goodbrey's reflections and conclusions are absolutely successful in the context of his research-through-design. Yet while the hybrid concept is a powerful asset for creation, as an analytical category, it is rather fraught, if not downright misleading.

At best, the concept is a meaningful starting point for the few examples that might be surmised to have been created with this particular idea in mind. *Comix Zone* (1995) is one of the earliest and best-known digital games to strongly and explicitly embrace comics in visuals, discourse, and gameplay logic. The game's premise is that a comic book artist swaps places with the arch villain of his stories and has to fight his way through the hordes of mutants that would otherwise have faced the protagonist of his comics. *Comix Zone*'s game mechanics are those of a side-scrolling fighting game with some puzzle-solving elements, but its game environments consequently adhere to the premise of being (inside) a comic book. Instead of rooms, the game has panels, and instead of levels, the player has to finish pages. The physicality of the printed page is essential to movement through the game world and to some game mechanics. The avatar has to forcefully jump or climb across the gutters separating individual panels, while the other comic book characters cannot cross them at all and the avatar can hurt them by throwing them into these virtual walls. Some gutters are even destructible, bursting into shreds of paper that rain across the page, the same way vanquished opponents do. Similarly, the villain paints opponents into the game world, his (black-and-white) hand hovering above the page. When the avatar reaches the very final panel of the game, it remains unfinished because the villain-cum-artist has to abandon his or her work and re-enter the comic book world. Apart from all these references to and transpositions of comic book materiality, narrative conventions of comics are a formative influence, as evidenced by the game progress being measured in a "superhero meter." *Comix Zone* unquestionably invites its players to think of it as a liminal space of digital game and comic book, yet it is, for all intents and purposes, a digital game as much as any other fighting game of its generation. If its creators had perceived it as an actual hybrid or even a comic book in its own right, there would hardly have been the need to create an additional promotional comic that turns the comics-based game into a game-based comic (Foster 2012).

Similar observations could be made about the few other games that explicitly embrace the logic and aesthetic of comics to a degree that suggests they are conceived as hybrids. The independent browser games *Treadsylvania* (2011) and *Strip 'Em All* (2013) as well as the perpetually in-development *Storyteller* (2013; see Benmergui 2013) are explicitly about comics and digital games, and they leave little doubt about their experimental nature. The only truly commercially successful pertinent example, the mobile game *Framed* (2014), blends comics and games in an equally interesting way but without foregrounding comics materiality or narrative traditions, drawing instead on film noir for stylistic inspiration while employing the spatio-temporal logic of closure through frame transition as a puzzle-solving mechanic. This strategy can be equally observed in *Lovecraft Quest: A Comix Game* (2018), which uses comics panels as an interface for a remake of the text-adventure *Hunt the Wumpus* (1973) and recontextualizes the narrative within Lovecraftian mythology. Approaching these examples with the a priori assumption that comics are of elevated importance for them is legitimate insofar as they often encourage such a reading through their titles or other paratexts. At the same time, this can distract from other, potentially more promising avenues of inquiry. During its development, the connection of *Lovecraft Quest: A Comix Game* to *Hunt the Wumpus* was made explicit, yet with its publication, the developers no longer referenced the inspiration (potentially because of copyright concerns), thus obscuring a crucial influence.

This is all the more true for examples where even the creators might not be aware of traditions into which they inscribe their products. Both Goodbrey's *A Duck Has an Adventure* (2012) and Jason Shiga's *Meanwhile* have been identified by their creators as hypercomics, yet their branching movement along paths of panels bears just as much resemblance to the century-old tradition of goose games in Europe (Ryan 2007) and the game of knowledge in India (Schmidt-Madsen 2019). Interpreting *Gorogoa* (2017) as alluding to comics is similarly not wrong yet still obscures the equally strong legacy of physical puzzles, from slide puzzles to Rubik's Cube. And discussing the obvious indebtedness of *Sentinels of the Multiverse* (2014) to superhero comics runs the risk of ignoring that it is, just as importantly, a digital game based on an analogue game.

The nexus of comics and digital games is such an accepted factor in popular culture at this point that it is easy to see comics everywhere, even if the reference is far from clear. *Darkest Dungeon* (2016) uses minimally animated characters in an animation style clearly inspired by motion comics, but its supernatural horror themes and its art style point just as much toward woodcut and stained-glass windows as influences. In the case of *What Remains of Edith Finch* (2017), the "Barbara" episode unambiguously references horror comics in content and style, while the ludic aesthetic of its context—an episodic walking simulator with varied game mechanics—appears at least as essential for its interpretation. An analogous case in which not the mere structure, but the level of material media needs to come into focus, is *Metal Gear Solid: Digital Graphic Novel* (2006). Interpreting this example as merely a software adaptation of the (game-based) print comic (Oprisko and Wood 2006) would exclude the motion comic's platform-dependence, as it was released exclusively on Sony's PlayStation Portable, making it a game-based comic that can only be read on gaming hardware by using an interface closely resembling that of the adapted game. All these factors combine when approaching the complex constellation of influences and sources in LEGO digital games: Attempting to analyze a self-conscious meta-game like *LEGO Batman 2: DC Super Heroes* (2012) as an adaptation of Batman comics without taking into account the material and cultural significance of the building block toys would be to drastically misread these games (Nørgård and Toft-Nielsen 2014; Wolf 2014).

This brief overview should show that a categorization of examples as game-comic hybrids is facile because the surface-level presence of both forms is easily spotted, more so than many other noteworthy influences. Instead of assuming that hybridization between digital games and comics is a stable category that constitutes the basis for a specific approach to these phenomena, the coincidence of perceived traits of both forms should prompt the granular analysis of artifacts as complex objects in their own right, reserving judgement on the significance of games or comics until a thorough analysis has been conducted.

Conclusion

This chapter has taken Goodbrey's exploration of the intersection of games and comics as a starting point to argue against the usefulness of "media hybrids" for analytical purposes. It bears stressing again that this in no way is meant to critique the quality or value of Goodbrey's work; his practice-driven approach simply has different goals, needs, and priorities than a purely analytical one.

The core argument presented here is that, when keeping in mind that both digital games and comics are always already hybridized, there is nothing to be gained by analyzing complex media artifacts based on an a priori classification as a "hybrid of hybrids." When used conscientiously for a very specific, clearly delimited phenomenon—as Goodbrey does in his own creative work, or as others have done with regard to other phenomena such as the "Comicfilm" (Sina 2016)—this strategy can be successful. Less method-aware research will, however, run the risk of mistaking a conceptual classification—heuristically identifying comics and digital games, two undefinable objects, by taking recourse to their prototypical understanding—as a systematic category with its own identity. There would be ample opportunity to explore related yet essentially different concepts like cognitive blends (Kankainen et al. 2017) as alternatives to hybrids, and one could obviously take completely different approaches to the issue, e.g., a discourse-historical one of analyzing self-statements of creators, descriptions of distributors, and characterizations of critics, as Philippe Gauthier (2011) does in an investigation of early animated drawings. What I tried here was to demonstrate where the concept of hybrids creates logical friction, to pinpoint potential analytical blind spots, and to show how both issues can be avoided through prototype theory and bias-aware analyses.

What this comes down to is a radicalization of Hayles's (2004) call for even more pervasively media-specific analysis. There is definitely the need to pay "increased attention to materiality" wherever "the specificity of the medium comes into play as its characteristics are flaunted, suppressed, subverted, reimagined" (Hayles 2004, 87). As this study of game-comic phenomena has shown, they cannot comfortably be identified either as a medium in their own right or as a hybrid of other media. They can be commensurately approached only by paying close attention to their particularity—not that of a genus or species, but that of an individual that might elude stable, meaningful categorization. Given how diverse the phenomena discussed here are—let alone the countless additional examples that already exist and will surely emerge in the years to come—Hayles's concluding observation rings equally true on a less generic and more individual level: "In the tangled web of medial ecology, change anywhere in the system stimulates change everywhere in the system" (2004, 87). Every new "hybrid" recombines the vast expressive repositories of its two alluded domains in new ways while situating itself in a far bigger context of potentially even more important influences.

Ultimately, the argument presented here is not without a certain irony because the insistence on the status of individual, highly specific examples instead of subsuming them under an ill-fitting umbrella term is, in spirit, very close to Bhabha's highly influential humanistic use of the hybrid-concept as "the empty third space, the other space of symbolic representation, at once bar and bearer of difference" (2004, 101). This abstract idea of hybridity is radical, revolutionary, and empowering—and maybe something that we should hold on to even if we abandon the idea of the comic-game hybrid.

Notes

1 This has created a tradition in which "hybrid" becomes a default categorization. One prominent example is Bolter and Grusin's mischaracterization of Mitchell's "imagetext" as a hybrid (Bolter and Grusin 1999, 30), a phenomenon for which he explicitly uses the term synthesis (Mitchell 2012, 1).

2 I'm indebted to Andreas Rauscher for pointing out another complicating factor: What McLuhan describes is the process of hybridization, out of which new singular and individual forms emerge. McLuhan and most other theorists, however, use hybrid as a noun, which solidifies the idea of a derivative, unoriginal form.

3 Adajian's critique is just as easily defused, though, by following his own logic: That cats and dogs are more prototypical of the concept of "pet" than lizards and snakes is surely correct, but particularly the types of dogs prototypical of the concept of "pet" will be rather terriers than shepherds (which might be pets, but more prototypical of working animals). As such, "pet dog" implies such attributes as small to medium size and a compatibility with an urban lifestyle—attributes that when applied to fish certainly don't suggest prototypical big fish like trouts or sharks.

4 There is, however, also a political component to the different understandings of conceptualization connected to different subject matters: The philosophical practice of establishing a framework for categorization is an abstract, objective, detached, and value-neutral process. For scholars of cultural products, the case is less abstract because including or excluding a particular specimen from a socially shared concept of diverse creators and recipients is tantamount to proclaiming authority over this discourse. In operations with abstract values and formulas, clear definitions are as essential as they are unproblematic. In discussions of socioculturally formed discursive categories, things are less simple.

Works cited

Aarseth, Espen J. 2004. "Genre Trouble: Narrativism and the Art of Simulation." In *First Person: New Media as Story, Performance, and Game*, edited by Noah Wardrip-Fruin and Pat Harrigan, 45–55. Cambridge, MA: MIT Press.

Aarseth, Espen J. 2012. "A Narrative Theory of Games." In *Proceedings of the International Conference on the Foundations of Digital Games*, edited by Magy S. El-Nasr, 129–133. New York: ACM.

Adajian, Thomas. 2005. "On the Prototype Theory of Concepts and the Definition of Art." *Journal of Aesthetics and Art Criticism* 63 (3): 231–236.

Andersen, Hanne, Peter Barker, and Xiang Chen. 1996. "Kuhn's Mature Philosophy of Science and Cognitive Psychology." *Philosophical Psychology* 9 (3): 347–363.

Arjoranta, Jonne. 2015. "Real-Time Hermeneutics: Meaning-Making in Ludonarrative Digital Games." PhD thesis, University of Jyväskylä, Finland. https://jonne.arjoranta.fi/repository/Arjoranta2015d.pdf (accessed 31 January 2020).

Arjoranta, Jonne. 2019. "How to Define Games and Why We Need To." *The Computer Games Journal* 8 (3–4): 109–120.

Bachmann, Christian A. 2016. *Metamedialität und Materialität im Comic: Zeitungscomic – Comicheft – Comicbuch*. Berlin: Ch. A. Bachmann Verlag.

Backe, Hans-Joachim. 2012. "Vom Yellow Kid zu Super Mario: Zum Verhältnis von Comics und Computerspielen." In *Comics Intermedial*, edited by Christian Bachmann, Véronique Sina, and Lars Banhold, 147–157. Essen: Ch. A. Bachmann Verlag.

Batman: Arkham Asylum. 2009. Developed by Rocksteady Studios. Published by Eidos Interactive and Warner Bros. Interactive Entertainment. Windows.

Benmergui, Daniel. 2013. "Storyteller: A Game about Building Stories." www.storyteller-game.com/p/about-storyteller.html (accessed 20 June 2019).

Bhabha, Homi K. 2004. *The Location of Culture*. Abingdon: Routledge.

Blok, Anders, and Torben E. Jensen. 2012. *Bruno Latour: Hybrid Thoughts in a Hybrid World*. Abingdon: Routledge.

Bolter, J. David, and Richard A. Grusin. 1999. *Remediation: Understanding New Media*. Cambridge, MA: MIT Press.

Borderlands. 2009. Developed by Gearbox. Published by 2K Games. Windows.

Brathwaite, Brenda, and Ian Schreiber. 2009. *Challenges for Game Designers*. Boston: Course Technology PTR.

Brooker, Will. 2012. *Hunting the Dark Knight: Twenty-First Century Batman*. London: I. B. Tauris.

Carey, Mike, and Peter Gross. 2010. *The Unwritten #17: The Many Lives of Lizzie Hexam: A Choose-a-Story Adventure*. New York: Vertigo.

Castle Wolfenstein. 1981. Developed and published by Muse Software. Apple II.

Cavallaro, Dani. 2010. *Anime and the Visual Novel: Narrative Structure, Design and Play at the Crossroads of Animation and Computer Games*. Jefferson: McFarland.

CED, and Boultanox. 2015. *Sherlock Holmes & Moriarty associés*. Pont-à-Mousson: Makaka Éditions.

City of Heroes. 2004. Developed by Cryptic Studios. Published by NCSOFT. Windows.

Cohn, Neil. 2013. *The Visual Language of Comics: Introduction to the Structure and Cognition of Sequential Images*. London: Bloomsbury.

Colley, Helen, and Frédérique Guéry. 2015. "Understanding New Hybrid Professions: Bourdieu, Illusio and the Case of Public Service Interpreters." *Cambridge Journal of Education* 45 (1): 113–131.

Comix Zone. 1995. Developed and published by Sega. Sega Genesis.

Corstorphine, Kevin. 2008. "'Killer7' and Comic Book Aesthetics in Contemporary Video Games." *International Journal of Comic Art* 10 (1): 68–73.

Corto Maltese: Secrets of Venice. 2014. Developed by Kids Up Hill. Published by BulkyPix. Windows.

Darkest Dungeon. 2016. Developed by Red Hook. Published by Merge Games. Windows.

Dead Space: Aftermath. 2011. Dir. Mike Disa. USA: Anchor Bay Entertainment.

Dead Space: Downfall. 2008. Dir. Chuck Patton. USA: Anchor Bay Entertainment.

Dear Esther. 2012. Developed and published by The Chinese Room. Windows.

Dragon's Lair. 1983. Developed and published by Cinematronics. Arcade Game.

A Duck Has an Adventure. 2012. Developed by Daniel M. Goodbrey. Published by E-merl.com. Android.

Du Hast Strife. 2016. Developed and published by Midnight Oil. Browser game.

Elleström, Lars. 2010. "Modalities of Media: A Model for Understanding Intermedial Relations." In *Media Borders, Multimodality and Intermediality*, edited by Lars Elleström, 11–48. Basingstoke: Palgrave Macmillan.

The Empty Kingdom. 2014. Developed by Daniel M. Goodbrey. Published by Kongregate. Browser. www.kongregate.com/games/stillmerlin/the-empty-kingdom (accessed 31 January 2020).

Foster, Aaron. 2012. "Comix Zone Promotional Comic Strip." http://sega-memories.blogspot.de/2012/02/comix-zone-promotional-comic-strip.html (accessed 20 June 2019).

Framed. 2014. Developed and published by Loveshack Games. iOS.

Freedom Force. 2002. Developed by Irrational Games. Published by Crave Entertainment. Windows.

Gauthier, Philippe. 2011. "A Trick Question: Are Early Animated Drawings a Film Genre or a Special Effect?" *Animation* 6 (2): 163–175.

Genette, Gérard. 1997. *Palimpsests: Literature in the Second Degree*. Lincoln: University of Nebraska Press.

Goodbrey, Daniel M. 2017. "The Impact of Digital Mediation and Hybridisation on the Form of Comics." PhD thesis, University of Hertfordshire, UK. http://e-merl.com/thesis/DMGthesis2017web.pdf (accessed 31 January 2020).

Goodman, Jonah. 2004. "Video Games to Comics: How to Make the Perfect Transition." *Sequential Tart* 7 (9). www.sequentialtart.com/archive/sept04/rdm_0904.shtml (accessed 14 February 2012).

Gorogoa. 2017. Developed by Jason Roberts. Published by Annapurna Interactive. Windows.

Groensteen, Thierry. 2009. "Why Are Comics Still in Search of Cultural Legitimization?" In *A Comics Studies Reader*, edited by Jeet Heer and Kent Worcester, 3–11. Jackson: University Press of Mississippi.

Hampton, James A. 2006. "Concepts as Prototypes." In *Psychology of Learning and Motivation* 46: 79–113.

Harvey, Robert C. 2001. "Comedy at the Juncture of Word and Image: The Emergence of the Modern Magazine Gag Cartoon Reveals the Vital Blend." In *The Language of Comics: Word and Image*, edited by Robin Varnum and Christina T. Gibbons, 75–96. Jackson: University Press of Mississippi.

Hatfield, Charles. 2009. "An Art of Tensions." In *A Comics Studies Reader*, edited by Jeet Heer and Kent Worcester, 132–148. Jackson: University Press of Mississippi.

Hayles, N. Katherine 2004. "Print Is Flat, Code Is Deep: The Importance of Media-Specific Analysis." *Poetics Today* 25 (1): 67–90.

Hjørland, Birger. 2017. "Classification." In *Encylopedia of Knowledge Organization*, edited by Birger Hjørland and Claudio Gnoli, n.p. Toronto: International Society for Knowledge Organization. www.isko.org/cyclo/classification (accessed 31 January 2020).

Holbo, John. 2014. "Redefining Comics." In *The Art of Comics: A Philosophical Approach*, edited by Aaron Meskin and Roy T. Cook, 3–30. Chichester: Wiley-Blackwell.

Hunt the Wumpus. 1973. Developed by Gregory Yob. Published by People's Computer Company. Basic.

Johnston, Antony, and Christopher Shy. 2010. *Dead Space: Salvage*. San Diego: IDW.

Johnston, Antony, and Ben Templesmith. 2013. *Dead Space*. London: Titan Books.

Jones, Roger D. 2018. *Developing Video Game Literacy in the EFL Classroom: A Qualitative Analysis of 10th Grade Classroom Game Discourse*. Tübingen: Narr.

Jost, Roland, and Axel Krommer, eds. 2011. *Comics und Computerspiele im Deutschunterricht: Fachwissenschaftliche und fachdidaktische Aspekte*. Baltmannsweiler: Schneider Hohengehren.

Juul, Jesper. 2005. *Half-Real: Video Games between Real Rules and Fictional Worlds*. Cambridge, MA: MIT Press.

Kankainen, Ville, Jonne Arjoranta, and Timo Nummenmaa. 2017. "Games as Blends: Understanding Hybrid Games." *Journal of Virtual Reality and Broadcasting* 14 (4): n.p. www.jvrb.org/past-issues/14.2017/4694 (accessed 31 January 2020).

Kukkonen, Karin. 2011. "Comics as a Test Case for Transmedial Narratology." *SubStance* 40 (124): 34–52.

Lakoff, George. 1987. *Women, Fire, and Dangerous Things: What Categories Reveal about the Mind*. Chicago: University of Chicago Press.

LEGO Batman 2: DC Super Heroes. 2012. Developed by Traveller's Tales. Published by Warner Bros. Interactive Entertainment. Windows.

Lovecraft Quest: A Comix Game. 2018. Developed and published by Ogurec Apps. Windows.

Malpas, Jeff. 2014. "With a Philosopher's Eye: A 'Naive' View on Animation." *Animation* 9 (1): 65–79.

Marradi, Alberto. 1990. "Classification, Typology, Taxonomy." *Quality and Quantity* 24 (2): 129–157.

Max Payne. 2001. Developed by Remedy. Published by Rockstar Games/Gathering of Developers. Windows.

McCloud, Scott. 1993. *Understanding Comics*. New York: Harper Collins

McLuhan, Marshall. 1964. *Understanding Media: The Extensions of Man*. New York: McGraw-Hill.

Meanwhile. 2013. Developed by Jason Shiga. Published by Zarfhome. iOS.

Meskin, Aaron. 2014. "The Ontology of Comics." In *The Art of Comics: A Philosophical Approach*, edited by Aaron Meskin and Roy T. Cook, 31–46. Chichester: Wiley-Blackwell.

Metal Gear Solid: Digital Graphic Novel. 2006. Developed by Kojima Productions. Published by Konami. PlayStation Portable.

Miodrag, Hannah. 2013. *Comics and Language: Reimagining Critical Discourse on the Form*. Jackson: University Press of Mississippi.

Mitchell, W. J. T. 2012. "Image X Text." In *The Future of Text and Image: Collected Essays on Literary and Visual Conjunctures*, edited by Ofra Amihay and Lauren Walsh, 1–11. Newcastle upon Tyne: Cambridge Scholars Publishing.

Moore, Alan, and Gene Ha. 2000. *Top 10* #8. La Jolla: Wildstorm.

Morrison, Grant, and Dave McKean. 2004. *Arkham Asylum: A Serious House on Serious Earth*. London: Titan Books.

Morton, Drew. 2015. "The Unfortunates: Towards a History and Definition of the Motion Comic." *Journal of Graphic Novels and Comics* 6 (4): 347–366.

Murray, Janet H. 1998. *Hamlet on the Holodeck: The Future of Narrative in Cyberspace*. Cambridge, MA: MIT Press.

Nørgård, Rikke T., and Claus Toft-Nielsen. 2014. "Gandalf on the Death Star: Levels of Seriality between Bricks, Bits, and Blockbusters." *Eludamos: Journal for Computer Game Culture* 8 (1): 171–198. www.eludamos.org/index.php/eludamos/article/view/vol8no1-11 (accessed 6 December 2015).

O'Malley, Bryan L. 2004. *Scott Pilgrim's Precious Little Life*. Portland: Oni Press.

Oprisko, Kris, and Ashley Wood. 2006. *The Complete Metal Gear Solid*. San Diego: IDW.

Proteus. 2013. Developed and published by Ed Key and David Kanaga. Windows.

Rajewsky, Irina O. 2005. "Intermediality, Intertextuality, and Remediation: A Literary Perspective on Intermediality." *Intermédialités* 6: 43–64.

Ryan, Marie-Laure. 2005. "Media and Narrative." In *The Routledge Encyclopedia of Narrative Theory*, edited by David Herman, Manfred Jahn, and Marie-Laure Ryan, 288–292. Abingdon: Routledge.

Ryan, Marie-Laure. 2007. "Jeux narratifs, fictions ludiques." *Intermédialités* 9: 15–34.

Schmidt-Madsen, Jacob. 2019. "The Game of Knowledge: Playing the Spiritual Liberation in 18th- and 19th-Century Western India." PhD thesis, University of Copenhagen, Denmark. https://static-curis.ku.dk/portal/files/221758034/Ph.d._afhandling_2019_Schmidt_Madsen_bd.1.pdf (accessed 31 January 2020).

Sentinels of the Multiverse. 2014. Developed by Handelabra and Greater Than Games. Published by Handelabra. Windows.

Sina, Véronique. 2016. *Comic – Film – Gender: Zur (Re-)Medialisierung von Geschlecht im Comicfilm*. Bielefeld: transcript.

Smith, Craig. 2015. "Motion Comics: The Emergence of a Hybrid Medium." *Writing Visual Culture* 7: n.p. www.herts.ac.uk/__data/assets/pdf_file/0018/100791/wvc-dc7-smith.pdf (accessed 31 January 2020).

Smolderen, Thierry. 2014. "Graphic Hybridization, the Crucible of Comics." In *The French Comics Theory Reader*, edited by Ann Miller and Bart Beaty, 47–61. Leuven: Leuven University Press.

Stenros, Jaakko. 2015. "Playfulness, Play, and Games: A Constructionist Ludology Approach." PhD thesis, Tampere University, Finland. https://trepo.tuni.fi/handle/10024/96986 (accessed 31 January 2020).

Storyteller. 2013. Developed by Daniel Benmergui. Unpublished [Alpha]. iOS.

Strip 'Em All. 2013. Developed by Ola Hansson. Published by Athletic Design. Browser. www.athleticarcade.com/stripemall/index.html (accessed 20 June 2019).

Taylor, Laurie N. 2004. "Compromised Divisions: Thresholds in Comic Books and Video Games." *ImageTexT: Interdisciplinary Comics Studies* 1 (1): n.p. www.english.ufl.edu/imagetext/archives/v1_1/taylor/index.shtml (accessed 20 June 2019).

Thomas, Eric. 2019. *Rolled and Told* Vol. 1. St. Louis, MO: Lion Forge.

Thon, Jan-Noël. 2014. "Mediality." In *The Johns Hopkins Guide to Digital Media*, edited by Marie-Laure Ryan, Lori Emerson, and Benjamin J. Robertson, 334–337. Baltimore: Johns Hopkins University Press.

Thon, Jan-Noël, and Lukas R. A. Wilde. 2016. "Mediality and Materiality of Contemporary Comics." *Journal of Graphic Novels and Comics* 7 (3): 233–241.

Treadsylvania. 2011. Developed by NMSUCC. Published by Kongregate. Browser. www.kongregate.com/games/NMSUCC/treadsylvania?acomplete=treadsyl (accessed 20 February 2012).

Vandermeersche, G. 2011. "Intermediality as Cultural Literacy and Teaching the Graphic Novel." *CLCWeb: Comparative Literature and Culture* 13 (3): n.p. https://docs.lib.purdue.edu/clcweb/vol13/iss3/20/ (accessed 31 January 2020).

Vaughan, Brian K., and Adrian Alphona. 2003. *Runaways* #1. New York: Marvel Comics.

What Remains of Edith Finch. 2017. Developed by Giant Sparrow. Published by Annapurna Interactive. Windows.

Wilde, Lukas R. A. 2015. "Distinguishing Mediality: The Problem of Identifying Forms and Functions of Digital Comics." *Networking Knowledge* 8 (4): 1–15. https://ojs.meccsa.org.uk/index.php/netknow/article/view/386 (accessed 31 January 2020).

Wittgenstein, Ludwig. 1958. *Philosophical Investigations*. 3rd edition. Oxford: Blackwell.

Wolf, Mark J. P., ed. 2014. *LEGO Studies: Examining the Building Blocks of a Transmedial Phenomenon*. New York: Routledge.

Wolf, Werner 2011. "(Inter)Mediality and the Study of Literature." *CLCWeb: Comparative Literature and Culture* 13 (3): n.p. https://docs.lib.purdue.edu/clcweb/vol13/iss3/2/ (accessed 31 January 2020).

Wolfenstein II: The New Colossus. 2017. Developed by MachineGames. Published by Bethesda Softworks. Windows.

Wolfenstein 3D. 1992. Developed by id Software. Published by Apogee Software. MS-DOS.

World of Warcraft. 2004. Developed and published by Blizzard Entertainment. Windows.

XIII. 2003. Developed and published by Ubisoft. Windows.

X-Men Legends II: Rise of Apocalypse. 2005. Developed by Raven Software. Published by Activision. Windows.

Zagal, José P., Michael Mateas, Clara Fernández-Vara, and Brian Hochhalter. 2008. "Towards an Ontological Language for Game Analysis." *Proceedings of DiGRA 2005 Conference: Changing Views—Worlds in Play*: n.p. www.digra.org/dl/db/06276.09313.pdf (accessed 30 January 2012).

6 Building stories

The interplay of comics and games in Chris Ware's works

Nina Eckhoff-Heindl

As Laurie N. Taylor has pointed out, "video games [...] have extremely close ties to comics" (2004, n.p.), a statement that is supported by the research of Hans-Joachim Backe (2012, 115) and Bryant Paul Johnson (2013, 145). What these three scholars have stated about the interrelation between digital games and comics can also be asserted for the analogous context of parlor games.[1] Characters like Batman, Hellboy, and many others appear in at least one parlor game as part of a bigger merchandizing strategy,[2] but as I will show in this chapter, parlor games are involved in the medium of comics in notable, if not always obvious, ways.

Recent examples of this involvement are works of the Franco-Belgian artists group called OuBaPo (short for *Ouvroir de bande dessinée potentielle*, "workshop of potential comic book art") that experiment with characteristics of games as they probe and expand the boundaries of the medium by applying a set of formal constraints (see also Kuhlman 2010, 79–80). For instance, Anne Baraou and Corinne Chalmeau's *Après tout, tant pis* (1991) addresses dice games quite directly. The comics object consists of three dice with a single panel on each face in a box. Every time the dice are rolled, a new narrative emerges (Groensteen 1997, 32). Another case is Patrice Killoffer's (1997, 66–67) *Bande dessinée en Tripoutre*, which contains a clear allusion to racing board games. Similarly, the English artists Alan Moore and Kevin O'Neill include a classical racing game within the *Black Dossier* of *The League of Extraordinary Gentlemen* (2008).

Whereas all of these examples have in common that they are solitary works of the mentioned artists, the interweaving of comics and game structures is an elementary part of Chris Ware's artistic approach. This chapter highlights the different intersections of comics and games in Ware's works, especially regarding conventions as well as socially constructed regulations and attributions within the comics and games cultures. It does so by comparing and contrasting two works that come from the opposite sites of this intersection: the game "'Fairy Tale' Road Rage" (2000), which interweaves game structures with comics elements; and the comic *Building Stories* (2012), which intermingles comics-specific narrations with game allusions.

In 2000, Chris Ware conceived the racing and grammar-learning board game "'Fairy Tale' Road Rage." It was published in the comics anthology *Little Lit: Folklore and Fairy Tale Funnies,* which is addressed at children and edited by Art Spiegelman and Françoise Mouly. It consists of a printed game board, cut-and-assemble game pieces, and a dice as well as a game manual and an accompanying comic strip with the origin story of the game characters. The comic *Building Stories* from 2012 consists of a box with 14 printed products, some of which vary greatly in form, including newspaper formats, magazines, a book whose design and format recalls a children's book, and a folded game board similar to that of a board game. In these different formats, the story of five inhabitants of a Chicago apartment building is told: a young woman, a middle-aged couple, the elderly woman who owns the house, and Branford the bee. The stories around these five protagonists are characterized by loneliness, depression, and a lack of interpersonal warmth. In contrast, the multicolored pages, the intricate page layouts, and the publication formats, some of which seem to be directed at children, carry a positive and playful undertone. This playful character is underlined by the triple-folded game board and the slip lid box as they resemble the classic arrangement of a board game.

In the preoccupation with the game board and the box, the recipients/players have to build stories. But whereas the board game "'Fairy Tale' Road Rage" with its complementary elements adapts comics structures and refers to aspects of comics culture on a social level (e.g., the valuing and collecting of comics), *Building Stories* adapts structures and mechanisms of games. By contrasting the board game with the comic, I argue that certain expectations connected with aesthetic, ludic, and narrative aspects of both works are invoked at first sight and disappointed on closer examination. Thereby, the reading viewers[3] and the players, respectively, have the possibility to ponder how communicative and social conventions regarding comics and games can be uncovered and even challenged.

"'Fairy Tale' Road Rage," or: How comics correlate with games

After assembling the game pieces, which represent vehicles driven by the characters Frog, Princess, Wolf, and Grandma, the game is ready.[4] The players of "'Fairy Tale' Road Rage" start at the corners of the game board with one out of four vehicles. By rolling the dice the players have to collect chits with different colors and words on them in order to fill up one's own so-called "storyboard" with a story in the format of a fairy tale. The different colors correspond to different word classes, and the first player to complete his or her story wins the game. Thereby, "'Fairy Tale' Road Rage" combines a classical racing game with a didactic approach to convey grammar-learning skills. The topic of tales emphasizes this concept by offering a typical and well-known sentence structure starting with "Once upon a time" and ending with "and so the moral of this story is... ." But whichever chits are combined to construe the story, the players will never get to know the moral conclusion, as it always ends with an ellipsis. The moral assumptions are left open. The heading of the playing rules advertises this matter of fact as an opportunity to shape moral assumptions out of one's own storyboard: "Hey Kids! Play… *'Fairy Tale' Road Rage* and trace a literary path to your own moral conclusion!" (Ware 2000, n.p.). Although the importance of the formation of ethics is stressed repeatedly within the manual and the other game components, the moral outcome has no consequences on winning or losing the game. While the social dimension of the parlor game is given by playing together with or against each other, the players are on their own in the final outcome of the game, the moral conclusion.

While we cannot make explicit statements about the moral dimensions of the constructed stories, at least the content of the colored chits reveals information on the stories' ending. The variety of verbs shows that in most cases the stories end unhappily, life-threateningly, or indeed with death (in six out of eight cases). These endings are diametrically opposed to the fairy tale format, which ideally provides a happy ending for the main characters and is epitomized in the phrase "and they lived happily ever after."[5] The negation of such an ending is reiterated in the comic that accompanies the game, which provides the interwoven background story of Frog, Wolf, Princess, and Grandma. The stories have four different starting points and are allocated in successive squares. Both idiosyncrasies resemble the game board context and refer directly to the structure of "'Fairy Tale' Road Rage," whereas the describing text evokes the association with children's books and, of course, fairy tales. Within this panel arrangement, the conventions and markers of comics, fairy tales, and board games are indissolubly intertwined. However, the reading viewers who are expecting a traditional ending may be left with frustration. Not only do all the protagonists live a sad and tragically miserable life (except for the fortunate Wolf), but Wolf is also not the stereotypical villain known from the fairy tale context. Although Wolf can partly be blamed for the unhappy lives of the others by his actions, he operates with a clear conscience and good intentions, as the text points out. A similar relation between the expectations of fairy tale content and their negation penetrates into the depictions on the game board: Instead of the enchanted forest, elves, and other places or characters of a magical world, the players confront buildings mostly taken from the American cityscape. But at least the names of the buildings remind us of fairy tales like the laundry "Snow White Cleaners" or "Jack's Beanstalk Gentlemen's Nightclub."[6]

"'Fairy Tale' Road Rage" thus frustrates conventional expectations of fairy tale content. This is noteworthy, especially since the expectations are not just not met, but actually disillusioned or, more fitting to the context of tales, disenchanted. Speaking of "disillusion," I do not want to highlight the negative connotations of being deprived of one's own ideas and wishes. Instead, I want to argue that in a neutral sense of the word, less charged with emotions, disillusionment is a precondition for the possibility to reveal and literally discover self-reflexive mechanisms and the prerequisites of our own perception and cultural imprint. This means, quite similar to genre conventions, but also in a broader understanding of cultural practices and techniques, that we are shaped by social and cultural regulations to expect certain things when we are confronted with specific markers, and in finding these expectations disappointed, we have to think about what seduced us to draw the disappointed conclusions in the first place.

While the motif of fairy tales within the game encourages the players to think about preconditions and socio-cultural expectations of fairy tale storytelling and the attribution to human and animal characters, the title already refers to this kind of questioning. Ware puts the fairy tale in quotation marks and highlights it as sarcastic, or at least as charged with another meaning. Not only do the expectations regarding fairy tales play a decisive role in "'Fairy Tale' Road Rage," but the anticipation of the entertainment value as well as the social dimension of the parlor game are crucial elements of the play experience as well.

Besides the fairy tale content, the title of the board game as well as the advertising statements accompanying the game make the social conventions of playing games a subject of self-reflection among the players. The title suggests a wild car chase and refers to the category of a racing game. In fact, this racing game has a very slow course of play due to the single dice used, with four being the highest number one can roll. In addition, the heading of the manual evokes some kind of excitement in the activity of "tracing a literary path" (Ware 2000, n.p.) while the description on the game board pledges recreation or at least an "agreeable tone of recreation for youth of both sexes" (Ware 2000, n.p.). In contrast, the personal liability statement at the bottom of the game manual indicates: "No insurance is made against potential alteration in moral constitution, world outlook, or temperament, nor is any child guaranteed a 'good time,' or even mild amusement" (Ware 2000, n.p.).

Besides these partially contradictory promises regarding fun and entertainment, this grammar-learning game directly refers to the discussion of educational games, which are often purported to fail to support learning processes to the same extent to which they entertain the players (Gros 2017; Stasieńko 2013). As Mizuko Itō (2008) maintains, the desire to learn something in passing while amusing oneself with gaming is relatively difficult to fulfill. Notwithstanding, there is a rich history of educational games, of which one of the earliest is the so-called *Kriegsspiel of Brunswick,* which was designed by the German mathematician Johann Christian Ludwig Hellwig, the master of pages at the court of the Duke of Brunswick. He developed the game on the basis of the rules and form of chess and published a rulebook in 1780. As part of a comprehensive compilation of European war games, H. D. S. Heistand translated Hellwig's rulebook into English and accompanied it by the translated excerpt of a letter from Hellwig, in which he stresses the goals he wants to achieve by his game. In particular, Hellwig formulates:

> That idea [for this tactical game] came to me first through a need which I experienced of rendering sensible, not to say palpable, a few principles and rules of the military art which my position as professor to the pages of the Duke of Brunswick required me to teach those young noblemen, destined some day for military service. Independently of this chief object my secondary one was to offer those who had no need of such resources an agreeable recreation by laying before them a game which, at first sight, presented different objects and operations, and which depended upon nothing but the rules and combinations made by the players.
>
> (Hellwig, quoted in Heistand 1898, 238)

Besides a strikingly similar wording in describing and even advertising the recovery effects of the games, Ware and Hellwig have in common that they combine an attractive gaming context for pleasure in the spare time (chess vs. racing game) with an educational purpose. But while Hellwig accomplishes this goal to some extent, as Rolf F. Nohr and Stefan Böhme (2009, 8–9) argue,[7] Ware uses the ruptures that evolve by confronting expectations with their disillusionment to point to the social regulations of playing games. For instance, as part of the game instructions, the single player option is not only not characterized as an opportunity for children who love to play games even if they are not in the company of others, but explicitly as the one for lonely desperate children who do not have any friends at all to play with. But in his usual ironic intonation, Chris Ware sees hope for the future of this stereotypical lonely youngster: "Do not, however, despair; someday you will grow up to be a famous cartoonist and all of the other kids who made fun of you will have miserable jobs and be desperately unhappy, but you will get to draw stories for lots of money about how you still hate them all" (2000, n.p.).[8]

As it echoes in the message to the lonely nerd and future cartoonist already, Ware also reflects on the relationship between children and adults. The manual is separated into two divisions, one for grown-ups and one for children only. The grown-ups are confronted with short sentences in a commanding accentuation and in bigger font size. The text for children has a smaller font size, fills the complete remaining page spread, and includes detailed information on the game as well as additional rules. The underlying assumptions of adults who can only understand the simplest sentence structures and children who do not have any problem with complex grammar, very formal language, and a variety of additional background information, reverses the conventional allocation of rules and regulations to different age groups (Meerhoff 2011, 31). Furthermore, it perverts the rules of comprehensibility of manuals according to a linguistic-semiotic viewpoint (Langer et al. 1999, 15–23; Nickl 2001, 65–66). As all of these examples show, the promises made in connection with the pleasure of playing, the social interaction, and the attribution of comprehensibility and adequacy to children and adults are disillusioned and partly reversed. Therefore, the preconditions of the process of socio-cultural attribution are exposed and even challenged.

However, not only is the gaming culture at issue here, but the sphere of comics culture is negotiated as well. In addition to the aesthetic matters in the context of the comic with the background stories of the fairy tale characters, the manual offers a short comics story with Rusty Brown and Chalky White, two of Chris Ware's recurring comics characters, as protagonists (Tinker 2009, 257–261). They are both collectors of comic books and action figures, and they fulfill all the stereotypes of lonely grown-up comics nerds. When Rusty notices in the comic strip that Chalky has cut out and assembled the "'Fairy Tale' Road Rage" characters and chits, he is on the verge of a nervous breakdown because the book is no longer near mint condition and has lost considerable value in his comics collection. Chalky can only calm him with the offer of one of his expensive action figures. In the end, Rusty, embracing his new action figure, plays the game with Chalky and realizes how much fun it is to play the game instead of storing it in a polyethylene storage bag in a cool, dark place.

Apart from the topic of collecting, the comic strip entitled "Collecteurs Extraordinaire" also satirizes adults: Rusty and Chalky have forgotten how to have fun and play games without worrying about the value of their collectables and toys. This is strongly emphasized by the additional explanatory note: "'Collectors' are 'adults' who like to have 'one of everything,' or, specifically, items which they were denied as children. 'Pristine' manufacturing condition and 'original packaging' are of a premium to them, as are 'rare' or 'hard-to-find' items. You should, under all conditions, avoid growing up to be a 'collector' " (Ware 2000, n.p.).

Thus, a close look at the title in combination with game elements, design, and the game manual in "'Fairy Tale' Road Rage" can foreground the game-related contexts of social conventions. In addition, as my analysis has shown, the social and communicative correlation of comics culture is intertwined with the disillusionment of expectations and the discovery of socio-cultural imprints regarding regulations for children and adults, conventions of specific parlor games, and fairy tales.

Building Stories, or: How game structures invade comics

Reading and viewing the individual parts of Chris Ware's *Building Stories* conveys quite a similar way of a discovering disillusionment. In contrast to "'Fairy Tale' Road Rage," however, *Building Stories* is clearly not a board game but offers some explicit board game references, for instance, by including a box with lid and base that is typical of board game packaging. This box represents an important part of *Building Stories* although its interpretative significance is often underestimated, as Andrew Kunka and Derek

Royal (2013) underscore. The back of the box features a text with an accompanying diagram entitled “Everything you need to read the new graphic novel *Building Stories*.” What initially reads like a manual does not provide the promised help with the complex structure of *Building Stories*. Taking the manual character seriously would mean that one would only need to know how to use the individual publication formats. The diagram shows how the publications can be unfolded and opened. What’s more, the proper positions for reception are addressed by depictions of the sitting, lying, standing, or traveling female protagonist. And, as a last structure of reference, arrows designate the filing locations of the publication formats within an apartment. The text, however, particularly pairs critical remarks of contemporary culture in the digital age with ironically fractured advertisements for the comic, and it contains a very rough summary with information on the production contexts. But fundamental questions such as in which order the elements of *Building Stories* should be read and viewed or what kind of stories can be expected are addressed neither by the diagram nor by the text. Thus, Ware takes up only the most obvious connections for his explanations, which can be summarized with Jasmin Meerhoff (2011, 32) as the presentation of knowledge of pre-inscriptive correlations that trivializes the function of manuals.

The foldable game board, the second game-related item of *Building Stories,* establishes the board game relation by its materiality, size, and visual appearance and has diagrammatical depictions of the apartment building and its inhabitants as its subject. The reverse side of the cardboard is covered with a structured blue paper and shows axonometric depictions of every single floor of the apartment building. The print on the inside of the folded cardboard shows the whole building during the four seasons. Every area focuses on one protagonist and the story this character inhabits, which corresponds to the blue cardboard back and the axonometric depiction of the floor in question. Through the diagrammatical structures and panel sequences, the reading viewers can gain insight into the relationships and activities of the five protagonists. The apartment building is introduced through the façade-less architectural depiction on the backside. The perception of this piece of *Building Stories* as a game element is invoked visually and materially, but there are neither pieces or tokens nor dice that would make this particular part of *Building Stories* usable as a game board. Furthermore, instead of playing within a community, as the allusion to a parlor game suggests, the recipients usually deal with *Building Stories* on their own, as is common for reading and viewing comics. This item rather complies with a manual that explains the connections and problems of the protagonists and supports the desire to structure all the information about the different plots.

Understanding the game board format as a manual points to a more abstract concept pertaining to the structural level of gameplay as well as to a notion of *Building Stories* that is informed by the approach to (video) games as "simulations of basic modes of real-life experiences" (Grodal 2003, 129), as Torben Grodal puts it. By taking this approach as a basis, reading viewers can comprehend *Building Stories* as experimental narrative (Gilmore 2012), as memory store (Sattler 2012), or archive of serialization (Crucifix 2018). Following Laurie N. Taylor's (2004) structural comparison between comics and videogames via the analysis of thresholds, I define gameplay as the framework consisting of game rules and the partly free interaction of players with the game.

By transferring the game-specific criteria of rules and regulations on a structural level, we can recognize the fourteen different items of *Building Stories* as simulations of the adopted publication format. In this context, I understand the basic concept of simulation as an "environment for experimentation," which Gonzalo Frasca defines as follows: "[T]o simulate is to model a (source) system through a different system which maintains (for somebody) some of the behaviors of the original system" (2003, 223). The sheets of the large, folded newspaper format, for instance, are loosely laid one inside the other and have to be unfolded. The reading and viewing process requires a broader space for handling as well as something to lay the newspaper piece down on in order to perceive the panel arrangements within. By contrast, the children's book format has the characteristic thick cardboard as book covers as well as a field located at the endpapers where the book owner's name can be inserted. Even though both items adapt structures of the underlying publication form of a newspaper as well as a children's book, the content appears in comics-specific panel arrangements.[9] Every piece of *Building Stories* is still part of the whole comics conglomeration. Yet the activity and the involvement of the reading viewers resembles the experiences we can gain with the forms of publications in real-life. In this sense, my argument is quite similar to the one of Torben Grodal (2003, 142) regarding the relationship between videogames and a possible real world by simulation.

Besides the regulations related to the mediality of the comic's items, the recipients also gain freedom in their interaction with *Building Stories*. It is up to the reading viewers to decide in which order they wish to place the individual elements of the work and how the narrative about the five protagonists and the apartment building evolves. Due to the nonlinearity of the perception process, the individual comics parts can consistently be rearranged and sequenced in new constellations, forming new references and revealing new systems of connection among the parts of *Building Stories*. Therefore, the reading viewers are permanently and actively influencing how the plot of each protagonist as well as the overall story of the whole ensemble is established and developed. The intriguing process of choosing items, ordering them and handling them under different conditions of perceiving, contrasts with the stories about sad and unfulfilled lives, for example, when the main protagonist, the nameless woman from the top floor, has an abortion, or when the couple's woman from the middle floor longs in her desperateness for the former mutual affection in her partnership.

Similar to the adaptation of structures of comics and tales in "'Fairy Tale' Road Rage," the referencing of game elements and mechanisms in *Building Stories* reveals socio-cultural imprints regarding elementary cultural techniques and learned knowledge about the usage of printed products. This process of generating meaning emerges from a process of disillusioning expectations and is deeply intertwined with game-specific mechanisms.

The interplay of games and comics in Ware's works, or: Some concluding thoughts

Ware's "'Fairy Tale' Road Rage" and *Building Stories* intermingle aspects of the framework of comics and games culture, in particular regarding conventions as well as socially constructed regulations and attributions. Both works seem to take up the promise of fun and entertainment through their design and game associations. In "'Fairy Tale' Road Rage," Ware raises expectations regarding the enjoyment and narrative of the game and counters these expectations by the slow manner in which the game develops, the staging of the magical world and its protagonists, and the way he comments on stereotypes about comics culture and its social settings. In *Building Stories,* the comics artist invokes playful characteristics and game structures that enrich the process of perception and stand clearly in contrast to the emotional and depressing content. By combining games with comics structures and, vice versa, comics with gaming strategies, the preoccupation with "'Fairy Tale' Road Rage" and *Building Stories* brings into focus the tension between game association, the expectations of fun and entertainment, and their disillusionment. Furthermore, it foregrounds the social and communicative dimension as well as the culturally imprinted implications of games and comics.

Acknowledgement

This chapter was written in connection with my PhD project, which has received funding from the European Union's Horizon 2020 research and innovation programme under the Marie Skłodowska-Curie grant agreement No. 713600. In addition to this generous support, I am very thankful to Julia Kuhlmann and Véronique Sina for their attentive reading and helpful suggestions.

Notes

1 For the particular context of board games within parlor games, see Johnson 2013, 147.

2 See, for example, the parlor games *Marvel Heroes* (2006), *Batman: Gotham City Strategy Game* (2013), and *Hellboy: The Board Game* (2019).

3 The expression "reading viewers" is used in order to describe more precisely the recipient and mechanisms of reception: When opening a comic book, the recipients are first viewers as they perceive the entire double page or the single page spread in its visual structure. Then they turn successively to the single panels, an action that is interrupted and expanded by the simultaneous observation of a single or double page.

4 The handicraft manual and the process of preparation would be quite interesting for an examination of Ware's work in the broader context of playfulness. For different approaches to Ware's cutouts, see Bachmann 2016, 176–184; Bredehoft 2006; Claudio 2011.

5 Although not all fairy tales possess a happy ending, Kathrin Pöge-Alder (2007, 27) points out that the happy ending is a typical feature of fairy tales. By using a quite characteristic preamble and complementary close in the story board, Ware refers to this kind of fairy tale.

6 This strategy of referencing is also known from other productions, for example Bill Willingham's comics series *Fables* (2002–2015) or the TV series *Once Upon a Time* (2011–2018).

7 There are also objections of Hellwig's contemporaries, as Sebastian Schwägele (2015, 19) describes.

8 It is noteworthy that this passage suggests a kind of self-reflection of the artist. Ware often ironically emphasizes his somewhat misfit youth, and it is no coincidence that Ware refers to the career of a comics artist (Ware 2017, 6–15). For a more detailed examination of Ware's self-portrayal in text and depiction, see Heindl 2018.

9 Of course, as several comics scholars have already mentioned, these publication formats are indissolubly entangled with the history of comics (Crucifix 2018; Ghosal 2015). It is also noteworthy that Ware adapts a specific children's book, namely the series *Little Golden Book*, which, as Julie Sinn Cassidy states, has been a "consistent [...] popular part of American children's literature and culture since [its] inception in 1942" (2008, 145). Its adaptation evokes the discussion of the entanglement of comics, childhood, and nostalgia as well as of trivialization and ennoblement (Cassidy 2008; Lanes 1976, 112–127).

Works cited

Bachmann, Christian. 2016. *Metamedialität und Materialität im Comic: Zeitungscomic – Comicheft – Comicbuch*. Berlin: Ch. A. Bachmann Verlag.

Backe, Hans-Joachim. 2012. "Vom Yellow Kid zu Super Mario: Zum Verhältnis von Comics und Computerspielen." In *Comics intermedial*, edited by Christian Bachmann, Véronique Sina, and Lars Banhold, 143–158. Essen: Ch. A. Bachmann Verlag.

Baraou, Anne, and Corinne Chalmeau. 1991. *Après tout, tant pis*. Paris: Hors gabarit.

Bredehoft, Thomas. 2006. "Comics Architecture, Multidimensionality, and Time: Chris Ware's 'Jimmy Corrigan: The Smartest Kid on Earth.'" *Modern Fiction Studies* 52 (4): 869–890.

Cassidy, Julie Sinn. 2008. "Transporting Nostalgia: The Little Golden Books as Souvenirs of Childhood." *Children's Literature* 36: 145–161.

Claudio, Esther. 2011. "Would You Admit It? On Chris Ware's Cut-Outs." *The Comics Grid: Journal of Comics Scholarship* 1: 28–30. https://issuu.com/ernestopriego/docs/comicsgridyearoneebook (accessed 31 January 2020).

Crucifix, Benoît. 2018. "From Loose to Boxed Fragments and Back Again: Seriality and Archive in Chris Ware's 'Building Stories.'" *Journal of Graphic Novels and Comics* 9 (1): 3–22.

Frasca, Gonzalo. 2003. "Simulation versus Narrative: Introduction to Ludology." In *The Video Game Theory Reader*, edited by Mark J. P. Wolf and Bernard Perron, 221–235. New York: Routledge.

Ghosal, Torsa. 2015. "Books with Bodies: Narrative Progression in Chris Ware's *Building Stories*." *Storyworlds: A Journal of Narrative Studies* 7 (1): 75–99.

Gilmore, Shawn. 2012. "Formal Disruption and Narrative Progress in *Building Stories*." *The Comics Journal*, 26 October. www.tcj.com/formal-disruption-and-narrative-progress-in-building-stories (accessed 31 January 2020).

Grodal, Torben. 2003. "Stories for Eye, Ear, and Muscles: Video Games, Media, and Embodied Experiences." In *The Video Game Theory Reader*, edited by Mark J. P. Wolf and Bernard Perron, 129–155. New York: Routledge.

Groensteen, Thierry. 1997. "Un premier bouquet de contraintes." *OuBaPo OuPus* 1: 13–59.

Gros, Begona. 2017. "Game Dimensions and Pedagogical Dimension in Serious Games." In *Handbook of Research on Serious Games for Educational Applications*, edited by Robert Zheng and Michael K. Gardner, 402–417. Hershey: IGI Global.

Heindl, Nina. 2018. "'Jimmy Corrigan has my grandfather's hair, Charlie Brown's eyes and my self-doubt': Autobiografische und autofiktionale Beziehungen in Chris Wares Comics." In *Autobiografie intermedial: Fallstudien zur Literatur und zum Comic*, edited by Kalina Kupczynska and Jadwiga Kita-Huber, 405–421. Bielefeld: Aisthesis.

Heistand, H. O. S. 1898. "Foreign Ware Games." In *Selected Papers Translated from European Military Publications*, 233–289. Washington: US Government Printing Office.

Itō, Mizuko. 2008. "Education vs. Entertainment: A Cultural History of Children's Software." In *The Ecology of Games: Connecting Youth, Games, and Learning*, edited by Katie Salen, 89–116. Cambridge, MA: MIT Press.

Johnson, Bryant Paul. 2013. "Equip Shield: The Role of Semipermeable Cultural Isolation in the History of Games and Comics." In *Gaming Globally: Production, Play, and Place*, edited by Nina B. Huntemann and Ben Aslinger, 141–161. New York: Palgrave Macmillan.

Killoffer, Patrice. 1997. "Bande dessinée en tripoutre." *OuBaPo OuPus* 1: 66–67

Kuhlman, Martha. 2010. "In the Comics Workshop: Chris Ware and the Oubapo." In *The Comics of Chris Ware: Drawing Is a Way of Thinking,* edited by David M. Ball and Martha B. Kuhlman, 78–89. Jackson: University Press of Mississippi.

Kunka, Andy, and Derek Royal. 2013. "Episode 21 Bonus Feature: A Closer Reading of 'Building Stories.'" *Comics Alternative Podcast*, 29 January. http://comicsalternative.com/episode-21-bonus (accessed 31 January 2020).

Lanes, Selma G. 1976. *Down the Rabbit Hole: Adventures and Misadventures in the Realm of Children's Literature*. New York: Atheneum.

Langer, Inghard, Friedemann Schulz von Thun, and Reinhard Tausch. 1999. *Sich verständlich ausdrücken*. Munich: Ernst Reinhardt.

Meerhoff, Jasmin. 2011. *Read me! Eine Kultur- und Mediengeschichte der Bedienungsanleitung*. Bielefeld: transcript.

Moore, Alan, and Kevin O'Neill. 2008. *The League of Extraordinary Gentlemen: Black Dossier*. La Jolla: America's Best Comics.

Nickl, Markus. 2001. *Gebrauchsanleitungen: Ein Beitrag zur Textsortengeschichte seit 1950*. Tübingen: Narr.

Nohr, Rolf F., and Stefan Böhme. 2009. *Die Auftritte des Krieges sinnlich machen: Johann C. L. Hellwig und das Braunschweiger Kriegsspiel*. Braunschweig: Appelhans-Verlag.

Pöge-Alder, Kathrin. 2007. *Märchenforschung: Theorien, Methoden, Interpretationen*. Tübingen: Narr.

Sattler, Peter. 2012. "Building Memories: Mine, Hers, and Ours." *The Comics Journal*, 2 November. www.tcj.com/building-memories-mine-hers-and-ours/ (accessed 31 January 2020).

Schwägele, Sebastian. 2015. *Planspiel – Lernen – Lerntransfer: Eine subjektorientierte Analyse von Einflussfaktoren*. Norderstedt: Books on Demand.

Stasieńko, Jan. 2013. "Why Are They So Boring? The Educational Context of Computer Games from a Design and a Research Perspective." *Neodidagmata* 35: 47–64.

Taylor, Laurie N. 2004. "Compromised Divisions: Thresholds in Comic Books and Video Games." *ImageTexT: Interdisciplinary Comics Studies* 1 (1): n.p. www.english.ufl.edu/imagetext/archives/v1_1/taylor/index.shtml (accessed 31 January 2020).

Tinker, Emma. 2009. "Identity and Form in Alternative Comics, 1967–2007." PhD thesis, University College London, UK. http://emmatinker.oxalto.co.uk/thesis (accessed 31 January 2020).

Ware, Chris. 2000. "'Fairy Tale' Road Rage." In *Little Lit: Folklore and Fairy Tale Funnies*, edited by Art Spiegelman and Françoise Mouly, endpapers. New York: RAW Junior.

Ware, Chris. 2012. *Building Stories*. New York: Pantheon.

Ware, Chris. 2017. *Monograph*. New York: Rizzoli.

7 *Homestuck* as a game

A webcomic between playful participation, digital technostalgia, and irritating inventory systems

Tim Glaser

Homestuck is a webcomic of truly epic proportions. Created by Andrew Hussie between 2009 and 2016, it consists of over 8,000 pages and contains various media formats. It has been called the "Ulysses of the Internet" (PBS Idea Channel 2012) and "a genre-fusing postmodern epic designed for and produced through the internet" (Litwhiler 2013, 1). As the creator himself put it: *Homestuck* is "a story about kids on the internet, that is told in a way that is like, *made of pure internet*" (O'Malley 2012, n.p., original emphasis). However, *Homestuck* not only utilizes the possibilities of digital production and reception, but the narration, style, and collaboration are themselves influenced by characteristics of digital media, especially game mechanics, obsolete technology, and playful interaction. For instance, the protagonists have to obey specific rules, such as a needlessly elaborate inventory system or leveling for inanimate objects, while simultaneously playing Sburb, a dangerous sandbox game that is superimposed over their real world. Furthermore, the first three chapters of *Homestuck* were created on the basis of various suggestions by readers, enabling them to directly participate in the game's gestation (Short 2014, 45).

This chapter argues that *Homestuck* is not only influenced by videogames and genre conventions, but that the webcomic can be understood as a playful yet critical appraisal of various aspects of gaming culture, digital technology, and fandom. Analyzing the interconnections between ludic, graphic, and narrative elements in this multilayered universe, which seems to be converging and diverging simultaneously, enables us to reflect on the interactions between metamedia elements and different modes of engagement. Hence, this chapter will first provide a very brief introduction to *Homestuck* and its story, production, and reception. The second section will focus on theories of metamedia storytelling and technostalgia and on their relation to webcomics and indie games. Finally, I analyze *Homestuck* as a *game*, with a focus on readers as players and references to gaming culture, tropes, and genres. The aim of this chapter is to demonstrate how *Homestuck* uses these different elements to encapsulate and reflect on the process of growing up in the age of online communities and digital communication.

Welcome to *Homestuck*

Homestuck is foremost a digital webcomic[1] created by Andrew Hussie, with assistance by various collaborators and fans who contributed pieces of music, artwork, ideas, and feedback.[2] The first page of *Homestuck*—not considering a short alpha run—was posted on 13 April 2009. *Homestuck* ran for seven years, and the official credits were posted on 25 October 2016.[3] On 13 April 2019—ten years after the initial start—a written epilogue to the webcomic was uploaded to the main page that also paid homage to self-hosted fan-fiction website *Archive of Our Own,* and in the same year *Homestuck 2: Beyond Canon* was released as an official sequel.[4] Beyond being a webcomic, *Homestuck* utilizes a range of digital media formats, everything from drawn images, animated GIFs, and chat logs to Flash animations, mini-games, and video files. In its entirety, *Homestuck* includes more than 8,000 pages, four hours of animation, and 800,000 words (Bailey 2018).

Homestuck was Hussie's fourth entry in the so-called *MS Paint Adventures* series,[5] after *Problem Sleuth* (2008–2009), *Bard Quest* (2007), and *Jailbreak* (2006–2007, 2011). All of them share the visual and logical imitation of old parser-based adventure games, while their plot development was shaped by audience participation via text-based inputs: "Hussie encouraged fans to share his role as author, allowing them to feel a sense of ownership and investment in the story" (Short 2014, 46). The "players" (readers and collaborators) suggest actions for the characters in the diegesis to perform—similar to commands typed into text prompts of adventure games. Hussie in turn chose a suggestion for the next panel. Primarily relying on a simple stick-figure style, Hussie was able to draw proposed actions quickly and could publish several panels per day.[6]

The narrative of *Homestuck* revolves around the friendship between and adventures of four thirteen-year-olds: John Egbert, Rose Lalonde, Dave Strider, and Jade Harley—respectively also known by their online handles ectoBiologist, tentacleTherapist, turntechGodhead, and gardenGnostic. While playing the immersive simulation sandbox game Sburb, a meteor shower appears and threatens to destroy planet earth. Before this happens, the game provides these teenagers with a complex alchemy system, an in-game collecting and crafting mechanic, to escape. Succeeding in this challenge transports them to a dimension called the "Medium." Advancing further, the four friends learn that Sburb was a mechanism designed to create a new universe. And the meteor shower and subsequent destruction of earth was initiated through the game and future versions of themselves. Many other important figures exist, such as the humanoid aliens called trolls (who also play a version of the game called Sgrub), guardian characters, clones, and the nonplayer character Lord English, who runs amok and threatens the protagonists.

Considering its scope and complexity, *Homestuck* appears to be an epic saga, including seemingly never-ending battles between good and evil, with the fate of the world at stake. Additionally, it incorporates tropes of fantasy, science-fiction, and horror genres, such as alien races, time traveling, strange artifacts, monsters, and mayhem. But beyond mere genre references, *Homestuck* oscillates between ironic dissociation and a serious examination of adolescence. Metaphors for growing up and elements from young adult fiction can be seen in the teenage protagonists and the focus on quirky internet friendship, shared memes, in-group jokes, awkwardness, and romance. In that sense, the emphasis of *Homestuck* lies on the experience of the characters—the kids and trolls—and their relationships among each other, and to their siblings and parents. This focus is echoed in the discourse and practices of the *Homestuck* fandom on questions of identity, LGBTIQ-themes and characters, especially in relation to the aforementioned trolls.[7]

These and other aspects of fandom were important factors for making *Homestuck* not only popular, but relevant. While the webcomic itself alluded to various aspects of geek, nerd, media, and internet cultures at large, the fan following "took over" this interconnected network of references and enhanced it through the usage of memes, running gags, *Tumblr* pages, fan art, fan fiction, and cosplay—and thus transformed the webcomic into a multifaceted participatory space.[8] With this in mind, it is important to understand that the "phenomenon" of *Homestuck* and the webcomic itself cannot be separated, especially since many of Hussie's design and story choices were influenced by readers, fans, and players. Therefore, this chapter addresses only a relatively small slice of *Homestuck* and the community experience it enabled. I will focus on the first three acts of *Homestuck*, including the webcomic, as well as interviews and paratexts written by Hussie. I will emphasize the relations between media, technology, and (web)comics as they relate to the concept of technostalgia and to modes of engagement. In addition, I will analyze the influence of videogame logic and tropes on *Homestuck* as well as different instances of interactivity, participation, and playfulness.

Forensic fandom and technostalgia in *Homestuck*

Homestuck's network of media formats, references, and genre tropes can be interconnected through what Kevin Veale names "metamedia storytelling," which he describes as "a technique where the audience's pre-existing and intuitive familiarity with modes of engagement from the wider landscape of mediated storytelling is used as a tool to shape and manipulate their experience of the text" (2019, 1029). Considering *Homestuck*, these different modes of engagement include—but are not limited to—webcomic, written fiction (and metafiction), animation (Flash, video, and GIF), puzzle solving, interactive (mini-)games, and other forms of participation. According to Veale, this multitude of modes and media formats, references, and literacies can be linked to the concept of "forensic fandom" (Mittell 2007), where the audience—the "players"—needs a detective mentality to engage with the comic, texts, and other media formats. This notion is echoed in Hussie's own description: "The thing is, Homestuck is both a story and a puzzle, by design and by definition. [...] There is a range of ways to interface with it, from the casual to the maniacal. Failing to grasp everything shouldn't preclude basic enjoyment, nor is it a symptom of failure by either the reader or the story" (Hussie 2014, n.p.). Those various modes of reception, forms of remediation, and different media elements expand on what can be understood as the media specificity[9] of (web)comics. This can be retraced in the way *Homestuck* reflects on media history, since outdated and obsolete digital technology and web-based media play an important part in the narration.

The relationship between personal history, generations, nostalgia, and media has been discussed by Göran Bolin, who concludes that technology is important for discussing the feeling of lost childhood and the desire to mediate intergenerational experience. In this context, Bolin introduces the term "technostalgia" (2016, 256) to describe a specific longing for outdated technology that is bound to devices and practices like analogue media and outdated communication forms. This longing can include technology as artifacts as well as the investment of personal struggle, time, and labor. One example would be the yearning for a "pre-digital connectedness that precedes contemporary social networking media" (Bolin 2016, 256). *Homestuck*, which started 2009, emerged during the reign of platform-based social media monopolies.[10] But contrary to these monopolies, the diegesis of and the references in *Homestuck* rely on technostalgic media and outdated "web 1.0" technology.

Technonostalgia appears most notably in the integration of various instant messaging systems as the primary medium for communication. This focus combines the sincere retelling of making friends in networked communities with poking fun at the limitations and peculiarities of this mode of communication. The conversations of the kids almost exclusively take place via Pesterchum[11] (see Figure 7.1). Using their different online handles—called Chumhandles—the kids converse not via speech bubbles but through a Pesterlog, which is placed on the page under the comics panel. The use of a chatlog changes the way the comic is read by utilizing the various media formats, such as the difference between animated panels and written text. The communication tends to be more extensive since the length of the Pesterlogs is not limited by the size of the panels.

Regarding aesthetics and practice, the design of Pesterchum resembles more outdated instant messaging services, such as ICQ, MSN, or AOL Instant Messenger, which were all created between 1995 and 1997 and shaped early communication on the internet (see Figure 7.1). The technostalgia element is not linked to an analogue area of social interaction but to a less centralized mode of communication, not bound to platforms and algorithmic optimization of content and advertisement. At the same time, the characters can

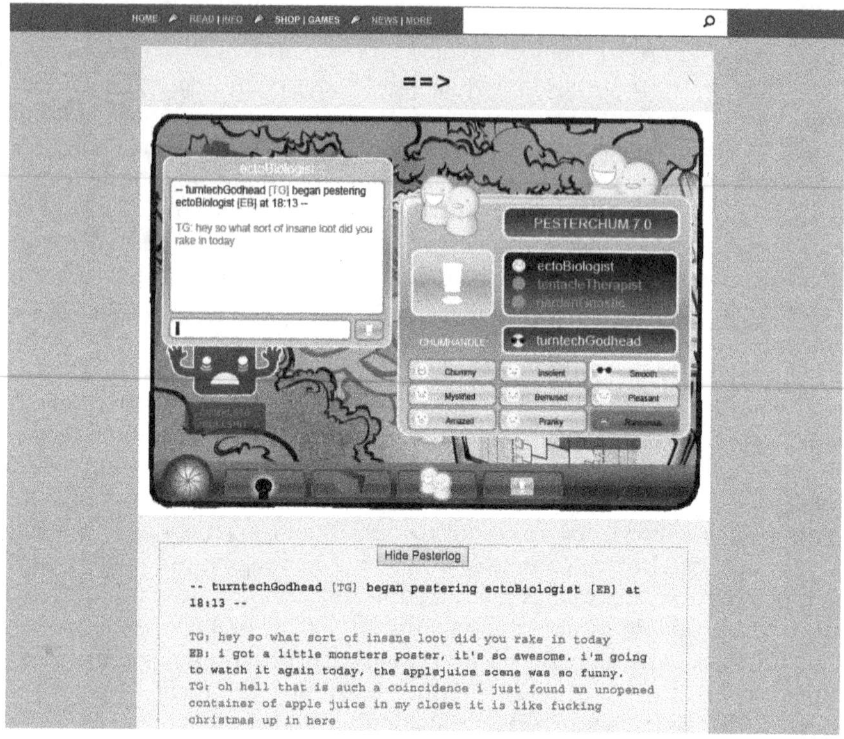

Figure 7.1 "-- turntechGodhead [TG] began pestering ectoBiologist [EB] at 18:13 --" (Hussie 2018, 324). © Homestuck and VIZ Media.

only express their individuality with their username, text color, and writing quirks.

This examination of early-twenty-first-century digital communication was also the starting point for several recent indie games,[12] which also remediated lost modes of communication and vacant online spaces.[13] One example is *Emily Is Away* (2015) developed by Kyle Seeley. The interactive visual novel tells the story of an unnamed protagonist and his relationship to Emily. Using a retro chat client interface, the game tells a (mostly linear) story, but the player is also able to change icons, profile information, and text color to fit the aesthetic style of the early-to-mid 2000s. As Julie Muncy described it in her review, *Emily Is Away* is "a game that conjures nostalgia for the pre-social media days of overwrought away messages and grating sound effects. It's a simulated conversation, a chat bot with the structure of an adventure game" (Muncy 2015, n.p.).

Nina Freeman's work is also linked to recreating lost media experiences, with a focus on personal history, fandom, and gaming. *Lost Memories Dot Net* (2017), for example, is a self-described "game about teen girls, blogs and love triangles in 2004" and was created for the Manchester International Festival in 2017.[14] Two years prior, she had released *Cibele* (2015), which fused personal experience, photography, a simulated desktop, and a remediated MMORPG. This can be understood as an interactive and mediate form of technostalgia, or, as Chartrand and Thériault describe it, as a blending of different virtual worlds: "[T]he game [*Cibele*] explores the creator's memories via a virtual world, which is a representation of the one in which she herself has lived these experiences" (2018, 7).[15]

These games shed some light on the relation between the internet as a timeless technology and certain practices of communication and representation that feel outmoded. Olia Lialina describes the lost amateur web of the 1990s as a vernacular web: "[I]t was bright, rich, personal, slow and under construction. It was a web of sudden connections and personal links. Pages were built on the edge of tomorrow, full of hope for a faster connection and a more powerful computer" (2015, n.p.).[16] *Homestuck*'s involvement in technostalgia also fuses the individual experiences of readers with different real and fictionalized media histories and modified versions of obsolete or outmoded technologies.

Pesterchum appears as a mimicry of early 2000s chat clients, but other references are more direct. Rose's first search for information on Sburb leads her to GameFAQs,[17] and later she writes her own walkthrough on the platform (Hussie 2018, 249).[18] While her walkthrough functions as a summary of the first act, it also appears on the extradiegetic page as "Sburb Beta Walkthrough," filed under the Simulation » Virtual » Virtual Life genre, connecting the fictionalized and the real digital spaces. Dave uses blogspot.com to host his "sweet bro's hella blog,"[19] where he reviews the latest issue of the gaming magazine *GameBro*,[20] among other things. Another reference is the intradiegetic webcomic "Sweet Bro and Hella Jeff," also created by Dave and read by the other three earthling protagonists.[21] Spanning 46 episodes, this webcomic features not only absurd storylines in the style of a nightmare-inducing GIF and glitch chaos, but it functions as a distorting mirror for various plot developments.

Finally, the webcomic *Homestuck* itself is facing forms of media loss and soon-to-be technostalgia. In 2017, the software company Adobe Inc. declared the end of life of Adobe Flash when they announced that they would "stop updating and distributing the Flash Player at the end of 2020" (Adobe Corporate Communications 2017, n.p.). Mozilla had already deactivated Flash plugin for the popular Firefox Browser. This affected various interactive elements in *Homestuck*. In the current version, most minigames have been replaced by images describing the experience—resembling a strategy guide.[22] This affects story-driven minigames, such as the point-and-click adventure in which John explores his house (Hussie 2018, 253) as well as smaller games, such as Jade playing her flute (Hussie 2018, 769). In addition, part of the *MS Paint Adventures* forums were lost, since during a server transfer data was corrupted.[23] While *Homestuck* lost an important element of interactivity and playfulness through this change in technology, there is still a lot of game left. Reading *Homestuck as a game* in the next segment does not imply that *Homestuck* is a game,[24] but that specific tropes, ideas, and modes of reception have game-like elements and, as such, reflect on our notion and understanding of game rules, genres, and tropes.

Homestuck as a game

> A young man stands in his bedroom. It just so happens that today, the 13th of April, 2009, is this young man's birthday. Though it was thirteen years ago he was given life, it is only today he will be given a name!
>
> (Hussie 2018, 1)

The first page of *Homestuck* starts with an opening that resembles the first interaction in many role-playing adventures: the naming of the protagonist (see Figure 7.2). This particular element of videogame logic is not only employed to draw the audience in but is ironically called upon in the accompanying text. With his thick glasses—and without hands—the unnamed young man is standing in front of a door, next to a cake. He is apparently waiting for a player input.

Observing the first page one notices that the first panel of *Homestuck* is not a still image, but an animation, a looping GIF animation to be exact.[25] The minor and repetitive movements of the yet unnamed young man might remind the audience of another videogame trope, the idling animation. Those mostly small, sometimes funny movements that happen "when a player leaves a game alone for a bit, are easy to overlook but key to conveying subtle (or not-so-subtle) aspects" (Couture 2018, n.p.) of videogames, their world, and their atmosphere. Galloway differentiates between different modes in videogames: "[M]achine actions are acts performed by the software and hardware of the game computer, while operator actions are acts performed by players" (Galloway 2006, 5). Even though this separation is "completely artificial—both the machine and the operator work together in a cybernetic relationship" (Galloway 2006, 5), the resemblance of "machine actions" reminds us of the world as a purposefully designed environment, waiting for our operator actions.

On the first page of *Homestuck*, the question, "What will the name of this young man be?" is central. *Homestuck* gives the player/reader only one option for an operator action: "> Enter name." The greater-than sign > refers to the aforementioned parser-based text games with the > signaling user input in the style of imperative commands.[26] Clicking on the "> Enter name." prompt brings players to the second page of *Homestuck*. Here, another GIF animation is looping, displaying the typing of "Zoosmell Pooplord," which prompts a negative reaction from the yet to be named character and a "try again, smartass" tool tip (Hussie 2018, 2). Something prevents this juvenile joke, or maybe the character demonstrates his own agency. Fortunately,

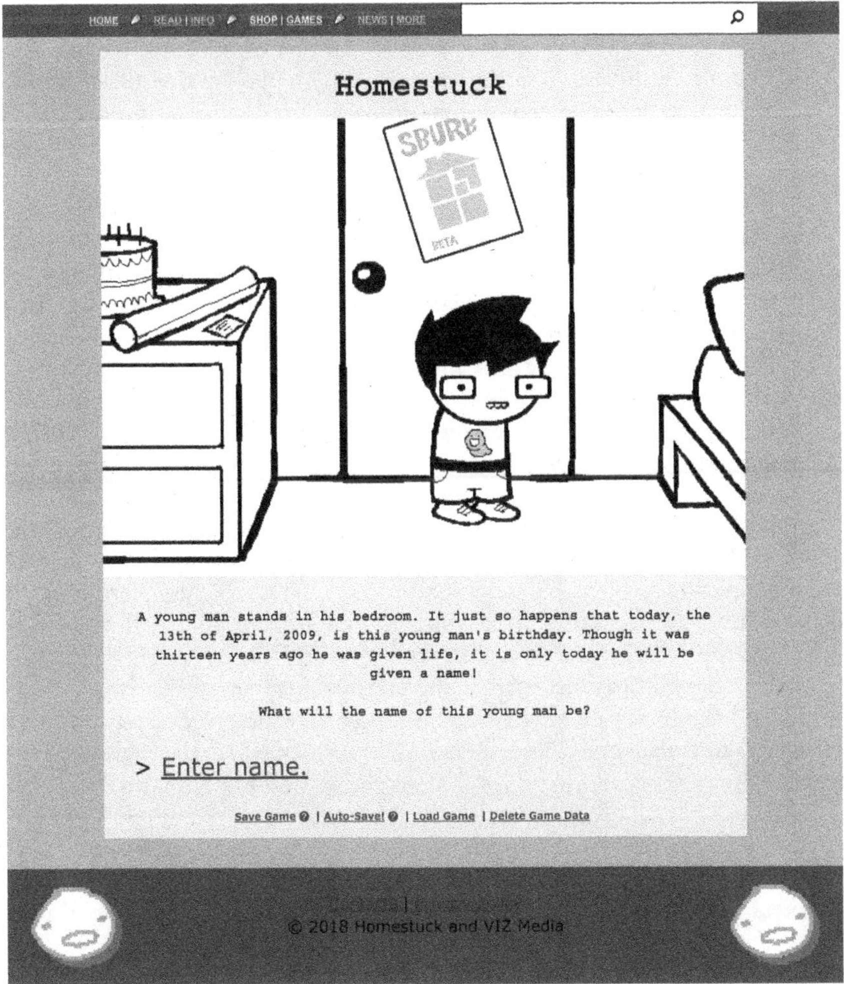

Figure 7.2 "*Homestuck* > Enter name." (Hussie 2018, 1). © Homestuck and VIZ Media.

the prompt on the second page enables the possibility for a revision: "> Try again." This leads to the third page, and the second suggestion "John Egbert" results in a smile by John and gets a green check (Hussie 2018, 3). The community successful named the first protagonist of *Homestuck*.[27] This all happened 2009, and we can only retrace those actions:

> Readers on the internet would suggest an action they wanted a character to take, and I would choose one from the pile and illustrate the results. All of book one [containing act 1 of the webcomic] was created

> this way, as will a number of books following it. You'll find this method generates quite the garden path through a story, leading to a good deal of meandering, silly diversions, gags, trial and error from the "player," and impromptu story crafting decisions. I am playing the role of a dungeon master, a game engine responding to input, and an improv comic all in one.
>
> (Hussie 2011, n.p.)

Homestuck, as noted, was Hussie's fourth webcomic in the *MS Paint Adventures* series, based on quick production and the possibility to participate. The first three acts of *Homestuck* were mostly written by using this suggestion-based system. In 2010 Hussie locked the suggestion boxes while he crafted longer story arcs, and the influence became more indirect—present through polls, forum entries, fan art, or other fan creations. One example is the naming of characters, for which Hussie used the *MS Paint Adventures* forums to gather recommendations. Another tool was online polls, for example, to conclude the outcome to the "WARDROBIFIER'S randomization mode" (Hussie 2018, 800), which automatically changes the symbol on Jade's shirt.[28] *Homestuck* evolved from a system that resembled a community-based let's play comic, in which the characters were under a chaotic hivemind control of the audience, to a more mediated approach, in which the creator and fans construct a world together and see which narrative possibilities emerge from the different elements.

Beyond the initial naming of the protagonist, *Homestuck* features more references to videogame culture. The whole world in which the four teenagers live functions according to rules that resemble well-known conventions of game genres, especially role-playing and adventure games: a leveling system, currencies, fighting system, and inventory management, to mention a few. Especially in the first chapters, those systems are paramount since these chapters act as the introduction, both for the readers/players and children. "This is common logic in game tutorials, where characters straddle postmodern awareness of the game mechanics on which they directly or indirectly seek to educate you, as well as themselves, strangely" (Hussie 2011, 6).

As with other elements of the webcomic, these gaming mechanics are mainly used to poke fun at existing tropes. For example, the leveling system is constructed around silly names and abstract numerical values. John starts with Greentike and levels up to Anklebiter, Pesky Urchin, and so forth.[29] The "Level up!" also provides Boondollars and upgrades such as "Gel Viscosity" or "Man Grit," thus overloading the readers with—seldom useful, mostly absurd—detailed information. Furthermore, inanimate objects, such as refrigerators or bathtubs (Hussie 2018, 557), can level up.

Sylladices are another nuisance for the four protagonists. Every kid has their own inventory system, with a spin on the classic management system popularized by point-and-click adventures. Referring to both syllabus and index, each Sylladex has a specific fetch mode that determines how artifacts—represented as captchalogued cards—are stored and retrieved. The different available modes refer to common data structures, board games, or other sorting systems. John starts with a Sylladex representing a stack, with only the option to interact with the card on top of his stack. Later he acquires the queue and array modes, which he combines to a queuestack array, enabling him to carry 24 cards at the same time and switching between accessing the top or bottom card of his six arrays.[30] His friends also use difficult-to-interact systems. Rose employs a tree fetch mode, which uses a binary system to store new cards on branches.[31] Board games, such as Memory, Jenga, or Pictionary, are the base for Jade's twelve fetch modes, and the hash map fetch mode that Dave uses can contain ten cards, with values ranging from 0 to 9 (Hussie 2018, 319). For Dave, every artifact that is captchalogued gets its hash value calculated, based on "valuing each consonant at 2, and each vowel at 1" (Hussie 2018, 319). Beyond that, each item can only be retrieved by an action with the same index value—which leads to accidents. At one time, Dave ejects his sword by yelling "stop" at a bird, killing the bird in the process.[32] As Hussie notes, those complicated Sylladices are part of a playful approach to videogames and interactivity: "Carefully educating you on needlessly complicated inventory systems that eventually get retired from a game you never get to play that doesn't actually exist. HOMESTUCK" (Hussie 2011, 10).

Superimposed over their world, the videogame Sburb becomes the point of departure for the main story arc. Playing Sburb starts the apocalypse and subsequent destruction of the earth, but it also provides the possibility to create a new reality. Sburb itself is best described as a multiplayer sandbox-style game with elements taken from building and simulation games. After a client player and server player connect, the server player can manipulate, create, and destroy objects in real time.[33] Using different obscure crafting material, such as numerous versions of Grist, artifacts can be constructed with which the client player can interact. This creates a multilayered world where different ludic systems interact and contradict each other. *The Sims* (2000) was an important inspiration for the mechanics and aesthetic of Sburb, as Hussie (2011, 105) himself notes. This can be seen in the isometric perspective, which itself mediates a specific set of genre expectations. Additionally, Hussie built a mock-up interactive menu for Sburb (Hussie 2018, 138) for the readers to play around with in order to convey the possibility of Sburb being a real game.[34] Those different levels of reference helped to manage different aspects of expectations and game-specific modes of reception. Furthermore, videogames—including tropes, participation, and genres—shaped the metamedia storytelling and development of *Homestuck*.

Conclusion

> There are a few moments in the earlier acts which seem to trick you into thinking Homestuck is all about getting cool gear, gaining levels,

> and kicking ass like you except to do in such games. This is kind of misleading though. In totality, HS isn't really about ass-kicking at all. It's about presenting awesome fantasy environments and situations in which ass-kicking could THEORETICALLY take place, but very rarely does except in dramatic hot points like this. Instead, those environments serve as backdrops for a huge amount of dicking around on the internet, babbling to friends about feelings, and being a bunch of stupid useless kids struggling to grow up. If you are ever under the impression HS is about anything else, you are invariably in for a world of hurt.
>
> (Hussie 2013, 257)

This statement underscores Hussie's playful approach to the limitations and capabilities of webcomics and videogames. Instead of creating a hybrid or hypermedium, Hussie relied on addressing themes such as obsolete technology and coming of age by utilizing media literacy, genre expectations, and audience participation. The "metamedia storytelling" of *Homestuck*—between technostalgia and community experience—uses videogames as material, discourse, and eventually to expand the understanding of what webcomics are and how they might evolve in the future. *Homestuck* demonstrates the illusion of a fully interactive experience, of a grand underlying logical system—as Chute and Jagoda summarize, *Homestuck* "repeatedly frustrates the user's desire for explicit interactivity, inviting and then curbing the type of agency promised by many new media projects" (2014, 10).

This frustration and the overall nonpersistence of mechanics, rules, and narrative elements contrasts with a long history of defining videogames as predictable rule-based systems that can be dismantled and theory-crafted. For instance, in *Homestuck,* countless rules are explained in detail, then soon forgotten or brought back in altered form—may it be the leveling system of inanimate objects or various currencies and building materials. In his book *The Toxic Meritocracy of Video Games* (2018), Christopher A. Paul describes the influence of merit on videogame narratives: "The story many games tell players is that if you work hard enough, if you are good enough, you can follow a straightforward path to power, wealth, and resources" (2018, 6). *Homestuck* is not only far away from a tale based on merit, but the webcomic also provides an example of gaming and gaming culture that is more than various forms of operator and machine action, input and output, winning and losing. *Homestuck* emphasizes the absurd and funny side of gaming tropes, such as the act of naming a character when he is already thirteen years old or almost-impossible-to-navigate inventory systems. In remediating the perspectives, aesthetics, and rules taken from different genres—from simulation, role-playing, and parser-based adventure games—it creates a world that is inventive and open-ended. The challenge of questioning videogame conventions, in particular meritocratic ideas, has been echoed in recent years by various indie games. We can therefore conclude that the similarities between *Homestuck* and games such as *Cibele* and *Emily is Away* go beyond remediating interfaces and seemingly lost digital communities as they altogether reflect on and criticize cultural assumptions on web-based communication and (sub)cultures. In *Homestuck*, communication and relationships between the main characters are based around real and fictionalized technostalgia media, creating a community in the diegesis and outside of it and demonstrating that playing together creates social spaces—both in world-destroying multiplayer sandbox-games and in forensic fandoms for webcomics. In relying on the community, using participation and influence, *Homestuck* established a relationship between author and players to build a shared world that spans across the webcomic itself, official and unofficial forums, wikis, and *Tumblr* pages. In this sense, *Homestuck* is not only a comic, but an alternative nexus of communication hubs.

With the end of the webcomic series in 2016 and the closure of the official forum, an important part of this mutual world is now stuck in time. In transforming a lived experience into a stable media format (digital or printed), *Homestuck* itself became part of technostalgic memory. Therefore, the notion that *Homestuck* is "*made of pure internet*" (O'Malley 2012, n.p., original emphasis) does not only convey the communities it helped to build during its active run and the various digital media aspects it utilized, but also the different modes of engagement, media literacies, and expectations it relied on and satirized to tell a truthful yet funny story about coming of age in an ever more interconnected world.

Notes

1 For an introduction to comics studies and webcomics in particular, see Hammel 2016; Wilde 2015.

2 The scope of this assistance led to a six-minute-plus-long official credit video (Homestuck Official 2016). Among others, Toby Fox, who lived in Hussie's basement, made music for *Homestuck*. In 2015, Toby Fox released *Undertale* (2015), which became popular and has some similarities to *Homestuck* in style and atmosphere. Both *Undertale* and *Homestuck* are heavily inspired by the Japanese role paying game *EarthBound* (1994), as Hussie himself states in the printed version (Hussie 2011, 21).

3 For the credits, see Homestuck Official 2016. Originally, *Homestuck* was hosted as part of the *MS Paint Adventures* homepage www.mspaintadventures.com (accessed 31 January 2020). In 2018, when Viz Media acquired the rights for publishing *Homestuck* and www.homestuck.com (accessed 31 January 2020), also owned by Viz, it became the new official homepage for the webcomic. Before that, the first three chapters were published by the Canadian online retailer Topato Corporation (Hussie 2011; 2012a; 2013).

4 After the webcomic had ended, two game spin-offs were developed by What Pumpkin Games, initially founded in 2010 by Hussie as a record label. The first act of *Hiveswap*, an old-school point-and-click adventure game, was released in

2017. The game had been a success on the crowdfunding platform Kickstarter. As Whitson and Salter note: "[*Homestuck*] has [...] a very strong fan following [...] and a Kickstarter campaign was funded to produce a video game around the comic's narrative. Such successes demonstrate that the addition of the web modality to the comic form can transform the core interaction of the experience" (2015, §8). Even though the videogame is set in the same universe, it features different characters, mainly a human girl named Joey, who switches places with a Dammek, a troll from another planet. *Hiveswap Friendsim*, a series of visual novel friendship dating sims, was released in 2018 for PCs and smartphones and consisted of 18 episodes and an epilogue.

5 The reference to MS Paint was kept even though he switched to Adobe Photoshop soon after drawing the first strips in the classic graphic editor.

6 The statistics show that the busiest day consisted of 66 pages and 111 panels. But Hussie also took long hiatuses, the longest lasting for over a year (Bailey 2018).

7 For a more in-depth analysis of gender and sex in *Homestuck*, see Wagner 2013. Also noteworthy is McInroy and Craig's (2018) exploration of the relation between fandom participation and LGBTIQ identities.

8 Fenty, Houp, and Taylor (2005) have analyzed the relationship between Underground Comix and webcomics. They conclude that both comics formats parody popular culture, but that Underground Comix rely more on "gender relations [and] drugs" while webcomics focus on "video games, and table-top role-playing games" (Fenty et al. 2005, n.p.). In this sense, *Homestuck* connects those two focal points as it combines nerdy, geeky topics and discussions on gender. See also Litwhiler 2013, 20–21.

9 As Noël Carroll wrote and critiqued in "The Specificity of Media in the Arts" (1985), the notion of media specificity or media essentialism is bound to the idea that different media forms can be distinguished from each other. In this unilateral perspective, media are seen as mere technology, with certain physical properties. Carroll shifts this focus to the usage and practices of media, since media should be understood in the context of the culture surrounding them, for example, limitations, definitions, styles, and genres that shape the exception and practices of media production and reception.

10 "The platform has emerged as a new business model, capable of extracting and controlling immense amounts of data, and with this shift we have seen the rise of large monopolistic firms" (Srnicek 2017, 6). Social media platforms include *Facebook*, *Twitter*, and *Instagram*. Concerning the relation between platform capitalism, comics production, and reception, see Glaser 2018.

11 Other characters also use different chat clients. For example, the trolls use Trollian to troll each other. The name is probably a reference to Trillian, a software that was created in 2000 and is able to connect different instant messaging protocols in one interface. Other chat clients in *Homestuck* include Delirious Biznasty, Rebelgram, and BettyBotherSee. Trollian also connects different timelines of the story (Hussie 2018, 4104).

12 On the history, (problematic) definition, and culture of indie games and independent games, see Parker 2014; Sharp 2016.

13 Understood as the "representation of one medium in another" (Bolter and Grusin 1999, 45), the term remediation here draws especially on the experience of different modes of media engagement.

14 See http://ninasays.so/lostmemoriesdotnet/ (accessed 31 January 2020).

15 Furthermore, simulated operating systems and nostalgic media usage play an important role in several other videogames. *Digital: A Love Story* (2010), for instance, alludes to the aesthetic and functionality of the AmigaOS Workbench and communication in Bulletin Board Systems. The interface of *A Normal Lost Phone* (2017) simulates that of a smartphone.
16 See also the project and blog *One Terabyte of Kilobyte Age* by Olia Lialina and Dragan Espenschied: https://blog.geocities.institute (accessed 31 January 2020).
17 GameFAQs is a dedicated community for people to share cheats, walkthroughs, tips, and of course FAQs for videogames. It was created in 1995 by Jeff Veasey.
18 Other examples include a later entry with screenshots (Hussie 2018, 510), an introduction to captcha codes and card alchemy (Hussie 2018, 845), and Rose's final entry: "In case it wasn't clear, magic is real" (Hussie 2018, 1942).
19 The latest post on the blog is a review on the March issue of *GameBro* (Hussie 2018, 325).
20 *GameBro* might be a reference to *GamePro*, a videogame magazine that was published by IDG between 1989 and 2011. *GamePro* is also the name of a German videogame magazine founded in 2002.
21 Examples of the webcomic can be found in *Homestuck* (Hussie 2018, 326, 459) and were simultaneously collected on a separate page: www.mspaintadventures.com/sweetbroandhellajeff (accessed 31 January 2020).
22 The same translation from interactive media to static images occurred in the printed version of *Homestuck*. Hussie describes this remediation as the difference between a game and a strategy guide: "This now somewhat resembles an old Nintendo Power strategy guide, with screenshots of the game and illustrations of the consequences of player actions" (Hussie 2012a, 11). The interactive version of those pages can still be accessed on browsers that support Flash—even though the future of those versions is unclear. See for example the Flash mini-games www.homestuck.com/story/253?fl=1 (accessed 31 January 2020) and www.homestuck.com/story/769?fl=1 (accessed 31 January 2020).
23 For the information on the "death" of the *MS Paint Adventures* forums, see www.reddit.com/r/homestuck/comments/do4cjj/rip_mspa_forums_20082016/ (accessed 31 January 2020).
24 One might even argue that those mini-games are not "real games" since they lack the possibility to fail. Therefore, they do not the fit the terms game comics or hypercomics as defined by Goodbrey 2015.
25 The history of GIF animations is tied to the notion of the internet as a realm of new aesthetics, beyond only technological innovations. As Jason Eppinks states: "It [the GIF] has an ethos, a utility, an evolving context, a set of aesthetics" (2014, 298). Using GIF animations therefore calls upon the idea of *Homestuck* being made out of and for the internet.
26 Hussie alludes to this connection in his introduction to the webcomic written for the crowdfunding campaign: "[*Homestuck*] heavily involves satire of internet culture, various game genres and systems, and most fundamentally, adventure games. The entire format is based on a parody of text-based and point-and-click adventure games" (Hussie 2012b, n.p.).
27 Below the command prompt, we find the last reference to videogame logic, the options to save and load the game, to toggle autosave or delete game data—javascript functions enabling the page to display us the last visited page.

28 Rose's wardrobifier settings were determined by a poll: "The decision was tough, but you think you came to the best possible conclusion" (Hussie 2018, 800). The following link leads to an image showing the result of the poll: www.homestuck.com/images/storyfiles/hs2/scraps/poll_jadeshirt.gif (accessed 31 January 2020).
29 The leveling up system is shown as a change in numbers, title, and amount of Boondollars (Hussie 2018, 405, 555, 1891).
30 It is a long journey for John from first captchaloguing fake arms (Hussie 2018, 7) to obtaining a control deck for easier access (Hussie 2018, 964).
31 Rose retrieves her laptop, which leads to her whole item tree collapsing and spilling the other items on the ground (Hussie 2018, 236).
32 Yelling "Stop!" (2+2+1+2) accidentally releases a ninja sword (Hussie 2018, 354).
33 After connecting to Sburb (Hussie 2018, 114), server players can create new objects—this possibility sometimes results in Escher-like buildings (Hussie 2018, 1081).
34 Hussie also refers to this in the paratext: "I believe the false menus like this actually felt quite convincing, and sort of activated the game-playing center of the reader's brain, making them want to use these tools, and on some level, causing them to actually believe they can" (Hussie 2011, 80).

Works cited

Adobe Corporate Communications. 2017. "Flash and the Future of Interactive Content." *Adobe Blog*, 25 July. http://theblog.adobe.com/adobe-flash-update (accessed 31 January 2020).

Bailey, Anthony. 2018. *MS Paint Adventures: Statistics*. http://readmspa.org/stats (accessed 31 January 2020).

Bolin, Göran. 2016. "Passion and Nostalgia in Generational Media Experiences." *European Journal of Cultural Studies* 19 (3): 250–264.

Bolter, J. David, and Richard Grusin. 1999. *Remediation: Understanding New Media*. Cambridge, MA: MIT Press.

Carroll, Noël. 1985. "The Specificity of Media in the Arts." *Journal of Aesthetic Education* 19 (4): 5–20.

Chartrand, Roxanne, and Pascale Thériault. 2018. "The Videoludic Cyborg: Queer/Feminist Reappropriations and Hybridity." *Proceedings of The Philosophy of Computer Games Conference 2018*: n.p. https://gameconference.itu.dk/papers/15%20-%20chartrand%20-%20the%20videoludic%20cyborg.pdf (accessed 31 January 2020).

Chute, Hillary, and Patrick Jagoda. 2014. "Introduction: Special Issue: Comics and Media." *Critical Inquiry* 40 (3): 1–10.

Cibele. 2015. Developed and published by Star Maid Games and Nina Freeman. Windows.

Couture, Joel. 2018. "What Makes a Great Idle Animation? Devs Share Their Favorites." *Gamasutra*, 21 May. www.gamasutra.com/view/news/318163/what_makes_a_great_idle_animation_devs_share_their_favorites.php (accessed 31 January 2020).

Digital: A Love Story. 2010. Developed and published by Love Conquers All Games. Windows.

EarthBound. 1994. Developed by Ape and HAL Laboratory. Published by Nintendo. SNES.

Emily Is Away. 2015. Developed and published by Kyle Seeley. Windows.

Eppink, Jason. 2014. "A Brief History of the GIF (So Far)." *Journal of Visual Culture* 13 (3): 298–306.

Fenty, Sean, Trena Houp, and Laurie N. Taylor. 2005. "Webcomics: The Influence and Continuation of the Comix Revolution" *ImageTexT: Interdisciplinary Comics Studies* 1 (2): n.p. http://imagetext.english.ufl.edu/archives/v1_2/group/ (accessed 31 January 2020).

Galloway, Alexander R. 2006. *Gaming: Essays on Algorithmic Culture*. Minneapolis: University of Minnesota Press.

Glaser, Tim. 2018. "oh no—this comic is literally me: Webcomics im Zeitalter ihrer memetischen Rezeption." *CLOSURE: Kieler e-Journal für Comicforschung* 4.5: n.p. www.closure.uni-kiel.de/closure4.5/glaser (accessed 31 January 2020).

Goodbrey, Daniel Merlin. 2015. "Game Comics: An Analysis of an Emergent Hybrid Form." *Journal of Graphic Novels and Comics* 6 (1): 3–14.

Hammel, Björn. 2016. "Webcomics." In *Comics und Graphic Novels: Eine Einführung*, edited by Julia Abel and Christian Klein, 169–180. Stuttgart: Metzler.

Hiveswap: Act 1. 2017. Developed by What Pumpkin Games. Published by Fellow Traveller. Windows.

Hiveswap Friendsim: Volume 1 to 18. 2018. Developed by What Pumpkin Games. Published by Fellow Traveller. Windows.

Homestuck Official. 2016. "Credits." *YouTube*, 24 October. www.youtube.com/watch?v=rMZU89jY2j8 (accessed 31 January 2020).

Hussie, Andrew. 2011. *Homestuck Book One*. Easthampton: Topatoco.

Hussie, Andrew. 2012a. *Homestuck Book Two*. Easthampton: Topatoco.

Hussie, Andrew. 2012b. "What Is Homestuck?" *MS Paint Adventures*, n.d. http://mspaintadventures.com/scraps2/homestuckKS.html (accessed 31 January 2020).

Hussie, Andrew. 2013. *Homestuck Book Three*. Easthampton: Topatoco.

Hussie, Andrew. 2014. "Answers (Archive)." *MS Paint Adventures Wiki Blog*, n.d. http://mspaintadventureswiki.tumblr.com/post/63803326538/answers-archive (accessed 31 January 2020).

Hussie, Andrew. 2018. *Homestuck*. www.homestuck.com (accessed 31 January 2020).

Lialina, Olia. 2015. *A Vernacular Web*. http://art.teleportacia.org/observation/vernacular/ (accessed 31 January 2020).

Litwhiler, Austin Gunner. 2013. "From Pulp to Webpage: *Homestuck* and Post-modern Digital Narrative." Honors thesis, State University of New York at Albany, US. https://scholarsarchive.library.albany.edu/honorscollege_eng/13/ (accessed 31 January 2020).

Lost Memories Dot Net. 2017. Developed and published by Nina Freeman and Aaron Freedman. Windows.

McInroy, Lauren B., and Shelly L. Craig. 2018. "Online Fandom: Identity Milestones, and Self-Identification of Sexual/Gender Minority Youth." *Journal of LGBT Youth* 15 (3): 1–18.

Mittell, Jason. 2007. "Lost in a Great Story." *Just TV* (blog), 23 October. http://justtv.wordpress.com/2007/10/23/lost-in-a-great-story (accessed 31 January 2020).

Muncy, Julie. 2015. "Return to the 2000s with This AIM-Inspired Chat Game." *Wired*, 30 October. www.wired.com/2015/10/emily-is-away (accessed 31 January 2020).

A Normal Lost Phone. 2017. Developed by Accidental Queens. Published by Plug in Digital. Windows.

O'Malley, Bryan Lee. 2012. "'Scott Pilgrim' Guy Interviews 'Homestuck' Guy: Bryan Lee O'Malley on Andrew Hussie." *ComicsAlliance*, 2 October. http://comicsalliance.com/homestuck-interview-andrew-hussie-bryan-lee-omalley-ms-paint-adventures (accessed 31 January 2020).

Parker, Felan. 2014. "Indie Game Studies Year Eleven." *Proceedings of DiGRA 2013: DeFragging Game Studies*: n.p. www.digra.org/digital-library/publications/indie-game-studies-year-eleven/ (accessed 31 January 2020).

Paul, Christopher A. 2018. *The Toxic Meritocracy of Video Games*. Minneapolis: University of Minnesota Press.

PBS Idea Channel. 2012. "Is Homestuck the Ulysses of the Internet? | Idea Channel | PBS Digital Studios." *YouTube*, 5 September. www.youtube.com/watch?v=MLK7RI_HW-E (accessed 31 January 2020).

Sharp, John. 2016. "Independent Games." In *Debugging Game History: A Critical Lexicon*, edited by Henry Lowood and Raiford Guins, 259–267. Cambridge, MA: MIT Press.

Short, Jennifer. 2014. "Let Me Tell You about *Homestuck*: The Online Production of Place." Master thesis, University of Central Florida, US. https://stars.library.ucf.edu/etd/4806/ (accessed 31 January 2020).

The Sims. 2000. Developed by Maxis. Published by Electronic Arts. Windows.

Srnicek, Nick. 2017. *Platform Capitalism*. Cambridge: Polity Press.

Undertale. 2015. Developed and published by Toby Fox. Windows.

Veale, Kevin. 2019. "'Friendship Isn't an Emotion Fucknuts': Manipulating Affective Materiality to Shape the Experience of *Homestuck*'s Story." *Convergence: The International Journal of Research into New Media Technologies* 25 (5–6): 1027–1043.

Wagner, Jamie. 2013. "The Webcomic *Homestuck* as Gender Fiction and Its Discourse on Gender Issues in the Narrative." Term paper, University of Konstanz, Germany.

Whitson, Roger Todd, and Anastasia Salter. 2015. "Introduction: Comics and the Digital Humanities." *Digital Humanities Quarterly* 9 (4): n.p. http://digitalhumanities.org/dhq/vol/9/4/000210/000210.html (accessed 31 January 2020).

Wilde, Lukas R. A. 2015. "Gibt es eine Ästhetik des Webcomic?" In *Webcomic im Fokus: Internationaler Comic-Salon Erlangen 2014*, edited by Lukas R. A. Wilde and Comic Solidarity, 4–15. Self-published.

8 *Metal Gear Solid* and its comics adaptations

Claudius Stemmler

Both popular discourse and academic scholarship have a tendency to consider the relationship between comics and videogames primarily from the angle of comics as the source for various elements in videogames. This is not surprising because, as a multimodal medium (Ryan and Thon 2014, 11), videogames are well suited to encompass elements from other media formats. Moving into the opposite direction, comics adaptations have to transpose complex multimodal systems into a combination of images and words. Perhaps this complexity has lessened their appeal since comics adaptations have, similar to film novelizations, rarely received scholarly attention and appear to be mostly treated as a mere side effect of today's integrated media industries. This, however, ignores the fact that such adaptations, independent of their artistic value, possess great potential to explore the relationship between comics and videogames as well as each medium's individual properties.

In 1998, the Japanese company Konami released *Metal Gear Solid* for the Sony PlayStation "to critical acclaim and commercial success" (Parkin 2012, n.p.). The game represented not only "an enormous leap forward in terms of what a story-driven action game could be" (Parish 2018, n.p.), but it also "formalize[d] and popularize[d] 'Stealth' as a kind of genre" (Parkin 2017, 147). Three years later, a sequel named *Metal Gear Solid 2: The Sons of Liberty* (2001) was released for the Sony PlayStation 2. Despite the fact that the game's narrative lead to a backlash (Holmes 2012, 135) and its "divisive nature clearly drove away a portion of the audience" (Holmes 2012, 144), it was a commercial success, with its ludic elements very much fulfilling expectations toward an improved sequel (Holmes 2012, 134). In 2004, the US-based company IDW Publishing began releasing a *Metal Gear Solid* comics series. Running for 24 issues, the series adapted both *Metal Gear Solid* (Oprisko and Wood 2014) and its sequel (Fraction and Wood 2014; Garner and Wood 2014). In a highly unusual move, Konami itself then began releasing further adaptations of these comics. Calling them digital graphic novels[1] and releasing them for the Sony PlayStation Portable (in 2006) and as feature films on DVD (in 2008), these adaptations reproduced the comics' narrative while taking advantage of their digital platforms' audiovisual capabilities. Taken together, this group of releases constitutes a unique object to study the relationship between videogames and comics.

In this chapter, I will analyze *Metal Gear Solid*, its sequel, and the aforementioned adaptations. These adaptations into linear narrative media are particularly intriguing because the reception of both games highlighted their ludic as well as their narrative elements. Alongside the question of how their multimodal aesthetics have been adapted, this invites asking if and how their distinctive ludic nature has been transposed. The first section of this chapter therefore analyzes the narration of these various incarnations while the second section examines their presentation. In both cases, this will reveal how their respective media format's properties shaped these elements. The conclusion presents an outlook on noticeable developments following this particular sequence of adaptations.

Narration and narrative

A general trait of adaptations is that they have "an overt and defining relationship to [a] prior tex[t]" (Hutcheon 2006, 3–4). At the same time, the broad range of existing adaptations makes it difficult to present a more specific definition of this relationship without losing its general applicability. Typically, theories of adaptation have assumed this relationship to center around the shared core of a work's narrative (Hutcheon 2006, 10). This assumption might, however, be more indebted to the fact such adaptations are, perhaps inadvertently, prioritized by scholars because they fit more easily into existing humanities frameworks. It is at this point that videogames as a source for adaptations are intriguing thanks to their contested narrativity. While the so-called ludology-narratology debate ended with blanket statements regarding videogames' narrativity being replaced by more moderate approaches acknowledging their potential narrativity (Mukherjee 2015, 7), its existence also highlighted the complexity of the issue. Analyzing adaptations of videogames into linear narrative media therefore begs the question of how their elements outside of narrative frameworks have been transposed. Does the process of adaptation resemble the extraction of a linear narrative from preexisting elements, or is it rather an addition of elements in order to create a coherent narration?

The games

In his essay "In Defense of Cutscenes," Rune Klevjer uses *Metal Gear Solid* as an example of a game that radical ludologists would consider "an artistic failure" (2002, 194). This is because a distinctive trait shared by the game and its sequel is the strong presence of embedded[2] narrative content. In both games, the process of playing is shaped by a structural interplay between three modes, *gameplay*, *cutscenes*, and *codec communication* (Holmes 2012, 86),[3] of which only one allows players to engage with the game's rule-based systems. The other two solely consist of embedded narrative elements whose presentation resembles earlier media formats.[4] *Cutscenes* are modeled in the audiovisual language of film, while *codec communication* with its sparse visual presentation accompanying voiced dialogue resembles radio drama (Holmes 2012, 86). Typically, the game switches between *gameplay* and these modes at predetermined points. Additionally, the player can actively switch from *gameplay* to *codec communication* to initiate a conversation with selected characters. While the avatar's specific situation influences which conversation occurs, the conversations themselves are linear. In this way, the player is granted access to a large number of optional embedded narrative segments. In the same vein, the game also features a small number of optional *cutscenes* triggered by circumstances not necessarily fulfilled during a playthrough. However, aside from these instances, both modes present a fixed sequence of diegetic events in which the player's position as recipient is akin to linear narratives.

In contrast, during *gameplay* the player engages with the games' rule-based systems through the avatar. The game's core mechanics (Salen and Zimmerman 2008, 317) constitute the avatar's abilities; they are applied to avoid detection while traversing the diegetic world. Furthermore, when detected and at predetermined points, the avatar has to fight his enemies. Besides these recurring elements, *gameplay* also encompasses singular events such as the avatar in *Metal Gear Solid* being subjected to torture. Typically, *gameplay* situations are emergent (Juul 2005, 73) and can be completed in various ways. However, aside from the torture sequence, the specific solution does not influence later embedded diegetic events. Together with the limited diversity of the emergent narrative events presented through *gameplay*, this might incline us to attribute to this mode a superficial role in terms of narration. This inclination, however, would ignore the narrative elements present in *gameplay*, which, similar to a film's mise-en-scène, often fail to be encompassed by models of linear narration. First, *gameplay* turns the diegetic world in a spatially realized fictional space full of narrative descriptors (Salen and Zimmerman 2008, 404) the player can explore through the avatar. Second, the game's rule-based systems constitute a procedural rhetoric (Bogost 2007, 3) in support of their thematic treatments. *Gameplay* also helps create an oscillating relationship between the avatar and the players as they switch between watching and performing as their digital embodiment (Backe 2008, 344). In both games, this relationship is effectively employed as part of the narration. Together, the three modes constitute a cycle in which embedded narrative events presented through *cutscenes* and *codec communication* introduce diegetic goals that the player's avatar then pursues in *gameplay*.

For the most part, the games' sequences of embedded narrative events are fixed and remain identical between playthroughs. There are, however, three noticeable exceptions. First, the aforementioned torture sequence in *Metal Gear Solid*, where the outcome decides which ally will later accompany the avatar. Not merely changing their sequential presentation, players here directly influence which of two embedded narrative endings will take place. Another exception is the optional briefing section in *Metal Gear Solid*. Here, the player can navigate a branching structure where some segments present the avatar being briefed through voiced dialogue and sparse animation while others consist solely of written text. While the player has control over the flow of narrative information, this does not influence the diegetic world's sequence of events. The same is true for the division of *Metal Gear Solid 2: Sons of Liberty* into two separately selectable chapters. In contrast to the optional briefing section, this presents a highly distinctive feature of modifying the diegetic events' sequential presentation. This is particularly noticeable in the game's original release, where only players acknowledging to be familiar with *Metal Gear Solid* played both chapters. What is remarkable about all these exceptions is that they strongly modify the player's reception through technologically simple means.

In summary, due to the strong presence of fixed sequences of embedded narration, both games generally fit well into classic models of narration. At the same time, they also feature various elements through which their narrative presentation exceeds the potential of established linear narrative media. An apt description of the process of playing would include the oscillation between classical textual and distinctively ludic elements, which is a structure typical of narrative videogames (Backe 2008, 109).

The comics

The specific choice of adapting *Metal Gear Solid* and *Metal Gear Solid 2: Sons of Liberty* into comics appears distinctly twofold. On the one hand, they appear as intuitive choices thanks to their large amount of embedded narrative elements set in a fixed sequence. On the other hand, both games feature several distinctive elements that cannot be replicated within a linear narrative presentation. Because of the relation of this dichotomy to the games' structured interplay, it is perhaps not surprising that the comics, despite not replicating this structured interplay, still appear distinctively shaped by it.

This is particularly evident in the comics version of *Metal Gear Solid*, where most of the panels are encapsulated visuals retraced from *cutscenes*. However, the source of these visuals is not *Metal Gear Solid* but the game's remake *Metal Gear Solid: The Twin Snakes* (2004).[5] This remake featured revised *cutscenes* that depict more flamboyant physical action, thereby moving the comic's presentation closer to the superhero genre. Furthermore, only in-game engine *cutscenes* were adapted while those employing film footage have been omitted. Through their dialogue and by presenting locations outside the closer diegetic setting, these *cutscenes* supported framing the game's fictional events within real-world circumstances. Their omission now makes the narrative of the comic appear not only more geographically enclosed but also more escapist than that of its source material. In comparison to *cutscenes*, only a small number of panels have been adapted from *gameplay*. Here, rather than concentrating on the game's core mechanic of sneaking, the focus lies on the protagonist's battles with various antagonists. The game's last mode, *codec communication*, has not been adapted as designated panels but rather as a distinctive set of speech balloons. Frequently, these have been added to panels adapted from *gameplay* where the game's presentation did not feature dialogue. Nonetheless, large parts of the game's dialogue presented through *codec communication* were dropped. This pattern of adaptation was generally retained for the comics version of *Metal Gear Solid 2: Sons of Liberty*. A major difference is, however, that more panels appear not directly retraced from the game's *cutscenes*. This goes hand in hand with the adaptation modifying the game's diegetic events to a larger degree, leading many panels to have no direct equivalent in the game. In general, the comics' pattern of adaptation can be described as extracting a narrative by concentrating on the games' elements suitable for linear narrative media. In its omission of large amounts of dialogue, this pattern highlights the visual primacy of comics. Furthermore, it also reveals the games' partial detachment between their narrative and their ludic core mechanic. Particularly the first games' adaptation shows that, even while only sparsely representing the sneaking mechanic, the narration remains coherent without adding new elements in its place.

As taken from their sources, the narratives of both comics adaptations could be described as twice restructured. First, a linear narrative was extracted from the games' potential variations. Then, a new layer of narrative structure was added through their episodic release. In *Metal Gear Solid*, the game's briefing section is partially adapted as the beginning of the narrative, and a combination of the game's two endings serves as the narrative's end. For *Metal Gear Solid: Sons of Liberty*, part of the game's first chapter follows a new prologue while more of its diegetic events are later presented through an intradiegetic retelling. Taking aside those changes necessarily facilitated by the transposition into a linear narrative, these decisions appear to lessen the risk of audiences being confused by the narration. Different from the games, where audiences might be expected to continue engaging with the work's ludic elements even when briefly losing interest in the narration, the comics lack such a "safety net." This lack can even present an economic risk because of the comics' episodic publishing, something that appears reflected in the work as with one exception each issue constitutes a single chapter ending on a cliffhanger-like situation. Typically, the protagonist has either received new information that will change the reader's understanding of previous events, or he is standing on the brink of a confrontation. Aside from the economic reality of publishing, this structure also reveals how the narratives of the games, even without explicit markers, have a typical videogame structure. The protagonists move from one short-term goal to the next (Salen and Zimmerman 2008, 343), with each goal supplying rewards such as information or equipment. The adaptations make this structure more clearly recognizable as many of the games' elements that have disguised it have been omitted.

The adaptations also present different relationships among the reader, the protagonist, and the text itself. By necessity refraining from replicating the games' oscillating player-avatar relationship, the comics also create greater distance between the recipient's and the protagonist's range of narrative knowledge. The games generally tie the recipient's knowledge to the protagonist, with only *cutscenes* sporadically featuring a more omniscient range. Compared to this, the comics regularly present diegetic events outside of the protagonist's presence. This greater distance becomes particular noticeable in *Metal Gear Solid: Sons of Liberty*, where the adaptation's restructuring of the narration leads to two characters functioning as protagonists. While many diegetic events have been remodeled to feature greater participation by returning protagonist Solid Snake, other events still necessarily center on newcomer Raiden. This change is distinctive because the game's narration did heavily build on the identification between the player and rookie operative Raiden. In the same mold, the adaptations also change the relationship between the text and the recipient by removing the games' various postmodern elements, such as direct references to their own materiality. Not only heightening their appeal as escapist entertainment, this also leads to one major theme of *Metal Gear Solid 2: Sons of Liberty* being diminished in its adaptation.

In summary, the changes in the adaptations lead to a more escapist narrative with a heavier emphasis on physical action. In doing this, the comics retain much of the narrative core of the games and remain recognizable as adaptations. However, many of the omitted elements were important in creating the games' unique identity and in moving their narration beyond generic predecessors in various media. Their omission makes the comics' narratives appear more generic in comparison.

The digital graphic novels

As adaptations, a remarkable element of the *Metal Gear Solid* digital graphic novels is that they completely reproduce the comics' visual images and texts without any additions, omissions, or changes in their sequence. They differ, however, in their presentation of these elements. The digital graphic novels present each panel by itself before being replaced by the next one, which creates a stricter sequential order of reception. While the first release for the Sony PlayStation Portable allowed readers to select between manually switching panels or automated playback, the second option became the standard for all later releases, leading to an approximately film-like presentation. In both cases, the adaptations feature a more restrictive reception and thereby reveal the freedom granted to the reader in the comics' reception. Aside from the complete reproduction of the previously published comic's visual images and text, there is one additional narrative element in the Sony PlayStation Portable version of the digital graphic novel. Here, the recipient can not only switch between playback modes but can also pause playback to "scan" panels. By locating the right visual cues, this then expands the material accessible inside a database full of narrative background information. As a structure of supplying optional narrative information running alongside a linear narration, this feature recalls the games' player-initiated *codec communication*.

Despite including complete textual reproductions of their source material, the digital graphic novels present a different narrative experience. This makes them an ideal example of how the adaptation into another format necessarily facilitates changes even when its creators appeared to have tried to abstain from modifying the content.

Presentation

In terms of their presentation, a major difference distinguishing videogames from comics is that they are "an inherently multimodal medium" that frequently includes "haptics, visuals, music, spoken language, and written text" (Ryan and Thon 2014, 11). In this particular sequence of adaptations, the comics adaptations first had to transpose such a multimodal experience into a combination of images and words before the digital graphic novels restored many of the semiotic systems available to videogames, while merging them onto the comics' preexisting elements. In all of this, it is important to note that any kind of audiovisual presentation has to balance aesthetic and functional needs. In videogames, players have to make decisions based on their "reading" of the situation, and wrong decisions can stop narrative progress. In contrast, while the aesthetic functions of linear narrative media might frustrate the recipient's comprehension, they do not stop the narrative progress. Therefore, the relevance of such a balance is especially important when creating the audiovisual presentation of videogames.

The games

Metal Gear Solid was released at a time when technological developments were leading to frequent changes in the presentation of videogames. A noticeable trend, particular on console systems, was the combination of different styles of presentation. This was mainly facilitated by the introduction of the CD-ROM, which allowed the inclusion and playback of audiovisual elements in a quality the same hardware could not process in real-time. Because these elements were stored in a fixed state, their application lacked flexibility. Many games therefore mixed elements in various styles and qualities to optimize their balance between aesthetic appeal and ludic functionality.

This is also the case in *Metal Gear Solid* and *Metal Gear Solid 2: Sons of Liberty*, where the audiovisual presentation changes between their different modes. The games' most common form of presentation consists of polygon-based graphics, which are not only used for all of *gameplay* but also for all *cutscenes* depicting events inside the diegetic setting.[6] Additionally, *Metal Gear Solid 2: Sons of Liberty* employs them for the character portraits in *codec communication*. During *gameplay*, the game's virtual camera typically presents a top-down viewpoint, with movements and additional angles dependent on context. While *gameplay* appears to prioritize the player's ability to oversee the avatar's situation, even here the games' approximation of cinematic aesthetics is recognizable in elements such as camera movements. The approximation of cinematic aesthetics is pushed further in *cutscenes*, where the games employ the audiovisual language of film while simultaneously removing visual markers of the games' rule-based systems. Throughout all of this, the visual assets are either identical or resemble those used in *gameplay* to a large degree. Aside from this, both games also feature stylistically different elements, such as animated and actual film footage in *cutscenes* and drawn character portraits during *codec communication* in *Metal Gear Solid*. Despite these exceptions, the general visual presentation appears in support of creating aesthetic coherence between the different modes. This is because, aside from the drawn character portraits, the use of film footage never presents the same characters and locations as the polygon-based graphics. Instead, these sequences generally connect the game's thematic treatments to real-world circumstances. Coupled with the games' general willingness to be self-referential, the stylistic difference appears appropriate, perhaps even supportive.

Another element enhancing the aesthetic coherence of the games is their aural presentation. The fact that all of the dialogue is performed by voice actors not only supports aesthetic coherence between modes but also marks the games' characters as performances. Musically, the repeated use of several themes, especially during *cutscenes*, resembles popular cinema's use of music, while the looped background music during *gameplay* is typical of videogames. Taken together, the audiovisual presentation of the games appears generally designed to "bridge the gaps" between the different modes and to support their perception as a unified whole, while distinctively taking advantage of practices established in film and other earlier media formats.

The comics

While lacking the games' syncretic (Groensteen 2007, 160) nature, the comics adaptations do not face the games' challenge of needing to unify different presentational modes. Indeed, in stark contrast to the games, the comics' presentation appears to actively undermine such an effect. There are constant switches between different styles, with drawings generally heavily stylized, panels often overflowing with jagged pencil lines, and the coloring sometimes appearing unfinished. The repeated stylistic changes between panels draw attention to the materiality of the comics (Schüwer

2008, 374) as they highlight the existence of the diegetic world as a set of representations. The color palette is monochromatic with color sparsely applied to highlight singular elements. This is most apparent in the use of red against the comics' usual palette of greens, blues, and grays. Another distinctive choice is the use of large soundwords to translate the more hectic diegetic events into a purely visual presentation. The visual presentation more closely resembles that of the games' concept artwork by Yoji Shinkawa than the games themselves.[7] This combination of stylistic choices amounts to an *art brut* (Duncan and Smith 2009, 161–162) style suitable for the harsh violent world represented.

That the comics panels are often initially hard to read highlights how the balance between aesthetic and functional needs differs between comics and videogames. Because reception is not internally timed, a comic can afford to include visuals readers might find hard to decipher in a brief moment. Taken together, the presentation stands in noticeable contrast to the comics' narration. This might have been motivated by their status as adaptations, whereby a distinctive presentation can heighten the appeal to potential audiences already familiar with the narrative.

The digital graphic novels

Simply speaking, the digital graphic novels reinstate the videogames' syncretic nature upon the comics adaptation while retaining a linear narrative. Aside from panels being placed into a strict sequential order, their presentation is altered to achieve a full screen presentation. This is accomplished through the use of film techniques like panning and zooming, whose application also leads to further regulation of individual panels' reading pattern. Furthermore, many panels now feature brief animations as well as gentle "camera" movements, which, combined with a layering of the existing visuals, produces an effect of a less flat diegetic space. An addition unique to the film versions is the presence of credit sequences akin to typical film presentations. In terms of audio, all versions feature a soundtrack that includes new versions of some of the compositions and sound effects taken from the games. Furthermore, the film versions feature all dialogue performed by voice actors, with most of the games' cast reprising their parts. All these choices strengthen the connection between the games and the digital graphic novels by creating a shared aural identity. Noticeably, even in versions with voiced dialogue, the digital graphic novels include speech balloons that remain fixed even when movement is applied to the presentation of the diegetic world. Particularly against the backdrop of the film versions' constant progress, this appears as a marker of the work's comics-specific identity. On the other hand, the version released for the Sony PlayStation Portable highlights the potential to interact with the visuals as the recipient can zoom through image layers while scanning panels.

In tune with their designation as digital graphic novels, the audiovisual presentation of these adaptations appears to walk the tightrope between presenting how digital media can evolve the experience of reading a comic while simultaneously retaining markers of being a comic. This is the case because the digital graphic novels must identify as comics to justify their existence against other media accessible on the same hardware.

Conclusion

Looking at *Metal Gear Solid*, *Metal Gear Solid 2: Sons of Liberty*, and their adaptations into comics and digital graphic novels reveals distinctive properties of these individual incarnations as well as of the various media formats. For one, they show that both games include a narrative core that remains recognizable throughout its transposition into other media formats. In both games, this core is mostly encompassed inside embedded narrative content and presented through two different modes of presentation. These modes introduce diegetic goals the player's avatar then pursues in another mode through engagement with the game's rule-based systems. In this mode, the player then actively controls the avatar inside emerging narrative events. Together, the structured interplay of these modes forms the general process of playing the games. While this structure is not replicated in the adaptations, it still appears to have had a lasting influence on the process of adaptation. This is because the adaptations prioritize the embedded narrative content that the games present through their film-like *cutscenes* mode. However, much of the games' lengthy dialogue, their postmodern sensibilities, their references outside of the closer diegetic setting, and their emergent narrative content have been omitted. The adaptations thereby retain many of the games' iconic narrative events but nonetheless feature a distinctively modified narrative. The choice of adapted materials leads to more escapist narratives with a stronger emphasis on physical action.

Both games, despite their general appearance as fixed linear narrations, also offer players various ways to access optional embedded narrative, modify the sequential presentation of narrative events, and even, in a single case, influence the narration's outcome. On these issues, their adaptations, however, show the limitations of their respective media formats. Aside from a single feature in one version of the digital graphic novels, all of these elements had to be removed or fixed into a singular sequence of events. While neither game might be anybody's poster child for nonlinear narration, it is illuminating to see that, despite their rather simple implementation of such features, they create a style of narration unique to videogames and not easily replicated in other forms of media.

In terms of presentation, the games and their adaptations seem to reflect vastly different intentions. The audiovisual presentation of the games appears designed to 'bridge the gaps' between their three modes. By keeping elements such as visual assets and the voiced dialogue consistent throughout all modes, they strive to present themselves as a unified experience. While they do not achieve this entirely in terms of their visual presentation, their narration and postmodern sensibilities are able to provide some motivation for the existing inconsistencies. Going into the opposite direction, the comics adaptations' visual presentation actively undermines the perception as a unified experience. Repeatedly switching between different styles, they feature heavily stylized panels overflowing with jagged pencil lines as well as sometimes seemingly unfinished coloring. This presentation also highlights the comics' own materiality, a choice curiously contrasting with the comics' narration completely omitting similar tendencies present in the games. The digital graphic novels, completely reproducing the comics' visuals as well as their text, expand this presentation through the use of cinematic techniques and a new aural presentation. This aural presentation connects these second-degree adaptations back to the games by referring to it in various ways. The complete reproduction of the comics inside this new multimodal shell of the digital graphic novels shows how the change of media format modifies content even when it is apparently identically reproduced.

In hindsight, the most distinctive and lasting effect of this sequence of adaptations appears to be on two later *Metal Gear Solid* titles for the Sony PlayStation Portable. Both games featured the participation of the comics' artist Ashley Wood for cutscenes stylistically similar to the digital graphic novels. Apart from this, the success of the comics adaptations appears to have been limited; despite the continued popularity of the videogame series, no further adaptations followed. However, the digital graphic novels appear to have fared even worse. Following the Sony PlayStation Portable version, their feature film versions initially did not even receive a release on Western markets. Their later Western release was then only as part of a collection to celebrate the series' 25th anniversary, where they found themselves stashed away as a bonus feature on one of the game discs. While it might not be possible to pinpoint a specific reason for the digital graphic novels' lack of success, it is intriguing to consider if and how this relates to their "misfit" nature. All their releases were for technological devices strongly associated with the playback of other forms of media. This might have led to audiences being unsure about the digital graphic novels' nature. Perhaps they might have fared better a few years later when multipurpose devices such as smart phones, tablets, and notebooks brought a distinctive change in how audiences consume media. Predating a general "liberation" of comics from print through digital distribution, the digital graphic novels do not just present a blueprint on how comics can take advantage of this liberation. In their subdued reception, they also present a warning and suggest the potential risks involved when giving up a well-established medial identity.

Notes

1 The first of these was published in Japan as *Metal Gear Solid: Bande Dessinée* (2006) and in Europe as *Metal Gear Solid: Digital Graphic Novel* (2006), while

the second was only published in Japan as *Metal Gear Solid 2: Bande Dessinée* (2008), the different titles leading to a markedly different paratextual framing.

2 The distinction between embedded and emergent game narratives goes back to Marc LeBlanc (Salen and Zimmermann 2008, 383). Katie Salen and Eric Zimmerman describe the difference as follows: "Embedded elements are narrative structures directly authored by game designers" while "emergent narrative approaches emphasize the ways that players interact with a game system to produce a narrative experience unique to each player" (2008, 384).

3 Holmes calls the three modes *active gameplay*, *cutscenes*, and *codec sequences*. I admit that neither mine nor his term for the player's interactions with the game's rule-based systems is ideal. By itself, *gameplay*, while often used in popular discourse, has the effect of implying some elements of the game to be not part of the experience of playing. While Holmes's use of *active gameplay* corrects this effect, it tends to mark the player's engagement with other modes as passive.

4 The degree to which these modes cover many of the narrative developments is even exemplified by *Metal Gear Solid* itself. After the player has first completed the game, it offers a mode where the narrative is presented through a combination of such embedded elements with brief written summaries.

5 Arguably, despite its title, this means that *Metal Gear Solid* could also be considered an adaptation of *Metal Gear Solid: The Twin Snakes*.

6 Here, both games differ from many other contemporary titles in their choice to use neither prerendered backgrounds during *gameplay* nor prerendered *cutscenes*. By doing this, the designers opted for a more unified and flexible visual presentation instead of higher quality visuals.

7 A dedication to him is even featured in one of the splash panels of *Metal Gear Solid*.

Works cited

Backe, Hans-Joachim. 2008. *Strukturen und Funktionen des Erzählens im Computerspiel: Eine typologische Einführung*. Würzburg: Königshausen und Neumann.

Bogost, Ian. 2007. *Persuasive Games: The Expressive Power of Videogames*. Cambridge, MA: MIT Press.

Duncan, Randy, and Matthew J. Smith. 2009. *The Power of Comics: History, Form and Culture*. New York: Continuum.

Fraction, Matt, and Ashley Wood. 2014. "Metal Gear Solid: Sons of Liberty #0." In *Metal Gear Solid: Deluxe Edition*, 298–327. San Diego: IDW Publishing.

Garner, Alex, and Ashley Wood. 2014. "Metal Gear Solid: Sons of Liberty." In *Metal Gear Solid: Deluxe Edition*, 328–593. San Diego: IDW Publishing.

Groensteen, Thierry. 2007. *The System of Comics*. Jackson: University Press of Mississippi.

Holmes, Dylan. 2012. *A Mind Forever Voyaging: A History of Storytelling in Video Games*. Self-published.

Hutcheon, Linda. 2006. *A Theory of Adaptation*. New York: Routledge.

Juul, Jesper. 2005. *Half-Real: Video Games between Real Rules and Fictional Worlds*. Cambridge, MA: MIT Press.

Klevjer, Rune. 2002. "In Defense of Cutscenes." In *Proceedings of Computer Games and Digital Cultures Conference*, edited by Frans Mäyrä, 191–202. Tampere: Tampere University Press.

Metal Gear Solid. 1998. Developed and published by Konami. PlayStation.

Metal Gear Solid: Bande Dessinée. 2006. Developed by Kojima Productions. Published by Konami. PlayStation Portable.

Metal Gear Solid: Digital Graphic Novel. 2006. Developed by Kojima Productions. Published by Konami. PlayStation Portable.

Metal Gear Solid: The Twin Snakes. 2004. Developed by Silicon Knights and Konami. Published by Konami. Nintendo GameCube.

Metal Gear Solid 2: Bande Dessinée. 2008. Developed by Kojima Productions. Published by Konami. DVD.

Metal Gear Solid 2: Sons of Liberty. 2001. Developed and published by Konami. PlayStation 2.

Mukherjee, Souvik. 2015. *Video Games and Storytelling: Reading Games and Playing Books*. New York: Palgrave Macmillan.

Oprisko, Kris, and Ashley Wood. 2014. "Metal Gear Solid." In *Metal Gear Solid: Deluxe Edition*, 4–297. San Diego: IDW Publishing.

Parish, Jeremy. 2018. "Ranking the *Metal Gear* Series." *Polygon*, 23 March. www.polygon.com/features/2018/2/19/17022700/best-metal-gear-games (accessed 31 January 2020).

Parkin, Simon. 2012. "Hideo Kojima: Video Game Drop-Out: Interview Part 1." *The Guardian*, 24 March. www.theguardian.com/technology/gamesblog/2012/may/23/hideo-kojima-interviewpart-1 (accessed 31 January 2020).

Parkin, Simon. 2017. *An Illustrated History of 151 Video Games*. London: Lorenz Books.

Ryan, Marie-Laure, and Jan-Noël Thon. 2014. "Storyworlds across Media: Introduction." In *Storyworlds across Media: Toward a Media-Conscious Narratology*, edited by Marie-Laure Ryan and Jan-Noël Thon, 1–21. Lincoln: University of Nebraska Press.

Salen, Katie, and Eric Zimmerman. 2008. *Rules of Play: Game Design Fundamentals*. Cambridge, MA: MIT Press.

Schüwer, Martin. 2008. *Wie Comics erzählen: Grundriss einer intermedialen Erzähltheorie der grafischen Literatur*. Trier: Wissenschaftlicher Verlag Trier.

Part II

Transmedia expansions

9 Many Spider-Men are better than one

Referencing as a narrative strategy

Dominik Mieth

Over the last 20 years, characters like Spider-Man, Batman, and Lara Croft have appeared in different iterations across several media such as comics, movies, and games. Usually, new iterations are introduced in the context of adaptation—e.g., via a new movie or videogame appearance. However, when characters have a long-running publication history, changes also take place in the medium of their origin, often to make the character more accessible for new audiences. Reiterating and recreating iconic characters for new and old audiences and adapting them for different media is a thin line to walk for creators, as their audience will include both long-term fans well-informed about previous appearances and potential new fans encountering the characters and their storyworlds for the first time.

Starting with theoretical perspectives on the elements that define a superhero character, I will outline a model of character components that should be applicable in both theory and practice. While this model should help us analyze several iterations of a character in comparison, it may also help creators to reflect on their decisions when working with similar IPs and hopefully to recreate a popular character successfully for a new comic book series, movie, or videogame. Using Spider-Man as an example, I will demonstrate how the comic books have dealt (or tried to deal) with the challenge of updating the character. While an attempt to introduce a new Spider-Man within the existing continuity failed, Marvel succeeded by establishing a multiplicity of Spider-Men across several comic book series and giving each iteration its own continuity. Next, I will look at cinematic iterations of Spider-Man since 2002. I will assess how these movies add to the multiplicity of the character while following the logic of adaptation. They choose different elements from the comic books as points of reference, creating different Spider-Men that share the same source material but present different elements from it. Lastly, I will look at some of the videogames featuring Spider-Man. I will demonstrate how the earlier games position themselves more or less clearly in relation to specific iterations of the character although they rarely reference complex events that would allow us to determine if they belong to the same storyworld. The newest installment ultimately applies an approach similar to the movies. In conclusion, I will emphasize the importance of continuity to reach new audiences and the relevance of including carefully curated references to appeal to audiences already familiar with popular characters like Spider-Man.

Theoretical perspectives

Studies across a variety of disciplines have touched upon the subject of one recognizable character appearing in various iterations across multiple texts or media. This includes adaptation studies (Burke 2015; Heinze 2019), transmedia studies (Jenkins 2009; Pearson 2019), media studies concerned with branding and franchising (Freeman 2017; Johnson 2012, 2017; Proctor 2012a, 2012b, 2017b), narratology (Eder 2015; Ryan 2013; Thon 2019), and fan studies (Tosca and Klastrup 2016). As expected, the focus of each of these studies varies depending on the discipline and its perspective on the subject. In the following, I will exclusively look at two specific aspects: What components define a character, and how are these components used in the creation of new iterations of the character?

In their seminal work on Batman, William Uricchio and Roberta E. Pearson summarize traits/attributes, events, recurrent characters, setting, and iconography as the five key components that define the core of the character (Uricchio and Pearson 2015, 209–210). They note that "without the presence of all five key components in some form, the Batman ceases to be the Batman, yet the primarily series nature of the character permits fairly wide variation in the treatment of these components across time and media" (Uricchio and Pearson 2015, 210). In the context of Spider-Man, the absence of events, recurrent characters, and setting draws a clear line between the superhero *character* that appears in comic books, movies, and videogames and a *figure* that is recognizable as a Spider-Man. One example might be the popular *YouTube* channel "Superhero-Spiderman-Frozen Compilations," in which a man in a costume appears as Spiderman [*sic*] but hardly presents any references to the Spider-Man metatext beyond this appearance (Beaumec1988 2020). Compared to the Spider-Man presented in any of the Marvel movies, it is indeed more a man in a costume than a Spider-Man.

In her examination of television characters like CSI's Gilbert Grissom, Pearson has developed a character template similar to the one she and Uricchio described for Batman. This template includes six key elements: psychological traits and habitual behaviors, physical traits and appearance, speech patterns and dialogue, interactions with other characters, environment, and biography (Pearson 2019, 150). These overlap with the five key components that Pearson and Uricchio constituted for the Batman but further specify attributes as psychological traits, habits, and powers and events into biographical events like the origin and events from popular storylines.

Henry Jenkins, commenting on Uricchio and Pearson, identifies three phases in the history of the superhero genre: the beginning as self-contained stories, the shift toward serialization and continuity, and finally a period of multiplicity in which "readers may consume multiple versions of the same franchise, each with different conceptions of the character" (2009, 20). Jenkins describes both the superhero genre and its iconic characters as flexible and able to absorb new contexts. These contexts may serve various different purposes—e.g., responding to the growing multiculturalism of American society (Jenkins 2009, 24). In reply, Uricchio and Pearson acknowledge multiplicity as the "industry's prime directive" (2015, 231) but add that the "multiplicity strategy requires key components as much if not more than did the continuity strategy; readers ignorant of a character's basic building blocks would be unable to take pleasure in their permutations" (2015, 232). Thus, they remain convinced that the origin story is a central aspect of the Batman (Uricchio and Pearson 2015, 233). I would agree in so far as *a* Batman contradicting the origin story (e.g., a Batman whose parents never died) might not get as close to being *the* Batman as *a* Batman embracing the origin story. However, it might be close enough as we have seen other characters than Bruce Wayne taking the mantle of Batman. They are perfectly acceptable as *the* Batman as long they are not compared to a competing version and the judgment heavily depends on the knowledge of the character.

In working toward a typology of transmedia characters, Paolo Bertetti argues against a "direct correspondence (or mutual implication) between transmedia worlds and transmedia characters" (2014, 2346). Using Conan the Barbarian as an example, he notes that the "identity of characters is a fuzzy concept, and some characters' occurrences are more typical than others" (Bertetti 2014, 2348). Bertetti identifies fictional identity (the character as actor inside a story) and existential identity (the character as being) as "two different main types of identity" (2014, 2348). He further divides existential identity into proper identity (as semantic identity consisting of elements that define the character's being) and relational identity (as syntactic identity based on the relationship to the world surrounding the character). Proper identity is divided into figurative identity (including the name and image) and thematic identity (including the roles a character plays, such as superhero or student) (Bertetti 2014, 2349). Finally, fictional identity is differentiated into actantial identity (e.g., hero of the story), modal identity (e.g., motivations, skills, knowledge in contrast to actions taken), and axiological identity (deep values that inspire actions taken) (Bertetti 2014, 2349)—and connected to actorial, temporal, and special variations on the relational levels of a character's identity (Bertetti 2014, 2356).

The components discussed by Uricchio and Pearson (2015) and Pearson (2019) can be allocated within Bertetti's model—think of iconography as part of the figurative identity or recurring characters as part of the relational identity. It is interesting to note that most of the components they describe (attributes, traits, events, biography) are part of what Bertetti describes as modal and relational aspects of a character's identity, which indicates that some parts of Bertetti's model are more likely to inspire creators. Vice versa, what Bertetti describes as actantial and axiological is hardly considered by Urrichio and Pearson, posing the question if and how these could be used by creators to fashion interesting new iterations of a character.

Discussing the appearance of Frankenstein's Monster in Marvel comic books, Shane Denson points out that new installments of iconic characters like Batman or Spider-Man "carry traces of their previous incarnations into their new worlds, where the strata of their previous lives accrue in a non-linear, non-diegetic manner" (2011, 537). He defines serial figures like Spider-Man in contrast to a series character that might never move beyond a single continuity, e.g., a character in a soap opera that is never rebooted or adapted to other media. Denson points out further that a serial figure extends beyond its diegetic domain via an "extra-diegetic link" (2011, 537). In other words: The existence of various Spider-Men (including the "Superhero-Spiderman-Frozen Compilations" channel's man in a costume; Beaumec1988 2020) thus frames Spider-Man as a serial figure as each new appearance makes its connection to other appearances transparent (e.g., by the man in the *YouTube* video wearing a costume designed after a specific version of Spider-Man). This means that while *a* Batman might be clearly identified as not being *the* Batman, he still strengthens Batman as a serial figure. The relevance of a single Batman or Spider-Man might then rather be determined by its reception—e.g., its popularity and the size of its audience, or justification, e.g., via canonicity (Proctor 2017a).

Pearson (2019) discusses transmedia characters, employing the concept of transfictionality introduced by Marie-Laure Ryan as the "migration of fictional entities across different texts" (2013, 383). Pearson analyzes transmedia characters in dimensions of additionality and cohesion. As she points out, additionality might not necessarily equal an expansion by introducing new settings or characters, but it might instead be a modification, e.g., reworking events, settings, or character details. Pearson discusses expansion and modification by the "points of contact" (2019, 149) on the fictional layer. She proposes a taxonomy consisting of "three structuring factors" (Pearson 2019, 149) by first separating time/place transfictions (e.g., a change of the setting) from character transfictions (e.g., a change of character traits), then realist from fantastic transfictions, and finally public domain (e.g., Sherlock Holmes) from proprietary (e.g., Batman) transfictions (Pearson 2019, 149–151). While Spider-Man is easily classified as proprietary and fantastic, I would argue that a new iteration of Spider-Man can introduce modifications on both the character and time/place domain at the same time. The notion of cohesion as quality that can be stronger/weaker seems to fit the evaluation of two or more versions of the same character in comparison.

Pearson's points of contact follow an idea similar to Jan-Noël Thon's (2019, 379) comparison of two single narratives within a transmedial franchise in terms of redundancy (both narratives present the same elements of a storyworld), expansion (one narrative adds previously unrepresented elements without leading to contradiction between both narratives), and modification (one narrative adds previously unrepresented elements, which leads to contradiction between both narratives, thus indicating them to be different storyworlds). Like storyworlds or narratives, two iterations of a single character like Spider-Man can be compared in these terms. From a creator's perspective, redundancy results in a possibly exact copy of an original. Modification makes sense in the context of transmedia storytelling, e.g., by filling in possible gaps left by another narrative, as many of the games developed with a movie license demonstrate by adding scenes that might take place between scenes in the movie. Finally, modification appears to be the strategy suggested by most recent appearances of Spider-Man, as the contradictions they create help turning what Denson describes as a series character into a serial figure.

A character component model

Building upon these distinctions, I suggest the following model that combines the components sorted by their importance regarding their cohesion to what could be considered a definitive version of the character. The order starts with cursory components like iconography, name, and license that can be judged more or less at a glance and moves on to more substantial and comprehensive components like canonicity, characteristics, settings, characters, and events that cannot be compared without a closer examination or previous knowledge of the character.

The deeper within a single component deviations or modifications appear in comparison to previous iterations of the character, the closer the character could be considered to the idea of a definitive Spider-Man rather than just being *a* Spider-Man, and the closer the iteration that serves as a benchmark in this comparison could be considered as the definitive Spider-Man. While definitive might suggest some sort of exclusivity, it is in fact possible that several Spider-Men might share this status, e.g., all four movie Spider-Men are perfectly acceptable as *the* Spider-Man as long as there is only one Spider-Man in the specific narrative.

The model takes into account that different recipients might compare a specific Spider-Man to different conceptions of the character depending on their previous exposure to Spider-Man fiction. While a truly definitive version of the character thus cannot exist, the question of definitiveness becomes a question of collective overlap between individual conceptions of the character. This resembles Jan-Noël Thon's observation that transmedial narratology can distinguish between the medial representation of a storyworld, its mental representation that is constructed during the reception by a single reader, and the storyworld as "intersubjective communicative construct" (2019, 376). Naturally, this collective overlap concurs with the popularity and spread of certain representations of the character. The clearer this collective overlap between the various Spider-Men becomes, the more cohesive the concept of Spider-Man becomes as a whole. These observations culminate in the following character component model:

Cursory components (requiring only superficial familiarity with the character):

1. *Iconography* (E.g., costume, recognizable pose or gesture: Does it look like Spider-Man?)
2. *Name* (Is it referred to as Spider-Man?)
3. *License* (Is it officially sanctioned by the holder of the franchise?)

Comprehensive components (requiring knowledge of existing narratives):

4. *Canonicity* (Is it part of an existing fictional world or timeline?)
5. *Characteristics*
    a. physical traits / powers (Can he/she do what Spider-Man can do?)
    b. psychological traits / habits (Does he/she behave like Spider-Man?)
    c. biography / origin (Has he/she experienced what Spider-Man has experienced?)
    d. speech patterns / dialogue (Does he/she talk like Spider-Man?)
6. *Setting* (Does it appear in a fictional world that evokes recognizable events from existing narratives? E.g., New York City)
7. *Supporting characters* (Do other characters related to events from existing narratives appear? E.g., Gwen Stacy)
8. *Events* (Does the narrative re-create or hint at events from existing narratives? E.g., the death of Gwen Stacy)

From a creator's perspective, the questions above can easily be reformulated, e.g., which supporting characters should a new iteration include and why? Such questions can lead not only toward a conscious decision regarding the selection of elements from existing iterations (e.g., who to include as Peter Parker's love interest and why) but also toward its potential benefits over other alternatives (e.g., the popularity of an element with an existing audience).

The comic books

Examining differences between Marvel and DC Comics, William Proctor notes that Marvel places greater emphasis on "continuity and ontological order," which offers a "vital component for many readers who enter the multiverse and demand rationality, cohesion, and consistency" (2017b, 344).

Reed Tucker echoes this in his history of the competition between Marvel and DC Comics. Developing a unified continuity between the different superheroes of the Marvel universe turned into one major advantage over the competition. The setup of their superheroes in a single universe "did not cause readers to abandon Marvel; in fact, they were being drawn deeper into this burgeoning fictional world, in some cases buying every title the company produced" (Tucker 2017, position 719 of 6685 Kindle eBook).

A character like Spider-Man, created in 1962, poses certain problems for creators, some of which Umberto Eco (1972) discusses in dissecting Superman. While a traditional mythological character like Hercules is defined by his "irreversible destiny," superheroes follow the logic of the modern novel, "in which the reader's main interest is transferred to the unpredictable nature of *what will happen* [emphasis in original] and, therefore, to the plot invention" (Eco 1972, 15). In addition, the "mythological character of comic strips [...] must be an archetype, the totality of certain collective aspirations, and therefore, he must necessarily become immobilized in an emblematic and fixed nature, which renders him easily recognizable" (Eco 1972, 15). On the one hand, writers of superhero narratives have to introduce unpredictable changes in the form of a plot twist; on the other hand, writers have to preserve the character resulting in a "narrative paradox" (Eco 1972, 16). Eco is still concerned with the Superman of the self-contained story area, which Jenkins (see above) refers to as the first phase of the superhero genre. Still, this observation holds true for characters like Spider-Man. As Sean Howe points out in his retelling of the competition between Marvel and DC Comics, the "average age of the monthly Marvel comic consumer now hovers at around thirty, which means that most readers have watched the narrative cycles repeat multiple times" (2013, position 7701 of 11016 Kindle eBook). Obviously, these readers seem to derive pleasure from the character staying the same.

Accordingly, in the mid-1990s, editor Terry Kavanagh argued that the writers had written Spider-Man "away from [their] audience" (Howe 2013, position 66562 of 11016 Kindle eBook) by getting him married and setting him up to become a father. He requested to bring the character "back to his essence" (Howe 2013, position 66562 of 11016 Kindle eBook). As a result, Marvel prepared a storyline in 1994 that would later be referred to as the "Clone Saga." The convoluted storyline and its production have been well documented by Goletz (2008). The "Clone Saga" went back to a storyline that concluded in *Amazing Spider-Man* Vol. 1 #149 (Conway and Andru 1975), in which Spider-Man fights a clone of himself that makes him doubt whether he himself is a clone. Marvel's intention was to reveal that clone to be the real Peter Parker and to install him as new Spider-Man under the name Ben Reilly. Sales dropped, and Marvel eventually decided to reinstall Peter Parker as Spider-Man by killing off Ben Reilly, revealing him to be the actual clone and leaving no room for any doubts that Peter was indeed the original Spider-Man.

Can the character component model explain why the audience rejected Ben Reilly? First of all, the obvious problem is the co-existence of two Spider-Men competing for the status of being *the* Spider-Man within a single continuity. Second, the fact that Ben Reilly is also competing with Peter Parker sharpens the conflict between the two Spider-Men. Marvel has indeed a hard time establishing the character as different from the previous Peter Parker. In *The Sensational Spider-Man* #0 (Jurgens and Janson 1996), in order to differentiate himself from the previous Spider-Man, Ben changes his costume and dyes his hair blond to prevent being confused with Peter Parker. Marvel also sets Ben Reilly up with new villains and a new cast of supporting characters. Nevertheless, a common situation in the narratives of the Ben Reilly storylines turns out to be Ben encountering characters whom Peter Parker has met and with whom he has grown familiar, and exploring the confusion resulting from their interaction. This serves as a constant reminder of the absence of Peter Parker. The changes made to set Ben Reilly apart from Peter Parker retain a constant reference to Peter Parker.

The "Clone Saga" storyline appears to be an example of a general pattern Marvel follows in the comic books to preserve what Eco described as "inexhaustible characters" (1972, 20). An impactful event triggers change (e.g., Peter being revealed to be the clone in 1995, Aunt May dying 1994), but the new status quo is only temporary and ultimately reverted after a certain time (Peter revealed to be the original in 1996, Aunt May revealed to be alive in 1998). It is important to note that in the case of Spider-Man, impactful events are in most cases events with consequences for the life of Peter Parker. Changes to his Spider-Man persona are less common but follow a similar pattern (e.g., his powers being extended as a result of the "The Other" storyline in 2005/2006, later repealed in the "One More Day" storyline in 2007/2008). Furthermore, the changes usually eliminate the occurrence of events that could be considered as bringing out "essential" components of the character (e.g., Aunt May lying in the hospital thus providing conflict between Peter's responsibilities as her nephew and being Spider-Man); thus, taking the changes back allows reintroducing what Eco describes as "recurrent stock situations" (1972, 20).

This pattern of reverting changes can also be interpreted in the context of conflicting concepts that form the characters and their relative importance. Using the character component model, this pattern can be discussed in terms of the aspects of the character that are involved. Is it more "essential" to Spider-Man that Peter Parker is married or that he is dating? How relevant are specific supporting characters like Mary Jane to bring out the "essence" of the character? Is making a deal with the devil to exchange his marriage with Mary Jane for the survival of Aunt May in line with the values and principles of Spider-Man?

Conflicts regarding these questions might arise between the various writers handling the books, their editors or other stakeholders involved in the franchise as a whole, as well as their audience. It is important to note that Marvel faced direct criticism from their audience through their letter columns long before fans had online media channels like *Twitter*. As one reaction, Marvel developed a practice to accommodate critics through additional publications. In 1997, they released a comic book with the title *Spider-Man: 101 Ways to End the Clone Saga* to assuage critics of the saga (Bernardo and Herrera 1997). This comic book presents the discussions of the various writers involved in the storyline as they are dealing with wrapping up the story, and it reveals some of the narrative strategies they considered. This story offered contemporary readers who felt invested in the discussion some form of acknowledgement and additional insights into the comic book industry.

While the *101 Ways to End the Clone Saga* book addressed the topic on a meta level, Marvel also launched new books to provide the audience with alternatives on a diegetic level. In 1998, Marvel explored the question of what could have happened if Peter and MJ's baby daughter had been born in *What If?* Vol. 2 #105 (Defalco and Frenz 1998) by introducing May Parker as Spider-Girl. The adventures of Spider-Girl then continued in her own books published until 2010 (DeFalco and Frenz 2010). In 2000, a new iteration of Spider-Man was created in the *Ultimate* line of comic books, in which Peter Parker is again a teenager gaining his powers for the first time (Bendis and Bagley 2000). This way, readers who had quit reading the main Spider-Man books in disagreement with the events that resolved the "Clone Saga" could pick and choose between two other iterations. Both Spider-Girl and the Ultimate Spider-Man referenced narratives from the original comic book continuity, either by adapting them as experiences of a young Peter Parker or as continuation of a shared past with a different future in the alternative universe of Spider-Girl. This way, Marvel was able to not only dodge the controversy caused by the two Spider-Men competing in a single continuity but also to keep their original Peter Parker relevant by following the logic of the serial figure described above. Introducing two new Peter Parkers in the father of Spider-Girl and the contemporary teenage Peter of the Ultimate continuity strengthened the original Peter Parker's status as the point of origin for these new iterations, while the stabilization of Peter Parker in the main continuity ultimately made the other two Peter Parkers obsolete. As a result, their books were canceled.

In spite of the controversy, the "Clone Saga" remains one of the staple storylines in the Spider-Man mythos and thus is one of the events that help define potential new iterations of Spider-Man. It was included in other iterations of Spider-Man, such as the *Ultimate Spider-Man* comic books and *Spider-Man: The Animated Series* (1994–1998). Writer Dan Slot picked up the "Clone Saga" in 2016 with the "Dead No More: The Clone Conspiracy" (Slott et al. 2017) storyline. This demonstrates that the quality of the storytelling is not as important as the notoriety of the story and its probability to be recognized by the audience. It is interesting to note that there is a similar timeframe between the original "Clone Saga" in the 1970s, its continuation in the 1990s, and its continuation in the 2010s. Of course, each storyline has provided Marvel with the chance to publish paperbacks of the older storylines. This recurrence of events not only satisfies what Eco describes as "pleasure from the non-story" (1972, 20) in audiences already familiar with the storylines. It also offers new readers an entry point to become familiar with the character and establishes links they can follow on their way to becoming expert audiences.

The concept of a multiverse allowing various versions of the characters to coexist not only in the comics but also across several media turned into another positive distinction for Marvel. Russell Backman describes the multiverse as "an established characteristic in Marvel's intellectual property" (2014, 206) that provides "a narrative principle that models the same type of processing required for transitioning between media forms" (2014, 218). It seems that somewhat controversial storylines like the "Clone Saga" inspire the creation of alternate realities and thus prepare audiences for the appearances of more Spider-Men across other media, to the point where the original Spider-Man from the comic books is no longer considered the definitive version of the character.

The movies

Writing about *Spider-Man: The Animated Series*, David Ray Carter comments on the "strength in its ability to take the best parts of the Spider-Man mythos and present them in a manner that still feels original" (2012, 212). The series loosely follows the timeline of the comic books but in recreating classic villains like the Lizard considers both classic and contemporary depictions in the comics. As Carter puts it, the show "privileged neither version over the other and operated with the realization that die-hard fans of Spider-Man would be familiar with both" (2012, 212). In some regards, *Spider-Man: The Animated Series* introduced the logic that the movies apply to the character in their adaptation of the comic books, although the movies further distance themselves from the continuity of the comic book as they pick from its material more freely.

Rebooting Spider-Man for the cinema with *The Amazing Spider-Man* (2012) only five years after the last movie in the Sam Raimi trilogy demonstrates the variety possible due to the vast extent of source material from comic books. While Tobey Maguire's Peter Parker is initially driven by his desire to impress the beautiful girl next door, Andrew Garfield's Peter Parker is initially driven by the mystery surrounding his parents' death and the feeling of being left behind. For the relationship between Peter and MJ, the Raimi trilogy seems to follow the logic of the comic books of the 1970s and 1980s. Marc Webb's Peter is allowed to explore different possibilities in the narration as he reveals his secret to Gwen Stacy on their first proper date, in turn allowing Gwen to support Spider-Man similar to the

MJ married to Peter Parker in the comic book storylines following their marriage in the 1990s.

The introduction of Spider-Man to the Marvel Cinematic Universe skips the origin story by introducing Peter as a supporting cast member in *Captain America: Civil War* (2016). Tom Holland's Peter Parker has Tony Stark and school friend Ned Leeds ask the necessary questions that are usually answered through the origin, including how he gained his powers and why he puts on the mask. The relationship between Peter and Tony Stark as his mentor echoes aspects of their relationship in the comic books of the mid-2000s.

Examining the various X-Men movies from the perspective of adaptation studies, Martin Zeller-Jacques points out that "references to the wider X-Men metatext [...] are included [...] to create a sense of density, of unexplored territory within the franchise" (2012, 155–156). Following this logic, all Spider-Man movies use references to various sources of the Spider-Man cosmos. The most obvious (and easily implemented) is namedropping to reference characters and locations that have been relevant throughout the history of Spider-Man, thus hinting at a larger world and potential events to be revealed for viewers familiar with the source material.

In general, the strategy of the movies in configuring their references is to condense the source material by creating new connections between characters, places, and events in order to entangle both Peter Parker and Spider-Man in the plot. In *Spider-Man* (2002), Norman Osborn is introduced as the father of Peter's high school friend who recognizes many of his own traits in the young Peter, thus giving both Peter and Spider-Man a relationship to the Green Goblin. In *The Amazing Spider-Man*, Peter's wish to find out more about his father's research makes him reveal the formula necessary for Curt Connor's transformation into the Lizard, which makes the Lizard part of his responsibility. In *Spider-Man: Homecoming* (2017), the Vulture turns out to be the father of Peter's love interest, a revelation that forces Spider-Man to choose between his moral obligation of stopping the bad guy and risking the bad guy's revenge. While the original comic books developed these villains without connection to Peter Parker, they did install some connections through retroactive continuity (e.g., Doctor Octopus dating Aunt May, the Green Goblin is revealed to be the father of Peter's best friend, scientist Curt Connor becoming a mentor to Peter Parker) in attempted retcons like *Spider-Man: Chapter One* (involving Doctor Octopus in Spider-Man's origin; Byrne 1998) or reboots like *Ultimate Spider-Man* (involving Norman Osborne in Spider-Man's origin; Bendis and Bagley 2000). The character constellation of a private relationship between Peter Parker and Spider-Man proved successful in the comic books, which is why it informed future versions of the character. As we will see, the most recent videogame also repeats this character constellation of the private relationship between Spider-Man and the main villain.

The movies also profit from the recognition of familiar events from the comic books, sometimes even toying with the expectations of viewers. When the Green Goblin kidnaps MJ in Raimi's *Spider-Man*, it is uncertain if this will result in the famous "The Night That Gwen Stacy Died" storyline. Vice versa, Captain Stacy's fate in *The Amazing Spider-Man* seems inevitable since he also died in the comic books, though until we see him die, we cannot be sure it will really happen. In *Spider-Man: Homecoming*, Jacob Batalon's character, who is clearly modeled after Ganke Lee from the *Ultimate Spider-Man* comics, is named after the comic book's Ned Leeds. In the comic books, Ned Leeds is revealed to be the Hobgoblin, one of Spider-Man's villains, upon his death, which is retroactively changed into him having been framed. This could imply that Jacob Batalon's character either dies, becomes a villain, or is framed to be a villain in further sequels. On the other hand, it also might lead to nothing. Again, it seems not as important how the reference is used as that it is obvious enough to be noted by long-term fans of the character. However, from a creator's perspective, this seems like a wasted opportunity.

The latest effort in recreating Spider-Man for the cinema is the animated movie *Spider-Man: Into the Spider-Verse* (2018), in which several Spider-Men and Spider-Women team up to prevent a catastrophic collapse of the multiverse caused by the Kingpin, who searches different realities to replace his dead wife and son. The story is loosely based on various sources. The comic book *Spider-Men II* (Bendis and Pichelli 2017) uses the same premise. A storyline from *Spider-Man: The Animated Series* that has several Spider-Men (including an actor without any superpowers who later introduces the "real" Spider-Man to Stan Lee) team up to prevent a similar event. The videogame *Spider-Man: Shattered Dimensions* (2010; see below) inspired an event in the Spider-Man comic books in 2014/2015 called "Spider-Verse," which includes several known Spider-Men (including Spider-Girl) and some newly created ones (Slott et al. 2014).

In his discussion of Batman, Jim Collins describes this as "narration by amalgamation" (2015, 166). According to Collins, the "popularity of these texts depends on their appeal not to a broad general audience, but a series of audiences varying in degrees of sophistication and stored cultural knowledge" (2015, 166). In this context it is of course relevant that a character like Spider-Man has been distributed long and broadly enough to be recognized by many audiences coming from different media and with different concepts of the character valuing (and acknowledging) different character components. Following this logic, *Spider-Man: Into the Spider-Verse* implements access points from various sources across various media.

From a creator's perspective, the underlying logic here seems to be that the broader the web of references becomes, the more accessible a new iteration of Spider-Man becomes for novice readers who are at least somewhat familiar with the character. They are offered more points of reference to what they might already know about Spider-Man. At the same time, the references make the adaptation more attractive to expert audiences that can trace the references back to their origin, recognize familiar patterns, and enjoy them as pleasure of the non-story (see above). Lastly, *Spider-Man: Into the Spider-Verse* demonstrates that the idea of a multiverse with competing facts has evolved past the comic books into the mainstream media. Again, the fidelity of the adaptation is not relevant, but rather the points of contact to previous iterations of the character in the context of additionality and cohesion. The character of Peter B. Parker can be interpreted as both a reference to Tobey Maguire's Peter Parker (he is shown kissing MJ while hanging upside down and stopping a train, thus evoking scenes from Sam Raimi's *Spider-Man* and *Spider-Man 2* [2004]) and as reference to the comic book Peter Parker who never got married and never had the child denied by the "Clone Saga." It does not matter which Spider-Man is referenced (though I'm sure it can be an interesting point of discussion for many fans) but that there are references that can be traced by comparing different versions of Spider-Men. The more the character appears across various media, the less important the relevance of the comic book becomes as point of origin. The fact that the comic books precede the other media appearances is more a historical sidenote than relevant to the conception of the character itself, even though tracing the steps in a chronological order might still help us understand the relationship of the different media appearances.

The games

Going through the list of Spider-Man's appearances in videogames, it becomes clear that the games published in the 1980s do work on the comic book license but do not really consider the comic book continuity. Comic books produced by Marvel were used to market games like *Questprobe Featuring Spider-Man* (1984) or *The Amazing Spider-Man and Captain America in Dr. Doom's Revenge* (1989) to appeal to the comic book audience but not to extend the comic book continuity. The storylines feature a prominent cast of heroes and villains from the comics, but the events displayed are without implications for the comic book continuity or the life of Peter Parker.

Many of the games released throughout the 1990s and beyond clearly represent adaptations of a specific license and narrative. Games like *Spider-Man: Return of the Sinister Six* (1992) or *Spider-Man and Venom: Maximum Carnage* (1994) are direct adaptations of storylines published in the comic books. Games like *Spider-Man: The Movie* (2002) or *The Amazing Spider-Man* (2012) are based on the specific movies. While the games based on the movies do expand the narration of their source, they hardly add to the narrative experience in a sense that might be considered as transmedia storytelling. They offer fans little reason to play them beyond the simple fact that they can engage in a game featuring the respective Spider-Man.

The game *Spider-Man* developed by Neversoft in 2000 marks a noteworthy exception. It toys with the comic book license by displaying comic book covers with the same layout as the contemporary books published by Marvel, including the Marvel Comics logo. The books presented start issue #1 as if the game had been a new comic book series. The opening cut scene shows Doctor Octopus giving a public presentation, and Eddie Brock aka Venom is planning to sell photos to the Daily Bugle newspaper. Both characters' configuration does not match the contemporary comic book continuity, while other facts, such as Peter being married to MJ and the Black Cat being familiar with his secret identity, do. The game also features the famous title song from the cartoon *Spider-Man* (1967–1970) and some of the voice actors from the contemporary *Spider-Man: The Animated Series* and *Spider-Man Unlimited* (1999–2001) for important roles like Spider-Man/Peter Parker and the Black Cat.

The game's first level comes with a voice-over from Stan Lee, who introduces himself as the creator of Spider-Man and welcomes "true-believers and newcomers alike," underlining the idea that the game considers both Spider-Man fans and players new to the character as its target audience. The game can be considered to present its own continuity (it is listed in the Marvel Database as Earth-TRN006), but the narrative presented is relatively straightforward and self-contained, and so it is difficult to describe it beyond its differences to other continuities presented by other Spider-Men.

The game extends its playtime beyond completing the story by allowing the player to collect additional suits for Spider-Man known from the comic books and TV shows. The player can collect covers of classic Spider-Man comic books that are easily recognized by avid readers and point newcomers to classic storylines and other iterations of Spider-Man, such as Spider-Man 2099. In many ways, the game provides a rough blueprint for modern superhero games like *Batman: Arkham Asylum* (2009) that introduce their own universe while referencing previous iterations across various media. However, *Batman: Arkham Asylum* does create a more complex and compelling universe by adding more relevant changes in contrast to other Batman media.

Ultimate Spider-Man, published by Activision in 2005, is an attempt to include a game into the continuity of the *Ultimate Spider-Man* comic book series. A making-of-video published by G4 advertised the game as including an unprecedented number of cameos from the comic book and entailing some Ultimate representations of characters that had not yet been introduced in the Ultimate comic books, like the villain Beetle and the mercenary Silver Sable. At the same time, Brian Michael Bendis, also writer of the *Ultimate Spider-Man* comic book, explained that the game would actually pick up the continuity of the book as a sequel to the "Ultimate Venom" storyline published in issues #33–38 throughout 2003. In 2006, Marvel advertised a storyline in the Ultimate comic book as a continuation of the game. In 2008, Bendis, however, decided to adapt the game into the comic book series and changed some events presented in the game, declaring it noncanonical (Marvel Database 2019). The *Ultimate Spider-Man* game therefore constitutes one of the few attempts of transmedia storytelling while at the same time demonstrating the challenges it provides for the creators involved in coordinating their efforts. As a result, Marvel did not repeat a similar attempt. Instead, they chose other, less demanding strategies linking the games to the franchise.

In 2010 and 2011, Activision released two videogames developed by Beenox that seem to build upon the comic book and have Spider-Man team up with Spider-Men from other dimensions. The first game, *Spider-Man: Shattered Dimensions*, was supervised by Dan Slott, the writer of the Spider-Man comic books at that time. It may have inspired his comic book event "Spider-Verse," published in 2014–2015, thus closing the circle of comics inspiring games back to the games inspiring new comic book storylines. While the presentation is much more elaborate, the storylines still are without implications for the comic book continuity and without events relevant to the life of Peter Parker and are thus hardly more relevant to fans attracted to the character through their interest in continuity as what happens next.

In 2018, the most recent game, *Marvel's Spider-Man*, developed by Insomniac Games, demonstrates the first attempt at creating a self-reliant and consistent continuity for Spider-Man within a videogame by including Peter Parker as a character with equal importance as Spider-Man and by closing the gap between the quality of the cut scenes to the movies. To emphasize this quality, the game features a Stan Lee cameo like a real Marvel movie.

Again, the game references storylines from the comic book continuity: Peter's Aunt May is working in a shelter for Martin Li, who is secretly the villain Mr. Negative, and the game's ending reminisces Aunt May's death in *The Amazing Spider-Man Vol. 1* #400 (DeMatteis and Bagley 1995). The game also toys with expectations of players already familiar with existing storylines as it teases the transformation of Doctor Octavius into Doctor Octopus, while referencing Sam Raimi's *Spider-Man 2* in the relationship between Peter and Octavius. It also introduces another genetically altered spider alongside Miles Morales, indicating that he might become another Spider-Man as seen in the *Ultimate Spider-Man* comic books and then suggesting that it might bite Mary Jane instead. This toying with the expectations of the audience again parallels similar strategies of the movies described above.

Like previous Spider-Man games featuring open world segments, the game offers various landmarks of the Marvel universe like the Avengers' tower. As such, it enables players to explore what other events and characters the storyworld might include. It often does not clarify whether the reference is just an Easter egg (e.g., a clock tower displaying the time of Gwen Stacy's death in *The Amazing Spider-Man 2: Rise of Electro* [2014]) or a possible hint at further developments (e.g., the actual appearance of heroes like the Black Panther and Daredevil). The game also includes collectibles that can be explored in the inventory. Again, these hint at the existence of other characters like Eddie Brock. These pieces offer long-term fans the opportunity to piece together the facts of the "Insomniverse" as distinct from other "Spider-Verses." This interacts nicely with the fact that the game allows the players to explore the world at their own pace, and its playtime easily extends beyond the runtime of all Spider-Man movies put together for players willing to devote the necessary attention to the game.

While the linear storytelling and timeframe of a feature film limits referencing, games have greater opportunities to include references by tying them to the game mechanics. In fact, with the growing number of Spider-Man-themed games, mechanics like web-swinging across an open world and collecting items become part of the benchmark to which new games are compared, similar to the way the components that define the character on the diegetic level become part of a collective concept of Spider-Man. In many ways, the games seem to indicate that, from a creator's perspective, the best strategy appears to create a new Spider-Man with its own continuity, both of which should be the result of careful curation of components from existing Spider-Men.

Conclusions

The title of this chapter itself is a reference. In 1963, Andy Warhol printed thirty black-and-white images of Leonardo da Vinci's Mona Lisa onto a canvas and called the piece *Thirty Are Better than One*. Warhol clearly frames his art as a form of reproduction, and the selection of the images he reproduces is an important part of the process. His silk-screening of Marilyn Monroe raises the question why he selected this particular image for reproduction, and for a younger generation, Warhol's Marylin may already have surpassed the original in relevance. Today, some might be more likely to see Warhol's art than the movies that made the actress famous. Similar things can be said about a superhero like Spider-Man that might someday move beyond its existence as a character in a comic book and will then be defined by the selection of elements creators have taken from various sources.

What we can learn from the many lives of Spider-Man is the importance of the web that links these different iterations of the characters together across their publication history. This web presents new pleasures to audiences willing to follow its strings across their various interconnections. While some iterations of Spider-Man are easily exposed as shallow representations with few ties to the existing continuities beyond naming conventions and appearances, others prove to be rich in references to their predecessors and thus demonstrate that their creators were equally invested in the character and its history as the fans they are trying to entangle in their narrative webs.

My goal was to point out opportunities and best practices for creators working with similar IPs. While reaching this goal will ultimately require a more thorough study focused on the specifics required by media as different as comic books, movies, and videogames and an extended look at the differences between the existing Spider-Men to identify recurrent components, a grounding principle has become clear: There is no definitive core concept of a character like Spider-Man, and its "essence" is subject to change as it depends on collective or individual interpretations of the character. However, a number of components are required in order to identify a character as Spider-Man, and they can be discussed using the model I have presented. While cursory components like iconography, name, and license are hardly a challenge to recreate, comprehensive components like characteristics, setting, characters, and events can be drawn from a large variety of material that creators can modify for their own iteration of the character.

Readers, viewers, or players encountering Spider-Man for the first time still need to be drawn in through compelling narratives until they have become acquainted with the character to the point where they are able to identify its differences from other superheroes on a substantial level. From there on out they are ready to navigate the tangled webs that link one iteration of the character to the others by comparing the different Spider-Men. At a time when mainstream audiences have learned to accept the multiplicity of a character like Spider-Man, these extradiegetic links have become as important as the intradiegetic narrative elements.

Works cited

The Amazing Spider-Man. 2012. Developed by Beenox. Published by Activision. Xbox 360.

The Amazing Spider-Man. 2012. Dir. Marc Webb. USA: Sony Pictures.

The Amazing Spider-Man 2: Rise of Electro. 2014. Dir. Marc Webb. USA: Sony Pictures.

The Amazing Spider-Man and Captain America in Dr. Doom's Revenge. 1989. Developed by Paragon Software Corporation. Published by Medalist International. MS-DOS.

Backmann, Russell. 2014. "In Franchise: Narrative Coherence, Alternates, and the Multiverse in *X-Men*." In *Superhero Synergies: Comic Book Characters Go Digital*, edited by James Gilmore and Matthias Stork, 201–219. Lanham, MD: Rowman and Littlefield.

Batman: Arkham Asylum. 2009. Developed by Rocksteady Studios. Published by Eidos Interactive and Warner Bros. Interactive Entertainment. Xbox 360.

Beaumec1988. 2020. "Superhero-Spiderman-Frozen Complilations." *YouTube*, 31 January 2020. www.youtube.com/user/beaumec1988 (accessed 31 January 2020).

Bendis, Brian M., and Mark Bagley. 2000. *Ultimate Spider-Man* Vol. 1 #1. New York: Marvel Comics.

Bendis, Brian M., and Sara Pichelli. 2017. *Spider-Men II* Vol 1 #1. New York: Marvel Comics.

Bernardo, Mark, and Ben Herrera. 1997. *Spider-Man: 101 Ways to End the Clone Saga* Vol. 1 #1. New York: Marvel Comics.

Bertetti, Paolo. 2014. "Toward a Typology of Transmedia Characters." *International Journal of Communication* 8 (20): 2344–2361.

Burke, Liam. 2015. *The Comic Book Film Adaptation: Exploring Modern Hollywood's Leading Genre*. Jackson: University Press of Mississippi.

Byrne, John. 1998. *Spider-Man: Chapter One*. New York: Marvel Comics.

Captain America: Civil War. 2016. Dir. Anthony Russo and Joe Russo. USA: Walt Disney Studios Motion Pictures.

Carter, David Ray. 2012. "Reinterpreting Myths in *Spider-Man: The Animated Series*." In *Web-Spinning Heroics*, edited by Robert M. Peaslee and Robert G. Weiner, 210–221. Jefferson: McFarland.

Collins, Jim. 2015. "*Batman: The Movie*: Narrative: The Hyperconsious." In *Many More Lives of the Batman*, edited by Roberta E. Pearson, William Uricchio, and Will Brooker, 151–170. New York: Palgrave Macmillan.

Conway, Gerry, and Ross Andru. 1975. *The Amazing Spider-Man* Vol 1 #149. New York: Marvel Comics.

Defalco, Tom, and Ron Frenz. 1998. *What If?* Vol 2 #105. New York: Marvel Comics.

Defalco, Tom, and Ron Frenz. 2010. *Spider-Girl: The End!* Vol. 1 #1. New York: Marvel Comics.

DeMatteis, J. M., and Mark Bagley. 1995. *The Amazing Spider-Man* Vol. 1 #400. New York: Marvel Comics.

Denson, Shane. 2011. "Marvel Comics' Frankenstein: A Case Study in the Media of Serial Figures." *Amerikastudien/American Studies* 56 (4): 531–553.

Eco, Umberto. 1972. "The Myth of Superman." *Diacritics* 2 (1): 14–22.

Eder, Jens. 2015. "Transmediality and the Politics of Adaptation: Concepts, Forms, and Strategies." In *The Politics of Adaptation*, edited by Dan Hassler-Forest and Nicklas Pascal, 66–81. London: Palgrave Macmillan.

Freeman, Matthew. 2017. "A World of Disney: Building a Transmedia Storyworld for Mickey and His Friends." In *World Building: Transmedia, Fans, Industries*, edited by Marta Boni, 93–108. Amsterdam: Amsterdam University Press.

Goletz, Andrew. 2008. "The Life of Reilly: An Introduction and Update." *The Life of Reilly*, 5 March. http://lifeofreillyarchives.blogspot.com/2008/03/introduction-and-update.html (accessed 31 January 2020).

Heinze, Rüdiger. 2019. "Alien Adapted (Again and Again): Fictional Universes between Difference and Repetition." In *Adaptation in the Age of Media Convergence*, edited by Johannes Fehrle and Werner Schäfke-Zell, 159–174. Amsterdam: Amsterdam University Press.

Howe, Sean. 2013. *Marvel Comics: The Untold Story*. Kindle eBook. New York: HarperCollins.

Jenkins, Henry. 2009. "'Just Men in Tights': Rewriting Silver Age Comics in an Era of Multiplicity." In *The Contemporary Comic Book Superhero*, edited by Angela Ndalianis, 30–57. New York: Routledge.

Johnson, Derek. 2012. "Cinematic Destiny: Marvel Studios and the Trade Stories of Industrial Convergence." *Cinema Journal* 52 (1): 1–24.

Johnson, Derek. 2017. "Battleworlds: The Management of Multiplicity." In *World Building: Transmedia, Fans, Industries*, edited by Marta Boni, 129–142. Amsterdam: Amsterdam University Press.

Jugens, Dan, and Klaus Janson. 1996. *The Sensational Spider-Man* Vol 1 #0. New York: Marvel Comics.

Marvel Database. 2019. "Ultimate Spider-Man (Video Game)." *Marvel Database*, 12 December. https://marvel.fandom.com/wiki/Ultimate_Spider-Man_(video_game) (accessed 31 January 2020).

Marvel's Spider-Man. 2018. Developed by Insomniac Games. Published by Sony Interactive Entertainment. PlayStation 4.

Pearson, Roberta E. 2019. "Additionality and Cohesion in Transfictional Heroes." In *The Routledge Companion to Transmedia Studies*, edited by Matthew Freeman and Renira Rampazzo Gambarato, 148–156. New York: Routledge.

Proctor, William. 2012a. "Beginning Again: The Reboot Phenomenon in Comic Books and Film." *Scan: Journal of Media Arts Culture* 9 (1): n.p. http://scan.net.au/scan/journal/display.php?journal_id=163 (accessed 31 January 2020).

Proctor, William. 2012b. "Regeneration and Rebirth: Anatomy of the Franchise Reboot." *Scope: An Online Journal of Film and Television Studies* 22: 1–19. www.nottingham.ac.uk/scope/documents/2012/february-2012/proctor.pdf (accessed 31 January 2020).

Proctor, William. 2017a. "Canonicity." In *The Routledge Companion to Imaginary Worlds*, edited by Mark J. P. Wolf, 236–245. New York: Routledge.

Proctor, William. 2017b. "Reboots and Retroactive Continuity." In *The Routledge Companion to Imaginary Worlds*, edited by Mark J. P. Wolf, 224–235. New York: Routledge.

Questprobe Featuring Spider-Man. 1984. Developed and published by Adventure International. Apple II.

Ryan, Marie-Laure. 2013. "Transmedial Storytelling and Transfictionality." *Poetics Today* 34 (3): 361–388.

Slott, Dan, Christos Gage, and Mike Costa. 2014. *Spider-Verse*. Modena: Panini.

Slott, Dan, Christos Gage, Sean Ryan, and Guiseppe Cammuncoli. 2017. *Amazing Spider-Man: Dead No More: The Clone Conspiracy*. Modena: Panini.

Spider-Man. 2000. Developed by Neversoft. Published by Activision. PlayStation.

Spider-Man. 2002. Dir. Sam Raimi. USA: Sony Pictures.

Spider-Man 2. 2004. Dir. Sam Raimi. USA: Sony Pictures.

Spider-Man 3. 2007. Dir. Sam Raimi. USA: Sony Pictures.

Spider-Man and Venom: Maximum Carnage. 1994. Developed by Software Creations. Published by Acclaim Entertainment. Genesis.

Spider-Man: Homecoming. 2017. Dir. Jon Watts. USA: Sony Pictures.

Spider-Man: Into the Spider-Verse. 2018. Dir. Bob Persichetti, Peter Ramsey, and Rodney Rothman. USA: Sony Pictures.

Spider-Man: Return of the Sinister Six. 1992. Developed by B.I.T.S. Published by LJN. Nintendo Entertainment System.

Spider-Man: Shattered Dimensions. 2010. Developed by Beenox. Published by Activision. Xbox 360.

Spider-Man: The Movie. 2002. Developed by Treyarch. Published by Activision. PlayStation 2.

Thon, Jan-Noël. 2019. "A Narratological Approach to Transmedial Storyworlds and Transmedial Universes." In *The Routledge Companion to Transmedia Studies*, edited by Matthew Freeman and Renira Rampazzo Gambarato, 375–382. New York: Routledge.

Tosca, Susana, and Lisbeth Klastrup. 2016. "The Networked Reception of Transmedial Universes: An Experience-Centered Approach." *MedieKultur: Journal of Media and Communication Research* 32 (60): 107–122.

Tucker, Reed. 2017. *Slugfest: Inside the Epic Fifty-Year Battle between Marvel and DC*. Kindle eBook. London: Sphere.

Ultimate Spider-Man. 2005. Developed by Treyarch. Published by Activision. PlayStation 2.

Uricchio, William, and Roberta E. Pearson. 2015. "'I'm Not Fooled by That Cheap Disguise.'" In *Many More Lives of the Batman*, edited by Roberta E. Pearson, William Uricchio, and Will Brooker, 205–236. New York: Palgrave Macmillan.

Zeller-Jacques, Martin. 2017. "Adapting the X-Men: Comic-Book Narratives in Film Franchises." In *A Companion to Literature, Film, and Adaptation*, edited by Deborah Cartmell, 143–158. Chichester: Blackwell.

10 The not-so *Fantastic Four* franchise

A critical history of the comic, the films, and the Disney/Fox merger

Robert Alan Brookey and Nan Zhang

When reviewing the 21st Century Fox 2015 release of the *Fantastic Four* franchise, Peter Travers of the *Rolling Stone* pulled no punches: "The latest reboot of the Fantastic Four—the cinematic equivalent of malware—is worse than worthless. It not only scrapes the bottom of the barrel; it knocks out the floor and sucks audiences into a black hole of soul-crushing, coma-inducing dullness" (2015, 1). Travers was not alone in his judgment. Todd McCarthy, in the *Hollywood Reporter*, characterized the film as "maddeningly lame and unimaginative" (2015, 1). *The New York Times* critic A. O. Scott was so displeased with the film that he willfully and admittedly recycled material from his review of the 2005 release of the *Fantastic Four* that he deemed "fantastic only in its commitment to mediocrity" (2015, 2). These critics' opinions did not differ much from the public's assessment of the film. While *Fantastic Four* (2015) only generated a 9 percent rating on *Rotten Tomatoes*, the website's audience score topped out at 18 percent. These scores placed the film on the website's list of the worst films of 2015 along such cinematic fare as *Paul Blart: Mall Cop* 2 (2015).

The real damage, however, was felt at the box office: The film only grossed $25 million its opening week, and then only went on to generate $167 million worldwide.[1] Given that the reported budget for the film was $120 million, and taking into account the unreported promotion budget, there is a good chance the film lost money. One thing is for certain: Any plans to produce a sequel from this reboot were scrapped by Fox.

One of the more visible critics of the film, Richard Roeper of the *Chicago Sun-Times*, dismissed the Fantastic Four as one of the "lesser teams in the Marvel Universe" (2015, 1). Anyone with a passing understanding of the history of Marvel comics knows that this is a mischaracterization. Still, Roeper's comment begs the question: Just how far has this franchise fallen? A rather definitive answer to that question came a few weeks prior, when Marvel published what was described as the "Triple Sized Final Issue 645" (Ching 2014, 1) of the *Fantastic Four* series (Robinson and Kirk 2015). While Marvel was a bit cagey about discussing the cancelation, Tom Brevoort, Senior Vice President of Publishing, seemed to allude to the decision on his *Tumblr* when he wrote:

> There are only so many hours in the day, and so many initiatives you can have going at once. So you need to pick and choose where you want to spend your time and your efforts. [...] If you had two things, and on one you earned 100% of the revenues from the efforts that you put into making it, and the other you earned a much smaller percentage for the same amount of time and effort, you'd be more likely to concentrate more heavily on the first, wouldn't you?
>
> (Brevoort 2014, 5)

Brevoort's rhetorical question is indeed rhetorical because it argues for the legitimacy of the commercial exigencies that drive the comic book industry. In the contemporary media landscape, comic book characters, and superheroes in particular, are extremely valuable intellectual property. In fact, the emergence of Marvel Studios, as we will discuss later, was orchestrated as an effort to capitalize on Marvel characters for the action figure toy market. We should also remember that Brevoort works for a company that was acquired by Disney in 2009, and that acquisition can be viewed not just as the ownership of a company, but also as the cultivation of intellectual property. Indeed, since Bob Iger took over as CEO of Disney in 2005, the company has been very acquisitive, buying up Pixar and Lucasfilm in addition to Marvel. These acquisitions can also be viewed as the accumulation of intellectual property, as both companies produce films that generate a good deal of ancillary products. The fact that Brevoort believes comics artists should primarily focus on properties that yield a great percentage of various revenue streams indicates that he is truly a company man, for both Marvel and Disney.

The decision to discontinue publication of the *Fantastic Four* proved to be a temporary one, because on 8 August 2018, a new *Fantastic Four* comic emerged, curiously resetting the publication history of the comic with the issue designation "#1" (Slott and Pichelli 2018). It would strain credulity to think that this reemergence of the Fantastic Four was not in some way related to Disney's acquisition of Fox. Indeed, the history of these two events lines up in an interesting manner. To put a finer point on it, while the *Fantastic Four* is not the prime motive for this acquisition, Disney's interest in Fox clearly had a great deal to do with what happened with the *Fantastic Four*, both its death and resurrection.

In this chapter, we provide a brief history of Disney, highlighting how and why the company began to value intellectual property early on. We will also discuss how Marvel Entertainment became Marvel Studios, and then a company that Disney was willing to purchase for over $4 billion. We then outline the unfortunate history of the *Fantastic Four* film franchise as executed by Fox Studios and explain how the *Fantastic Four* became a property caught up in the corporate machinations between Disney and Fox.

Our method is best described as a critical historical/descriptive analysis, one that links historic events to contemporary outcomes. Our theoretical lens is decidedly informed by political economy, or at least the part of that school that focuses on how corporate interests shape production and content (Mosco 1996). Our purpose is to show how corporate ownership and intellectual property rights drove the decision regarding the *Fantastic Four*. One of the outcomes of our inquiry is to challenge the dubious division between the study of political economy and the study of fan culture. In fact, we hope to demonstrate that fans can be active and empowered when they identify and challenge corporate decisions that impact fan cultures.

The trouble with Oswald

Walt Disney's animation career began in Kansas City, but in 1923, he decided to move to Hollywood to make it big. Like many who made this move before him, and after, Disney first struggled to find employment and recognition as an animator. After some qualified success with the *Alice Comedies* series (1923–1927), which combined animation and live action footage, Disney landed a contract with Universal to produce the *Oswald the Lucky Rabbit* cartoons (1927–1938). The contract was negotiated with Disney's distributor Charles Mintz, but Disney's charge was rather vague: Universal wanted a cartoon about a rabbit. Disney and his fledgling animation team created the character of Oswald, and the cartoon series proved popular with audiences and critics. This success, however, did not seem to generate respect from either Mintz or Universal. In fact, when it came time to negotiate the contract for the next series of Oswald cartoons, Mintz dropped his price from $2,250 per cartoon to $1,800. When Disney balked at this significant drop in compensation, Mintz threatened to take both the studio and the series away from him. Disney soon learned that most of the members of his animation team had already committed to Mintz and that Universal owned the intellectual property rights to Oswald (Thomas 1994). In other words, Mintz was already set to move forward with the production of more Oswald cartoons, without Disney's involvement.[2]

It was a humiliating loss for Disney, particularly given that he had to work with his disloyal animation team to finish his commitment to the Oswald series. Yet, simultaneously and surreptitiously, Disney was working on a cartoon entitled *Plane Crazy* (1928), which featured his new creation Mickey Mouse. Unfortunately, *Plane Crazy* failed to find a distributor, but when Mickey Mouse later appeared in the sound production cartoon *Steamboat Willie*, released in 1928, a cultural icon was born (Thomas 1994).

Disney learned an important lesson from this experience; the ownership of intellectual property is necessary for artistic control. Disney would also learn that intellectual property was a valuable commodity. Mickey Mouse began to move merchandise shortly after *Steamboat Willie* appeared in theaters, with the Ingersoll company producing its first Mickey Mouse watch in 1933 (Thomas 1994). Indeed, Disney was a pioneer in the practices of licensing and distributing ancillary products, and those practices have been expanded and accelerated over the years. More than 50 years after his passing, the Disney company is still committed to the development and exploitation of intellectual property, and any visit to a Disney park reveals how much space is devoted to the retailing of these ancillary products.

Consequently, Disney as a company has become notoriously protective and litigious when its intellectual property is concerned. A few years ago, the Walt Disney Company thought nothing of suing day-care centers in Florida for painting Disney characters on their walls, or going after any other companies (either small or large) that appropriated their intellectual property (Fort Lauderdale News and Sun-Sentinel 1989). More recently, a Michigan baker was sued by Disney for using Marvel and Star Wars characters on his cakes for copyright and trademark infringement (Gardner 2015). In other words, Disney's early lessons are not lost on the current custodians of his company and have clearly informed the company's corporate culture. It is not difficult to see how this commitment to intellectual property, and the understanding of its value, has informed the acquisitions the company has made over the past years.

Soon after Bob Iger took over as CEO of Disney, one of his first major actions was to acquire Pixar in a $7.4 billion deal. The significance of this deal was compounded by the fact that Iger's predecessor, Michael Eisner, failed to negotiate with then Pixar CEO Steve Jobs on a contract to continue the relationship between Disney and Pixar. Disney and Pixar had enjoyed a successful collaboration beginning with *Toy Story* (1995), but this success also contributed to its undoing. After the success of *Toy Story*, Jobs had signed a multipicture contract with Disney that allowed the companies to share costs and revenue, with the provision that Disney received a cut of the box office receipts prior to the division of this revenue stream. Jobs was looking to secure a new contract, with more favorable terms for Pixar, and Eisner was unwilling to meet his demands (Brookey and Westerfelhaus 2005). Consequently, Jobs had broken off talks with Eisner and was negotiating with the other studios for a distribution deal for Pixar. With Eisner out of the company, Iger was free to negotiate with Jobs, and the deal they cut not only allowed Disney to buy Pixar outright but also gave Jobs a seat on the Disney board and a sizeable share of Disney stock (Holson 2006). Iger's move to acquire Pixar secured all the existing intellectual property associated with the Disney/Pixar collaboration (*Toy Story*, *A Bug's Life* [1998], *Monsters, Inc.* [2001], and *Finding Nemo* [2003]), as well as any and all future productions from the animation studio.

Disney's next big acquisition was the $4.24 billion purchase of Marvel in 2009. About a decade earlier, Marvel Studios had emerged and had begun developing some significant film franchises, including *X-Men*, *Spider-Man*, and *Iron Man*. Disney's acquisition has accelerated the production of Marvel Studio films, drawing on a variety of Marvel characters and combinations of those characters, as well as an expansion into television production and live stage production. Disney's 2012 acquisition of Lucasfilm has yielded a similar expansion in the production of content tied to the *Star Wars* franchise. One of the primary drivers of these acquisitions was the intellectual property that already had a dedicated fan base and could thereby be deployed across a variety of ancillary markets (toys, clothing, and videogames) in which Disney already had a sizable footprint.

Disney's acquisition of Fox is a bit more complex. For example, Fox is a studio with a history as old as Disney's, and it has been a major production film studio for several decades. After it was taken over by Rupert Murdoch in the mid-1980s, the film studio became a subsidiary of the larger Fox/Newscorp conglomerate. That conglomerate was then split into two companies in 2013, with the publishing concerns spun off into News Corporation and the media holdings renamed 21st Century Fox (Ellingson 2013). The acquisition of 21st Century Fox secures for Disney the Fox film and television production studios, many of its cable channels, and international systems such as Sky and Star India, but it does not include the Fox broadcast network, the Fox Sports channels, nor the Fox News or Fox Business channels. Where Marvel is concerned, the acquisition means that Marvel will now retrieve the film rights to some important properties including *X-Men* and *Deadpool*, but the circumstances surrounding the rights to the *Fantastic Four* are more complex, as we will discuss later. Although clearly not the only factor, like the other Disney acquisitions, the Marvel intellectual property was likely an important driver for the $71 billion deal. In fact, the recent history of the *Fantastic Four* franchise provides support for this claim. Before we make that case, however, it may be helpful to revisit the events that turned Marvel into a film studio.

The rise of Marvel Studios

Marvel Comics was founded in 1939, but its brand did not really begin to emerge until 1961, when Stan Lee and Jack Kirby began developing *Spider-Man* and the *Fantastic Four*. In fact, these were some of the first Marvel characters to make the jump to other media, with the first Marvel cartoons and animated television shows appearing in 1966/1967. Because the company began to be more involved in animated production, it was purchased by New World Entertainment in 1986. New World was an independent film production company founded by Roger Corman (a name that will figure prominently in the history of the *Fantastic Four*), but after experiencing financial difficulties, the company would sell Marvel to the notorious Ron Perelman.

Perelman was infamous on Wall Street for acquiring companies and then turning a profit by selling off parts of these companies and their assets; in other words, he bought companies in order to dismantle them. In fact, that appeared to be exactly what was happening to Marvel under Perelman's ownership. By 1995, Marvel's stock had lost half its value and was heading toward bankruptcy. Perelman also fired one-third of Marvel's publishing office staff, and he was threatening to cease publication of Marvel comic books (Raviv 2004).

While these plans were disturbing to Marvel's fan base, they would spell disaster for some of the companies that did business with Marvel. For example, Toy Biz was a company with an exclusive contract to produce Marvel action figures, a contract secured by giving up 46 percent of the company to Perelman. Fearful that Toy Biz would soon meet the same fate as the other companies Perelman had acquired, the top partners of Toy Biz, Isaac Perlmutter, and Avi Arad, approached Perelman with an idea: to make movies based on Marvel comics (Raviv 2004). If Marvel ceased publishing, the value of the intellectual property rights (the characters) would significantly diminish over time. While this was a loss Perelman could well afford, the situation was quite different for Perlmutter and Arad as their financial futures were at stake. Perlmutter and Arad believed that if the Marvel characters were spun off into films, it would open up a variety of ancillary markets and thereby increase the value of the intellectual property.

One of the sticking points in the efforts to turn Marvel into a film studio was the fact that the film rights for many of their superhero characters had already been sold off to other studios. After several very contentious legal battles, including a corporate bankruptcy, Marvel emerged with Perlmutter and Arad at liberty to pursue film production. The bankruptcy voided many of the previous licensing contracts, so Marvel could negotiate new deals with film studios (Raviv 2004). Those deals involved co-production of the Marvel Studio films with other major studios such as Fox and Columbia.

As was the plan all along, Marvel Studios was also heavily involved in the ancillary product market, with a special emphasis on videogame spin-offs. Even before Disney acquired the studio in 2009, releasing videogames in conjunction with their films was a common practice at Marvel. Games were released for the *X-Men* films (starting with *X-Men* [2000], all three of the original *Spider-Man* films (2002; 2004; 2007), and the original *Iron Man* (2008) film. Videogames were also released from the *Fantastic Four* (2005) and *Fantastic Four: Rise of the Silver Surfer* (2007). Since the Disney acquisition, videogame releases have continued apace with spin-offs for *Iron Man 2* (2010), *Thor* (2011), and *Captain America: The First Avenger* (2011), just to name a few.

In fact, since the Disney acquisition, the performance of Marvel Studio films has been historic. For 2018, the two highest grossing films were *Black Panther* and *Avengers: Infinity War*, with a combined box office revenue total of $1.3 billion. *Deadpool 2* and *Ant-Man and the Wasp* were also among the top ten grossing films for 2018 with $318 million and $216 million in box office receipts, respectively.[3] This was a significant improvement from the year before, when Marvel characters only held the sixth (*Spider-Man: Homecoming*) and eighth (*Thor: Ragnarok*) place spots on top grossing films, but generally the studio's track record has been solid. Due to the success of their early films, including the *X-Men* and *Spider-Man* franchises, Marvel was able to produce *Iron Man* independently, securing a distribution deal with Paramount. Perlmutter and Arad had planned to model Marvel Studios on Disney, and that effort was fully validated when Disney acquired the studio.

Although Marvel no longer publishes annual financial reports as an independent company and Disney does not break out the revenue generated by Marvel specifically, the success of Marvel's films in 2018 alone indicates the value of the acquisition. Tucked away in Disney's 2017 report is this interesting passage about Marvel:

> Prior to the Company's acquisition of Marvel in fiscal year 2010, Marvel had licensed the rights to third-party studios to produce and distribute feature films based on certain Marvel properties including Spider-Man, The Fantastic Four and X-Men. Under the licensing arrangements, the third-party studios incur the costs to produce and distribute the films, and the Company retains the merchandise licensing rights. Under the licensing arrangement for Spider-Man, the Company pays the third-party studio a licensing fee based on each film's box office receipts, subject to specified limits. Under the licensing arrangements for The Fantastic Four and X-Men, the third-party studio pays the Company a licensing fee and receives a share of the Company's merchandise revenue on these properties.
>
> (The Walt Disney Company 2017, 11)

Therefore, almost seven years after the acquisition of Marvel, the value for Disney is still the intellectual property rights and the licensing fees. This point brings us back to the Fox acquisition and the *Fantastic Four*.

From the *Fantastic Four* to the not-so-fantastic

The *Fantastic Four* film franchise has had a rather ignoble history. The film rights for the characters were acquired by Bernd Eichinger for the German film production company Constantin Film. It was with these rights that a low-budget *Fantastic Four* film was put into production with Roger Corman in 1992. This production has become part of comics and film culture legend, due in no small part to the fact that the final film was never given a full release to theaters. In fact, many have speculated that the film was only put into production in order to maintain the film rights. The 2015 documentary *Doomed! The Untold Story of Roger Corman's Fantastic Four* interviews several cast and crew members who were involved in the production, and their sense of disappointment in a project they imagined would launch their careers is an uncomfortable combination of the comic and the tragic. The film and the film's trailer are currently (and perhaps illegally) available on *YouTube*, and even a cursory viewing reveals a production that at best could be described as slip-shod. The abysmal production values alone provide sufficient evidence to suggest the film was never meant for a theatrical release, and the fact the film is not even listed on imdb.com is also telling.

In spite of this dubious cinematic venture, the film rights were retained by Eichinger, who then partnered with 20th Century Fox to produce the big-budget *Fantastic Four* release in 2005 and the *Fantastic Four: Rise of the Silver Surfer* in 2007. These films actually had the support of the studio and had production budgets of $100 million and $130 million, respectively. Admittedly, the cast was heavy with television talent, and the films appeared well before Chris Evans would have the box office draw to play Captain America, but the studio's commitment to the productions was still exponentially greater than their predecessor. In addition, Fox made sure the film exploited the ancillary market, and among the products spun-off from the films were two videogames mentioned above: *Fantastic Four* (2005), published by Activision, and *Fantastic Four: Rise of the Silver Surfer* (2007), published by 2K Games. In spite of this commitment, the first film was only moderately successful, with a worldwide box office gross of $330 million, and the second film fared even worse with a $289 million worldwide gross. Neither of the films received much critical praise, with the first film only receiving a 27 percent score on Rotten Tomatoes, and the second only performing slightly above that, at 37 percent. From a critical standpoint, the videogames did not do much better. In his review for *IGN.com*, Juan Castro warns readers that while *Fantastic Four* is a "passable action game," players should "rent this one first" (2005, 22). The review for the second game, authored by Greg Miller, was subtitled: "A game so bad it puts Dr. Doom to shame" (2007, 1). Given the disappointing response, Fox passed on the option for a third film in the franchise. Fox decided to reboot the franchise with the 2015 release, a film that was, as noted above, savaged by the critics and only generated $167 in box office receipts worldwide.

To put it bluntly, Eichinger and Fox have been very poor stewards of the *Fantastic Four* franchise. After nearly 25 years and four productions, the studio has yet to turn this Marvel property into a franchise that stands with other properties from the Marvel universe, most notably the *Avengers*, *Spider-Man*, and *Black Panther*. This is surprising given that the *Fantastic Four* was considered to be one of the first and most enduring successes for Marvel comics. Marvel, too, could not have been happy with the *Fantastic Four* productions, but what the company chose to do about it surprised and disappointed the comic book's fans: Marvel announced it was ceasing publication of the *Fantastic Four*, with the last issue appearing in May 2015, just a few months prior to the release of the last film. The timing was suspect, and certain fan sites voiced their suspicion, referencing the *Tumblr* post by Brevoort we have already quoted. Brevoort (2014) was responding to an inquiry regarding the *X-Men*, a franchise for which Fox also owned the film rights. While fans speculated that Brevoort was also referring to the Fantastic Four, even putting his intentions to one side, the comment is certainly applicable. As long as Fox maintained the film rights to the Fantastic

Four, Marvel would have limited control over the direction of the franchise and enjoy limited compensation at the box office. This compensation would be further limited for those films that performed poorly at the box office, with the last *Fantastic Four* film being a case in point.

When Marvel Studios began, it was completely dependent on studios like Fox and Sony to finance productions and handle distribution. Even when Marvel started self-financing with *Iron Man* in 2008, it was still dependent on Paramount for distribution. After Disney acquired Marvel in 2009, Marvel was no longer dependent on other partnerships, either for financing or distribution. Instead, Disney had the corporate infrastructure to produce and distribute the films, and manage all of the ancillary products associated with the Marvel universe. In addition, given Disney's history and corporate culture regarding intellectual property, it is not difficult to imagine that they would want to retain the rights to the Fantastic Four at a cost; or more to the point, at the cost of the comic's publication. In fact, when the revenues of the film franchises are placed against the revenues generated by comic book publishing, it is clear that Disney had less to lose by pulling the publication of *Fantastic Four*, and much more to gain.

Disney and Fox

Drawing lines of causation can often be a dubious proposition, so in this section, we offer our points as speculative. Nevertheless, the timing of events related to Disney's efforts to acquire Fox and the recent publication history of the Fantastic Four certainly invite speculation because they align very closely with important events. For example, the announcement to discontinue the publication of *Fantastic Four* was made in October 2014, during the New York Comic Con, less than a year before the last film was released by Fox. At this point, the film had not generated much buzz, either positive or negative, so the motive behind this move raised suspicion. As Anita Busch, writing for *Deadline Hollywood*, observed: "We had heard that Marvel wanted to use the Fantastic Four characters in future Avengers films, so it could be a way for Marvel to put pressure on the studio. Or maybe it doesn't want the competition at the box office as 2015 is gearing up to be one helluva [*sic*] crowded market […] and Marvel will be vying against Fox and others on a number of tentpole films. Marvel spokespeople could not be reached for comment" (Busch 2014, 1).

Marvel's silence on this issue is not surprising, and to be fair, Brevoort would at least speak to the issue indirectly, as noted earlier. If, however, Marvel wanted to put pressure on Fox, then ceasing publication of *Fantastic Four* had the effect, intended or not, to significantly lower the value of the comic's intellectual property. Indeed, it is important to remember that Marvel Studios was conceived in reaction to Perelman's threat to close down publication of all Marvel comics. This history most likely has not been forgotten at Marvel, even after its acquisition by Disney. And given

Disney's understanding of the value of intellectual property, and its hardball tactics with day-care centers, it is not unimaginable that the cancelation was strategic.

Clearly, Disney's motive to buy out Fox was not completely driven by the rights to the Fantastic Four because the deal put much more on the table. Negotiations between Bob Iger and Rupert Murdoch began in August 2017 and continued for the next few months. The boards of both companies came to a preliminary agreement that was announced in December 2017. The deal was finalized in July 2018; on 20 March 2019, the acquisition was officially announced, and the assets not acquired by Disney were formed into a new company called the Fox Corporation. A day prior, the new Fox Corporation began trading on the NASDAQ, and former US House Speaker Paul Ryan was appointed to the new corporate board (Stelter 2019).

As for the timing of this deal, it is worth noting that only three months prior to the July announcement finalizing the merger, Marvel announced that it was putting *Fantastic Four* back into publication. The first new issue of the *Fantastic Four* was released on 8 August 2018, less than two months after the merger was approved by the US Department of Justice. The fact that the comic book was put back into publication at this time seems to signify a renewed interest in this intellectual property. As discussed above, while the Fantastic Four may have had little to do with the merger, the merger seems to have had everything to do with the Fantastic Four.

Although Disney's acquisition does not secure the Fantastic Four film rights for Marvel, they will have the international distribution rights, without which Constantin's production rights have very limited value. For example, with the 2015 reboot, Fox handled theatrical distribution in the US and 18 other territories, including important markets in Europe and Asia.[4] Furthermore, given the abysmal performance of the last reboot, the *Fantastic Four* film franchise is not very attractive to the other Hollywood studios with international distribution infrastructures (keeping in mind there are now only four others). In other words, even if Constantin does not sell the film rights to Marvel, they may have no other options for distribution partners but Disney, moving forward.

A word about fan culture and political economy

There has been an ongoing and, we would argue, dubious division between the celebration of fan culture as a point of consumer empowerment and the critique of capitalism in the current media climate. Christian Fuchs (2017) provides a strong analysis of this division in his book on social media, particularly when he discusses the way Henry Jenkins imagines participatory culture. As he notes, although Jenkins acknowledges the presence of capital as a driver in media decisions, Jenkins continually positions consumer empowerment as a satisfactory check on those in power. While we would not agree with Fuchs's references to fascism, we make no apologies for our alignment with the political economists. In addition, it is important to search for moments when consumer empowerment and the critique of capitalism align, not as a satisfactory challenge, but as an opportunity when consumers recognize that their interests are not what drives the decisions of media conglomerates.

When announcements about the cancelation of *Fantastic Four* appeared, one of the most exacting critics of this move was Rick Johnson, founder of the comic book blog *Bleeding Cool*. Johnson first posted about the absence of the Fantastic Four on the cover of Marvel's 75th Anniversary Issue, noting that the absence was a "deliberate, if understandable choice," perhaps indicating Marvel's intention to promote other superheroes in its films and television shows (2014a, 5). Later, Johnson would also comment on the *Fantastic Four* cancelation: "Twentieth Century Fox pretty much has an eternal claim on Fantastic Four and X-Men movies, if they keep making them, after the deal was done during Marvel's bankruptcy days, with very little benefit to Marvel. The belief inside the higher echelons of Marvel is that promoting these properties in comics only benefits Fox's movies at the expense of those from Marvel Studios" (Johnson 2014b, 3–4).

When it was announced that the comic would go back into production, Johnson authored a post in which he provided an extensive analysis of Marvel's efforts to scrub the Fantastic Four from fan culture. In addition to canceling the comic, Marvel shut down the production of posters, stature lines, trading cards, and t-shirts; Marvel even pulled permission for the Fantastic Four characters to appear in an art show. As Johnson (2018) notes, all of this was motivated by Marvel's dissatisfaction with Fox, and he saves his harshest criticism for Brevoort for his obfuscation and deceit regarding the motives behind the cancelation. In other words, Johnson provided a sustained critique of Marvel's cancelation of *Fantastic Four*, one that was fully in step with the practices of political economy. The difference that Johnson provides, and it is an important one, is that his critique is posed to demand better fan service from Disney, which is in contrast to those critics who regard Disney's cultural production in very negative terms (Giroux and Pollock 2010).

Johnson would also fall fully within the camp of the empowered fan, one who has created and monetized an ongoing tertiary text informed by his own love for comic books. Although Brevoort acknowledges Johnson's efforts, his acknowledgment is at best dismissive, and the Fantastic Four is a case that illustrates how easy it was for Marvel (and in turn Disney) to dismiss and disregard the interests of fans. Yes, Johnson had agency; and, yes, his complaints gained attention from Marvel. Yet, in the final analysis, the Fantastic Four disappeared from comic book culture for three years, and its disappearance and reemergence have everything to do with Disney's, and in turn Marvel's, relationship with Fox. In other words, when it comes to the bottom line, fan culture often takes a back seat.

Conclusion

The takeaway from the case of the *Fantastic Four* is not to disregard the importance of fan culture, or to overstate the power of media conglomerates. In fact, to suggest that fan culture may take a back seat to corporate interest is not an overstatement, and it should serve as a call for fan culture to continue to be aware of that fact. We would argue that we need fans like Johnson to continue to recognize when and how their interests are being underserved by media conglomerates, and to continue to challenge those companies and their representatives. It is in the interests of fans to not only celebrate their cultures but also to critique the corporate practices that put those cultures at risk. Admittedly, fans may not have power over corporations. They may not always win, and often they may lose. We would still maintain, however, that this kind of romantic struggle is at the heart of the superhero comic book narrative, and as in those narratives, the struggle must continue.

In fact, the struggle may become more important as media consolidation continues apace, and again, Disney and Fox are a case in point. Now that the deal is secured, Disney has roughly a 30 percent market share of the global film market. Also, with controlling interest in Hulu, Disney will be in a much better position to launch its proprietary streaming service, moving its content off other services, including Pixar films, and the content from the *Star Wars* and Marvel universes. In fact, all of the live action Marvel shows on Netflix have been canceled, including *Luke Cage* (2016–2018), *Iron Fist* (2017–2018), *Jessica Jones* (2015–2019), *The Punisher* (2017–2019), and *The Defenders* (2017). As Julia Alexander (2019) notes, while some of these shows are jointly owned by Netflix and will continue to stream on the service, these cancelations will allow Disney to reboot these series for the launch of their own streaming service. So, unsurprisingly, it seems that Disney plans to use the merger to exercise even more control over the media market. Therefore, it is important for fans to be even more mindful, even more suspicious, and even more vocal in their challenges of corporate maneuvers, particularly when those maneuvers put fan culture at risk.

As for the Fantastic Four, in January 2019, Marvel Comics celebrated "Fantastic Four: World's Greatest Week" on its webpage (www.marvel.com/fantastic-four-week; accessed 31 January 2020), revisiting the history of the comic book and making various announcements about its future. During this week, the webpage posted videos including tips on how to play the Fantastic Four characters in the new *Marvel: Future Fight* (2015) mobile videogame, and how to beat Dr. Doom in *Marvel Strike Force* (2018). Therefore, Marvel has already incorporated these characters into their latest videogame releases. Although no plans for a future film were disclosed during this week, there was a special video in which Brevoort is identified as the new editor of the revived *Fantastic Four*. Perhaps we should note that this particular video was preceded with an advertisement for Disney+, the new streaming service that includes a special section for Marvel. In that section, Disney+ offers up old episodes of the *Fantastic Four* cartoon that aired from 1994 to 1996. Clearly, with the acquisition of Fox and the revival by Marvel, Disney is allowing the Fantastic Four to return with a vengeance, and eager to exploit its intellectual property. As Ben Grimm might say: "It's clobberin' time!"

Notes

1 All box office data was retrieved from www.boxofficemojo.com/ on 23 March 2019.
2 One of Bob Iger's first actions as Disney CEO was to acquire the rights to Oswald the Rabbit back in 2006. Universal still owned the character, and in an interesting trade, Disney gave NBC Universal ESPN sportscaster to NBC Sports for the intellectual property rights to Oswald. Disney would then incorporate the character into the *Epic Mickey* (2010) videogame, and Oswald merchandise is readily available in the Disney theme parks.
3 All box office data was retrieved from www.boxofficemojo.com/ on 23 March 2019.
4 This is the information listed on *IMDB* for the film. On an interesting note, and one that illustrates the odd ways of international film distribution, Warner Bros. handled distribution for Belgium, Switzerland, and the Netherlands.

Works cited

Alexander, Julia. 2018. "Netflix Cancels *Jessica Jones* and *The Punisher*." *The Verge*, 18 February. www.theverge.com/2019/2/18/18229507/jessica-jones-punisher-netflix-canceled-iron-fist-daredevil-luke-cage-defenders-disney (accessed 31 January 2020).

Ant-Man and the Wasp. 2018. Dir. Peyton Reed. USA: Walt Disney Studios Motion Pictures.

Avengers: Infinity Wars. 2018. Dir. Anthony Russo and Joe Russo. USA: Walt Disney Studios Motion Pictures.

Black Panther. 2018. Dir. Ryan Coogler. USA: Walt Disney Studios Motion Pictures.

Brevoort, Tom. 2014. "New Brevoort Formspring." *Tumblr*, 31 July. http://brevoortformspring.tumblr.com/post/93403610623/so-i-will-ask-a-different-question-why-isnt (accessed 31 January 2020).

Brookey, Robert Alan, and Robert Westerfelhaus. 2005. "The Digital *auteur*: Branding Identity on the *Monsters, Inc.* DVD." *Western Journal of Communication* 69 (2): 109–128.

A Bug's Life. 1998. Dir. John Lasseter. USA: Buena Vista Pictures Distribution.

Busch, Anita. 2014. "Marvel Cancels 'Fantastic Four' Comic Book Series before Fox 2015 Movie Launch." *Deadline Hollywood*, 13 October. https://deadline.com/2014/10/fantastic-four-comics-cancelled-2015-movie-850498/ (accessed 31 January 2020).

Captain America: The First Avenger. 2011. Dir. Joe Johnston. USA: Paramount Pictures.

Castro, Juan. 2005. "Fantastic Four." *IGN*, 28 June. www.ign.com/articles/2005/06/29/fantastic-4-2 (accessed 31 January 2020).

Ching, Albert. 2014. "Final Issue of *Fantastic Four* Listed for 2015." *CBR*, 5 October. www.cbr.com/final-issue-of-fantastic-four-listed-for-2015/ (accessed 31 January 2020).

Deadpool 2. 2018. Dir. David Leitch. USA: 20th Century Fox.

Doomed! The Untold Story of Roger Corman's Fantastic Four. 2015. Dir. Marty Langford. USA: Uncork'd Entertainment.

Ellingson, Annlee. 2013. "It's Official: 21st Century Fox and Newscorp Spilt, With New Shares to Be Issued Monday." *L. A. Biz*, 30 June. www.bizjournals.com/losangeles/news/2013/06/28/its-official-21st-century-fox-splits.html (accessed 31 January 2020).

Epic Mickey. 2010. Developed by Junction Point Studios. Published by Disney Interactive Studios. Nintendo Wii.

Fantastic Four. 2005. Developed by 7 Studios. Published by Activision. PlayStation 2.

Fantastic Four. 2005. Dir. Tim Story. USA: 20th Century Fox.

Fantastic Four. 2015. Dir. Josh Trank. USA: 20th Century Fox.

Fantastic Four: Rise of the Silver Surfer. 2007. Developed by 7 Studios. Published by 2K Games. PlayStation 2.

Fantastic Four: Rise of the Silver Surfer. 2007. Dir. Tim Story. USA: 20th Century Fox.

Finding Nemo. 2003. Dir. Andrew Stanton. USA: Buena Vista Pictures Distribution.

Fort Lauderdale News, and Sun-Sentinel. 1989. "Cartoon Figures Run Afoul of Law." *Chicago Tribune*, 27 April. www.chicagotribune.com/news/ct-xpm-1989-04-27-8904070716-story.html (accessed 31 January 2020).

Fuchs, Christian. 2017. *Social Media: A Critical Introduction*. London: Sage.

Gardner, Eriq. 2015. "Disney Sues over Edible Cake Frosting Featuring Marvel, Lucasfilm Characters." *The Hollywood Reporter*, 3 September. www.hollywoodreporter.com/thr-esq/disney-sues-edible-cake-frosting-820032 (accessed 31 January 2020).

Giroux, Henry, and Pollock, Grace. 2010. *The Mouse That Roared: Disney and the End of Innocence*. Lanham, MD: Rowman and Littlefield.

Holson, Laura. 2006. "Disney Agrees to Acquire Pixar in a $7.4 Billion Deal." *The New York Times*, 25 January. www.nytimes.com/2006/01/25/business/disney-agrees-to-acquire-pixar-in-a-74-billion-deal.html (accessed 31 January 2020).

Iron Man. 2008. Dir. Jon Favreau. USA: Paramount Pictures.

Iron Man 2. 2010. Dir. Jon Favreau. USA: Paramount Pictures.

Johnson, Rich. 2014a. "Reboots, Guardians and No More Mutants." *Bleeding Cool*, 23 May. www.bleedingcool.com/2014/05/23/reboots-guardians-and-no-more-mutants/ (accessed 31 January 2020).

Johnson, Rich. 2014b. "Would Marvel Really Cancel *Fantastic Four* to Snub Fox?" *Bleeding Cool*, 29 May. www.bleedingcool.com/2014/05/29/would-marvel-really-cancel-fantastic-four-to-snub-fox/ (accessed 31 January 2020).

Johnson, Rich. 2018. "A History of Why Marvel Comics Didn't Publish the *Fantastic Four* for 3 Years." *Bleeding Cool*, 29 March. www.bleedingcool.com/2018/03/29/history-marvel-comics-fantastic-four/ (accessed 31 January 2020).

Marvel: Future Fight. 2015. Developed and published by Netmarble Games. iOS.

Marvel Strike Force. 2018. Developed and published by FoxNext Games Los Angeles. iOS.

McCarthy, Todd. 2015. "'Fantastic Four' Film Review." *The Hollywood Reporter*, 8 August. www.hollywoodreporter.com/review/film-review-fantastic-four-813140 (accessed 31 January 2020).

Miller, Greg. 2007. "'Fantastic Four: Rise of the Silver Surfer' Review." *IGN*, 18 June. www.ign.com/articles/2007/06/18/fantastic-4-rise-of-the-silver-surfer-review-3 (accessed 31 January 2020).
Monsters, Inc. 2001. Dir. Pete Docter. USA: Buena Vista Pictures Distribution.
Mosco, Vincent. 1996. *The Political Economy of Communication: Rethinking and Renewal*. Los Angeles: Sage.
Paul Blart: Mall Cop 2. 2015. Dir. Andy Fickman. USA: Columbia Pictures.
Plane Crazy. 1928. Dir. Walt Disney and Ub Iwerks. USA: Celebrity Productions.
Raviv, Dan. 2004. *Comic Wars: Marvel's Battle for Survival*. Sea Cliff: Levant Book.
Robinson, James, and Leonard Kirk. 2015. *Fantastic Four* Vol. 4: *The End Is Fourever*. New York: Marvel Comics.
Roeper, Richard. 2015. "'Fantastic Four': A Lightweight Marvel Origin Story Flames Out." *Chicago Sun Times*, 6 August. https://chicago.suntimes.com/entertainment/fantastic-four-a-lightweight-marvel-origin-story-flames-out/ (accessed 31 January 2020).
Scott, A. O. 2015. "Review: 'Fantastic Four,' the Reboot (Wanted or Not)." *The New York Times*, 6 August. www.nytimes.com/2015/08/07/movies/review-fantastic-four-the-reboot-wanted-or-not.html (accessed 31 January 2020).
Slott, Dan, and Sara Pichelli. 2018. *Fantastic Four* #1. New York: Marvel Comics.
Spider-Man. 2002. Dir. Sam Raimi. USA: Sony Pictures.
Spider-Man 2. 2004. Dir. Sam Raimi. USA: Sony Pictures.
Spider-Man 3. 2007. Dir. Sam Raimi. USA: Sony Pictures.
Spider-Man: Homecoming. 2017. Dir. Jon Watts. USA: Sony Pictures.
Steamboat Willie. 1928. Dir. Walt Disney and Ub Iwerks. USA: Celebrity Productions.
Stelter, Brian. 2019. "Former Speaker of the House Paul Ryan Joins Board of Fox Corporation." *CNN Business*, 19 March. www.cnn.com/2019/03/19/media/paul-ryan-fox-corporation/index.html (accessed 31 January 2020).
Thomas, Bob. 1994. *An American Original: Walt Disney*. Glendale: Disney Editions.
Thor. 2011. Dir. Kenneth Branagh. USA: Paramount Pictures.
Thor: Ragnarok. 2017. Dir. Taika Waititi. USA: Walt Disney Studios Motion Pictures.
Toy Story. 1995. Dir. John Lasseter. USA: Buena Vista Pictures Distribution.
Travers, Peter. 2015. "*Fantastic Four* Movie Review." *Rolling Stone*, 6 August. www.rollingstone.com/movies/movie-reviews/fantastic-four-movie-review-246262/ (accessed 31 January 2020).
X-Men. 2000. Dir. Bryan Singer. USA: 20th Century Fox.

11 The road to *Arkham Asylum*

Batman: Dark Tomorrow and transitional transmedia

James Fleury

The period of 1997 to 2005 represented a branding crisis for the Batman intellectual property (IP), or brand. During this time, Warner Bros., DC Comics, and their conglomerate parents Time Warner and AOL Time Warner struggled to revive the character as a film franchise after the disappointing critical and commercial performance of *Batman and Robin* (1997).[1] Prior to the reboot *Batman Begins* (2005), Batman continued to appear in comic books (e.g., crossover arcs such as 1999's "No Man's Land") and animated television series (e.g., *Justice League* [2001–2004]). This left Time Warner and AOL Time Warner without a theatrical film release capable of powering a "synergy" campaign, where they could use different corporate holdings to cross-promote one another.

Dating back to *Superman: The Movie* (1978), the conglomerate then known as Warner Communications Inc. (WCI)—which became Time Warner in 1990, after merging with Time Inc.—had used its comic book IP as the basis for synergistic films. *Superman: The Movie* not only adapted an internal IP, but it also demonstrated to WCI the cost efficiency of repurposing a product across its divisions. The film drew from and added to DC Comics stories while also inspiring a Warner Bros. Records soundtrack, tie-ins from Warner Books, and a 1978 Atari videogame.[2] The game, with a plot that loosely adapts a sequence from the film—in which an earthquake endangers a bridge—but with promotional art taken from the comics, reflects a dual licensing strategy involving separate rights to *Superman: The Movie* and the comics (see Figure 11.1).

This allowed WCI to collect a greater portion of the comics-licensing profits compared to the film-licensing rights that were shared with independent producers Alexander and Ilya Salkind (Screen International 1978, 12). As Eileen Meehan (2015, 78) has analyzed, WCI took a similar approach with *Batman* (1989), with Warner Bros. licensing out the film rights and DC licensing out rights to the character's comics incarnation. As part of this dual licensing strategy, Sunsoft published a pair of multiplatform videogame tie-ins: 1990's *Batman: The Video Game*, which adapted the film's narrative, and 1991's *Batman: Return of the Joker*, whose licensing from DC Comics—and not Warner Bros.—positioned it as a sequel to the

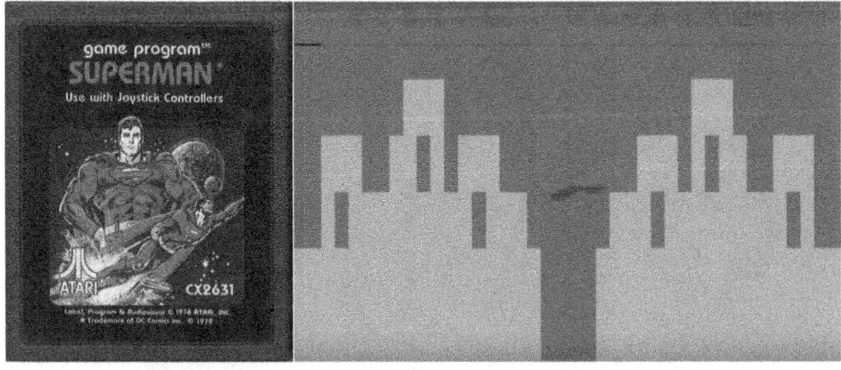

Figure 11.1 Dual film and comic book licensing in *Superman* (1978) (composite by the author).

1990 game rather than to the film despite using the film's font and vehicular designs (see Figure 11.2).

The licensing program for the sequels *Batman Returns* (1992), *Batman Forever* (1995), and *Batman and Robin* focused more on the films themselves. As such, the tie-in videogames—from publishers Acclaim Entertainment, Atari, Konami, Sega, and Tiger Electronics—all adapted their respective film's plot, characters, and settings. By the late 1990s, tie-in games had become an expected component of a film's network of ancillary, or paratextual, material. With the cinematic future of Batman in limbo after *Batman and Robin*, Time Warner and AOL Time Warner returned to a dual licensing strategy to maintain the IP's gaming presence. First, Warner Bros. partnered with publishers on games set in the "DC Animated Universe." Ubisoft, for instance, released *Batman: Vengeance* in 2001 and *Batman: Rise of Sin Tzu* two years later, with each featuring an original story set in the world of *The New Batman Adventures* animated series (1997–1999). Second, DC Comics separately licensed out the rights for comics-based games, including 2003's *Batman: Dark Tomorrow* from publisher Kemco and developer Hot Gen. Like Ubisoft's titles, *Batman: Dark Tomorrow* presents a new story, one whose characters and storyworld derive from the comics and that extends into a two-issue series. Then, in 2004, Warner Bros. formed the Warner Bros. Interactive Entertainment (WBIE) videogame subsidiary, which has embraced in-house development and publishing over licensing partnerships while also focusing on Batman games not tied to other media, such as the *LEGO Batman* (2008–), *Injustice* (2013–), and *Arkhamverse* (2009–2016) transmedia franchises.

As *Batman: Vengeance*, *Batman: Rise of Sin Tzu*, and *Batman: Dark Tomorrow* all suggest, the positioning of licensed videogames—whether created internally by the IP owner or externally by a vendor—had started

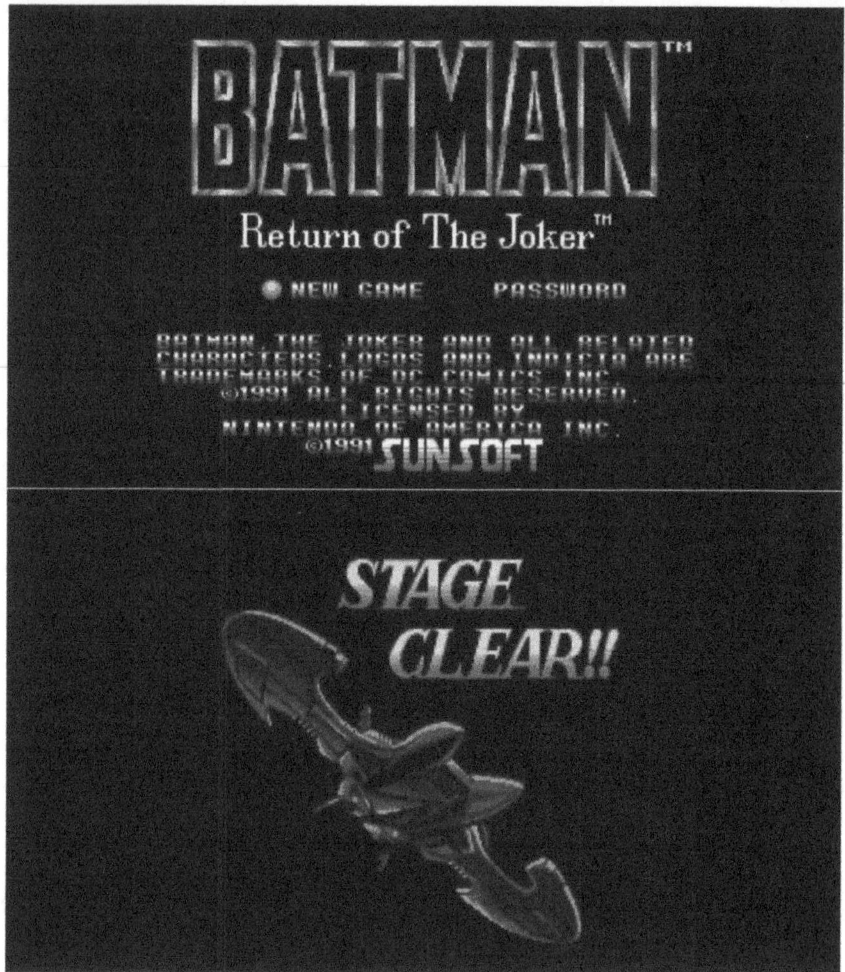

Figure 11.2 Comic book licensing combined with film elements in *Batman: Return of the Joker* (1991) (composite by the author).

to shift from "multimedia" to "transmedia" by the early 2000s. That is, whereas earlier Batman tie-ins had *replicated* film narratives, these newer games *expanded* the storyworlds of their respective franchise. More recently, as WBIE's Batman projects demonstrate, licensed games have shifted even further away from replication; instead of adapting elements from a *single* text (e.g., a film, TV show, or comic book arc), *LEGO Batman, Injustice*, and the *Arkhamverse* adapt elements from *multiple* texts to present amalgamated, unique interpretations of Batman that have inspired their own distinct franchises.

In this chapter, I analyze how *Batman: Dark Tomorrow* reflects changes in tie-in videogame production in the early 2000s and also prefigures the transmedia storytelling framework of the *Arkhamverse* franchise that began with *Batman: Arkham Asylum* (2009). While *Batman: Dark Tomorrow* anchored itself to the comic books, *Batman: Arkham Asylum* arrived in a different gaming landscape and consolidated elements from across the history of Batman media, including not just the comics but also the film and TV incarnations. Both games express how media franchises have turned to paratexts to sustain IP in between film releases, with *Batman: Dark Tomorrow* debuting prior to *Batman Begins* and *Batman: Arkham Asylum* arriving in between *The Dark Knight* (2008) and *The Dark Knight Rises* (2012). After providing an overview of developments in scholarly and management approaches to transmedia storytelling, I examine how the Batman IP represents a complex web of multiple—sometimes intersecting, sometimes isolated—franchises. I then analyze the transmedia elements of *Batman: Dark Tomorrow* before concluding with an exploration as to why *Batman: Arkham Asylum* went on to receive a decidedly more enthusiastic response from critics and audiences. Together, these games demonstrate that efforts to implement transmedia storytelling in relation to Batman have proven challenging due to the IP's multifranchisality. Based on a political economy of the media perspective and close readings of the games themselves, I argue that the difference in reception for *Batman: Dark Tomorrow* and *Batman: Arkham Asylum* lies in a combination of adaptation approaches and changes in managing media industry convergence.

Approaches to studying and franchising Batman

Developments in transmedia studies and media franchise management have followed a similar path of prioritizing narrative development before focusing on "storyworld" development. Introduced in Marsha Kinder's *Playing with Power in Television, Movies and Video Games: From Muppet Babies to Teenage Mutant Ninja Turtles* (1991), the concept of transmedia storytelling—as Henry Jenkins defines it in *Convergence Culture: Where Old and New Media Collide*—refers to a narrative that "unfolds across multiple media platforms, with each new text making a distinctive and valuable contribution to the whole" (2006, 97–98). Jenkins argues that transmedia storytelling represents "a new aesthetic that has emerged in response to media convergence" (Jenkins 2006, 20–21). By convergence, he means "a situation in which multiple media systems coexist and where media content flows fluidly across them" (2006, 20, 322). Whereas Jenkins focuses on late-twentieth and early-twenty-first-century examples of convergence, encouraged by then-emergent technologies like the internet and mobile devices, Avi Santo (2015) as well as Kristin Fast and Henrik Örnebring (2017) have reminded us that pre-digital media convergence also supported an industrial strategy of transmedia (e.g., introduced on the radio in 1930, *The Shadow* brought together pulp magazines, comic strips, and film shorts).

In addition to exploring the analogue origins of transmedia, scholars—including Jenkins himself—have expanded their attention from *narratives* carried across media texts to the development of *storyworlds* across media texts (Ryan and Thon 2014, 1). Based on this more recent scholarship, Matthew Freeman has defined transmedia storytelling as a set of industry "strategies for holding fictional story worlds [*sic*] together across multiple media and for pointing audiences across those media" (2016, 3). This definition encourages a more expansive view of transmedia not just for scholars but also for industry practitioners. In the narrative-centric model of transmedia, as Jenkins puts it, "each medium does what it does best," and "[e]ach franchise entry needs to be self-contained" without being redundant. However, even he describes this as an "ideal form of transmedia storytelling" (Jenkins 2006, 98). To achieve this "ideal," creative stakeholders (e.g., the IP owner and any licensees), according to Fast and Örnebring, need to take a "planned (i.e., strategic, coordinated)" (2017, 637) approach. Prioritizing the expansion of a storyworld instead of a narrative, though, leaves more room for an "emergent (i.e., unplanned, contingent, organic)" approach that can better respond to creative developments and market trends while also encouraging closer engagement with the audience, permitting, for instance, fan contributions to media franchises (Fast and Örnebring 2017, 637).

For scholars, broadening the focus from narrative-building to world-building takes account of not only the value of fan practices (e.g., as Marta Boni explains, digital technologies have underscored the extent to which "textual poaching, participatory culture and sharing activities can also complement official marketing strategies" [2017, 18]) but also the practical challenges of coordinating transmedia campaigns. In the introduction to their edited collection *Star Wars and the History of Transmedia Storytelling* (2017), Sean Guynes and Dan Hassler-Forest write regarding the collection's essays: "While it may seem as though transmedia franchises such as *Star Wars* have become all-powerful entertainment empires, these analyses of key moments show how precarious, unpredictable, and strangely unstable the *Star Wars* storyworld has truly been" (2017, 13). Studying world-building instead of just narrative, then, helps draw attention to the difficulties of establishing and sustaining transmedia franchises. If the narrative-based form of transmedia assumes a "top-down" model in which rights-owners exercise complete control, the more expansive perspective of world-building acknowledges their lack of control.[3]

In fact, the shift from multimedia to transmedia represents a franchise management strategy designed to compensate for this lack of control. As I have discussed elsewhere (with Bryan Hikari Hartzheim and Stephen Mamber), multimedia involves texts that "adapt shared material (e.g., a novelization or tie-in videogame that retells a film's story)" whereas transmedia texts deliver "different material so that the totality of a franchise presents an overarching story" (Fleury et al. 2019, 1). In general, moving from multimedia to transmedia management helps IP owners "create heightened interest across their brands [...] in response to shifting audience and technological trends" (Fleury et al. 2019, 1). Tie-in videogames, for example, moved from multimedia replication to transmedia expansion to address changes in consumer taste and hardware developments.

Typically released in time for a film's theatrical opening weekend or arrival on home video, tie-ins are designed to leverage the accompanying marketing budget and provide cross-promotion. By the 1990s, technological advancements (e.g., more photorealistic graphics and higher-capacity memory) encouraged games that could more faithfully recreate the look, sound, and scope of a given film at the expense of a longer development period. At the same time, tie-in developers have tended to struggle with limited access to film material like scripts and footage, which has restricted the ability for tie-ins to provide a faithful adaptation. This limited access and the increasingly long time needed for development made it difficult for tie-ins to appear in time for a film's theatrical or home video release date without sacrificing gameplay or presentation quality. As a result, tie-ins that directly adapted a film's narrative developed a negative reputation among players and critics.[4] A compensatory trend that became especially common in the 2000s, fewer tie-ins adapted film narratives and instead began to present original stories (e.g., sequels and prequels) set in the same world. Transmedia, then, allowed for tie-ins to still exploit a film's accompanying publicity without needing to gain access to a script or footage. With no new Batman films at the time, *Batman: Dark Tomorrow* served as the main text, or what Jenkins (2014) has called the "mothership," of its own transmedia constellation connected to the franchise's comics.

By the end of the 2000s, tie-ins had begun to migrate from home consoles (e.g., Microsoft's Xbox and Sony's PlayStation hardware) to mobile platforms (i.e., smartphones and tablets). For developers and IP owners, mobile devices allow for faster and less expensive development so that games can more easily arrive in time for a film release. For consumers, the low, or even free (with "in-app purchases"), download cost of these apps presents a lower barrier to entry than a $60 console game (Kohler 2013). Despite the film tie-in market moving more and more to mobile, consoles continue to receive licensed games. Unlike multimedia and transmedia products that directly adapt a film's elements, games such as those within the *Arkhamverse* take a more "general" approach that uses a nonspecific version of an IP.

This approach simultaneously promotes a larger media brand, rather than just a single film of that brand, and can serve as the foundation for a new transmedia franchise in its own right. Although these general licensed games do not directly adapt specific aspects of other franchise texts, they still function as world-building for an IP. As such, they avoid some of the problems associated with transmedia tie-ins to films, such as a tendency for subsequent film releases to supersede the contributions of paratexts (e.g., *The Amazing Spider-Man 2* [2014] presents a version of the Rhino [played by Paul Giamatti] that contradicts the characterization from the previous tie-in game *The Amazing Spider-Man* [2012]). As Freeman notes, when focused on extending a narrative rather than a world, "transmedia storytelling is often a messy system of contingencies, alternatives, and reboots" (2017, 63). By not adding to a film's narrative, general licensed games follow what Jenkins describes as a transmedia storytelling trend in which continuity matters less than "multiplicity—the possibility of alternative versions of the characters or parallel universe versions of the stories" (2009b, n.p.). As Clare Parody puts it, multiplicity is "often a rewarding form of mastery over a franchise text, not a source of tension" (2011, 216). General licensed games, then, present a new version of an IP not beholden to the expectations of other media texts. With Batman, *Batman: Dark Tomorrow* represents an early attempt at this generic concept, albeit one still tied to the character's comic books; subsequently, *Batman: Arkham Asylum* would deviate from any single pre-existing version of Batman while inspiring its own, *Arkhamverse* transmedia storyworld.

Based on these shifts in franchise management in general and tie-in game approaches in particular, I propose a model that seeks to make sense of the seemingly multiple Batman franchises. Back in 1991, William Uricchio and Roberta E. Pearson (2015) analyzed how, throughout the late 1980s, the Batman franchise had noticeably splintered, transitioning from an organizational logic of continuity to one of multiplicity due to the economic strategy of synergy—which, as in the case of *Superman: The Movie*, encouraged variations of the same IP. For decades, the Batman comics already had presented a continuity distinct from other media (e.g., the TV series *Batman* [1966–1968]), and this practice continued with the film franchise that began in 1989. However, by the late 1980s, the comics no longer shared a single continuity; instead, standalone mini-series like *The Dark Knight Returns* (1986) and one-shots like *Batman: Gotham by Gaslight* (1989) presented narratives set outside the "canon" of the comics. This splintering prompted Uricchio and Pearson to observe that, because Batman lacks a "primary urtext," multiple versions of the character tend to exist simultaneously at any given time (2015, 207). As Jenkins has noted, "rather than fragmenting or confusing the audience, this multiplicity of Batmen helped fans learn to live in a universe where there were diverse, competing images of their favorite characters and indeed, to appreciate the pleasures of seeing familiar fictions transformed in unpredicted ways" (2009a, n.p.). Over time, the concept of multiplicity has become a common practice within the comic book industry, especially as a way to attract new consumers and offer novelty to existing fans (Pearson 2017, 121).

Because of this, there now exist multiple "Batmen," each of which, I contend, comprise a different franchise. To organize the network of Batman texts, I draw from Nick Browne's "The Political Economy of the Television (Super) Text" (1984). Browne (1984, 176–180) presents several ways to

Category	Description	Examples
Megatext	Everything featuring elements of the Batman intellectual property, whether licensed or unlicensed	All Batman comic books, films, video games, animated series, fan fiction
Supertext	Each Batman franchise, whether licensed or unlicensed	The *Dark Knight* trilogy, the *Arkhamverse*
Individual texts	Each Batman franchise text, whether licensed or unlicensed	*Batman* (Tim Burton, 1989), *Batman: Dead End* (Sandy Collora, 2003)

Figure 11.3 Categories of Batman texts, derived from Nick Browne's "The Political Economy of the Television (Super) Text" (1984).

describe a "television text" and its "context," from the "megatext" ("the text of television," or "everything that has appeared on television") to the "supertext" ("the particular program and all the introductory and interstitial materials," such as advertisements) to "the program proper" (e.g., individual TV series). I apply this framework to distinguish between the Batman "megatext" (everything featuring elements of the IP, whether licensed or unlicensed), Batman "supertexts" (individual Batman franchises, such as the *Arkhamverse*), and individual texts (e.g., each film) (see Figure 11.3). In addition to accounting for IP-owner and audience contributions as well as for overlaps between the categories, this model also helps to emphasize the distinction between the franchise management strategies of *Batman: Dark Tomorrow* and *Batman: Arkham Asylum*.

The transmedia "failure" of *Batman: Dark Tomorrow* and the transmedia "success" of *Batman: Arkham Asylum*

Having splintered in the 1980s, the Batman megatext between 1997 and 2005 followed a trend of dormant film brands embracing paratexts as a form of franchise management. In 1991, Timothy Zahn's novel *Heir to the Empire* had reinvigorated interest in *Star Wars* during the cinematically fallow period between *Star Wars Episode VI: Return of the Jedi* (1983) and *Star Wars Episode I: The Phantom Menace* (1999). More broadly, Zahn's novel popularized the "Expanded Universe" concept, in which paratexts contribute to a larger narrative and storyworld. This model depends on the transmedia integration of multiple platforms to sustain a single, grand story and world. Compared to *Star Wars*, however, industrial and textual circumstances have limited the ability of the Batman brand to embrace a similar, overarching transmedia model.

Specifically, the larger Batman megatext comprises multiple transmedia supertexts, including not just the *Arkhamverse* but also, for instance, the DC Animated Universe and *Injustice*. As the dual licensing strategy between Warner Bros. and DC for *Superman: The Movie* and the 1989 *Batman* film suggests, divisions in the Warner conglomerates historically have competed, rather than cooperated, with each other. This extends from a corporate practice of Warner "siloing" its units to provide each with greater flexibility against the volatile nature of the market for their respective products (Flint 2019; Littleton 2013). Furthermore, whereas *Star Wars* revolves around its films, the Batman IP has long maintained a distinct presence in different media, which has created a decentralized constellation of texts. That is, while the films drive the transmedia storytelling for *Star Wars*, the Batman megatext includes multiple, unrelated supertexts, or different sub-franchises within the larger franchise. As Time Warner, AOL Time Warner, and AT&T have horizontally and vertically expanded across media, these sub-franchises have transitioned from a multimedia format—in which paratexts repeat the narratives of a source text—to a transmedia model—in which paratexts contribute unique narrative and world-building material and enrich one another. *Batman: Dark Tomorrow* and *Batman: Arkham Asylum* demonstrate how the Batman megatext gradually adopted a transmedia model for its supertexts as a management strategy to sustain audience interest in between film releases.

Despite its rather limited multiplatform storytelling and negative reception, *Batman: Dark Tomorrow* paved the road to the *Arkhamverse* transmedia franchise due to its independence from the Batman films and TV series. Throughout the 1990s, few superhero films appeared outside of the four live-action *Batman* installments due to the troubled development on a new *Superman* film and rights complications on Marvel adaptations. While Batman appeared only in games tied to either the films or *Batman: The Animated Series* (1992–1995), other superheroes headlined games based on both their animated and comics incarnations, with some even adapting specific comic book arcs (e.g., *The Death and Return of Superman* [1994] and *Spider-Man and Venom: Maximum Carnage* [1994]). In the early 2000s, as Warner Bros. continued to struggle with launching new superhero films, DC chose to capitalize on its characters. This led to licensed games that adapted general comic book elements (e.g., characters, settings, and art styles) without adapting specific stories, including *Superman: The Man of Steel* (2002), *Aquaman: Battle for Atlantis* (2003), and *Batman: Dark Tomorrow*.

Batman: Dark Tomorrow, in fact, represented the first Batman videogame to have no film or TV ties since the comics-licensed *Batman: The Caped Crusader* (1988). As a press release put it, "'Batman: Dark Tomorrow' is the first modern Batman video game to date based not on the movie or animation series, but on the original DC Comics comic book" (Kombo 2012, n.p.). To distinguish *Batman: Dark Tomorrow* from recent Batman games, Kemco leaned into the DC Comics license. To compensate for the lack of a source film, the publisher hired comics veteran Scott Peterson—who, at the time, was writing *Batman: Gotham Adventures* for DC—and Kenji Terada—the co-writer of the first three installments of the *Final Fantasy* series (1987–1990)—to develop the script. Notably, *Batman: Dark Tomorrow* represents one of the first games to come from a comics writer. This continued a trend at the time of publishers partnering with creative stakeholders from other media to add legitimacy to their licensed products, such as the participation of actors Tobey Maguire and Willem Dafoe in the film tie-in *Spider-Man* (2002) or the involvement of the Wachowskis in the transmedia text *Enter the Matrix* (2003). With a script from writers associated with comics and videogames, *Batman: Dark Tomorrow* distinguishes itself from previous, film- and TV-based Batman titles (see Figure 11.4).

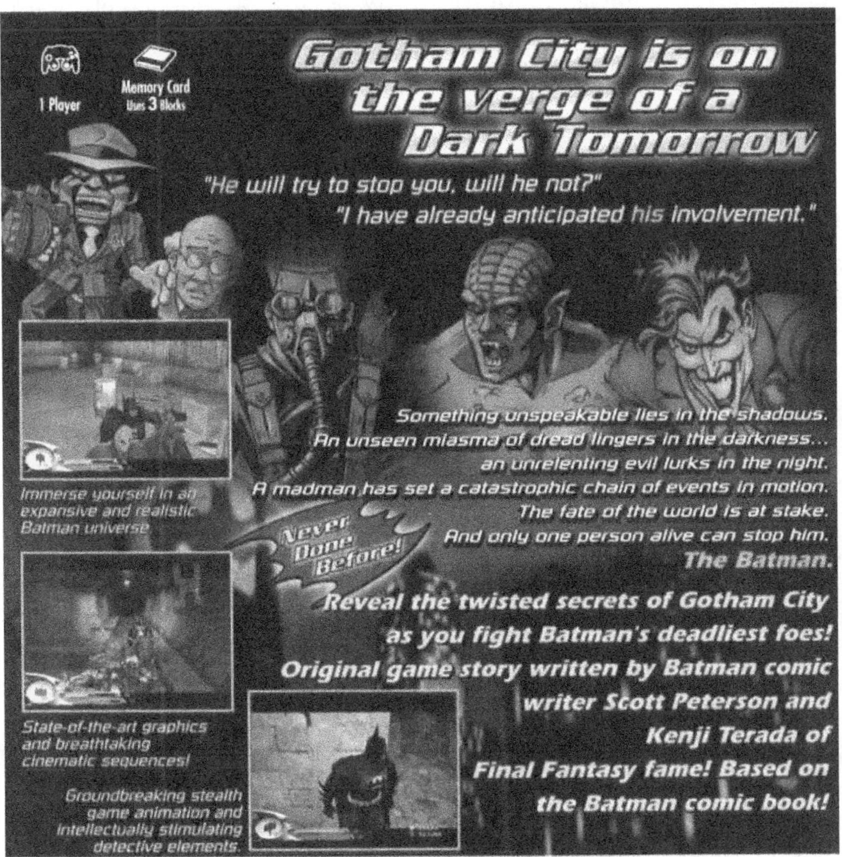

Figure 11.4 The packaging for *Batman: Dark Tomorrow* (2003) emphasizes its ties to the comic books.

The story itself also works to appeal to multiple demographics. It begins with Batman attempting to thwart a gang war between the Ventriloquist, Scarface, and Black Mask while the Joker abducts Commissioner Gordon and holds him hostage at Arkham Asylum. To rescue Gordon, the player—as Batman—must defeat a series of enemies like Poison Ivy, Killer Croc, and Mr. Freeze. Batman eventually discovers that Ra's al Ghul had orchestrated the kidnapping as a distraction from his plot to dominate the world by detonating a number of bombs that will cause natural disasters. As this summary suggests, the story relies on encounters with characters familiar to film audiences as well as characters better known among comics aficionados. With appeals to general audiences, comic book readers, and gaming enthusiasts alike, the game provides several levels of access and meaning.[5]

To expand the game's appeal beyond comic book fans, Kemco also took advantage of the promotional hype machine that powers the videogame industry press. *Batman: Dark Tomorrow* received a considerably warm reception at the 2001 edition of the Electronic Entertainment Expo (E3) trade show, where the publisher announced the project's pedigree of comics and gaming talent and also showcased a non-playable demo featuring computer-animated cutscenes (see Figure 11.5).

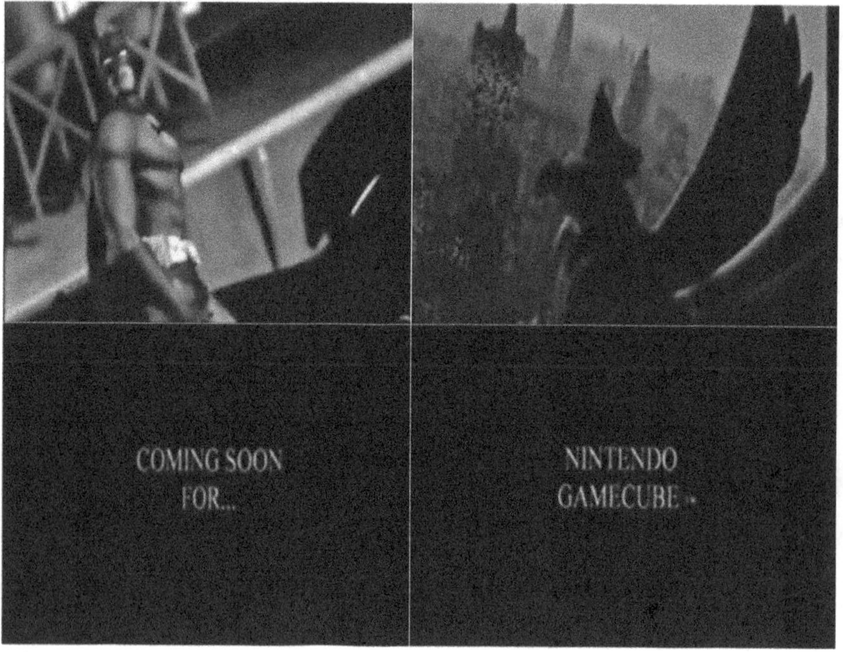

Figure 11.5 Images from the 2001 E3 preview of *Batman: Dark Tomorrow* (composite by the author).

This trailer, however, provided no indication of what the playable portions of the game would look like. This speaks to the emphasis placed on visuals at the time among the gaming press in anticipation of the Fall 2001 releases of the Microsoft Xbox and Nintendo GameCube—consoles that, like the Sony PlayStation 2 that had debuted a year earlier, could achieve more photorealistic graphics than earlier hardware. Justin Speer of *GameSpot*, for instance, wrote the following about the *Batman: Dark Tomorrow* preview video: "While no obvious gameplay elements were demonstrated, beautiful action-packed cutscenes gave proof of the GameCube's rendering power" (2006, n.p.). Although game industry previews allow us to chart a game's development, they tend to be tightly controlled and misleading experiences (Pitts 2016).[6] This often results in published previews that resemble thinly veiled promotions. In the case of *Batman: Dark Tomorrow*, Kemco's focus on production values worked to create an aura of prestige around the visuals and talent involved.

By not highlighting actual gameplay, the publisher withheld a series of problems plaguing the project's development. After announcing *Batman: Dark Tomorrow* as a GameCube exclusive that would arrive in November 2001, Kemco expanded development to the Xbox. Once Microsoft became involved, the company demanded changes to the story and gameplay. This delayed the development process, with Peterson needing to provide rewrites and developer Hot Gen needing to make gameplay and presentation compromises in order to meet the demands of a growing list of stakeholders that included Kemco, Nintendo, Microsoft, and DC. Ultimately, by the time it was released in March 2003, *Batman: Dark Tomorrow* had spent four years in development (Clow 2016; IGN Staff 2001; Speer 2006).

In addition to preview events, Kemco promoted *Batman: Dark Tomorrow* with a two-issue comic book prequel. This collaboration with DC and Peterson added to the project's legitimacy. Reflecting the game's dual address to gamers and comics fans, the first issue arrived as a supplement to gaming magazines like *Nintendo Power* and *GamePro* in November 2002, and the second issue appeared as a pack-in with the game itself. As Glenn Halseth, Kemco's vice president of sales and marketing, stated in a press release: "Creating this custom, limited-edition collectible comic book assures core gamers and Batman fans alike that we are developing and publishing a game that will represent Batman as intended by his original creators" (Kombo 2012, n.p.). Despite representing *Batman: Dark Tomorrow*'s only form of transmedia storytelling expansion, these comics add little to the game's narrative. What story exists merely serves as a vehicle for Batman to encounter a collection of familiar characters. Structurally, the two comics rely on foreshadowing to remind readers of their marketing function as prequels intended to tie-in to a videogame (see Figure 11.6).

In addition to the heavy-handedness of this foreshadowing, the comics fail as transmedia in other areas as well. Specifically, not only do some aspects in the game and the comics contradict each other, but the game also neglects

Figure 11.6 Examples of foreshadowing in the *Batman: Dark Tomorrow* comic books (composite by the author).

to reference events covered in the comics. For instance, both the game and the first issue of the comic feature a flashback depicting the murder of Thomas and Martha Wayne; however, the killer uses a different type of gun in the game compared to the comic book. Additionally, even though Killer Croc is hospitalized after a fight with Batman in the second prequel comic, in the videogame, he and Batman fight again with no reference to their recent duel or his hospitalization. This all suggests a lack of coordination between the videogame and comic book teams and, therefore, indicates the practical challenges of implementing a transmedia project centered on narrative extension rather than world-building.

In several respects, *Batman: Dark Tomorrow* ultimately failed to live up to its gaming press hype or to its comic book origins. As M. J. Clarke (2013) has noted of transmedia TV videogame tie-ins, paratexts tend to bear the marks of their production context. First, Kemco had announced back at E3 2001 that it would follow an ambitious open-world format, with Batman able to freely explore Gotham City in various vehicles like the Batmobile and Batplane. However, the finished product features strictly linear gameplay and no vehicle segments aside from a sequence in which Batman uses a hang-glider. The developers proved unable to realize this ambition, even with the delayed release date—potentially due to competing stakeholder demands.

Second, *Batman: Dark Tomorrow* presents one of four closing cutscenes following the final level. These endings depend on the player taking certain actions in this level, namely preventing Ra's al Ghul from detonating a series of bombs placed around the world and also defeating Ra's in a sword fight. If the player does not succeed in either of these situations, Batman dies from a stab wound and Ra's attains world domination. The other bleak endings feature Batman either dying or failing to save the world (even the version in which Batman only loses in battle shows that the explosions merely have been delayed by seventeen hours). In the victorious ending, Batman both saves the world and wins the duel, while Ra's accidentally dies at the hand of his own sword; however, so as to not kill off a major villain and thereby dictate the continuity of the comic book supertext going forward, Talia al Ghul revives her father in the "Lazarus Pit" after promising Batman: "We shall meet again." Although the opportunity for different endings provides a sense of variety, the game does not make clear how to achieve the victorious variation. Without consulting a gameplay "walkthrough" (i.e., a guide that explains how to progress), the player would not realize the necessity of disarming the bombs' signal device prior to the sword fight with Ra's. Because of this, the player initially will either lose entirely or defeat Ra's but not stop the bombs; at best, then, as Ra's says in the accompanying cutscene, Batman will "have won the battle, but … lost the war." Although the script may provide the requisite high stakes expected in a Batman narrative, the lack of player instruction reflects the flawed game design and troubled development of *Batman: Dark Tomorrow*.

Third, the game lacks camera controls and instead features "fixed" angles whereby the player can adjust the Batman avatar but not the position of the camera. Likely implemented as a strategy to reduce development time, the changing perspective that occurs with each new screen creates a disconnect between the direction the player's thumb moves and that of the avatar. With each screen, the player will need to reorient in order to navigate Batman. When coupled with the unresponsive controls, the fixed camera renders narrative progression nearly impossible. Both of these flaws also make Batman appear inept, having seemingly lost his ability to swing across rooftops or even defend himself against generic goons.

With such an inept presentation of Batman, the game fails to capture the core of the character, despite the visuals presenting an aesthetic authentic to the comics of the time. As a frustrating gaming experience and as a problematic adaptation of the comic book storyworld, *Batman: Dark Tomorrow* achieves what Trevor Elkington has termed "negative synergy" (2009, 222). In other words, it fails to please either players or fans of the source material. Even with the promising presentation and concept that appeared in prerelease material, once *Batman: Dark Tomorrow* became playable, it joined a long line of poorly received Batman games.

Nonetheless, *Batman: Dark Tomorrow* represents a precursor to the direction of the *Arkhamverse*. In 2004—following the release of *Batman: Dark Tomorrow* and other maligned licensed titles like *Superman: The New Superman Adventures* (1999)—Time Warner formed WBIE as a videogame subsidiary of Warner Bros. Significantly, with WBIE, Warner Bros. became the first Hollywood studio to maintain an in-house game division (Fritz 2005). In contrast, other media conglomerates had traditionally kept their videogame units separate from their film studios and even used different names to distinguish between them (e.g., Columbia Pictures and Sony Imagesoft). This corporate positioning underscored that Warner Bros. had established WBIE to control the use of its IP in licensed games—in addition to taking advantage of the fact that, as Randy Nichols (2008, 132) points out, games revenues had continued to outpace those of the American film industry by 2004. To increase its chances of success, Time Warner installed games industry veteran Jason Hall, co-founder of Monolith Productions, as the head of WBIE; in the past, media conglomerate-owned game divisions (e.g., Atari at WCI) typically hired executives from outside the games industry. With Hall's guidance, WBIE worked to improve the reputation of Warner IP among players by instituting a policy in 2004 that tied vendors' royalties to review scores (Gaudiosi 2004). By the time *Batman: Arkham Asylum* arrived five years later, WBIE also had reduced its reliance on licensing by moving into game development itself. Because of the negative critical and commercial reception it and other licensed games had received in the early 2000s, *Batman: Dark Tomorrow* inspired WBIE to take more control over the use of its IP in videogames.

By 2009, licensed games were beginning to move away from direct adaptations of films and TV series in favor of *Batman: Dark Tomorrow*'s more general approach to IP. To minimize risk and to account for the migration of tie-ins to mobile platforms, WBIE started to follow a bifurcated strategy for its home console products (Batchelor 2012).[7] On the one hand, its family-friendly *LEGO* titles have served as tie-ins directly related to films (e.g., *LEGO Harry Potter: Years 5–7* [2011] adapted the last four *Harry Potter* cinematic installments while also cross-promoting the home video release of *Harry Potter and the Deathly Hallows—Part 2* [2011]). On the other hand, games intended for an older, "core" demographic have taken an approach that WBIE's Senior Vice President of International Games Olivier Wolff has explained as "a gaming expression of an IP which stands by itself" (Weber 2013). These games, including the *Arkhamverse* series and *Middle-earth: Shadow of Mordor* (2014), function independently from other media within their respective franchises. Like *Batman: Dark Tomorrow*, *Batman: Arkham Asylum* originally had embraced a generic adaptation approach due to its publisher—Eidos—having only the DC Comics license while Electronic Arts retained the film license from Warner Bros.[8]

Although both *Batman: Dark Tomorrow* and *Batman: Arkham Asylum* relied on the Batman comic book license and not on the films, they met drastically different receptions, with *Batman: Dark Tomorrow*, *Game Informer*'s 0.75-out-of-10 review criticizing the gameplay as "incomprehensible and littered with bugs" (Reiner 2003, n.p.) and even *IGN*'s slightly more optimistic 2.2-out-of-10 review concluding: "This game is crap" (Goldstein 2003, n.p.). By contrast, *Game Informer* called *Batman: Arkham Asylum* "The Best Batman Game Ever Made" (Reiner 2009, n.p.), and *IGN*'s 9.3-out-of-10 review referred to it as "the greatest comic book videogame of all time" (Miller 2010, n.p.). Like *Batman: Dark Tomorrow*, *Batman: Arkham Asylum* and its sequels debuted in years devoid of a Batman film and worked to keep the character in the public consciousness. Whereas tie-ins previously had served as multimedia paratexts to Batman films, the *Arkham* games—as centers of a unique supertext—represented transmedia mothership texts supported by their own paratexts. This suggests how WBIE positioned each *Arkhamverse* game as a blockbuster entertainment in its own right whereas *Batman: Dark Tomorrow*'s development and marketing issues suggest a lack of care on behalf of DC Comics and Time Warner.

Furthermore, while *Batman: Dark Tomorrow* represents a Batman videogame supertext prototype, its transmedia presence was limited only to the comics. Not only does the game's content reflect only the comics of the time, but also its transmedia extensions include just the two prequel comics. *Batman: Arkham Asylum*, both diegetically and extradiegetically, represents a much more ambitious venture. On the level of content, the open-world *Batman: Arkham Asylum* and the larger *Arkhamverse* leverage the inherent multiplicity of the Batman megatext that had become increasingly prevalent since the 1980s. Whereas *Batman: Dark Tomorrow* presents only the comic book incarnation, the *Arkhamverse* consolidates material from multiple Batman media to form what Kalvero A. Sinervo has described as a "palimpsest" (2016). In his transmedia storytelling guide *Comics for Film, Games and Animation: Using Comics to Construct Your Transmedia Storyworld* (2013), Tyler Weaver presents a case study of *Batman: Arkham City* (2011), the second game released as part of the *Arkhamverse*. He notes, "*Arkham Asylum* created an entirely new Batman storyworld, one that blended the best of the comics with the best of the movies and the best of the animated incarnation" (Weaver 2013, 247). This description emphasizes how the *Arkhamverse* consolidates not just any element from across the Batman megatext but specifically those elements that fans tend to regard as "the best," such as acting and writing talent from *Batman: The Animated Series*, the tone of the *Dark Knight* film trilogy, and characters and locations derived from the comic books. Compared to *Batman: Dark Tomorrow*, the *Arkhamverse* presents a much more expansive transmedia storytelling context spread across comic books, mobile apps, a virtual reality experience, and a direct-to-video animated film (see Figure 11.7).

Conclusion

Even though videogame players and Batman fans have long criticized *Batman: Dark Tomorrow*, it nonetheless inspired—however indirectly—the transmedia approach of the *Arkhamverse*.[9] From this perspective, *Batman: Dark Tomorrow* provides the opportunity for a media industries failure study. Matt Hills (2013) and John Thornton Caldwell (2015) have advocated for looking at examples of failure, such as discontinued products or incompatible production cultures, to gain insight on what does not work.

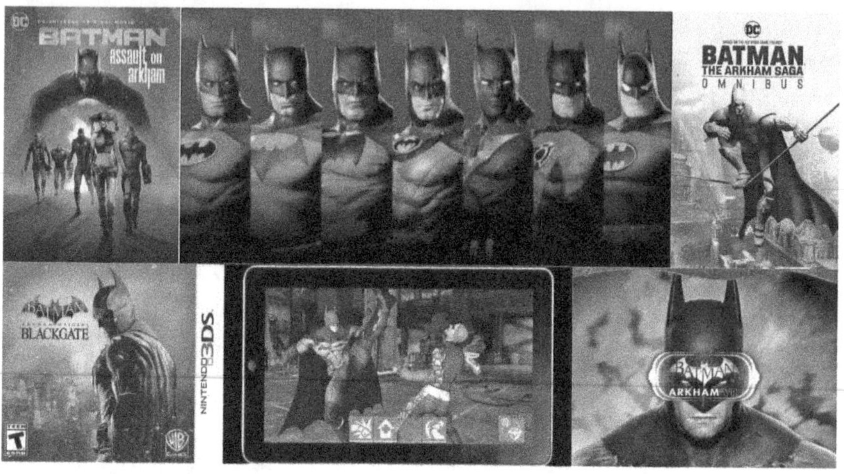

Figure 11.7 Transmedia components of the *Arkhamverse* (composite by the author).

In particular, *Batman: Dark Tomorrow* demonstrated how a videogame could stand apart from other Batman media and form the center of its own transmedia supertext. With the *Arkhamverse*, the games represent the central, mothership text and not an ancillary like a traditional tie-in. More broadly, *Batman: Arkham Asylum* inspired WBIE to approach its IP-based games as distinct; according to Senior Vice President of Digital Gaming Glen Ballard, they "transcend" individual films, such that games featuring a particular IP can adapt a megatext instead of needing to adapt an individual supertext or text featuring that IP. For WBIE, then, the *Arkhamverse* has demonstrated that licensed games can achieve success without explicit textual connections. Just as its licensing penalty had helped legitimize WBIE and the gaming presence of Warner brands, so has the decision to position its games as distinct from other media. Beyond legitimization, the generic adaptation approach helps to promote multiple, related media through a single text. 2015's *Batman: Arkham Knight*, for instance, features content related to the TV series *Batman*, comic book arcs like *Batman: Under the Red Hood* (2004–2006), and films like *Batman v Superman: Dawn of Justice* (2016) (IGN 2016).

Batman: Dark Tomorrow showed how videogames like *Batman: Arkham Asylum* could help maintain brand awareness in years without *Batman* film installments and thereby stimulate sales of previous texts and paratexts. In other words, the generic approach provides these games with a timeless quality that can benefit from, but does not necessarily depend on, the marketing hype for another, related product like a theatrical film release. Other licensors have adopted this approach; for Sony and Marvel, the PlayStation 4–exclusive *Marvel's Spider-Man* (2018) does not directly adapt any pre-existing *Spider-Man* text but instead integrates elements from across the character's megatext. As such, it sustained public awareness about the character in advance of his next film appearance while also driving audiences to other Spider-Man texts. General adaptations like these contrast early media-licensed games from the Atari 2600 era (e.g., 1978's *Superman*), when limited technology meant providing a small narrative around gameplay. Today, the open-world *Arkham* games and *Marvel's Spider-Man* demonstrate how contemporary media-licensed software tends to place gameplay over an expansive, multistory narrative.

Despite its perceived failures, *Batman: Dark Tomorrow* did succeed in sustaining the Batman megatext in between film releases. Its greatest legacy lay in disconnecting from the Batman films or animated series and in demonstrating how a videogame could launch a transmedia extension. In both of these ways, the transitional paratext of *Batman: Dark Tomorrow* paved the road to *Batman: Arkham Asylum* and a more expansive transmedia enterprise.

Notes

1 Internet Service Provider AOL and the Time Warner media conglomerate merged in 2000; however, due to AOL's loss of market value, the corporate masthead reverted back to "Time Warner" in 2003. In 2009, Time Warner divested itself of AOL.

2 The Superman comics exploited the film's marketing hype by reintegrating previously abandoned elements, such as a weakness to kryptonite and Clark Kent's role as a newspaper reporter at *The Daily Planet* (Tye 2012, 544).

3 As Boni writes, "the elements of transmedia storytelling all too often remain part of a designed, top-down experience. Commercial transmedia worlds are often built upon a deterministic vision" (2017, 17).

4 See, for instance, Elkington 2009, who argues that story in tie-ins typically takes precedence over gameplay.

5 This recalls the multiquadrant demographic targeting strategies that blockbuster films often employ, such as 1989's *Batman* appealing to older audiences with a decades-old IP and the casting of Jack Nicholson as well as appealing to young audiences with a young director, Tim Burton, and original music from Prince.

6 Pitts notes that publishers at preview events tend to use the highest-quality hardware within a strictly controlled environment. He warns: "Suffice it to say, take previews with a grain of salt" (Pitts 2016, 132).

7 As an executive from Ubisoft explains: "In our industry, product development is expensive, which means that along with big opportunities there are significant industrial risks [...] World-famous and high-potential IPs aimed at dedicated targets (kids, young male adults, etc.) usually allow a minimisation of these risks" (Batchelor 2012).

8 Electronic Arts held the rights to adapt the *Dark Knight* film trilogy; however, the publisher released only a 2005 tie-in to *Batman Begins* and canceled development on a game based on *The Dark Knight*. By the time *The Dark Knight Rises* was released in 2012, Electronic Arts had lost the rights to the *Batman* film license;

instead, the film's tie-in arrived only on phones and tablets, from mobile developer and publisher Kabam.

9 For examples of critical perspectives on *Batman: Dark Tomorrow*, see Psykhophear 2008; and Crappy Games Wiki Uncensored 2018.

Works cited

The Amazing Spider-Man. 2012. Developed by Beenox. Published by Activision. PlayStation 3.

The Amazing Spider-Man 2. 2014. Dir. Marc Webb. USA: Sony Pictures.

Aquaman: Battle for Atlantis. 2003. Developed by Lucky Chicken Games. Published by TDK Interactive. GameCube.

Batchelor, James. 2012. "Ubisoft: Strong Licences Need Strong Concepts." *MCV*, 20 December. www.mcvuk.com/ubisoft-strong-licences-need-strong-concepts/ (accessed 31 January 2020).

Batman. 1989. Dir. Tim Burton. USA: Warner Bros. Pictures.

Batman: Arkham Asylum. 2009. Developed by Rocksteady Studios. Published by Eidos Interactive and Warner Bros. Interactive Entertainment. PlayStation 3.

Batman: Arkham City. 2011. Developed by Rocksteady Studios. Published by Warner Bros. Interactive Entertainment. PlayStation 3.

Batman: Arkham Knight. 2015. Developed by Rocksteady Studios. Published by Warner Bros. Interactive Entertainment. Xbox One.

Batman: The Caped Crusader. 1988. Developed by Special FX Software Ltd. Published by Data East. MS-DOS.

Batman: Dark Tomorrow. 2003. Developed by Hot Gen. Published by Kemco. GameCube.

Batman: Return of the Joker. 1991. Developed and published by Sunsoft. Nintendo Entertainment System.

Batman: Rise of Sin Tzu. 2003. Developed and published by Ubisoft. GameCube.

Batman: Vengeance. 2001. Developed and published by Ubisoft. GameCube.

Batman: The Video Game. 1990. Developed and published by Sunsoft. Nintendo Entertainment System.

Batman and Robin. 1997. Dir. Joel Schumacher. USA: Warner Bros. Pictures.

Batman Begins. 2005. Developed by Eurocom. Published by Electronic Arts. PlayStation 2.

Batman Begins. 2005. Dir. Christopher Nolan. USA: Warner Bros. Pictures.

Batman Forever. 1995. Dir. Joel Schumacher. USA: Warner Bros. Pictures.

Batman Returns. 1992. Dir. Tim Burton. USA: Warner Bros. Pictures.

Boni, Marta. 2017. "Introduction." In *World Building: Transmedia, Fans, Industries*, edited by Marta Boni, 9–27. Amsterdam: Amsterdam University Press.

Browne, Nick. 1984. "The Political Economy of the Television (Super) Text." *Quarterly Review of Film and Video* 9 (3): 174–182.

Caldwell, John Thornton. 2015. "Production Studies: Where Do We Go from Here?" Paper presented at the Conference of New Directions in Film and Television Production Studies, 14–15 April, Bristol, UK.

Clarke, M. J. 2013. *Transmedia Television: New Trends in Network Serial Production*. New York: Bloomsbury.

Clow, Chris. 2016. "*Batman: Dark Tomorrow* (with Special Guest Scott Peterson)." *Comics on Consoles*, 26 March. Podcast.

Crappy Games Wiki Uncensored. 2018. "*Batman: Dark Tomorrow*." *Crappy Games Wiki Uncensored*, 26 July. https://crappygames.miraheze.org/wiki/Batman:_Dark_Tomorrow (accessed 31 January 2020).

The Dark Knight. 2008. Dir. Christopher Nolan. USA: Warner Bros. Pictures.

The Dark Knight Rises. 2012. Dir. Christopher Nolan. USA: Warner Bros. Pictures.

The Death and Return of Superman. 1994. Developed by Blizzard Entertainment. Published by Sunsoft. SNES.

Elkington, Trevor. 2009. "Too Many Cooks: Media Convergence and Self-Defeating Adaptations." In *The Video Game Theory Reader 2*, edited by Bernard Perron and Mark J. P. Wolf, 213–235. New York: Routledge.

Enter the Matrix. 2003. Developed by Shiny Entertainment. Published by Atari. GameCube.

Fast, Kristin, and Henrik Örnebring. 2017. "Transmedia World-Building: *The Shadow* (1931–Present) and *Transformers* (1984–Present)." *The International Journal of Cultural Studies* 20 (6): 636–652.

Fleury, James, Bryan Hikari Hartzheim, and Stephen Mamber. 2019. "Introduction: The Franchise Era." In *The Franchise Era: Managing Media in the Digital Economy*, edited by James Fleury, Bryan Hikari Hartzheim, and Stephen Mamber, 1–28. Edinburgh: Edinburgh University Press.

Flint, Joe. 2019. "AT&T to HBO, Turner: No More Fiefdoms." *The Wall Street Journal*, 1 March. www.wsj.com/articles/at-t-readying-overhaul-of-warnermedia-11551483138 (accessed 31 January 2020).

Freeman, Matthew. 2016. *Historicising Transmedia Storytelling: Early Twentieth-Century Transmedia Story Worlds*. New York: Routledge.

Freeman, Matthew. 2017. "From Sequel to Quasi-Novelization: *Splinter of the Mind's Eye* and the 1970s Culture of Transmedia Contingency." In Star Wars *and the History of Transmedia Storytelling*, edited by Sean Guynes and Dan Hassler-Forest, 61–72. Amsterdam: Amsterdam University Press.

Fritz, Ben. 2005. "Warner Plays Its Own Game." *Variety*, 9 January. https://variety.com/2005/film/news/warners-plays-its-own-game-1117915856/ (accessed 31 January 2020).

Gaudiosi, John. 2004 "Warner Interactive Aims for Better Film–Game Synergy." *Home Media Magazine*, 19 July. https://web.archive.org/web/20160303221353/www.homemediamagazine.com/news/warner-interactive-aims-better-film-game-synergy-6420 (accessed 31 January 2020).

Goldstein, Hilary. 2003. "*Batman: Dark Tomorrow* Review." *IGN*, 24 March. www.ign.com/articles/2003/03/24/batman-dark-tomorrow-review (accessed 31 January 2020).

Guynes, Sean, and Dan Hassler-Forest. 2017. "Introduction: What Is This Strange World We've Come To?" In Star Wars *and the History of Transmedia Storytelling*, edited by Sean Guynes and Dan Hassler-Forest, 11–13. Amsterdam: Amsterdam University Press.

Harry Potter and the Deathly Hallows—Part 2. 2011. Dir. David Yates. USA: Warner Bros. Pictures.

Hills, Matt. 2013. "TV Aesthetics in Transition: 'Bad' TV Dramas and Discourses of Failure." Paper presented at the Society for Cinema and Media Studies Conference, 7 March, Chicago, US.

IGN. 2016. "*Batman Arkham Knight* Wiki Guide." *IGN*, 3 November. www.ign.com/wikis/batman-arkham-knight/ (accessed 31 January 2020).

IGN Staff. 2001. "Tomorrow Delayed." *IGN*, 25 September. https://au.ign.com/articles/2001/09/25/tomorrow-delayed (accessed 31 January 2020).

Jenkins, Henry. 2006. *Convergence Culture: Where Old and New Media Collide.* New York: New York University Press.

Jenkins, Henry. 2009a. "The Many Lives of the Batman (Revisited): Multiplicity, Manga, and Anime." *Confessions of an Aca-Fan*, 2 February. http://henryjenkins.org/blog/2009/02/the_many_lives_of_the_batman_r.html (accessed 31 January 2020).

Jenkins, Henry. 2009b. "The Revenge of the Origami Unicorn: Seven Principles of Transmedia Storytelling." *Confessions of an Aca-Fan*, 12 December. http://henryjenkins.org/blog/2009/12/the_revenge_of_the_origami_uni.html (accessed 31 January 2020).

Jenkins, Henry. 2014. "The Reign of the Mothership: Transmedia's Past, Present, and Possible Futures." In *Wired TV: Laboring over an Interactive Future*, edited by Denise Mann, 244–268. New Brunswick: Rutgers University Press.

Kinder, Marsha. 1991. *Playing with Power in Television, Movies and Video Games: From Muppet Babies to Teenage Mutant Ninja Turtles.* Berkeley: University of California Press.

Kohler, Chris. 2013. "Why Games Based on Movies Disappeared (and Why They're Coming Back)." *Wired*, 15 February. www.wired.com/2013/02/movie-games/ (accessed 31 January 2020).

Kombo. 2012. "Kemco and DC Comics to Create Limited Edition Comic Book for 'Batman: Dark Tomorrow.'" *GameZone*, 4 May. www.gamezone.com/originals/kemco-and-dc-comics-to-create-limited-edition-comic-book-for-quot-batman-dark-tomorrow-39/ (accessed 31 January 2020).

LEGO Harry Potter: Years 5–7. 2011. Developed by Traveller's Tales. Published by Warner Bros. Interactive Entertainment. PlayStation 3.

Littleton, Cynthia. 2013. "Warner Bros. Embraced Digital Future with Choice of Kevin Tsujihara as CEO." *Variety*, 27 March. https://variety.com/2013/biz/news/warner-bros-embraces-digital-future-in-selecting-kevin-tsujihara-as-ceo-1200328738/ (accessed 31 January 2020).

Marvel's Spider-Man. 2018. Developed by Insomniac Games. Published by Sony Interactive Entertainment. PlayStation 4.

Meehan, Eileen. 2015. "'Holy Commodity Fetish, Batman!': The Political Economy of a Commercial Intertext." In *Many More Lives of the Batman*, edited by Roberta E. Pearson, William Uricchio, and Will Brooker, 69–87. New York: Palgrave Macmillan.

Middle-earth: Shadow of Mordor. 2014. Developed by Monolith Productions. Published by Warner Bros. Interactive Entertainment. Xbox One.

Miller, Greg. 2010. "*Batman: Arkham Asylum* (Game of the Year) Review." *IGN*, 26 May. www.ign.com/articles/2010/05/27/batman-arkham-asylum-game-of-the-year-review (accessed 31 January 2020).

Nichols, Randy. 2008. "Ancillary Markets: Merchandising and Video Games." In *The Contemporary Hollywood Film Industry*, edited by Janet Wasko and Paul McDonald, 132–142. Malden: Wiley-Blackwell.

Parody, Clare. 2011. "Franchising/Adaptation." *Adaptation* 4 (2): 210–218.

Pearson, Roberta E. 2017. "World-Building Logics and Copyright: The Dark Knight and the Great Detective." In *World Building: Transmedia, Fans, Industries*, edited by Marta Boni, 109–128. Amsterdam: Amsterdam University Press.

Pitts, Russ. 2016. *Sex, Drugs, and Cartoon Violence: My Decade as a Video Game Journalist*. Self-published.

Psykhophear. 2008. "Possibly the Worst Batman Game You'll Ever Play." *Giant Bomb*, 5 December.

Reiner, Andrew. 2003. "*Batman: Dark Tomorrow* (GC)." *Game Informer* 121: 87.

Reiner, Andrew. 2009. "*Batman: Arkham Asylum*." *Game Informer*, 27 September.

Ryan, Marie-Laure, and Jan-Noël Thon. 2014. "Storyworlds across Media: Introduction." In *Storyworlds across Media: Toward a Media-Conscious Narratology*, edited by Marie-Laure Ryan and Jan-Noël Thon, 1–21. Lincoln: University of Nebraska Press.

Screen International. 1978. "Selling 'Superman,'" *Screen International* (9 December): 12.

Sinervo, Kalervo A. 2016. "Gotham on the Ground: Transmedia Meets Topography in the Environments of the *Arkham* Videogame Series." *Wide Screen Journal* 6 (1): n.p. http://widescreenjournal.org/index.php/journal/article/view/103/140 (accessed 31 January 2020).

Speer, Justin. 2006. "E3 2001 First Impression: *Batman: Dark Tomorrow*." *GameSpot*, 17 May.

Spider-Man. 2002. Developed by Treyarch. Published by Activision. GameCube.

Spider-Man and Venom: Maximum Carnage. 1994. Developed by Software Creations. Published by LJN. SNES.

Star Wars Episode I: The Phantom Menace. 1999. Dir. George Lucas. USA: 20th Century Fox.

Star Wars Episode VI: Return of the Jedi. 1983. Dir. Richard Marquand. USA: 20th Century Fox.

Superman. 1978. Developed and published by Atari. Atari 2600.

Superman: The Man of Steel. 2002. Developed by Circus Freak. Published by Infogrames. Xbox.

Superman: The Movie. 1978. Dir. Richard Donner. USA: Warner Bros. Pictures.

Superman: The New Superman Adventures. 1999. Developed and published by Titus Interactive. Nintendo 64.

Tye, Larry. 2012. *Superman: The High-Flying History of America's Most Enduring Hero*. New York: Random House.

Uricchio, William, and Roberta E. Pearson. 2015. "I'm Not Fooled by That Cheap Disguise." In *Many More Lives of the Batman*, edited by Roberta E. Pearson, William Uricchio, and Will Brooker, 205–236. New York: Palgrave Macmillan.

Weaver, Tyler. 2013. *Comics for Film, Games and Animation: Using Comics to Construct Your Transmedia Storyworld*. New York: Focal Press.

Weber, Rachel. 2013. "Warner's Wolff: 'We Really Have a Competitive Advantage.'" *GamesIndustry.biz*, 7 October. www.gamesindustry.biz/articles/2013-10-07-olivier-wolff (accessed 31 January 2020).

Zahn, Timothy. 1991. *Heir to the Empire*. New York: Bantam Spectra.

12 When rules collide

Definitional strategies for superheroes across comic books and games

William Uricchio

The summer of 2019 saw Spider-Man in an unlikely position: a pawn, struggled over by Sony, Disney, and Disney's subsidiary Marvel Entertainment. Sony, owner of the character's film rights, but not of the comic book rights, did well with Spider-Man, enjoying its all-time largest global box office earnings in the summer of 2019 with *Spider-Man: Far from Home*. Unfortunately, about the same time, the 2015 deal-sharing agreement between Sony and Marvel that allowed Spider-Man and the Avengers to appear in one another's films collapsed, as Disney sought to tighten the terms of Marvel's collaboration.[1] Ironically, even though *Spider-Man: Far from Home* set the stage for the next major Avengers' storyline, for a time, it seemed as though Spider-Man and the Avengers were unlikely to share screen space. Sony's film Spider-Man was barred from inhabiting the same narrative space as his Marvel colleagues, much as actors with studio contracts were once blocked from working with other studios in the classic Hollywood era.

There are storyworlds and financial worlds, and occasionally they collide. This collision illustrates an underlying law of the universe: The financial world dictates the terms of the storyworld and determines which characters get to interact with others. Rules—in this case emerging from financial and intellectual property considerations—determine the existential conditions of superheroes, their actions, and even their friends. Rules set the conditions for creativity and demarcate the horizon of narrative possibility. For all of the scholarly focus on superhero texts and worlds, rules delimit the behaviors of superheroes, shape their relationship to their worlds, and deserve greater attention as determining elements in the production process.

Rules matter, as this example from the Realpolitik of financial and legal rules shows. And just as they can constrain who makes what and whose storyworld a particular character can inhabit, they can also constrain the creative work of authors and artists of superhero comic books. In this latter case, rules take the form of writers' and artists' *bibles* that define the possibilities of the text. But beyond simply constraining textual possibility, they can also be generative, articulating key components that can be recombined to produce countless variations and that enable those variants to still be understood as manifestations of a particular superhero. They provide coherence to a multiply-authored, multiply-depicted character, world, and narrative. As such, they are relatively rare literary artifacts, most commonly used both to articulate the contours of corporate-owned intellectual property and to guide the creative expression of comic book artists.

Superhero games are also rule-bound. Yet game rules tend to be less character and world specific, and more concerned with the actions of the player and the performance of the platform. Designers of superhero games focus on the possibilities of gameplay, usually on the level of mechanics and user interface. They define the movements and operations that can be enacted in the "skinned" domain of character, world, and story. But because the rule sets can be character-agnostic and re-deployed to games skinned with other characters and inhabiting other genres, the rules seem looser than those found in comic book bibles. "Good" games, I will assert, seek some consistency between the rules of play and defining elements of the character and narrative, using mechanics to enhance expression. By these criteria, there are plenty of "bad" games...

Together—or so I will argue in this chapter—these combined rules have the capacity not only to inhibit and constrain, but also to shape and create subsequent narratives—particularly with the help of emerging media technologies. "Emerging" is a key word and means this chapter will necessarily be speculative. But speculative or not, the rules that bind character and world combined with the rules that define the mechanics of play offer a best-case scenario for the assimilation of existing textual worlds into story-generating technologies.

This chapter addresses competing strategies for character/world definition and coherence in comic books (bibles) and games (rules), as a way of getting to larger questions regarding the operations of narrative in fixed and authored texts (comic books) and dynamic and experientially generated texts (games). The challenges posed by the latter, including collaborative authorship with the user, are in the process of taking a new turn with algorithmically produced stories, offering a speculative twist on existing definitional strategies. Using examples drawn from Batman and Spider-Man, I explore bibles/rules and fixed/dynamic manifestations as a way of speculating about the conditions necessary to algorithmically generate stories. The constrained and formulaic nature of both superhero bibles and game rules offers a "best case" on which to base speculation about this new turn in narrative production.

Superheroes and story generators...

The connection may not at first glance seem obvious, but as Roberta Pearson and I argued in our work on the Batman, certain superhero characters effectively work as narrative generators (Uricchio and Pearson 1991, 2015). Their origin stories and character definitions echo through and indeed shape the construction of their world, their enemies (each with equivalent and parallel origin stories), and their stories (drawing on the underlying narrative tension encapsulated by the character). The reification and codification of these traits into what the industry terms "bibles" speak to the formulaic nature of character, world, iconography… and their locus in an industrial mode of production. That these elegantly crystallized formulas are capable of yielding endless story variations (eighty years' worth in the Batman's case) that remain coherent, is nothing short of remarkable.[2]

This narrative-generating capacity, hard wired in character definition and articulated through bibles (and intellectual property litigation), makes this sector of superheroes compelling in terms of thinking through current developments in algorithmically-driven story generators. As the key building blocks of this technology begin to emerge and interact with one another as prototypes, we can see the conceptual and practical contours of a new generation of story machines, even if they do not yet exist in any compelling way. This condition renders the comments that follow emphatically speculative; but the speculation is grounded. The thesis in a nutshell is a) that technologists involved with story generators can learn from superhero story construction; and b) that superhero bibles together with the rule sets from certain superhero games can serve as "best-case" experimental fodder for these emerging technologies. All to say, the fantasy worlds of superheroes may hold the developmental keys for the next frontier of storytelling systems.

Before looking more closely at what superhero bibles and game rules might contribute to this emerging narrative technology, it is worth considering the state of story generators. They are complicated and interdependent systems, and many of their components already infuse and shape our textual encounters in one way or another. Consider the behaviors of procedurally-generated characters in computer games, where entities interact with and even challenge players while inhabiting narrative roles and displaying various skill levels without any player intervention. Consider Google and other search engines, where our search results, their appearance, and their sequencing include choices made on the basis of server location (language settings; geographical priority) and the presumed relevance of search terms based on prior usage. Those whose settings allow can experience prompts derived from Google's many services including Gmail, maps, and one's history of past purchases. In this case, a "text"—a selection made from near infinite data sets—is constructed on-the-fly for individual users. Consider Netflix, Amazon, and Spotify, all of which operate in a similar way, putting the user's data-trails and stated preferences to work by guiding the interaction of algorithms with large data sets to select and push the texts to which we have access, serving as recommendation systems. In this context, "recommendation" both makes particular texts available (or occludes them) and orders textual sequence. These are not stories, of course, but they are responsive assemblages—textual elements pulled together and uniquely sequenced in real time on the basis of assumptions about the user. And they are ubiquitous in today's digital world.

Lab experiments have recently extended this reasoning, but for narrative ends, focusing on what might best be described as physiologically-navigated texts. Virtual Reality goggles equipped with pupil-trackers use algorithms to calculate what the user is viewing and extrapolate an assumed level of user interest by observing pupillary dilation, heartrate, and, in some use cases, even temperature, movement, and galvanic skin response.[3] These data points add a responsive layer to the more predictive data set acquired from past behaviors, combining to construct an "appropriate" pathing of the algorithmically-extrapolated user through a branched narrative environment. Branched narratives offer a tried and true approach to interactive stories, but their interfaces, which pause the action and require the viewer to make a choice before continuing, are clunky. But instead, imagine *Black Mirror: Bandersnatch*,[4] where navigational choices are intuited by the system and the viewer experiences a smooth and continuous narrative according to her or his preferences... rather than fumbling with the remote control at every decision point.

In addition to curating a story from data trails (like Google) and pathing users through a branched story environment based on physiological responses, a third approach to story draws on user data to actually construct and configure the text itself. That is, rather than shaping the user's textual access and environment, the algorithm, again, drawing upon user data, anticipates user interests and preemptively makes decisions regarding the textual structure. It acts as a third party, standing between the audience and a set of textual elements and brokering the two by extrapolating insights from user data and a pre-existing textual environment, which in turn are selectively called upon to construct a text. From a world of textual possibility, the user simply experiences a made-to-measure linear text, a text that generally masks the fact that it has been algorithmically compiled on-the-fly.

The algorithmic creation of texts-on-demand for individual users has had a robust presence in the realm of print since about 2012. Companies such as Narrative Science, Yseop, and Automated Insights mine and analyze data, using natural language processing to deliver it to the user as story. Millions of these stories are produced and sold each year. Although still primarily deployed in business settings, by the traditional printed press for structured data sets (sports and finance), and on sites such as BuzzFeed as narrative reductions, they are perfectly capable of targeting uniquely configured stories to individual participants. Algorithmic video production, while far behind, is fast making use of advances in image recognition software to analyze shots for content and emotional register and suggesting edited sequences for narrative material, as evidenced by recent automated video editing developments emerging from a Stanford-Adobe partnership (Leake et al. 2017, 1–14). These are extremely promising developments, and if one adds into the mix the ability to synthesize sound and image of known personages, the possibilities are near infinite. These latter technologies, the backbone of "deepfake," can be extremely problematic (not the least, amplifying a sense of epistemological uncertainty regarding what is real and unreal in our news environment), but my endeavor here is to point to their possibilities for the creation of narrative texts.

These three techniques (curation, pathing, narrative generation) are driving advances in new forms of responsive storytelling. All three are making significant advances thanks to ongoing developments in artificial intelligence. They inhabit a larger ecosystem in which convergent media industries seek to optimize ways of putting their "content" on different platforms. Companies like Unity are reinventing the production pipeline and are offering ways to output the same "content" in film and television, virtual reality, and game formats. In the process, the computer environment permits myriad digital assets—special effects, backgrounds, shadow rendering, and more—to be experimented with and layered in as desired. These changes herald a radically new configuration of production that will inevitably be informed by advances in storytelling technologies. So, while in a sense speculative, these developments are both immanent and increasingly tangible. My argument is that as they develop, the most relevant domain for continued experimentation will be the superhero genre, bound as it is by rules and enabled as it is by self-generating narrative logics.[5]

In the beginning was the word: Bibles

Authored and drawn by different hands, appearing over decades and across multiple series, superhero comic book characters and their worlds can easily be rendered incoherent, little more than icon-branded caricatures. And because the narratives are more often than not generated by the character (often in concert with the world), coherence and consistency matter. Enter the comic book "bible," a compendium of editorial guidelines that define behavior, motivation, history, imagery, and setting across authors, artists, and time.

In an age of media convergence, however, characters inhabit not only multiple and multiply-authored series, but multimedia worlds, with comic books, film, games, toys, and merchandizing each having their own affordances and specificities. "Bibles" are usually designed to contain the variables within comic books; but what about the character's other media manifestations? Some media, such as film, benefit from the bible's editorial conventions, albeit with some exceptions and explanations regarding alternate storyworlds. Other media, toys for example, have character attributes constrained largely by the rules of intellectual property (IP), which dictate the terms of inclusion (the right to bear, for example, the Batman logo) and transgression and thus exclusion (trademark violation and litigation). But the terms of IP control are both limited and reflect legal constraints rather than narratological control, as evidenced by the licensing of superhero characters to LEGOs, where concern with story, motivation, and world are abandoned (or celebrated, tongue-in-cheek, with a nod to meta-narrative), and few to none of the bible's concerns are evident. Character, in this setting, is reduced to a few trademarked iconographic elements, some arbitrary intertextual associations, and above all the invocation of the character's name.

Alas, bibles are hard to come by. They are one of the tricks of the trade, keys to all that is doable in the superhero's world. They articulate the rules that bind, and while intended to guide human creatives, they could also easily be extended to guide the algorithmic construction of character-bound narratives. Let's take a closer look at a bible—in particular, *A Brief Batbible: Notes on the Dark Knight Detective*, revised April 1989 under the guidance of Dennis O'Neil, editor of DC Comics' various Batman titles between 1986 and 2000. The unpublished nine-page document is broken into such sections as: "Who He Is," "Where He Lives," "The Batcave," "His Associates," "His Character," "Bruce or Batman?" (Batman! "Wayne has become part of his toolkit, an identity he finds useful."), "His Gear," "His City," "Writing His Stories," and "Drawing His Stories."

The instructions to writers are straightforward: Batman's physical characteristics are carefully demarcated (how fast he can run, for example), as is his intelligence level ("comfortably in the genius numbers"), his obsessions ("the elimination of crime," "the inviolability of life"), his sexual behavior ("celibate"), and even his limits (he "might not be able to explain the differences between the ideas of Freud and Jung"). And so it goes, with detailed explanations of Batman's utility belt, the Batmobile and Batcopter, and, of course, his costume. Regarding "His City," the bible decrees: "Gotham is a distillation of everything that's dark, moody and frightening about New York. It is Hell's Kitchen. The Lower East Side. Bed Stuy. The South Bronx. Soho and Tribeca off the main thoroughfares at three in the morning."

Writers are advised on how to make use of these many elements: "It is necessary to devise plots which use many if not most of the skills and attributes outlined above… . Batman is a detective … . We should achieve a balance between ratiocination and action, neglecting neither, but perhaps emphasizing the latter. Stories should, above all, *move*. Batman should never do something sitting that he can do running or leaping or jumping off a rooftop." And artists, too, are given clear guidance: "Artists are encouraged to remember mood, action and grotesquerie. Panels should be textured and backgrounds should not be slighted; in any Batman series, Gotham City is a *character*, and should be treated as such. Clarity is essential. Readers should never wonder which panel to read next, nor have any doubt about exactly what's happening here." The bible articulates the origin story and its relationship to character, elucidating the narrative mechanism at the core of Batman's motivation and thus the nature of his encounters with his peculiar world. It provides the guardrails for written and drawn versions of the character, containing and protecting the character from those who might veer off the road of coherence. In addition, it translates into words and values the distinctive trait of narrative generation associated with superheroes like the Batman, codifying them and, in the process, articulating a rule system that could be of eventual use to algorithmic story generators.

The rules of play: Games

Games offer an increasingly interesting set of options for character/world definition and operation as we move into an era of computer-generated content. Digital games generally require *assets* (characters and settings, for example), *mechanics* (the systems operating characters in the game world), and *rules* (action and interaction parameters for the game to proceed and for the user to achieve an outcome). Games are usually genre-specific (i.e., the mechanics and rules adhere to a particular form of game such as a first-person shooter), and they can range from tightly scripted play to the exploration of open worlds. Superhero games are usually coordinated with the commandments of a comic book bible with regard to their assets and occasionally rules. A game's mechanics and rules can work in tandem to develop an additional dimension to the rules that define a comic book superhero, helping to reinforce that character within the game medium.

A determining aesthetic question is: Does a superhero character define the mechanics and rules of play, or does it conform to the mechanics and rules of a pre-existing game genre? The working hypothesis of this chapter privileges an aesthetic of consistency and coherency. It considers overall game design as a "better" and "more satisfying" experience—from the character's and user's perspectives—when the game rules and character rules align, and when the game's mechanics seem consistent with the character. Alignment can take many forms, and they are worth teasing out. I will draw from two games generally seen as successful extensions of superheroes into the game medium[6]: *Batman: Arkham Asylum* (2009) and *Spider-Man 2* (2004).

Batman: Arkham Asylum was a hit with reviewers, who called it the "greatest comic book game of all time" (Miller 2010, n.p.) and the "best superhero game of modern times" (Edge Staff 2009, n.p.). It won several awards, including Best Action Adventure Game, Best Game, and Game of the Year from various media outlets, and it held the 2009 Guinness World Record for "Most Critically Acclaimed Superhero Game Ever." The game is indeed a "comic book game," partly because the developers only had access to the rights for the original Batman license—not the film. Thus, on the asset level, the game is consistent with the previously discussed bible. Batman's design was heavily influenced by the work of comics artist Jim Lee, who drew Batman as a strong, muscular character with a modern black and dark gray costume and an industrial look. Artists avoided film interpretations of the Joker, turning instead to Alan Moore's 1988 graphic novel *Batman: The Killing Joke* (Moore 1988). And the game's overall aesthetic combined a comic book style with realism. The environmental architecture and characters had to be extravagant enough to represent the Batman's world, Gotham, but also needed realistic texture and detail. The second aim was to recreate the dark, Gothic imagery inherent to the Batman universe, something that the biblically-endorsed Arkham Asylum provided (in addition to providing a way to contain many of Batman's iconic foes in one space). The game world's design and attention to detail were well received by critics.[7]

On the level of mechanics, the game won kudos for extending traditional character attributes to the play design. Unlike many other "action-adventure" Batman games, *Batman: Arkham Asylum* has a primary focus on Batman's combat and stealth abilities and the gadgets that can be used in combat and exploration. It acknowledges that Batman is a detective with a long history of teammates, not just a brooding brawler (though there is also plenty of brooding and brawling). And it does this by providing innovative mechanics such as "Detective Vision," a visual mode that provides contextual information, highlights interactive objects like removable grates, and shows the number of enemies in an area and their status (including their awareness of Batman's presence). The mode is also used to follow footprints, investigate odors, and solve puzzles—detective work.[8] Another defining Batman trait, the character's use of stealth, is translated into a mechanic for attacking well-armed enemies. "Stealth mode" enables Batman to swoop in unexpectedly from the shadowy folds of Gotham's gargoyles and subdue the heavily armed enemies beneath, and it was called out for praise by game critics. Andy Robinson declared the mechanic to be the centerpiece of the game and called it "a thinking man's stealth game" (2009, n.p.).

Just as the mechanics of the game transformed the spirit of Batman's character and world into interactive play, so too did the game rules. For example, a defining Batman dictum is that the character does not kill. And the game's rules reinforce that—Batman merely "incapacitates" the villain-inmates (a number of whom are armed with lethal weapons).

For all the praise that the game generated, it was also criticized—and in a revealing way. Many reviewers labeled the "boss battles" as the game's biggest failing. They found that the battles often relied on old-fashioned, tedious, and repetitive game tropes that required the player to learn monotonous routines in confrontations that were ultimately anticlimactic. Standard fight mechanics, typical of the action-adventure genre and having no direct tie-ins to the Batman's character or world, failed to win over fans.

For further exemplification, particularly regarding characterization through game mechanics and user interface, we must leave the DC universe and return to the Marvel universe with which this chapter opened. Writes Daniel Alvarez from *The Gamer*: "Repetitive combat, mediocre graphics, and an overall 'cash-in' feel are some of the reasons why a lot of film games have received negative feedback. These things don't apply to *Spider-Man 2*'s videogame adaptation. Released in 2004, *Spider-Man 2* was an achievement for the character. It set the standard for all the future games, and is the definitive game based on a movie" (Alvarez 2017, n.p.). *Spider-Man 2* remains a high-water mark for superhero games, particularly in the way the character moves through New York. The console versions in particular received critical acclaim.[9] There has not been another Spider-Man game that has captured the verticality of Manhattan, and the user interface requires the player to use both hands to fire off webs at skyscrapers simply to move forward. The physics are forgiving but reinforce the fact that Spider-Man is a living pendulum. And just to cement the correlation of character attributes and game mechanics, Spider-Man can also crawl up walls faster than he can run on the ground. The Spidey sense kicks in during combat, giving players a warning before the enemy lands a punch, allowing them to dodge hits the way the comic book depicts Spider-Man doing the same.

Inverse reviewer Matt Kim described the game as "basically *Grand Theft Auto* starring Spider-Man, and you are free to explore a huge Manhattan, accepting quests from people on the streets and fighting random street crimes. It was truly an open-world game with great villains to encounter, like Black Cat and Mysterio. Unlike GTA, there's no need to hijack a car: Spider-Man swinging around huge skyscrapers is the preferred method of travel here" (2016, n.p.). Kim adds that the game is "a fan favorite for its ambitious scale, and unprecedented mechanical success" (2016, n.p.). Indeed, based on an overview of the game's reviews, its most popular aspect was the web-swinging mechanic, where Spider-Man had to shoot webbing at actual targets, unlike previous games where he simply shot webbing up into the sky. *Screenrant*'s Chris Hodges adds:

> It's interesting that, while web-swinging has always been one of the most fundamental aspects of Spider-Man as a character, most of his games kind of treated it as an afterthought. It wasn't until the games based on the second *Spider-Man* movie that an advanced, physics-based system was built to allow for true three-dimensional web-swinging. In fact, the web-swinging system in *Spider-Man 2* was so well done that you could have fun literally just swinging around the city for hours and hours.
> (2017, n.p.)

And indeed, it's the stuff of legends. The title of Austin Wood's *Eurogamer* article says it all: "13 Years Later, *Spider-Man 2*'s Swinging Has Never Been Bettered—Here's Its Story" (2017, n.p.). Wood writes:

> Treyarch's Spider-Man 2 was first released on 28 June 2004. More than 13 years later, it still holds up as a yardstick for both Spider-Man and superhero videogames. But it's not the combat people remember. It's not the balloon kid or pizza delivery side missions. It's not the amazing

> cast of villains, either. It's the swinging, the sheer exhilaration of flying over, around, between and often smack into buildings. Spider-Man 2 is a tantalising playground of needles to thread, a true-to-life Spidey simulation.
>
> (2017, n.p.)[10]

"Swinging around" as a mechanic (like running up walls) enabled the user to explore the city and "feel" the comic book superhero's dynamic trajectories through urban space. Like the Batman's "Stealth Mode" and "Detective Vision," it transformed characterization into action and play. As noted by the reviewers, the effect of the game physics was effective to the point that it enabled free-form exploration of the city as Spider-Man, rather than simply following the progression of the game. This was partly enabled by the game's user interface, which, like the mechanics, harkened directly back to the character. As mentioned, using both hands, like Spider-Man, enabled the user to cast webs and swing rapidly through the city. The user-as-Spidey can cast a web to the left or right with the corresponding trigger button, but hitting both controls acceleration. A complicated slingshot move can also be unlocked. The point is that the game's user interface requires the player to enact the character's gestures, enhancing the effect of targeting and connecting the web, and swinging through urban space.

The briefly noted Batman and Spider-Man games are both bound by rules and enabled by mechanics and realized by the player's ensuing actions. As we have seen, some of these overlap with the characteristics articulated in the comic book bibles discussed above. To the point of this chapter, the enabling of characteristics through play mechanics and rules, like the strictures of the comic book bibles, formalizes elements that are relevant for algorithmic story generators. Batman's "Detective Vision" and aversion to killing transform commandments from the bible into actionable mechanics. Spider-Man's abilities to climb walls, project webbing, and swing through urban canyons are transformed into the mechanics of play. Players enact superhero abilities—a point made particularly tangible with *Spider-Man 2*'s controller interface. And they are constrained by the same constraints faced by the superhero (the inability to kill, in Batman's case). These elements not only provide for aesthetically satisfying superhero games but are key components for ongoing character generation.

Alas, most superhero games do not make use of this opportunity. The pressures of tight production schedules (including user testing), cost, and stability of play encourage most producers to fall back on standard game conventions and make use of existing mechanics (the just referenced article by Wood offers a case study). Yet, while not the norm, there is sufficient evidence in anecdotes such as players swinging around for hours in *Spider-Man 2*'s open world to suggest that character expression through mechanics and rules offers a powerful and medium-specific counterpart to comic book bibles, and thus the larger project of narrative generation.

Pulling the pieces together

Thus far, we have considered two types of rules: those codified into a bible and pertaining to the comic book, a fixed text; and those operationalized in the mechanics and rules of play and pertaining to games, an interactive experience. One of these rule sets fits flawlessly onto theories of narrative as they have been developed by literary and film theorists. The comic book, like literature and film, is a fixed medium bearing a fixed story. The only real interaction takes place in the act of reading and interpretation—but the stability of the text is a given.[11] Games, by contrast, are played and not read. They are composed of assets, mechanics, and rules for their deployment. The "text," should we want to invoke the term to make use of dominant narrative theory, emerges from a particular enactment of the game's elements. But any particular game is capable of supporting myriad enactments, myriad texts, which are then in turn open to the interpretive latitude enjoyed by fixed texts.

Comic books and games... reading and playing... stable configurations of medium-text and instable... the contrast between these two systems is profound. This raises a pointed question: What is narrative? Is narrative something to be found in the structure of a text, as most of us have learned in school? Or is it also an experience, a particular way of organizing events in the world (an emphatically minority view)? In other writing on this topic, I have likened the distinction to the difference between reading a wonderful book and playing, for example, pirates with one's friends (ok, think back to age 6...). Both worlds unfold, with the reader and player uncertain and deeply curious about what will follow on the next page or in the next move. Both worlds are bound by rules, the book by the conventions of genre, and the play as well, where the rules are inhabited ("if the sword hits you, you're dead"; "the table is the captain's HQ"). And both experiences can be retold as coherent narratives and analyzed only at the end of the run.

To be clear, I think that both of these approaches are legitimate and, indeed, that in many settings, they are complementary. A tour bus, guiding its passengers through the sights of a new city and regaling them with informational details can be wonderful; but so too can wandering on one's own through the streets and shops of a new city. One, like the book, is a fixed text for all; the other, like a game, is a unique experience. Together, they are powerful.

Our culture has shown a marked preference for fixed texts, even if the reality is more malleable than many would like to admit (Uricchio 2016, 155–170). Our educational systems focus almost exclusively on the book, relegating play to the margins. And this is not without reason if one's goal is to share a canon of textual references (Matthew Arnold's "best which has been thought and said in the world" [2006, 5]) with as wide a cohort as possible. This behavior is also historically grounded, with the "fixity" at the base of dominant media until the last decades of the twentieth century (print, recorded sound, photography, film, television) only recently being complemented by interactive media (digital games, VR and AR, and various interactive textual systems). Earlier interactive media—the telephone and post, for example—tended to be framed as "communications," as processes, rather than as texts. Their textual ephemerality bracketed them off from the analytic modalities enjoyed by fixed media and texts. That strategy has by default been extended to today's newly prominent interactive media. But game studies, work on VR and AR, and efforts to understand various interactive narrative systems have all begun to push back, offering alternative ways to think about narrative.[12] And game developments such as *Spider-Man 2*'s "open world," with players swinging around the city "for hours," and seeking out malefactors of one kind or another and swooping in to reconcile them with justice—*and finding pleasure in it*—offers some intriguing insights.

The question of what constitutes narrative is pressing if one is in the business of conceiving story generators. Is the goal to create a machine that will produce fixed texts, like comic books? Or to design and populate an environment within which the reader/player/user can discover narratively satisfying experiences? Framed another way, is narrative agency the exclusive purview of an author/creator? Or is it something to be shared between an author/creator and reader/user?

As I write this in 2019, the verdict is still out. Developers of story generators are pursuing both approaches, and at least at this stage of things, it seems as though putting the onus on the user to find a satisfying path through a world of narrative potential is the way to go. That implies an interactive world, a world that can be appropriately bounded by rules that are in comic book bibles, and that can be enabled by game rules and mechanics that amplify and enable elements of the narrative. The story, in this case, is only as good as the user. By contrast, fixed story generators are perfectly capable of producing coherent narratives that hew to the rule set. But they are not necessarily satisfying or elegant.[13] That said, we can expect rapid developments in both approaches thanks to advances in machine learning and the increasing datafication of human experiences.[14]

Where does that leave us? First, technologists involved with story generators have much to learn from superhero story construction. As we have seen, both superhero comic books and some game creators have developed systems—rules—to articulate character, iconography, behavior, and worlds. These systems, and above all the superheroes on which they are based, serve as elegant strands of DNA that are capable of generating countless story variants. Second, superhero bibles together with the rule sets from certain superhero games can serve as "best-case" experimental fodder for these emerging technologies. Whether fixed story or narrative world, story technologists have a ready-made repository of rules, techniques, and experiences to fall back on as they seek to implement their own systems. In the world of narrative fiction, this is, as far as I know, a unique situation.

The fantasy worlds of superhero comic books and games may indeed hold the developmental keys for the next frontier of storytelling systems!

Notes

1 Disney acquired Marvel in 2009 for USD 4 billion. The corporate disagreement between Sony and Disney/Marvel that was in effect when this chapter was drafted was resolved in late September 2019.
2 One can imagine a range of critical responses to the countless variations enabled by these characters and their attendant industries, ranging from Vladimir Propp (1968) and the structural underpinnings of folk narratives to Theodor W. Adorno's (1941) critique of "structural standardization" in popular music.
3 Typically, these goggle-based systems have been developed for purposes of foveated rendering, that is, the high-definition rendering of only what the eye sees, and not the entire 360-degree world. The efficiencies in computational and rendering processes are significant; but so, too, is the added value of such systems for tracking what the viewer sees and how the viewer's pupils respond.
4 The project was released on Netflix on 28 December 2018, and its producers claimed that over one trillion paths were available for its viewers (see Wikipedia 2020).
5 This domain could also be interesting from an archival perspective, permitting new configurations of content generated from the libraries of DC, Marvel, and others, and adapting the storylines and character arcs from the last eight decades.
6 I am indebted to Philip Tan, Creative Director of the MIT Game Lab, for generously sharing his insights into the vast world of superhero-based games.
7 *Game Informer*'s Andrew Reiner said the game's setting had "a taut and mesmerizing atmosphere, and was a place of wonder and inexplicable horror" (2009, n.p.).
8 In some ways, *Batman: Arkham Asylum* is a refinement of ideas from the James Bond game *James Bond 007: Everything or Nothing* (2003). In that game, Bond has a mechanic to detect the precise location where a single bullet would cause the most damage, even in the middle of being charged by a mob of minions. But in *Batman*, the mechanic is reworked in the interests of reinforcing and rendering playable the detective qualities so important to the character.
9 The other versions of the game have also received generally positive reviews with the exception of the PC/Mac version, which was "dumbed down" for a young audience and thus featured more simplistic and less challenging gameplay.
10 Wood also notes that Activision abandoned this still unparalleled swinging technique: "In its pursuit of mass-market appeal, Activision threw out what most consider to be the secret ingredient to the Spider-Man videogame recipe."
11 There are, of course, crucial exceptions such as the Oulipo, and specifically one of the founding works of the movement: *A Hundred Thousand Billion Poems* by Raymond Queneau (originally published as *Cent mille milliards de poèmes* in 1961). It is a book of sonnets in which each line is written with the same rhyme sound so that they can all be combined, meaning there is a possibility to generate 100,000,000,000,000 poems, specifically emphasizing that it is strict constraint that allows for such great variation and exploration. The book itself was printed as ten sonnets with each line cut out so that the reader can manually

flip through and create all of the permutations. Despite being in a printed and relatively "fixed" form, this book falls into the category of "designing and populating an environment within which the reader/player/user can discover narratively satisfying experiences." Thanks to Judy Ann Heflin for calling my attention to this precedent.

12 Examples of developed discourse regarding interactive media range from scholarship, such as Montfort 2003, to the work of research labs such as my own on interactive and immersive documentaries, the MIT Open Documentary Lab (http://opendoclab.mit.edu; accessed 31 January 2020).

13 There are a number of popular "first steps" in superhero generation. Under the rubric "Create Your Own Experiences," Marvel offers its users a tool kit to "Create Your Own Web Warrior" (https://spiderman.marvelhq.com/games/create-your-own-web-warrior; accessed 31 January 2020). For a time, the Batman Meme Generator enjoyed a certain popularity (https://batmancomic.info/; accessed 31 January 2020), as did websites that generated villains' names, superhero names, etc. (such as www.name-generator.org.uk/hero; accessed 31 January 2020). My reference to story generators pertains to a still largely lab-bound set of developments, not these. See, for example, this proposal for a narrative generator from UCLA's School of Arts and Architecture: https://publicityreform.github.io/findbyimage/generative-narrative-project-proposal.html (accessed 31 January 2020).

14 Consider the response to OpenAI's GPT2 text generator. OpenAI's backers, including Elon Musk, have not released their work publicly for fear of misuse (Hern 2019).

Works cited

Adorno, Theodor W. 1941. "On Popular Music." *Studies in Philosophy and Social Science* 9: 17–48.

Alvarez, Daniel. 2017. "The 8 Best and 7 Worst Spider-Man Games." *The Gamer*, 11 May. www.thegamer.com/the-8-best-and-7-worst-spider-man-games/ (accessed 31 January 2020).

Arnold, Matthew. 2006. *Culture and Anarchy*. Oxford: Oxford University Press.

Batman: Arkham Asylum. 2009. Developed by Rocksteady Studios. Published by Eidos Interactive and Warner Bros. Interactive Entertainment. PlayStation 3.

Black Mirror: Bandersnatch. 2018. Dir. David Slade. USA: Netflix.

Edge Staff. 2009. "Review: *Batman: Arkham Asylum*." *Edge*, 1 September.

Hern, Alex. 2019. "New AI Fake Text Generator May Be Too Dangerous to Release, Say Creators." *The Guardian*, 14 February. www.theguardian.com/technology/2019/feb/14/elon-musk-backed-ai-writes-convincing-news-fiction (accessed 31 January 2020).

Hodges, Chris. 2017. "Every Spider-Man Video Game, Ranked from Worst to Best." *Screenrant*, 10 July. https://screenrant.com/every-spider-man-video-game-ranked-worst-best/ (accessed 31 January 2020).

James Bond 007: Everything or Nothing. 2003. Developed by Griptonite Games. Published by Electronic Arts. Game Boy Advance.

Kim, Matt. 2016. "Ranking the Best Spider-Man Video Games of All Time." *Inverse*, 28 April. www.inverse.com/article/14913-ranking-the-10-best-spider-man-video-games-of-all-time (accessed 31 January 2020).

Leake, MacKenzie, Abe Davis, Anh Truong, and Maneesh Agrawala. 2017. "Computational Video Editing for Dialogue-Driven Scenes." *ACM Transactions on Graphics* 36 (4): Article 130, 1–14.

Miller, Greg. 2010. "*Batman: Arkham Asylum* (Game of the Year) Review." *IGN*, 26 May. www.ign.com/articles/2010/05/27/batman-arkham-asylum-game-of-the-year-review (accessed 31 January 2020).

Montfort, Nick. 2003. *Twisty Little Passages: An Approach to Interactive Fiction*. Cambridge, MA: MIT Press.

Moore, Alan. 1988. *Batman: The Killing Joke*. New York: DC Comics.

Propp, Vladimir. 1968. *Morphology of the Folktale*. Revised edition. Austin: University of Texas Press.

Queneau, Raymond. 1961. *Cent mille milliards de poèmes*. Paris: Gallimard.

Reiner, Andrew. 2009. "*Batman: Arkham Asylum*." *Game Informer*, 27 September.

Robinson, Andy. 2009. "*Batman: Arkham Asylum* Review." *Computer and Video Games*, 21 August.

Spider-Man 2. 2004. Developed by Treyarch. Published by Activision. PlayStation 2.

Spider-Man: Far from Home. 2019. Dir. John Watts. USA: Sony Pictures.

Uricchio, William. 2016. "Interactivity and the Modalities of Textual Hacking: From the Bible to Algorithmically Generated Stories." In *The Politics of Ephemeral Digital Media*, edited by Sara Pesce and Paolo Nolo, 155–170. New York: Routledge.

Uricchio, William, and Roberta E. Pearson. 1991. "'I'm Not Fooled by That Cheap Disguise.'" In *The Many Lives of the Batman: Critical Approaches to a Superhero and His Media*, edited by Roberta E. Pearson and William Uricchio, 182–213. New York: Routledge.

Uricchio, William, and Roberta E. Pearson. 2015. "'I'm Not Fooled by That Cheap Disguise.'" In *Many More Lives of the Batman*, edited by Roberta E. Pearson, William Uricchio, and Will Brooker, 205–236. New York: Palgrave Macmillan.

Wikipedia. 2020. "*Black Mirror: Bandersnatch*." *Wikipedia*, 31 January. https://en.wikipedia.org/wiki/Black_Mirror:_Bandersnatch (accessed 31 January 2020).

Woods, Austin. 2017. "13 Years Later, *Spider-Man 2*'s Swinging Has Never Been Bettered—Here's Its Story." *Eurogamer*, 12 July 2017. https://www.eurogamer.net/articles/2017-07-12-13-years-later-spider-man-2s-swinging-has-never-been-bettered-heres-its-story (accessed 31 January 2020).

13 The manifestations of game characters in a media mix strategy

Joleen Blom

Media-crossing characters dominate contemporary transmedia practices. Defined as quasi-persons within a social assemblage that motivates the reader to endow them with a form of personhood (Frow 2014; 2018, x), these characters span the media gamut from novels to television series and comics to games. They shape a transmedia ecology whose complex relations and structures challenge scholars from Western Europe and the USA (the "West"), as well as from Japan, where franchises distribute these characters across as many media as possible, following a strategy known as the *media mix* (Steinberg 2012).

One of the academic discourses that discusses transmedia texts as identified by Eder (2015) emerges from recent studies on the structure and production of transmedia works known as transmedia storytelling (Jenkins 2006), transmedia practice, or transmedia world-building (Klastrup and Tosca 2004; Wolf 2012). This largely Western discourse focuses on consistency between fictional worlds, primarily via stories, especially characters, and iconography (Harvey 2014), and it is only beginning to engage with the scholarship on these issues that has been conducted in Japan since the late 1980s.[1] This discourse tends to reevaluate the identity and narrative continuity of a character as a requirement for stories (Brooker 2012; Denson 2011; Geraghty 2017; Pearson 2019; Rosendo 2016; Tosca and Klastrup 2019; Uricchio and Pearson 1991). As such, it is based on two assumptions: First, that characters are foremost elements of a diegetic world (Eder, Jannidis, and Schneider 2010; Margolin 1983; 1986); and second, that as quasi-persons (Frow 2014), it is a prerequisite for characters to have a consistent identity analogous to human persons.

This chapter diverges from these assumptions by moving beyond the Westernized discourse of transmedia storytelling, looking instead at popular characters whose coherence of identity becomes discontinuous when they appear in a variety of media within a media mix strategy, especially when it comes to the unstable relation between games and narrative media such as manga or anime. The Pokémon franchise's Pikachu, for instance, does not represent the same character in all the media in which it appears. In the *Pokémon* anime TV series (1997–), its identity is that of the Pokémon of trainer Ash Ketchum, while in other cases, the character functions as the mascot for the Nintendo Company or represents one of the many Pokémon creatures the player can catch and train in *Pokémon* games like *Pokémon Sword and Shield* (2019).

In Japan's historical development of media convergence, such types of *media mix* represent a popular commercial strategy aimed at dispersing content across a variety of media to stimulate their consumption. Marc Steinberg's *The Anime Media Mix* (2012) created an expanding awareness about Japan's media practices as part of the current global media ecology. According to Steinberg (2012, 84), the character is the focus of the media mix, whose proliferation across media allows these media to connect and communicate. The point of departure is not any striving for consistency. Rather, character proliferation is the node that combines transmedia and crossmedia practices. Characters become autonomous from any particular story, and their appearances across media do not have to be coherent in terms of narrative continuity. Instead, characters continually reappear across media platforms akin to the life of game characters existing in a continuous loop of dying and respawning after their initial death (Azuma 2007; Kascuk 2016).

The proliferation of the character seems to stand in stark contrast to the ideal of consistency on the Western side of the discourse, but both transmedia practices from the West and from Japan face a similar challenge when characters appear in digital games. The challenge is caused by the structural differences between games and media with narrative affinities, like comics, novels, or animation (Aarseth 2006). Despite the fact that games can and do represent worlds and characters, game characters have multiple functions at the same time. They can be at once the representation of the players inside the game world, a fictional entity of the game world's story, ludic game pieces, and proprietary symbols of a larger franchise (Aarseth 2012; Aldred 2014; Klevjer 2006; Schröter and Thon 2014; Vella 2014, 2015). It would be easy to generalize digital games in terms of how they communicate characters; however, each game can vary to a great extent from other games in how they present characters. For example, *Thomas Was Alone* (2012) and *Overwatch* (2016) use different means to invoke characters; the former depends primarily on an extradiegetic narrator, whereas the latter uses visual design techniques to tell the player that the characters they see on screen are person-like entities.

This chapter utilizes the position of game characters inside the media mix strategy in order to explore the challenge digital games pose to contemporary transmedia practices and structures when a media mix strategy attempts to converge games with various narrative media. It addresses the following questions:

1. What is the relation between transmedia characters and characters in the media mix?

2. What do game characters contribute to a media mix, and how do they influence the distribution of the game character in other media?
3. How do game characters affect the identity of the character in the media mix?

I will first provide a theoretical foundation for the relation between characters in the media mix and transmedial characters, then use a case study of the *Persona 5* franchise to assess the challenges game characters bring to a media mix, and finally conclude how game characters affect the identity of the character when characters are distributed across multiple media.

Transmedia characters

The primary difference between transmedia storytelling and a media mix is that the former focuses on narrative continuity between stories as they are told via various media, whereas a media mix concentrates on the distribution of characters without the need for any coherence between their appearances. In this section, I discuss the theoretical basis of transmedia characters before turning to their counterparts in the media mix.

Inspired by Kinder's (1991) term of transmedia intertextuality, Jenkins (2006) popularized transmedia storytelling as a technique to tell stories across multiple media platforms that each contribute something new to a (fictional) world. This is not to say that these worlds can only be created via stories, but according to Klastrup and Tosca (2004) and Wolf (2012), stories are the dominant method of creating these worlds. When creating new fictional worlds, producers tend to use so-called bibles, or world databases (Harvey 2015; Rosendo 2015), to preserve the narrative thread, which ensures the coherence of the world as it is constructed across multiple media platforms. These practices are not limited to stories; the bibles can also come in the form of character profiles, art, sound, references, combat explanations, and more in order to facilitate the communication between different teams as the world is being developed (Francis 2019).

These practices resonate with the process of canonization. Backe (2015) explains that during the construction of a canon, many different "invisible hands" attempt to establish a set of works as normative and fixed, which happens on a micro level by individuals and on a macro level by institutions. The creation of a world bible is primarily enforced on a macro level where institutions attempt to create consistency in the fictional world by attributing to that bible an almost sacred meaning and where the institution attains a position that becomes "associated with unquestionable authority and the totality of knowledge on a subject, outside which only heresy remains" (Backe 2015, 6).

Transmedia characters appear in different works across multiple media platforms, but they are subject to the same desire for coherence and consistency. Their main issue is their transtextual identity because the various manifestations of a character in multiple works create incoherence and inconsistency between the character's appearances. Over the years, characters such as Batman, Superman, Buffy, Lara Croft, Sherlock Holmes, Harry Potter, or Bella Swan have appeared repeatedly across a wide range of media. This multiplicity of manifestations creates diverse and competing identities with different continuities; sometimes the characters appear in different franchises; at other times, the competing manifestations only make sense in different timelines or parallel universes.

Characters appearing in multiverses, or standalone issues in comics, and films are far from being the exception in the everyday business of contemporary transmedia practice. The audience watching *Into the Spiderverse* (2019) will likely not wonder if Spider-Man character Miles Morales will appear in the current Spider-Man films starring Tom Holland as Peter Parker. Yet theories about transmedia characters like these assume that a character must be the same individual between stories in which it appears (Rosendo 2016). Wilde describes the position of the transmedia character in "Western" theories as follows: "Transmedia character theories in the narrower sense clearly prefer the theoretical option that a 'character' must first and foremost be thought of as a coherent, contextualized entity (although always presented *incomplete*), which is presumed to exist within a diegetic world" (2019, 8, original emphasis).

These conventional theories of characters derive mostly from the field of literary studies, where they are presumed to exist in a diegetic world constructed via stories (Bal 1979; Eder et al. 2010; Jannidis 2012; Margolin 1983; Reicher 2010). According to Wilde (2019), strategies that theorists adopt to provide a theoretical explanation of transtextual identity tend to construct the character as a semiotic object belonging to a transmedial storyworld (Thon 2015) that consists of multiple works instead of a single narrative work, or they conceptualize the character as an intersubjective communicative construct (Eder 2008; 2010). Other strategies to tackle the issue of a coherent identity tend to define a "core" to the character that provides a framework to determine the cohesion between each character manifestation (Brooker 2012; Pearson 2019; Uricchio and Pearson 1991). However, these kinds of strategies tend to create hierarchy between character manifestations; if one identity of a character's manifestation does not cohere on enough points with the established core, then that manifestation is automatically lower in the hierarchy and thus less of that character.

Within this Western discourse, only few theorists advocate the dispersion of the character identity in terms of a constellation; once inconsistencies in continuity occur, the manifestations are perceived as different characters with different identities. For example, Denson (2011) differentiates between a series character and a serial figure, whereas Bertetti (2014) presents an extensive typology of character identities when the character travels between works; the typology distinguishes between character manifestations over a single course of events and multiple courses of events.

Characters in the media mix

As Wilde (2019) suggests, the contingency of a character's identity is commonplace in Japan, where the character functions akin to a character instance, or a character role that changes depending on the work in which it appears. It is only fairly recently that Japanese theory about characters is trickling into the West. Early works by Napier (2001), Allison (2006), and Lamarre (2009) discuss characters in the media mix, but they do not clearly address the media mix. It was not until Steinberg (2012) that the media mix, and the role of characters within it, took a prominent spot in the discussion about contemporary transmedia practices.

In a media mix strategy, Steinberg explains, the character is a "a device that simultaneously allows audiovisual media and objects to connect and forces their proliferation" (2012, 84). He contributes two main attributes to the discussion of characters: First, the character is mobile; it transfers from one medium to the next. Second, the character allows for communication between different media and modalities. The character functions as a network of different nodes, where each node—that is, each of the character's manifestations—connects to its other manifestations. As Steinberg also states, the media mix in Japan has its own historical development alongside the term media convergence in the West (2012, viii). Among the most prevalent works are those by Ōtsuka (1989, 2010), Itō (2005, 2011), and Azuma (2007, 2009). Ōtsuka (1989, 2010) is an early authority who examines a narrative-oriented media mix from the 1980s. In this media mix, the role of the character is one that allows readers to attain a *grand narrative*, the single totality of all individual narratives of the world accumulated. Readers obtain this grand narrative by gathering information about the world, following the multiple manifestations of the character(s) appearing in individual narratives.

Responding to Ōtsuka's concept of the grand narrative, Azuma (2009) argues that the media mix trend of the early 2000s shifted from being narrative-oriented to being character-oriented. Azuma describes the consumers of the character-oriented media mix as *otaku*, (male) consumers obsessed with aspects of popular culture who do not attempt to obtain any grand narrative but only absorb smaller narratives. They consume the character itself without the goal of gaining a larger understanding of the world to which it is connected. The character exists separated from its world in a multiplicity of manifestations, only to be consumed by *otaku* as the primary goal of its existence. Itō's revolutionary book *Tetsuka izu deddo*[2] (2005, 2011) further changes perspectives on the media mix. Itō uses the concept of the symbolic body (*kigō shintai*), described by Tezuka—who is commonly known as the father of manga—to differentiate between the *kyara* and the *kyarakutā* (character) in the character-oriented media mix. The *kyara* is the symbolic body, that is, the visual representation of a body but not yet a character (Itō 2005, 116). Using Ōtsuka's idea that the character has to be akin to a real person (Itō 2005, 130), the *kyarakutā* is what Itō considers to be a *dramatis persona* (*tōjō jinbutsu*) that gives the impression that it is a human-like figure and therefore mortal, whereas a *kyara* is not (Itō 2005, 120).

Unfortunately, most of the works from Japan about characters remain untranslated to this day. Azuma (2007), for example, contradicts Itō's distinction between the *kyara* and the *kyarakutā* specifically on the point of the death of characters, proposing instead that the character has overcome death as it lives multiple lives. He connects the ongoing reappearances of the character across media platforms to the life of game characters that tend to exist in a continuous loop of dying and respawning after their initial death.[3] However, Saitō (2014) objects to Azuma's idea of the character overcoming death. Instead, he proposes that a character can transfer from one work to another but that its life cannot be reproduced. Saitō considers it an essential element to the character that every time the character transfers to another work, it becomes a different character. This element he calls "*tensō kanō/fukusei fukanō*" (Saitō 2014, 109, original emphasis), the possibility to transfer and the impossibility of reproduction. The *kyara*, on the other hand, can be reproduced, but not transferred, due to their extradiegetic existence. Considering *kyara* phantoms that reside in a network of plurality, Saitō concludes that "even if we try to transfer a *kyara* from one work to another, each time we transfer a *kyara*, it will just multiply, and as a result, the act of transferring a *kyara* is just reproducing the same *kyara*" (2014, 110, my translation). *Kyara* do not become different characters when they move from one work to another, but instead the *kyara* operates in a network in which the same symbolic body is constantly repeated in each work, while none of these bodies are characters at all. Saitō calls the *kyara*'s impossibility to transfer as a character "*fukusei kanō/tensō fukanō*" (2014, 109, original emphasis), the possibility of reproduction and the impossibility to transfer.

In his translated discussion of Itō's notion of the *kyara*, Wilde (2019) explains that Itō perceives the entity to be "pre-narrative" that exists outside of a narrative context, and outside of a diegetic world. According to Wilde, although in the West the serial figure—a character with multiple identities—is perceived as the result of inconsistent character manifestations, the current debate could profit from the Japanese concept of the *kyara*. *Kyara* are not bound to a "default mode" of a diegetic incarnation and "can accordingly be seen as 'mediated performers' or 'virtual celebrities' […]. Fictitious actors that can take on any *role* (usually, but not always likewise, fictional) attributed to them" (Wilde 2019, 13, original emphasis).

The problem with games and narrative media

Game characters have been discussed primarily in terms of the differences between the avatar—as the locus of agency or the representation of the player—and the character, which were often used as interchangeable terms particularly in the early years of game studies (Aarseth 1997; Bartle 1996;

Bayliss 2007; Calleja 2011; Newman 2002; Klevjer 2006; Tosca 2003). Later, the dual identity between the player and the character became a topic of discussion, where the character is considered to be an inhabitant of a game world while simultaneously embodying the player as its locus of agency (Tronstad 2008; Vella 2014, 2015). Following from this, the general consensus seems to be that characters have multiple functions at the same time. Depending on the genre, these functions range from the representation of the player to ludic pieces as well as to fictional beings in a narrative world (Egenfeldt-Nielsen et al. 2008; Linderoth 2005; Schröter and Thon 2014). However, even within this discussion, there is a lack of engagement with game characters that players do not control as a player-character. An exception is Jørgensen's (2010) work about supporting characters to provide a coherent narrative experience in games. However, when characters are addressed as textual beings with a life on their own, they are discussed in terms of the story or narrative that the game supposedly has to have.

With a few exceptions, there seems to be a relative lack of engagement with games and game characters despite their visible presence in contemporary transmedia practices. Games seem to be relatively left out of the debate, although they do participate in media mixes. According to Picard and Pelletier-Gagnon (2015), Japanese games (*gēmu* in Japanese) are not bound to any essence that defines their "Japaneseness" but are subject to a market that develops and fluctuates under the influences of macro cultures (institutions and industrial structures) and micro cultures (player communities, fans of popular culture, etc.) in a technological environment developed globally. *Gēmu* develop in a media ecology characterized by commercial strategies, in particular the media mix (Picard and Pelletier-Gagnon 2015, 3).

A few Western scholars argue that games and narrative media have an unstable relation when they are involved in a trans- or crossmedia strategy. For example, Aarseth states that "narrative affinities and affordances shared by books and films are not shared by games" (2006, 207). He uses Cawelti's (1976) distinction between two levels of popular fiction: (1) the level of cultural convention where characters, stereotypes, themes, and environments are located; and, (2) the level of structure where a series of events happen. According to Aarseth, the story is told in the latter, but games only contain the first without affording the latter.

Aarseth's argument against games as a storytelling medium resides inside the Western context that accentuates the coherence of stories. This discussion of coherence is also present in Aldred's (2012, 101) work about the connection between game characters and film characters. She argues that game characters in a crossmedia production are forced to be doubles for their filmic counterparts and therefore function more in terms of aesthetic contemplation than as the locus of agency for players. In a later work, Aldred adds that game characters in crossmedia productions function simultaneously as "interactive representatives of the players in the game world, fictional entities that serve to advance the story of the game world, and the proprietary symbols of the larger game franchise they belong to" (2014, 355). She explains that these kinds of characters lack the affordances of player modification in order to enable their translation across multiple media platforms and merchandise (Aldred 2014, 359). In other words, game characters in a crossmedia production have to be structurally regulated to resonate with their counterparts in media with narrative affinities because any modification to the character that games can do structurally causes turmoil in the effort toward coherence in the character's identity.

Reflecting on the place of Japanese games inside a media mix, Steinberg (2015) argues that games are central. The 1980s *Madara* franchise illustrates this centrality. Here, the manga mimicked the visual aesthetics of digital games and in turn enabled crossmedia development. This resonates with Aarseth's (2006) argument that crossmedia transfers only happen on the level of cultural convention. Games in this particular case are used as additional works to stimulate the consumption of the *Madara* manga media mix (Steinberg 2015, 47). However, games have become increasingly common as the primary medium around which the rest of a media mix is built, recent examples of such media mix strategies being *Danganronpa: Trigger Happy Havoc* (2010), *Persona 5* (2016), *Pokémon Sun and Moon* (2016), *Final Fantasy XV* (2016), or *Nier: Automata* (2017), to name just a few.

Within these games, characters continuously switch back and forth between different segments. Each segment declares that the player expects something different from the characters, which could be exploration, battle, or narrative development, or something else. To use Lamarre's (2018) term, game characters are in a constant state of switching between codes where we expect something different from them within each segment. These segments function as games within the overall game, consisting of their own mechanics, rules, and goals that contribute to the game's larger structural process so that the player can reach the game's endstate. The sum of the different segments provides the player with a plurality of possibilities that do not only affect the overall progress of the game but also provide the player creative agency to influence game characters in the process toward the endstate. For example, in *Fire Emblem: Three Houses* (2019), the player has to choose a house at the start of the game: Golden Deer, Blue Lion, or Black Eagles. The choice determines which characters the player will initially develop, recruit, and, as the game's plot progresses, kill. The game is divided into different modes, each with its own goals and rules, but all contributing to the characters' development. The battle mode gives the characters experience points in battles; during the school class mode, the player will teach the characters new skills or develop already attained skills; in the courtyard, the player-character can walk around completing quests for these characters; and the game's various simulation modes allow the player to have characters bond with each other as they cook, dine, and have tea parties together. Each segment develops the characters in a specific way so that they not only become stronger as pawns in the battle mode, but it also allows the player to influence the outcome of their connection to each other.

It is therefore relevant to discuss the contribution of games in the debate about the coherence of character identity in contemporary media practices. Games structurally differ from media with a stronger affinity to narrative. As a result, game characters have to adhere to their narrative counterparts, but a lack of scholarly engagement exists about those cases where games are the first platform on which a particular character identity manifests itself. In the next section, I will analyze *Persona 5* to explore the influence of game characters when they appear in other media inside a media mix strategy, and I will provide a preliminary conclusion about how they affect the transtextual identity of the character.

Characters in *Persona 5*

After waiting for ten years, fans of the *Shin Megami Tensei: Persona* videogame franchise were rewarded for their patience: Developer Atlus finally released the next game installment of the series, *Persona 5*, in September 2016. As was custom in the previous game installments, the player takes control over the game's silent teenage protagonist, whose mission is to rid the world of those corrupted adults who deprive others of their much-needed freedom. Together with his friends, Joker, the protagonist, creates a vigilante group called *Kaitōdan,* with whom he roams the palaces of the shadow world to steal the hearts from corrupted individuals.

Persona 5 is more than a game; it is a media mix strategy with the game as its focal point. The game has been adapted into a manga serialization (see Murasaki 2017 for the first volume) and an anime[4] television series (2018–2019). The characters also appear in a rhythm game, *Persona 5: Dancing in Starlight* (2018), in the dungeon crawler game *Persona Q2: New Cinema Labyrinth* (2018), and Joker appears in the crossover fighting game *Super Smash Bros. Ultimate* (2018). In October 2019, Atlus released an expanded version of the original game, called *Persona 5 Royal* (2019), that includes added content such as new dungeons, new activities, and new characters. The characters are also sold as merchandise.

In the *Persona 5* game, the player directs Joker and his group of friends through a variety of segments: In the dungeon exploration, the player moves Joker through the palaces where they plan to steal the hearts of their enemies, while trying to perform actions of stealth to avoid detection. Once they engage an enemy, the characters enter a battle segment in which players can command the characters to attack, avoid, defend, and more in order to win and return to the dungeon exploration. Any won battle provides the characters experience points, money, and sometimes new *personae*, creatures the Joker can use in battle. Outside of the dungeons, the player engages with Joker's everyday school life, and they can modify the character's attributes (called *social stats*) in terms of numerical value by participating in school classes, working part-time jobs, and hanging out with his friends. These attributes characterize Joker in five different aspects: guts, knowledge, charm, kindness, and proficiency. Once the player manages to increase the numerical value of the protagonist's charm aspect from one to two, the characterization changes semantically from "existent" to "head-turning." The player cannot change the attributes any other way, nor can they lower them. They only increase in one direction, but the player can determine how far the attributes rise—until they reach their maximum. All these segments contribute to the overall process to smooth the way to the game's endstate.

The main events that take place in the game progress in a fixed sequence and do not differ per gameplay; they will always take place in the same order. The player has no influence over what will happen and how. For example, Joker's classmate Ann Takamaki will always follow Joker, his friend Ryūji, and cat mascot Morgana inside Kamoshida's palace, where she will be captured by their teacher Kamoshida. When Joker and Ryūji enter Kamoshida's hideout, they find Ann and Kamoshida. Kamoshida speaks down to her, telling her that her best friend's suicide attempt was Ann's fault because Ann had refused Kamoshida's sexual advances. Ann stands up to him and awakens her inner *persona*. The player will then enter a battle segment. The player has to win this battle; although the player could potentially lose the battle against the enemy, this will only lead to a game over screen so that one has to try the battle again if one wants to progress the game. After the battle, Ann joins the Joker's group of *Kaitōdan*. The same goes for all the other characters the player will recruit: Morgana, Yusuke, Makoto, Futaba, Haru, and Goro will all join the *Kaitōdan*, regardless of how the player performs in the game.

Persona 5 consists of a macro structure that connects fixed major events in a sequence (Backe 2012, 254) over which the player has little to no influence, and of a micro structure, several smaller segments that allow the player to modify the characters. In the macro structure, the characters function as fictional beings with their own inner life and motivations, whereas the segments in the micro structure present the characters as ludic pieces that the player cultivates on a structural level to smooth the process to the game's endstate. This gives the impression that there is a strict distinction between the identity of the characters as quasi-persons in the game's macro structure and as ludic pieces in the game's micro structure. However, there is a particular segment in *Persona 5* in which the character as a quasi-person and as a ludic piece converge, which I call the *system of affection* (SA).

Persona 5's system of affection

The SA is a ludic process inherently procedural in nature in which the player creates relationships of love and friendship between characters. The relationships are embedded in structural systematic game design, which players affect by performing sets of actions. Kelly (2015, 47) refers to the simulation of love in *Dragon Age II* (2011) as a system of courtship, but also as a system in which the game characters are integrated and bound to the game and its rules so that they only have to execute a certain strategy in order to successfully woo a nonplayable character.

In *Persona 5*, the SA is presented in the so-called *confidant* segments of the game; over the course of the game's main events, the player has opportunities to have Joker establish several relationships of friendship and/or love with characters, whom the game calls *confidants*. These include all the characters with whom Joker roams the palaces, but also characters he meets in his daily life, such as classmate Yuuki Mishima, *shōgi*[5], player Hifumi Togo, or his landlord Sojiro Sakura. As ludic game pieces, the player just needs to execute the right strategy to successfully develop these relationships. The player executes this strategy by having Joker give the confidants gifts they like and by choosing the correct dialogue option in order to raise the confidant's affection. The degree of affection is presented via a tier-rank with the maximum level of ten. Each rank gives the player certain benefits that help reaching the game's endstate. For example, reaching the second rank with Ann allows her to perform a follow-up attack in the battle segments, while reaching rank nine provides a chance that she saves Joker from a fatal attack. When the player has reached a character's tenth rank, they have "maxed out" the relationship with that character. This means that the relationship will not develop any further during the game. While possible, it is incredibly difficult to "max out" each confidant's relationship over the course of a single gameplay. It is much more likely that players need to start playing the game again, for which they can import the data from a previous gameplay to max out all the confidant relationships.

The events that unfold in the SA differ per *confidant*, but they always concern the personal issues the character faces. After a relationship is maxed out, the confidants will confront their issues. The segments with Ann revolve around Ann trying to come to terms with her friend Shiho's attempted suicide. As the relationship progresses, Ann opens up to Joker, informing him about Shiho's recovery as well as confiding in him how she changed as a person. Before "maxing out" the relationship, the player can decide to have her as a friend to Joker or have them become lovers. While the events over the course of the relationship development are fixed sequences, the player has agency over whether they pursue these relationships at all, and how far they will bring the relationship. The player can stop leveling up the ranks at any time over the course of the game.[6] Another choice the player has concerns the nature of the relationship; in the case of female characters, the player can choose for the relationship to become romantic or one of friendship. Due to the heteronormative nature of the SA in this game, the nature of relationships with male characters is always one of friendship. Regardless, the relationship segments are not required to play and reach the game's endstate; they only provide additional benefits.

The SA provides the player with agency that allows them to choose the extent to which characters develop as quasi-persons, while they can simultaneously develop these characters as ludic pieces to support the progress of the game. Because the player has this agency in the game, they are partially involved in the characterization of the character. Developments such as Ann Takamaki having resolved her concerns about her friend's attempted suicide, or having entered a relationship of romance with Joker, depend on the actions of each player. This kind of agency is not present in the other media version of *Persona 5*. In the next section, I will therefore look at how two examples in *Persona 5*'s media mix strategy engage with the SA of the game: the *Persona 5* manga and the *Persona 5 Comic Anthology*.

The system of affection in the *Persona 5* media mix strategy

The *Persona 5* manga (Murasaki 2017) is an adaptation that translates the game into comic book format. The manga is drawn by *mangaka*[7] Hisato Murasaki, but the cover of each volume contains the words *gensaku*[8] followed by the Atlus logo. This implies that this serial release is officially recognized as an adaptation by the game's intellectual property owner (IP) Atlus. At this moment, the manga consists of four volumes, all of which I have analyzed to see if they contain traces or references to the game's SA.

The manga presents a close adaptation of the game's macro structure with little variation to the fixed events. For example, as in the game, Ann Takamaki follows Ryūji, Morgana, and Joker into Kamoshida's palace and is captured. In the manga, Ryūji and Joker are held down to the ground by enemies to prevent them from rescuing Ann, an action that does not occur in the game. Aside from small differences like these, Ann does stand up to her teacher and awakens her inner *persona*. That said, the battle segment of the game is replaced by a boss battle between Ann, Ryūji, Morgana, Joker, and Kamoshida, which in the game takes place after Ann has officially joined the *Kaitōdan*. Battles such as those against the palace's boss will happen in the game regardless of whether the player intends to fight them; however, the translation of the battle to comics format occurs mostly on the level of convention. On a structural level, the manga does not implement the actions the player could have undertaken during the battle segments.

No volume of the *Persona 5's* manga adaptation acknowledges the existence of the source work's system of affection. I cannot find a trace of Joker developing relationships with the *confidants* beyond what the game's macro structure presents—it omits even entire scripted sequences of the events that happen during the SA segments. For example, after the boss battle with Kamoshida, Ann convinces Ryūji, Morgana, and Joker that she should join their team so that she can fight against corrupted individuals like Kamoshida. When they accept her offer, she is introduced as a *confidant*. This entire sequence is skipped in the manga. The transition to a new chapter where the team celebrates their victory suggests instead that she has become part of the *Kaitōdan*.

The *Persona 5 Comic Anthology* is a series of short stories in comic book format written and drawn by multiple artists. I managed to obtain two volumes, volume one and two, on which I base my analysis (DNA Media Comics 2017a; 2017b). Although the Atlus logo is absent from the cover, the publisher, DNA Media Comics, has received the copyright license to use the *Persona 5* characters for their manga, which is stated on the last page of each volume. According to Tosca and Nakamura (2019), character proliferation in a media mix strategy happens via the selling of copyright licenses to other creators, who can then use the franchise's characters to create their own works within that strategy, such as manga or anime, but also games and mobile phone applications. The *Persona 5* media mix strategy operates exactly on these principles; although the manga volumes by DNA Media Comics are not recognized by Atlus as official adaptations, DNA Media Comics has required Atlus's official authorization to use the *Persona 5's* characters for their own works, making these volumes part of the *Persona 5* media mix strategy.

The content of the manga anthology consists of parody and pastiche stories about the game, and it is presented in either of the two following comics formats:

- The *yonkoma*; four-panel comics with the intention to provoke laughter. The last panel usually presents the punchline of the joke. They come in a set of eight pages (one page contains two *yonkoma*) written by an individual author.
- Short stories; fixed sequences of events that range between eight to twelve pages. Each story is written by a different author.

All of the short stories present "what if" scenarios, and not a single story imitates the events of the game. For both male and female characters, the SA is addressed in terms of background explorations, in which stories present additional events about the relationships between Joker and the *confidants*. For the female characters, the relationship explorations tend to be of a romantic nature, although the game allows the relationship to be one of friendship. For example, the story "Na mo shiranu kafetomo"[9] by KyūZIP (2017) in the anthology's first volume tells about the encounter between medical doctor Tae Takemi and Goro Akechi in café Leblanc, where Joker lives. Tae, in a moment of doubt about her relation to Joker, interrogates Goro about Joker's favorite food, places he likes to go, and things he likes. Tae is happy to hear she is closer to Joker than Goro. At the end of the story, she decides to text Joker to invite him over to her clinic. Although this event does not occur in the game, it does correspond to the scripted events during the SA segments between Joker and Tae Takemi, where she regularly texts him, asking him to come over to her clinic.

In the rest of the comics, including the *yonkoma*, the SA is addressed in a humorous light, specifically to make fun of the possibility that in the game Joker can date nine female characters at the same time, and the requirements for dating all of them simultaneously. In the short stories, poking fun at this possibility comes in passing. For instance, in "Morugana kagekiha"[10] by Tamura Mutō (2017), Morgana expresses his desire to date Ann. This is problematic, however, since Morgana is a talking anthropomorphic cat and can only date her when he returns to his human form. In a single panel, Joker thinks about Morgana's lack of realization about how much money dating would cost and all the skills Morgana would need: that he would need the courage of a lion, a charm level that has to be extremely high, kindness like that of a female goddess, extreme knowledge, and high skills in magic. This text is shown over a flashback of the multiple dates Joker has had with the female *confidant* characters. Both the visual flashback and the Joker's written thoughts are references to the SA system. In order for Joker to engage with the SA of some of these confidants, he does indeed need to have a high level of these attributes. To raise the rank of Tae Takemi, for example, Joker must have level four "charismatic" of the charm attribute—which is the second highest level for an attribute and requires quite some time and in-game training to obtain. Although the joke about the possibility to date all nine women simultaneously only occurs in passing in the short stories, in the *yonkama* it tends to be the punchline. In "Saigo no kotoba"[11] by Kinoko Mori (2017), Joker's infidelity is discovered by his female teammates, Ann, Makoto, Haru, and Futaba. When Ann tells him that he is the worst for dating all four of them, Joker denies it and delivers the punchline: He had been dating nine women at the same time, not four.

In short, any translation of the SA into the *Persona 5* manga adaptation seems to be absent, as the manga only adapts the fixed events in the game's macro structure. However, the *Persona 5 Comic Anthology* does refer to the SA system, but every translation of this system remains on the level of convention; the jokes and "what-if" background stories do acknowledge the existence of the system, but they do not incorporate it. Following Aarseth's (2006) conclusion about the friction between games and media with narrative affinity, the structure that games have influences what narrative media can and cannot do. In the final section, I will therefore focus on how game characters affect the identity of the character in the media mix.

The identities of the characters

In a media mix strategy, the contingency of a character's identity is common; the character does not have to have a coherent fixed identity. At first glance, the proliferation of the characters in the Atlus media mix of *Persona 5* seems to be following just that contingency. The variety of media that deliver *Persona 5*, such as the official adaptation from game to manga, suggests that Atlus just wants to distribute the franchise over as many media as possible.

However, a close reading of the official manga adaptation reveals that the SA segments of the game that structurally merge the characters as quasi-persons and as ludic pieces is not adapted—its existence is not even hinted at.

This is not to say that Atlus does not acknowledge their game's system of affection at all. The *Persona 5 Comic Anthology*'s official use of the *Persona 5* characters suggests that Atlus is relatively comfortable with the exploration of the characters' relationships in peripheral nonludic media that have legally obtained copyright licenses. However, I have to stress that the acknowledgment only occurs on the condition that the relationships correspond to the relationships represented by the game. The anthology shows a "what-if" story about the relationship between Joker and Tae Takemi, but it does not show a "what-if" story of a romantic relationship between Joker and Goro Akechi. To provide a counterexample, the *dōjinshi*[12] *Pelsona 5 unofficial fanbook: Koko ni ai ga aru akashi o: Joker X Akechi* (Banyu 2017a) and *Perusona 5 unofficial fanbook: Futari de aruita ano hi no hoshizora: Joker X Gori Akechi* (Banyu 2017b)[13] have not received any official license, but—as the titles suggest—depict a queer reading of the relationship between Joker and Goro Akechi. Besides the fact that these *dōjinshi* recognize, on the level of convention, the game's SA, they add another layer to the relationship and make it explicitly romantic and sexual.

The paradox is that a media mix strategy with a game at its center in which players can influence the character's development has to take the role of the player into consideration. The role of the player causes friction between the game and crossmedia distributions. Atlus might not want to tinker with the player's own experience from a commercial point of view because it could devalue that experience and could establish a dominant reading that retroactively affects the game. However, Atlus's lack of any engagement with the SA in the official manga adaptation and the subsequent relocation of the depiction of their game's SA to a peripheral publication still establishes a dominant reading because it implies that the experience the player gains by playing with the SA in the game is of secondary value to the game's macro structure.

One can say that contingency of character identity in the media mix should not require coherence. Of relevance here is that Atlus only officially acknowledges the relationships in the *Persona 5 Comic Anthology* as they adhere to the representation of relationships in the source work. Although the anthology seems to illustrate an exploration of the possible romantic relationship between Tae Takemi and Joker, the anthology does not explore any queer readings of the relationships between Joker and other *confidants*. These queer readings only happen in *dōjinshi* that do not have obtained Atlus's legal copyrights to use their characters and that are, in this sense, not part of the *Persona 5* media mix strategy. This means that Atlus maintains a position of authority that decides which publications of *Persona 5* should be counted as normative and which ones regarded as heresy. In other words, any *Persona 5* character that is not officially recognized by Atlus is not counted as part of the identity of the character.[14]

Acknowledgments

This research has received funding from the European Research Council (ERC) under the European Union's Horizon 2020 research and innovation programme (Grant Agreement No [695528]—Making Sense of Games).

Notes

1 This engagement is mostly confined to the field of Japanese studies, not in the least because of the language barrier between Japan and the West. As English translations and contributions become more and more available, knowledge about media practices and structures from Japan becomes increasingly accessible to media scholars without proficiency of the Japanese language.
2 The translation of the title is "Tezuka Is Dead."
3 For an English-language summarized explanation, see Kascuk 2016.
4 *Anime* (アニメ) are hand or computer drawn animations that can appear as film and/or television series.
5 *Shōgi* is known as Japanese chess.
6 With a few exceptions, such as Goro Akechi, Sae Niijima, and Morgana, these SA are mandatory and will rank up regardless of the player's performance in the game.
7 A *mangaka* is a comic book writer or comic book artist.
8 原作（げんさく）means "original source."
9 「名も知らぬカフェとも」（なもしらぬカフェとも）translates as "My café buddy whose name I do not know."
10 「モルガナ過激派」（モルガナかげきは）translates as something like "Morgana the Extremist."
11 「最後の言葉」（さいごのことば） means "Final Words."
12 *Dōjinshi* (同人誌) are self-published works such as magazines, comics, or novels usually containing fan fiction.
13 Spelling mistakes in the titles are intended and reproduced exactly as the titles of the *dōjinshi*'s covers spell them.
14 In this chapter, I focus on the character proliferation of a Japanese media mix model only. This is not to say that this kind of model has not already reached Western comics and games culture in some sense. The *Mass Effect* game series (2007–2012) also contains a system of affection. The developer Bioware has migrated the characters of these games to the *Mass Effect* comics that also do not present the game series' system of affection. However, unlike the *Persona 5* media mix strategy, where the coherence of characters does not seem to matter in terms of narrative continuity, the *Mass Effect* comics avoid any expansion of the world, as they only depict a character's background stories as told or hinted at by the events of the game. Moreover, the comics avoid any visual depiction of Shepard and any indication of their gender in order to create a sense of narrative continuity between the character's manifestations.

Works cited

Aarseth, Espen J. 1997. *Cybertext: Perspectives on Ergodic Literature*. Baltimore: Johns Hopkins University Press.

Aarseth, Espen J. 2006. "The Culture and Business of Cross-Media Productions." *Popular Communication* 4 (3): 203–211.

Aarseth, Espen J. 2012. "A Narrative Theory of Games." In *Proceedings of the International Conference on the Foundations of Digital Games*, edited by Magy S. El-Nasr, 129–133. New York: ACM.

Aldred, Jessica. 2012. "A Question of Character: Transmediation, Abstraction, and Identification in Early Games Licensed from Movies." In *Before the Crash: Early Video Game History*, edited by Mark J. P. Wolf, 90–104. Detroit: Wayne State University Press.

Aldred, Jessica. 2014. "Characters." In *The Routledge Companion to Video Game Studies*, edited by Mark J. P. Wolf and Bernard Perron, 355–363. New York: Routledge.

Allison, Anne. 2006. *Millennial Monsters: Japanese Toys and the Global Imagination*. Berkeley: University of California Press.

Azuma, Hiroki. 2007. *Gēmuteki riarizmu no tanjō: Dōbutsuka suru posutomodan 2*. Tokyo: Kōdansha.

Azuma, Hiroki. 2009. *Otaku: Japan's Database Animals*. Minneapolis: University of Minnesota Press.

Backe, Hans-Joachim. 2012. "Narrative Rules? Story Logic and the Structures of Games." *Literary and Linguistic Computing* 27 (3): 243–260.

Backe, Hans-Joachim. 2015. "The Literary Canon in the Age of New Media." *Poetics Today* 36 (1–2): 1–31.

Bal, Mieke. 1979. "Inleiding: Wat zijn personages en wat doen we ermee?" In *Mensen van papier: Over personages in de literatuur*, edited by Mieke Bal, 1–13. Assen: Van Gorcum.

Banyu. 2017a. *Pelsona 5 unofficial fanbook: Koko ni ai ga aru akashi o: Joker X Akechi*. http://banyu.info/ (accessed 31 January 2020).

Banyu. 2017b. *Perusona 5 unofficial fanbook: Futari de aruita ano hi no hoshizora: Joker X Gori Akechi*. http://banyu.info/ (accessed 31 January 2020).

Bartle, Richard. 1996. "Avatar, Character, Persona." http://mud.co.uk/richard/acp.htm (accessed 31 January 2020).

Bayliss, Peter. 2007. "Beings in the Game-World: Characters, Avatars, and Players." *IE '07: Proceedings of the 4th Australasian Conference on Interactive Entertainment*: Article 4. https://dl.acm.org/citation.cfm?id=1367960 (accessed 31 January 2020).

Bertetti, Paolo. 2014. "Toward a Typology of Transmedia Characters." *International Journal of Communication* 8: 2344–2361.

Brooker, Will. 2012. *Hunting the Dark Knight: Twenty-First Century Batman*. London: I. B. Tauris.

Calleja, Gordon. 2011. *In-Game: From Immersion to Incorporation*. Cambridge, MA: MIT Press.

Cawelti, John. 1976. *Adventure, Mystery, and Romance: Formula Stories as Art and Popular Culture*. Chicago: University of Chicago Press.

Danganronpa: Trigger Happy Havoc. 2010. Developed and published by Spike. PlayStation Portable.

Denson, Shane. 2011. "Marvel Comics' Frankenstein: A Case Study in the Media of Serial Figures." *Amerikastudien/American Studies* 56 (4): 531–553.

DNA Media Comics. 2017a. *Persona 5 Comic Anthology* Vol. 1. Tokyo: DNA Media Comics.

DNA Media Comics. 2017b. *Persona 5 Comic Anthology* Vol. 2. Tokyo: DNA Media Comics.

Dragon Age II. 2011. Developed by Bioware. Published by Electronic Arts. Windows.

Eder, Jens. 2008. *Die Figur im Film: Grundlagen der Figurenanalyse*. Marburg: Schüren.

Eder, Jens. 2010. "Understanding Characters." *Projections* 4 (1): 16–40.

Eder, Jens. 2015. "Transmediality and the Politics of Adaptation: Concepts, Forms, and Strategies." In *The Politics of Adaptation: Media Convergence and Ideology*, edited by Dan Hassler-Forest and Pascal Nicklas, 66–81. London: Palgrave Macmillan.

Eder, Jens, Fotis Jannidis, and Ralf Schneider. 2010. "Introduction." In *Characters in Fictional Worlds: Understanding Imaginary Beings in Literature, Film, and Other Media*, edited by Jens Eder, Fotis Jannidis, and Ralf Schneider, 3–64. Berlin: De Gruyter.

Egenfeldt-Nielsen, Simon, Jonas Heide Smith, and Susana Pajares Tosca. 2008. *Understanding Video Games: The Essential Introduction*. New York: Routledge.

Final Fantasy XV. 2016. Developed and published by Square Enix. PlayStation 4.

Fire Emblem: Three Houses. 2019. Developed by Intelligent Systems and Koei Tecmo. Published by Nintendo. Nintendo Switch.

Francis, Bryant. 2019. "Building a Basic Story Bible for Your Game." *Gamasutra*, 18 October. www.gamasutra.com/view/news/352517/Building_a_basic_story_bible_for_your_game.php (accessed 31 January 2020).

Frow, John. 2014. *Character and Person*. Oxford: Oxford University Press.

Frow, John. 2018. "Character." In *The Cambridge Companion to Narrative Theory*, edited by Matthew Garret, 105–119. Cambridge: Cambridge University Press.

Geraghty, Lincoln. 2017. "Transmedia Character Building: Textual Crossovers in the *Star Wars* Universe." In Star Wars *and the History of Transmedia Storytelling*, edited by Sean Guynes and Dan Hassler-Forest, 117–128. Amsterdam: Amsterdam University Press.

Harvey, Colin, B. 2014. "A Taxonomy of Transmedia Storytelling." In *Storyworlds across Media: Toward a Media-Conscious Narratology*, edited by Marie-Laure Ryan and Jan-Noël Thon, 278–294. Lincoln: University of Nebraska Press.

Harvey, Colin, B. 2015. *Fantastic Transmedia: Narrative, Play and Memory across Science Fiction and Fantasy Storyworlds*. London: Palgrave Macmillan.

Into the Spiderverse. 2018. Dir. Bob Persichetti, Peter Ramsey, and Rodney Rothman. USA: Sony Pictures.

Itō, Gō. 2005. *Tetsuka izu deddo*. Tokyo: Seikaisha Shinsho.

Jannidis, Fotis. 2012. "Character." In *The Living Handbook of Narratology*, edited by Peter Hühn, Jan Christoph Meister, John Pier, and Wolf Schmid, n.p. Hamburg: Hamburg University Press. www.lhn.uni-hamburg.de/article/character (accessed 31 January 2020).

Jenkins, Henry. 2006. *Convergence Culture: Where Old and New Media Collide*. New York: New York University Press.

Jørgensen, Kristine. 2010. "Game Characters as Narrative Devices: A Comparative Analysis of *Dragon Age: Origins* and *Mass Effect 2*." *Eludamos: Journal for Computer Game Culture* 4 (2): 315–331. www.eludamos.org/index.php/eludamos/article/view/vol4no2-13 (accessed 31 January 2020).

Kascuk, Zoltan. 2016. "From 'Game-Life Realism' to the 'Imagination-Oriented Aesthetic': Reconsidering Bordieu's Contibution to Fan Studies in the Light of Japanese Manga and Otaku Theory." *Kritika Kultura* 26: 274–292.

Kelly, Peter. 2015. "Approaching the Digital Courting Process in *Dragon Age 2*." In *Game Love: Essays on Play and Affection*, edited by Jessica Enevold and Esther MacCallum-Stewart, 46–62. Jefferson: McFarland.

Kinder, Marsha. 1991. *Playing with Power in Movies, Television, and Video Games: From Muppet Babies to Teenage Mutant Ninja Turtles*. Berkeley: University of California Press.

Klastrup, Lisbeth, and Susana Tosca. 2004. "Transmedial Worlds—Rethinking Cyberworld Design." *CW '04: Proceedings of the 2004 International Conference on Cyberworlds*: 409–416. https://dl.acm.org/doi/10.1109/CW.2004.67 (accessed 31 January 2020).

Klevjer, Rune. 2006. "What Is the Avatar? Fiction and Embodiment in Avatar-Based Singleplayer Computer Games." PhD thesis, University of Bergen, Norway. http://bora.uib.no/handle/1956/2234 (accessed 31 January 2020).

KyūZIP. 2017. "Na mo shiranu kafetomo." In *Persona 5 Comic Anthology* Vol. 1, edited by DNA Media Comics, 123–130. Tokyo: DNA Media Comics.

Lamarre, Thomas. 2009. *The Anime Machine: A Media Theory of Animation*. Minneapolis: University of Minnesota Press.

Lamarre, Thomas. 2018. *Anime Technology*. Minneapolis: University of Minnesota Press.

Linderoth, Jonas. 2005. "Animated Game Pieces: Avatars as Roles, Tools and Props." *Proceedings of the Aesthetics of Play Conference*: n.p. www.aestheticsofplay.org/linderoth.php (accessed 31 January 2020).

Margolin, Uri. 1983. "Characterization in Narrative: Some Theoretical Prolegomena." *Neophilologus* 67 (1): 1–14.

Margolin, Uri. 1986. "The Doer and the Deed: Action as a Basis for Characterization in Narrative." *Poetics Today* 7 (2): 205–225.

Mori, Kinoko. 2017. "Saigo no kotoba." In *Persona 5 Comic Anthology* Vol. 1, edited by DNA Media Comics, 5. Tokyo: DNA Media Comics.

Murasaki, Hisato. 2017. *Persona 5* Vol. 1. Tokyo: Shogakukan.

Mutō, Tamura. 2017. "Morugana kagekiha." In *Persona 5 Comic Anthology* Vol. 2, edited by DNA Media Comics, 40–52. Tokyo: DNA Media Comics.

Nakamura, Akinori, and Susana Tosca. 2019. "The *Mobile Suit Gundam* Franchise: A Case Study of Transmedia Storytelling Practices and the Role of Digital Games in Japan." *DiGRA '19: Proceedings of the 2019 DiGRA International Conference: Game, Play and the Emerging Ludo-Mix*: n.p. www.digra.org/wp-content/uploads/digital-library/DiGRA_2019_paper_235.pdf (accessed 31 January 2020).

Napier, Susan J. 2001. *Anime from* Akira *to* Princess Monoke*: Experiencing Contemporary Japanese Animation*. New York: Palgrave Macmillan.

Newman, James. 2002. "The Myth of the Ergodic Videogame: Some Thoughts on Player-Character Relationships in Videogames." *Game Studies: The International Journal of Computer Game Research* 2 (1): n.p. www.gamestudies.org/0102/newman/ (accessed 31 January 2020).

Nier: Automata. 2017. Developed by PlatinumGames. Published by Square Enix. PlayStation 4.

Ōtsuka, Eiji. 1989. *Monogatari shōhiron*. Tokyo: Asuki Shinsho.

Ōtsuka, Eiji. 2010. "World and Variation: The Reproduction and Consumption of Narrative." *Mechademia: Fanthropologies* 5: 99–118.

Overwatch. 2016. Developed and published by Blizzard Entertainment. Windows.

Pearson, Roberta E. 2019. "Transmedia Characters: Additionality and Cohesion in Transfictional Heroes." In *The Routledge Companion to Transmedia Studies*, edited by Matthew Freeman and Renira Rampazzo Gambarato, 148–156. New York: Routledge.

Persona 5. 2016. Developed by P-Studio. Published by Atlus. PlayStation 4.

Persona 5: Dancing in Starlight. 2018. Developed by P-Studio. Published by Atlus. PlayStation 4.

Persona 5 Royal. 2019. Developed by P-Studio. Published by Atlus. PlayStation 4.

Persona Q2: New Cinema Labyrinth. 2018. Developed by P-Studio. Published by Atlus. Nintendo 3DS.

Picard, Martin, and Jérémie Pelletier-Gagnon. 2015. "Introduction: Geemu, Media Mix, and the State of Japanese Video Game Studies." *Kinephanos: Journal of Media Studies and Popular Culture* 5 (December): 1–19.

Pokémon Sun and Moon. 2016. Developed by Game Freak. Published by The Pokémon Company and Nintendo. Nintendo 3DS.

Pokémon Sword and Shield. 2019. Developed by Game Freak. Published by The Pokémon Company and Nintendo. Nintendo Switch.

Reicher, Maria E. 2010. "The Ontology of Fictional Characters." In *Characters in Fictional Worlds: Understanding Imaginary Beings in Literature, Film, and Other Media*, edited by Jens Eder, Fotis Jannidis, and Ralf Schneider, 111–133. Berlin: De Gruyter.

Rosendo, Nieves. 2015. "The Map Is Not the Territory: Bible and Canon in the Transmedial World of *Halo*." *IMAGE: Zeitschrift für interdisziplinäre Bildwissenschaft* Special Issue 22 (July): 54–64.

Rosendo, Nieves. 2016. "Character-Centred Transmedia Narratives: *Sherlock Holmes* in the 21st Century." *Artnodes* 18 (November): 20–27.

Saitō, Tamaki. 2014. *Kyarakutā seishin bunseki: Manga, bungaku, nihonjin*. Tokyo: Chikuma Sobo.

Schröter, Felix, and Jan-Noël Thon. 2014. "Video Game Characters: Theory and Analysis." *DIEGESIS: Interdisciplinary E-Journal for Narrative Research* 3 (1): 40–77.

Steinberg, Marc. 2012. *Anime's Media Mix: Franchising Toys and Characters in Japan*. Minneapolis: University of Minnesota Press.

Steinberg, Marc. 2015. "8-Bit Manga: Kadokawa's Madara, or, the Gameic Media Mix." *Kinephanos: Journal of Media Studies and Popular Culture* 5 (December): 40–52.

Super Smash Bros. Ultimate. 2018. Developed by Bandai Namco and Sora Ltd. Published by Nintendo. Nintendo Switch.

Thomas Was Alone. 2012. Developed and published by Mike Bithell. Windows.

Thon, Jan-Noël. 2015. "Converging Worlds: From Transmedia Storyworlds to Transmedial Universes." *Storyworlds: A Journal of Narrative Studies* 7 (2): 21–53.

Tosca, Susana. 2003. "The Appeal of Cute Monkeys." In *Proceedings of Level Up: Digital Games Research Conference*, edited by Marinka Copier and Joost Raessens, 392–403. Utrecht: Utrecht University Press.

Tosca, Susana, and Lisbeth Klastrup. 2019. *Transmedial Worlds in Everyday Life: Networked Reception, Social Media and Fictional Worlds*. New York: Routledge.

Tronstad, Ragnhild. 2008. "Character Identification in *World of Warcraft*: The Relationship between Capacity and Appearance." In *Digital Culture, Play, and*

Identity: A World of Warcraft *Reader*, edited by Hilde G. Corneliussen and Jill Walker Rettberg, 249–264. Cambridge, MA: MIT Press.

Uricchio, William, and Roberta E. Pearson. 1991. "'I'm Not Fooled by That Cheap Disguise.'" In *The Many Lives of the Batman: Critical Approaches to a Superhero and His Media*, edited by Roberta E. Pearson and William Uricchio, 182–213. New York: Routledge.

Vella, Daniel. 2014. "Modeling the Semiotic Structure of Game Characters." *DiGRA '14: Proceedings of the 2014 DiGRA Conference*: n.p. www.digra.org/digital-library/publications/modeling-the-semiotic-structure-of-game-characters/ (31 January 2020).

Vella, Daniel. 2015. "The Ludic Subject and the Ludic Self: Analyzing the 'I-in-the-Gameworld.' " PhD thesis, IT University of Copenhagen, Denmark. https://en.itu.dk/~/media/en/research/phd-programme/phd-defences/2015/daniel-vella---the-ludic-subject-and-the-ludic-self-final-print-pdf.pdf (accessed 31 January 2020).

Wilde, Lukas R. A. 2019. "Recontextualizing Characters: Media Convergence and Pre-/Meta-Narrative Character Circulation." *IMAGE: Zeitschrift für interdisziplinäre Bildwissenschaft* Special Issue 29 (January): 3–21.

Wolf, Mark, J. P. 2012. *Building Imaginary Worlds: The Theory and History of Subcreation*. New York: Routledge.

14 Creating Lara Croft

The meaning of the comic books for the *Tomb Raider* franchise

Josefa Much

Since the creation of Lara Croft in 1996, it seems impossible to imagine the game industry without her. Her pop-cultural impact certainly affected the gaming industry, but the expansion of her character into a whole franchise has also immortalized her through action figures, cosplay, music videos, and appearances in many other media. If you take a closer look at the franchise, you will find a number of different videogames for different gaming platforms as well as three action films, six novels, and many comic books. Shortly after the release of the very first *Tomb Raider* game in 1996, the comic book publisher Top Cow released a crossover with their own heroine Sara Pezzini aka Witchblade and Lara Croft: *Tomb Raider/Witchblade* (Turner 1997, 1998). The *Witchblade* comic books were one of Top Cow's most prominent series. As a result, something very interesting happened: Lara Croft was introduced into a new universe beyond her own games, and thus into a new storyworld. She became part of the Top Cow universe as both franchises collided. Two years later, the Tomb Raider received her own stand-alone comic book series. It not only focused on her adventures, but also on her personal thoughts and approach, introducing different characters and friends of hers. Later on, this would be used to create new crossovers with different Top Cow characters (e.g., *Dark Crossing* [Holland and Turner 2000a, 2000b]; *Endgame* [Rieber and Green 2003a, 2003b, 2003c; Silvestri and Tan 2003; Turner 2002c]; the Magdalena crossover [Bonny and Basaldua 2004a, 2004b, 2004c]; the Fathom/Witchblade/Tomb Raider crossover [Turner 2000, 2002a, 2002b]). And since one stand-alone comic book series apparently is not enough, another Tomb Raider comics series was introduced: *Tomb Raider: Journeys* (2001–2003), a series of different Tomb Raider stories.

This begs the question why the comic book series, of all things, is so important to this big universe with all its ongoing stories that can be played on different gaming platforms. There are different ways to approach the significance of the comic books, but there is a major difference between the comics released before and after the reboot of the *Tomb Raider* franchise in 2013. Before the reboot, the comic books served as another entry point (Jenkins 2006, 95–99) to the *Tomb Raider* franchise, which was commercially successful but also gathered its own fan base. Followers of the comic book series were so fascinated with it that they even started their own small comic book series about all things Lara Croft. I will explore this series below, but before I do so, I will first provide an overview of the different *Tomb Raider* games and the attempt of the *Tomb Raider* creators to change the storytelling of the games to create a transmedia event within the franchise. Second, I will compare comic book and game, and the transition of the comic books within the franchise, following different perspectives on the performance of Lara Croft. An additional perspective on the franchise, especially on learning and educational potentials of the current game series, follows. Finally, I will take a closer look at the essential functions that the comic book fulfills and then end with concluding remarks. Overall, this chapter seeks to show the significance of different media and the role of fans and the appropriation of original content (see Deterding 2009). Furthermore, it aims to demonstrate how different aspects of storytelling work in a more mixed style in early *Tomb Raider* games and adaptations in comparison to the comic books of the 2013 reboot, in which the storyworld is closer to the used media. I will argue that the reboot invests the story and background of Lara Croft with a more credible character and a deeper storytelling.

Overview

After six stand-alone games and the commercial failure of *Tomb Raider: The Angel of Darkness* in 2003, a "small" reboot of the series was in order: *Tomb Raider: Legend* (2006), *Tomb Raider: Anniversary* (2007) (a remake of the very first *Tomb Raider* game), and the concluding part of the trilogy, *Tomb Raider: Underworld* (2008) were produced by a new developer. These reboots signified a new direction for the franchise by placing greater emphasis on the storytelling and the main character. Lara Croft was no longer just a badass adventurous grave robber but also someone who lost her parents at a young age (the death of her parents is an established, unalterable event within the *Tomb Raider* franchise, maybe comparable to the death of Uncle Ben in the Spider-Man universe and the murder of Bruce Wayne's parents). The focus on her mother's death ultimately amounted to trite conversations, dramatic actions, and forced facial expressions. Something similar was attempted with the sixth game of the series, *Tomb Raider: The Angel of Darkness*. A new look, a new way to tell a story, even a male counterpart. Also, *Tomb Raider: The Angel of Darkness* marked the first attempt at creating a transmedia event with books (and in some way with a comic book arc) that bridged the game story after her apparent death in *Tomb Raider IV: The Last Revelation* (1999).

None of this really contributed to the storytelling in the games. Kennedy points out for the first-generation games: "The creation and maintenance of a fairly complex backstory for Lara is an attempt to secure control of her virtual identity—she is a commercial product after all. Providing Lara with a (fairly) plausible history gives her some ontological coherence and helps to enhance the immersion of the player in the *Tomb Raider* world, and abets the identification with Lara" (2002, n.p.). The comic books, however, were quite literally a different story. The medium offers enough time to tell a story, to develop reasonable characters and stage credible character developments. The storytelling in the comic books offers not just a stage for Lara Croft and the different authors and artists with a vision for this strong female character; it also offers something for the fans, who can enjoy new stories told in a different medium. Of course, it is also important for videogames to tell a story, and it matters just as much how the story is told. But there are many more mechanisms and approaches in videogames that have to succeed, especially on a ludological level (Juul 2005). There are, for instance, the gameplay, the expectations of the publisher, and the audience's expectations of the games, as well as a bug-free environment. In short: It is quite a task to entertain consumers in such a complex medium. The comic books offer an opportunity to shape a flat character that originally lacked in personality but has extraordinary physical abilities into a rounded character with a credible and believable life (while also living through exciting adventures besides representing a hero's saga; Campbell 1990). Moreover, every medium has a different role and use of mechanics, as Thon points out in regard of subjective representation: "Despite differences with regard to the mediality of conventionally distinct media and the idiosyncrasies of individual narrative representations, however, the subjective representation of consciousness can be considered a genuinely transmedial phenomenon in that it is realized across wide range of media, each with its own specific limitations and affordances" (2014, 67). Thus, it is no surprise that there is a different approach for the videogames and the comic books.

What worked well for the first and second series of *Tomb Raider* games also worked for the 2013 *Tomb Raider* reboot. The comic books are no longer published by Top Cow Comics, but by Dark Horse Comics. Now, Lara's adventures take place in her own universe, not in two different universes. This time, the comic books also fulfill a different role: They tell the story between the games.

Learning and educational potentials

Over the past few years, Lara Croft and *Tomb Raider* have often been the focus of academic research, for example in gender studies (Deuber-Mankowsky 2005; Kennedy 2002). But there are other aspects of the franchise worth looking at. From a broader perspective, it is fair to say that videogames can create learning and educational potentials (Fromme and Könitz 2014). The same holds true for comic books. A strong indicator for this can be what Fromme describes as irritations: the creation of an alienating distance that disrupts the immersion. In videogames, such irritations allow for the use of world-references and self-references, such as references to other media worlds (Fromme 2006, 193). The *Tomb Raider* franchise includes not only videogames, but also three films and a multitude of comics, in all of which Lara Croft is interpreted and contextualized over and over. This happens either through different actresses or, in the case of the comics, through different artists who interpret Lara Croft in their respective art style (and also through the stories told by the authors). Indeed, there are some memorable characteristics and items that seem to be an integral part of Lara Croft across all the different representations: the iconic dual pistols, the holsters, the brown hot pants with a greenish top, and the long brown ponytail.[1] Other media references can be found even beyond the videogames. For example, in *Shadow of the Tomb Raider* (2018), it is possible to play the avatar with skins from the old *Tomb Raider* videogames (*Tomb Raider* [1996]; *Tomb Raider: The Angel of Darkness*). Alicia Vikander's Lara Croft makes a reference to Angelina Jolie's Lara Croft as she is interested in two of the iconic pistols from the first film (and wears the same braid as Jolie's Lara), and newspaper articles in *Rise of the Tomb Raide*r (2015) describe events from the comic book series. Here, it becomes obvious how compressed the storyworld truly is. The game can serve as a starting point, but every now and then there are references to franchise spin-offs. These irritations enable the consumers to constantly scrutinize the character of Lara Croft and her personal development, and they also allow them to examine how realistically and authentically she is portrayed. In addition, there are many Easter eggs, such as Lara quoting her other iterations, for example, "I think I am not strong enough," a statement from Lara Croft in *Tomb Raider: The Angel of Darkness*. These ironic, sometimes self-ironic, references can, in turn, be taken up again and cause more irritations (Fromme 2006, 199).[2] But we see references beyond Lara's own universe: Every now and then you can find a dead Indiana Jones (in *Tomb Raider IV: The Last Revelation*) or Nathan Drake from the *Uncharted* series (2007–2017) (in *Lara Croft and the Guardian of Light* [2010]). These characters share the same game genre.[3]

If you take a formal look at the videogames and comic books, it becomes clear that these media often reflect on their own genres and forms. Hereafter, I will focus on the latest reboot of the series, both the videogame and the comic books, in order to explore the complexity of the transmedia franchise.

Jörissen and Marotzki have worked out four dimensions to analyze educational potentials, referring to questions raised by Immanuel Kant: What can I know? What should I do? What may I hope? What is the human being? The first dimension, the dimension of knowledge (What can I know?), refers to a critical contemplation of the limits and conditions of knowledge (Jörissen and Marotzki 2009, 31), but also to factual knowledge and orienting knowledge as well as intermedia and self-references (Fromme and Könitz 2014). The second dimension, the dimension of action (What should I do?), exposes us to ethical and moral questions concerning our own or someone else's actions (Jörissen and Marotzki 2009, 31). The third dimension, the dimension of limits, refers to things that cannot be explained reasonably, for example, the loss of control or the breaking of the fourth wall in media (Fromme and Könitz 2014). In the final dimension, everything comes together: the dimension of biography or identity (What is the human being?) and reflecting on one's identity (Jörissen and Marotzki 2009, 31). It is the most complex dimension because all previous questions lead to this question.

A closer look at these dimensions indicates their applicability to the latest reboot of *Tomb Raider* and foregrounds interesting connections to the comic books. Over the course of the game, Lara Croft finds different everyday objects (Fromme and Könitz 2014, 254). When she enters a village, she stumbles over artifacts left behind by the former inhabitants, such as toys or photographs. She may also find antique boxes, old swords, or jewelry, like old jade necklaces. Not all of these objects stem from the same time period, but the game menu reveals more details about them. In the inventory, Lara comments on all the objects. She names and identifies them and sorts them into different time periods. Thus, you can reimage who lived there, identify enemies, and gain factual knowledge about the different time periods. All of this relates to the dimension of knowledge (Jörissen and Marotzki 2009, 31). It also shows a difference compared to the other *Tomb Raider* eras because the artifacts never took such a big role as describing the object within the games.

The dimension of action is present throughout the game and the whole game series because Lara gets into dangerous, life-threatening situations and has to make decisions to survive. At certain points, the gamer can take action, mostly in the form of quick-time events in which the player has a short moment to decide how to proceed in a given situation. Likewise, the decision to save her friends and colleagues is a complex task. Throughout the whole series, Lara has to make challenging decisions, and these decisions build upon each other. For example, in every game of the series, an apocalypse has to be stopped to save the world. In *Tomb Raider* (2013), set on an island, the world is threatened by an ancient weather goddess named Himiko; in *Rise of the Tomb Raider*, Lara has to prevent someone from finding the promise of immortality; and in the final part of the new *Tomb Raider* trilogy, *Shadow of the Tomb Raider*, Lara herself accidentally starts the countdown to the apocalypse by stealing a precious Maya artifact. The dimension of limits is tied strongly to the dimension of action because the main themes revolve around issues like survival or the loss of control and how to deal with it. The portrayal of these limits is often very emotional and brutal, but also crucial to the staging—one of the reasons the game has been rated PG18.[4] At the very beginning of *Tomb Raider* (2013), Lara encounters a mystical Oni-Warrior who will kill her if the player does not react fast enough. Every possible cause of death has its own special cutscene. But if Lara finds a way out of the encounter, she has to crawl through a cave filled with blood and bones—a rather well-made illustration of the dimension of limits.

All of these dimensions lead to the dimension of biography, for which they form the basis. Throughout the series, Lara Croft is established as a young adult, traumatized by all of her life-threatening experiences. The omnipresent antagonist of thc videogame series is an organization named Trinity, which she has to face in every game. Another focus of the series is the research into her father's death and heritage, which she has to reprocess time and again. This topic is explored through flashback scenes, but also through a level in *Shadow of the Tomb Raider*. A playable flashback scene designed as a whole game level is experienced from the perspective of a very young Lara Croft. At the end of the *Rise of the Tomb Raider* game, the player can decide the fate of the main antagonist (after the final battle). At this point, the antagonist reveals that he is the reason for her father's death. After that, the player can decide to leave the antagonist for dead or to kill him. On the one hand, her father's biography is in the focus of the protagonist because Lara Croft wants to reveal the truth behind her father's death. On the other hand, she also wants to know more because she is constantly comparing herself to him. This leads to a narrative construction of biography throughout the series (Marotzki 2004, 368). These four dimensions are not only present in the videogames; they can appear in the comic books, albeit not in an interactive form.

Furthermore, the revelation of biographical aspects in the comics happens from a different point of view than in the videogame series. One could almost consider the comic books a kind of diary or log book (Krüger 1999, 14–18; Marotzki 1999, 114–120). They offer a glimpse into the reasons behind certain actions of a character because the comic books themselves contain references to the videogames. References to oneself and the world can be transferred into videogames (Fromme and Könitz 2014). Comic books can enhance these references or serve as separate starting points. In the latter case, they would also serve as independent entry points into the story (Jenkins 2006, 111).

Significance of the comic books

After this overview of the franchise and the different connections between the individual elements and media, I turn to the significance of the comic books (see Figure 14.1). Altogether there are three essential functions that the comic books fulfill: extension of the storyworld, fan-generated content, and closure of gaps in the videogames/storyworld (Jenkins 2006; Ryan 2013).

Extension of the storyworld

As already mentioned, the franchise extends to many different levels of storytelling in different media, including the first run of the comic book series from 1999 to 2005, with 50 issues, a 12-issue comic book miniseries called *Tomb Raider: Journeys*, and miscellaneous specials and crossovers. The first comic book series ended two years after the commercial disaster of *Tomb Raider: The Angel of Darkness*.[5] Interestingly, the series addresses events

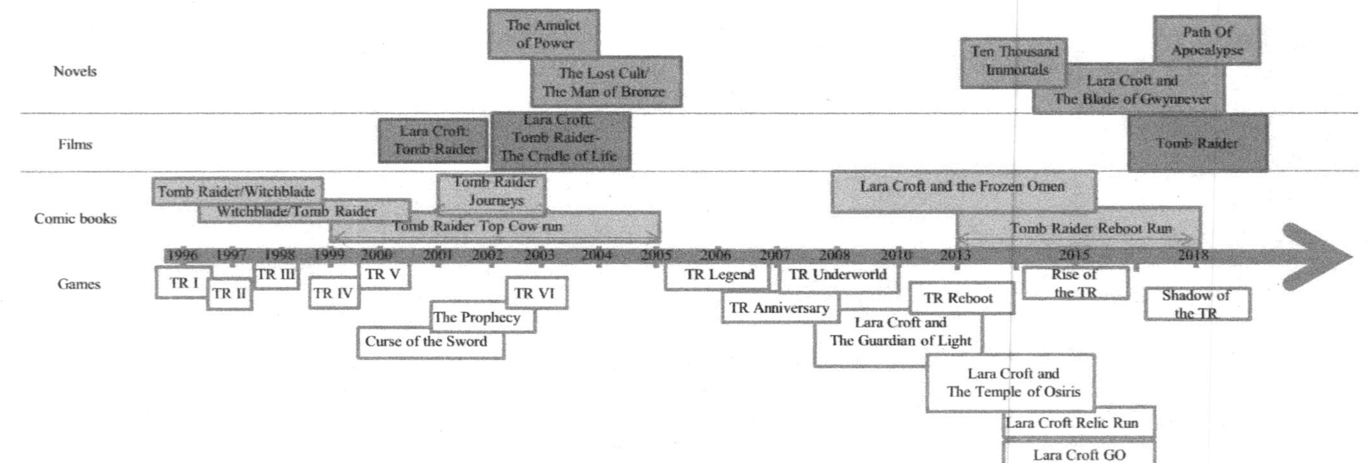

Figure 14.1 Overview of the *Tomb Raider* franchise.

from the videogame storyline for the first time. Many of the characters, locations, and concepts are transferred to the comic books. In contrast to *Tomb Raider: The Angel of Darkness*, the comic book series does not end at this point but continues to tell the story beyond the videogame's end until the last issue two years later. This represents the biggest extension of the *Tomb Raider* franchise because *Tomb Raider: The Angel of Darkness* is an open-ended story and writers can simply go on and keep following the tale of Lara Croft.

As of yet, there are no signs that the comic book series is running out of material. Little signs and cues in the videogame series and tutorial levels as well as certain objects hint at even more adventures Lara might have experienced. All around Lara Croft's virtual house, we find a multitude of exhibited artifacts one might conclude are souvenirs from still unknown travels. For example, you can find the Ark of the Covenant in the first *Tomb Raider* game (maybe also an Indiana Jones Easter egg), located in the main hall, and there is also a trophy room with figures of Egyptian cats or human figures. In *Tomb Raider: Anniversary*, there is also a trophy room with Greek flagstones behind glass and relics from different cultures and different areas of the world. In the hidden trophy room in *Tomb Raider III: Adventures of Lara Croft* (1998), you can find floating objects, also from her past adventures (e.g., the Dagger of Xiang from *Tomb Raider II* [1997]) and still unknown objects.

The comic book series offers the reader an intimate insight into the character by telling the stories from a first-person perspective. In a way, they document and explore the biography and identity of Lara Croft—a kind of illustrated, accompanying diary. In the videogames, the player can merely guess at her emotions through physical or verbal cues designed to help the player (nods, "I can't do this," "aahh"). The sound design also grants the player some insights (Fromme and Könitz 2014, 267). Special sounds indicate an unlocked secret, such as finding additional hidden objects, like the jade dragons in *Tomb Raider II,* or the discovery of hidden medi-packs. Furthermore, the relationships between characters are only explained through cutscenes or flashbacks. In *Tomb Raider* (2013), Lara reflects on herself and her own actions at campfires/saving points and after special game stages. In the comic book series, she interacts directly with other characters. Thus, the other characters receive more reasonable background stories and can introduce themselves. Alternatively, a narrator introduces the characters or Lara Croft herself comments on characters or actions in text panels, speech bubbles, or thought bubbles (McCloud 2005). This form of speech that has been converted into text (Dittmar 2011, 97–98) shows how Lara thinks about the characters. Through this form it is also possible to make conclusions about the content.[6] The text panels and bubbles also offer more room to interpret and analyze, and they can be seen as a cross-cutting to the comic books. As mentioned above, the comic book series follows its own storyline with hints to or parables from the videogame series, as exemplified by *Tomb Raider* #26 to #28 (Rieber and Green 2003a, 2003b, 2003c). After the events of *Tomb Raider IV: The Last Revelation,* the story finishes with an open ending, regardless of whether the protagonist survived her destiny in Egypt or not. Lara also dies in the comic book series, but her resurrection differs from the one in the videogame series.

The comic book series starts the way it ends: as a complementary story to the videogames or a collection of stories of Lara Croft as the Tomb Raider. The ongoing series was published two months after the release of *Tomb Raider IV: The Last Revelation*. The fourth videogame marks the temporary end of the heroine, but only in her digital incarnation. The ongoing comic book series has its own point of view, its own story, and a lot more background information. It also introduces old and new characters. The role of a "storyteller" was also introduced in the game *Tomb Raider V: Chronicles* (2000), following *Tomb Raider IV: The Last Revelation*. Some friends of Lara Croft's come together after her funeral and share stories about her adventures. The two recurring devices of the videogame/narrative style are: the death of Lara Croft and the retrospective narrative of the life of Lara Croft.[7]

In the Top Cow universe, Lara Croft's death is staged as a big crossover event. It had such a big impact that three comic book series were affected by it, most notably the *Witchblade* series, in which the main protagonist Sara Pezzini has to deal with the loss of a friend and her own feelings of guilt, remembering shared experiences and reflecting on their friendship. The two devices mentioned above are processed and concluded in the *Tomb Raider* series. Lara Croft's death is staged in an Egyptian twilight zone where she has to justify her grave robbery (see parallel to *Tomb Raider IV: The Last Revelation*). This is another way of explaining how Lara Croft survived her own death and how she was resurrected from the dead.

The second start of the series in 2006, when Crystal Dynamics published *Tomb Raider: Legend*, *Tomb Raider: Anniversary*, and *Tomb Raider: Underworld*, was not accompanied by a second run of the comic book series, even though it had been planned by Crystal Dynamics.[8] With the reboot of the *Tomb Raider* franchise and Lara Croft's origin story, a new comic book series, this time published by Dark Horse Comics, emerged. In this series, Lara Croft has just started her archaeological career, and the player accompanies her on her first big expedition. In the videogames before the reboot, Lara Croft already had an origin story, but now we can accompany her on her way to becoming the Tomb Raider—a development mirrored in the videogame titles: *Tomb Raider*, *Rise of the Tomb Raider*, and *Shadow of the Tomb Raider*. The comic books are now tied more closely to the videogames than in the previous run before the reboot, but they also fulfill the role of a first-person narrative focusing on Lara Croft's point of view and on how the characters relate to each other. In addition, there is more room to discuss and reflect on the grief about a lost or dead character.

Fan-generated content

Successful major videogame franchises with strong and recognizable characters often go hand in hand with fan-generated content. There are, for example, many *Tomb Raider* fansites around the world, complete with huge fan communities that are often interconnected. The official *Tomb Raider* website also offers a community board to exchange with other fans and community managers. In addition, it is possible to register your own fansite. These communities offer the possibility to share fan art and fan content, but there is also fan art beyond the "official" boards.

Notably, many big *Tomb Raider* fan communities do not exist anymore or have officially been closed by the admins (e.g., *PlanetLara.com*). Reasons for the closure of the sites differ, but most of the time it is due to other projects or other commitments.[9] Nevertheless, there is a large amount of fan art on the world wide web. The artist community DeviantArt lists 78,007 entries with the tag "Tomb Raider," 77,554 entries with the tag "Lara Croft," and roundabout 3,100 entries tagged as "tomb raider comic." A vast number of entries can also be found on *Tumblr* (also the official *Tomb Raider Blog*, which awards an annual community prize), and the Google image search reveals a multitude of search results on thematic fan art and community art. There is not only much art for the videogame series, but also fan art relating to the comic book series: fan-generated art for story arcs, new colorizations of sketches, copies and imitations of a certain art style or a certain artist in the comic book series, but also cosplays of the different interpretations of Lara Croft from the comic book series. If you also consider fan fiction, the world's largest database for fan fiction, fanfiction.net, lists 500 entries on Lara Croft, among them some ongoing comics stories. But within the *Tomb Raider* community, something very extraordinary happened: the creation of an original, fan-generated comic book series called *Tales of Lara Croft* (2003–2007). This artistic, participatory project arose in collaboration with fans, artists, and the publisher of the *Tomb Raider* videogames.

To take a closer look at this phenomenon, one can apply one of the seven "principles of transmedia storytelling," namely the principle of performance: "The ability of transmedia extensions to lead to fan produced performances that can become part of the transmedia narrative itself. Some performances are invited by the creator while others are not; fans actively search for sites of potential performance" (Jenkins 2010, n.p.). *Tales of Lara Croft* was a non-profit project that distributed copies of the comics through a now closed fan site (*PlanetLara.com*). Fans created their own little stories around Lara Croft. These were not just tales about and with the action heroine, but also stories about how fans discovered the fandom, what they thought about the strong female lead character, and what *Tomb Raider* and Lara Croft meant to them. It is a reflection on being a fan, packed into fan fiction stories paired with fan art (and thus, first attempts at professionalization).

Closure of gaps in the videogames/storyworld

The fan-generated content (not only in *Tales of Lara Croft*) tries to close some gaps in the storyworld, but it does so from a fan perspective. The most recent comics series is closer to the videogames than ever before. The storyworld is more open, offers many entry points, and, thus, lots of room for interpretation, thanks to the multitude of different authors who generate stories. After the reboot of the game series, this was planned differently. The start of the reboot did not coincide with the first videogame *Tomb Raider* (2013); the first published medium was actually the comic book *Tomb Raider: The Beginning* (Pratchett and Mutti 2013). This is the first entry point after the new start of the franchise, and it is set immediately before the beginning of the videogame's story. All the crew members and new characters are introduced, and Lara Croft ponders the current events. Lara now stays in her very own universe, and the comic books thus serve a different purpose: They show what happens in-between the games and therefore serve as new entry points. They are not just fillers to bridge the time between publications but fulfill an important role in the franchise in regard to development of the characters (if you want to get a clue what happens in between and around the game). The game does work for itself, and in most aspects, this also works for the comic books if you are familiar with Lara Croft and *Tomb Raider*.

In *Tomb Raider* (2013), Lara and a group of friends and scientists are stranded on a forgotten island, which is also the focus of the videogame. In the two subsequent games, of all her island friends, only Jonah is left to accompany Lara and support her on her adventures. If you want to know what happened between the 2013 game and the 2015 follow-up, you have to read the comic books. They explore every character's background in greater detail and deal with the aftermath of the events in the videogames. Another hint at the more straightforward storytelling can be found via the authors of the comic book stories. One of them is Rhianna Pratchett, who also wrote the story for *Tomb Raider* (2013). The same authors who contribute to the videogame series also write stories for the comic book series and therefore have a better overview over the entire series/franchise and narrative. How well everything comes together becomes apparent at the end of the reboot trilogy: One month after the publication of the final videogame *Shadow of the Tomb Raider,* the associated comic book run was also finalized and the last issue published (see Figure 14.2).

Conclusion

This chapter sought to provide a better overview of and insight into the *Tomb Raider* franchise, detailing how the comic books fit into this franchise and determining what constitutes their significance for transmedia storytelling. It offers but a glimpse of this phenomenon because I left out some comic

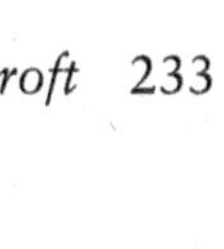

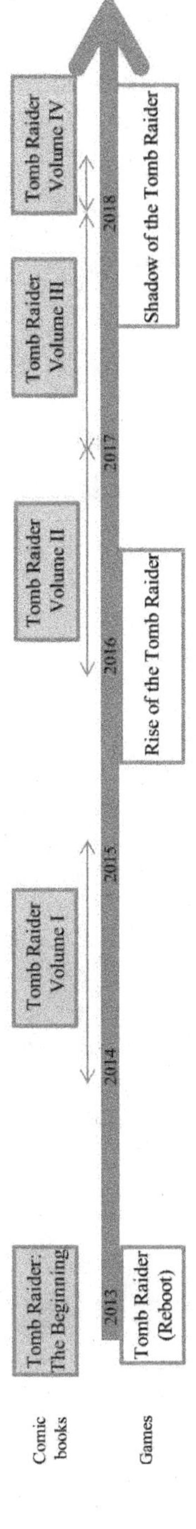

Figure 14.2 Overview of the *Tomb Raider* reboot franchise.

book series focusing on Lara Croft, among them *Tomb Raider: Journeys* and the *Tomb Raider* spin-off *Lara Croft and the Frozen Omen* (Bechko and Carnero 2015)—the comic book series based on *Lara Croft and the Guardian of Light* and *Lara Croft and the Temple of Osiris* (2014). In addition, we have to consider the significance of other spin-offs such as *Lara Croft Go* (2015), the handheld series (*Tomb Raider: Curse of the Sword* [2001] and *Tomb Raider: The Prophecy* [2002]), and the *Tomb Raider* films (*Lara Croft: Tomb Raider* [2001], *Lara Croft: Tomb Raider: The Cradle of Life* [2003], and *Tomb Raider* [2018]) as well as their position within the franchise. The comic books establish many connections to the films and videogames—in many cases, it is the storyline (the story arc of the *Angel of Darkness* comics [Bonny and Daniel 2003a, 2003b, 2003c, 2003d] or the *Tomb Raider* reboot arc)—and they impact the franchise, for example, with the death of Lara Croft and its adaptation in different media (the "Endgame" story arc in the *Tomb Raider* comics). The importance of the character Lara Croft and the series shapes the "Endgame" story arc (Turner 2002c) because the events in this arc impact a whole comics universe. Furthermore, out of this story arc arises a whole new comic book series in the Top Cow universe (Silvestri and Tan 2003).

During the first run of the comic book series set in the Top Cow universe, the storyworld Lara Croft inhabits is very open and rather loosely defined, but it marks a very remarkable entry point for the franchise. Every story is relevant for the storyworld (Ryan 2013, 92). Lara Croft is a strong female lead character who experiences adventures all around the world. The authors of the stories have much creative space to tell these stories, even though the first main volume (1999–2005) follows a straightforward storyline. They are supported by one-shots (e.g., Avery and Tan 2004; Bonny and Daniel 2004; Jurgens and Jusko 2005) or by the more independent storytelling in *Tomb Raider: Journeys*. Within the stories, one can find references to the videogames and the films; this happens most notably through the visual representation of Lara Croft (clothes, hairstyle, choice of weapons). At a second glance, even more can be discovered: Easter eggs, hints at events in the videogames, or artifacts.

After the reboot of *Tomb Raider*, the *Tomb Raider* universe reinvented itself, and all of the stories are interwoven and connected to each other. The new *Tomb Raider* universe "starts" with the comic book *Tomb Raider: The Beginning*, an introduction to the main game. All other media are interconnected and tell a chronological story if read and/or played in the right order. At the end of the comic books, the videogame picks up the story almost gapless, and the same goes for the novels that were published (Abnett and Vincent 2014; Perry 2018). This continuous narrative style is paralleled by the producers and writers of the videogames series, such as Rhianna Pratchett, who are also working on different media within the franchise. As a result, the storyworld is more tightly woven together. There are fewer possibilities for plot holes than in the pre-reboot storyworld.

However, the diversity of the characters and the storytelling is, to an extent, lost. On the other hand, there is a gain in the credibility of the franchise and the events that happen in this world. Most significantly, the comic books are the glue of the franchise. They present new stories, fill in the gaps, and create a space for fan desires as well as new entry points to the transmedia world(-building).

Notes

1 This not only holds true for the different media in the franchise but is also acknowledged by the fan community. A look at the cosplayers reveals a range of different representations of Lara Croft. Cosplays of this character receive so much positive reception that the publisher even released instructions on how to do a proper Lara Croft cosplay (with information on the fabric, color, materials, etc., for instance at https://cdn.sqexeu.com/files/tombraider/files/GearGuide.pdf; accessed 31 January 2020).

2 Other irritations named by Fromme are references to different media worlds, ironic play with meanings, breaking the fourth wall, performance of gameworld and interface-elements, and paradoxical expressions of NPCs (Fromme 2006, 193–199)

3 Indiana Jones also served as model for the creation of Lara Croft, while the game adapts elements of the Indiana Jones movies: "As we already know, Lara Croft was modeled after a Hollywood figure. Listening to the way Jeremy Heath-Smith tells it, the transformation of Indiana Jones into Lara Croft was simply due to concerns that similarities between a male protagonist and his Hollywood prototype 'could cause trouble with George Lucas'" (Deuber-Mankowsky 2005, 23). As Rauscher (2012, 167) points out, she does not only adapt elements of Indiana Jones but also of James Bond.

4 According to most computer game rating systems: PEGI 18 Years (European Union), USK 18 (Germany), ESRB: Mature 17+ (USA)—except *Rise of the Tomb Raider* and *Shadow of the Tomb Raider* with a USK 16 (Germany).

5 The long-awaited game after the apparent death of Lara Croft tried to explain everything through transmedia events, including three books (Gardner 2004; Knight 2004; Resnick 2003) to bridge the story between *Tomb Raider IV: The Last Revelation* and *Tomb Raider: The Angel of Darkness* (and in some way the comic book series). They tried to create a more serious and darker version of *Tomb Raider* but failed because most of the audience ignored the additional story material (Rauscher 2011, 175). Another reason was a very buggy game with confusing gameplay.

6 As Thon points out: "Contemporary graphic novels may be considered a multimodal medium with strong visual emphasis. Comparable to both feature films and computer games, however, they use not only pictorial but also various verbal elements representing characters' speech and thought in speech or thought bubbles as part of the verbal-pictorial mode of representation that prototypically defines their mediality as well as representing narratorial voices or the 'inner voice' of characters through the use of narration boxes or thought boxes typically located above or below the verbal pictorial representation in the panel body" (Thon 2014, 78).

7 Or, in other words, the narrative style as flashback, as Bordwell and Thompson write: "An alteration of *story* order in which the *plot* moves back to show events that have taken place earlier than ones already shown" (2017, 515, original emphases; see also Bordwell and Thompson 2017, 79).

8 In 2007, it was planned to publish a new *Tomb Raider* comics series about the second *Tomb Raider* videogame reboot (*Tomb Raider: Legend*, *Tomb Raider: Anniversary*, *Tomb Raider: Underworld*), but it was canceled due to licensing problems.

9 This was one of many reasons for the closure of *PlanetLara.com*. If you follow the thread on the *Tomb Raider* forums you can also see the significance of this special Lara Croft fanpage. They delivered a lot of fan-generated content like fan art but also official *Tomb Raider* game materials such as game music, soundtracks, official wallpapers, or interviews with the developers of the *Tomb Raider* games (www.tombraiderforums.com/showthread.php?t=171288; accessed 31 January 2020).

Works cited

Abnett, Dan, and Nik Vincent. 2014. *Tomb Raider: The Ten Thousand Immortals*. London: DK.

Avery, Fiona, and Billy Tan. 2004. *Tomb Raider: Arabian Nights*. Los Angeles: Top Cow Productions.

Bechko, Corinna, and Carmen Carnero. 2015. *Lara Croft and the Frozen Omen*. Milwaukie: Dark Horse Comics.

Bonny, James, and Eric Basaldua. 2004a. *Tomb Raider #46: Gathering Storm: Part 1*. Los Angeles: Top Cow Productions.

Bonny, James, and Eric Basaldua. 2004b. *Tomb Raider #47: Gathering Storm: Part 2*. Los Angeles: Top Cow Productions.

Bonny, James, and Eric Basaldua. 2004c. *Tomb Raider #48: Gathering Storm: Part 3*. Los Angeles: Top Cow Productions.

Bonny, James, and Tony Daniel. 2003a. *Tomb Raider #32: Angel of Darkness: Part 1*. Los Angeles: Top Cow Productions.

Bonny, James, and Tony Daniel. 2003b. *Tomb Raider #33: Angel of Darkness: Part 2*: Los Angeles: Top Cow Productions.

Bonny, James, and Tony Daniel. 2003c. *Tomb Raider #34: Angel of Darkness: Part 3*. Los Angeles: Top Cow Productions.

Bonny, James, and Tony Daniel. 2003d. *Tomb Raider #35: The Black Legion: Part 1*. Los Angeles: Top Cow Productions.

Bonny, James, and Tony Daniel. 2004. *Tomb Raider: Takeover*. Los Angeles: Top Cow Productions.

Bordwell, David, and Kristin Thompson. 2017. *Film Art: An Introduction*. 11th edition. New York: McGraw-Hill Education.

Campbell, Joseph. 1990. *The Hero's Journey: The World of Joseph Campbell*. New York: HarperCollins.

Deterding, Sebastian. 2009: "Henry Jenkins: Textuelles Wildern und Konvergenzkultur." In *Schlüsselwerke der Cultural Studies*, edited by Andreas Hepp, Friedrich Krotz, and Tanja Thomas, 235–234. Wiesbaden: Springer VS.

Deuber-Mankowsky, Astrid. 2005. *Lara Croft: Cyber Heroine*. Minneapolis: University of Minnesota Press.

Dittmar, Jakob. 2011. *Comic-Analyse*. Konstanz: UVK.

Fromme, Johannes. 2006. "Zwischen Immersion und Distanz: Lern- und Bildungspotenziale von Computerspielen." *In Clash of Realities: Computerspiele und soziale Wirklichkeit*, edited by Winfried Kaminski and Martin Lorber, 177–209. Munich: kopaed.

Fromme, Johannes, and Christopher Könitz. 2014. "Bildungspotenziale von Computerspielen: Überlegungen zur Analyse und bildungstheoretischen Einschätzung eines hybriden Medienphänomens." In *Perspektiven der Medienbildung*, edited by Winfried Marotzki and Norbert Meder, 235–286. Wiesbaden: Springer VS.

Gardner, James Alan. 2004. *Lara Croft: Tomb Raider: The Man of Bronze*. Los Angeles: Del Rey.

Holland, Charles, and Dwayne Turner. 2000a. *Dark Crossing #1: Dark Clouds Rising*. Los Angeles: Top Cow Productions.

Holland, Charles, and Dwayne Turner. 2000b. *Dark Crossing #2: Dark Clouds Overhead*. Los Angeles: Top Cow Productions.

Jenkins, Henry. 2006. *Convergence Culture: Where Old and New Media Collide*. New York: New York University Press.

Jenkins, Henry. 2010. "Transmedia Education: 7 Principles Revisited." *Confessions of an Aca-Fan*, 21 June. http://henryjenkins.org/blog/2010/06/transmedia_education_the_7_pri.html (accessed 31 January 2020).

Jörissen, Benjamin, and Winfried Marotzki. 2009. *Medienbildung: Eine Einführung: Theorie – Methoden – Analysen*. Bad Heilbrunn: Klinkhardt.

Jurgens, Dan, and Joe Jusko. 2005. *Tomb Raider: The Greatest Treasure of All*. Los Angeles: Top Cow Productions.

Juul, Jesper 2005. *Half-Real: Video Games between Real Rules and Fictional Worlds*. Cambridge, MA: MIT Press.

Kennedy, Helen W. 2002. "Lara Croft: Feminist Icon or Cyberbimbo? On the Limits of Textual Analysis." *Game Studies: The International Journal of Computer Game Research* 2 (2): n.p. http://gamestudies.org/0202/kennedy/ (accessed 31 January 2020).

Knight, E. E. 2004. *Lara Croft: Tomb Raider: The Lost Cult*. Los Angeles: Del Rey.

Krüger, Heinz-Hermann. 1999. "Entwicklungslinien, Forschungsfelder und Perspektiven der erziehungswissenschaflichen Biographieforschung." In *Handbuch erziehungswissenschaftliche Biographieforschung*, edited by Winfried Marotzki and Heinz-Hermann Krüger, 13–33. Wiesbaden: VS Verlag für Sozialwissenschaften.

Lara Croft and the Guardian of Light. 2010. Developed by Crystal Dynamics. Published by Square Enix. Windows.

Lara Croft and the Temple of Osiris. 2014. Developed by Crystal Dynamics. Published by Square Enix. Windows.

Lara Croft Go. 2015. Developed and published by Square Enix. iOS.

Lara Croft: Tomb Raider. 2001. Dir. Simon West. USA: Paramount Pictures.

Lara Croft: Tomb Raider: The Cradle of Life. 2003. Dir. Jan de Bont. USA: Paramount Pictures.

Marotzki, Winfried. 1999. "Forschungsmethoden und -methodologie der Erziehungswissenschaflichen Biographieforschung." In *Handbuch erziehungswissenschaftliche Biographieforschung*, edited by Winfried Marotzki and Heinz-Hermann Krüger, 111–135. Wiesbaden: VS Verlag für Sozialwissenschaften.

Marotzki, Winfried. 2004. "Bildung und Orientierung im Zeichen neuer Informationstechnologien oder: Warum Lara Croft eine kulturelle Ikone ist." In *Kontinuität, Krise und Zukunft der Bildung: Analysen und Perspektiven*, edited by Petra Korte, 363–379. Münster: LIT Verlag.

McCloud, Scott. 2005. *Understanding Comics: The Invisible Art*. New York: Harper Perennial.

Pratchett, Rhianna, and Andreas Mutti. 2013. *Tomb Raider: The Beginning*. Milwaukie: Dark Horse Comics.

Perry, S. D. 2018. *Shadow of the Tomb Raider: Path of the Apocalypse*. London: Titan Books.

Rauscher, Andreas 2012. *Spielerische Fiktionen: Transmediale Genrekonzepte in Videospielen*. Marburg: Schüren.

Resnick, Mike. 2003. *Lara Croft: Tomb Raider: The Amulet of Power*. Los Angeles: Del Rey.

Rieber, John N., and Randy Green. 2003a. *Tomb Raider #26: Abyss: Part 1*. Los Angeles: Top Cow Productions.

Rieber, John N., and Randy Green. 2003b. *Tomb Raider #27: Abyss: Part 2*. Los Angeles: Top Cow Productions.

Rieber, John N., and Randy Green. 2003c. *Tomb Raider #28: Abyss: Part 3*. Los Angeles: Top Cow Productions.

Rise of the Tomb Raider. 2015. Developed by Crystal Dynamics. Published by Square Enix. Windows.

Ryan, Marie-Laure. 2013. "Transmediales Storytelling und Transfiktionalität." In *Medien – Erzählen – Gesellschaft: Transmediales Erzählen im Zeitalter der Medienkonvergenz*, edited by Karl Renner, Dagmar von Hoff, and Matthias Krings, 88–117. Berlin: De Gruyter.

Shadow of the Tomb Raider. 2018. Developed by Crystal Dynamics. Published by Square Enix. Windows.

Silvestri, Marc, and Billy Tan. 2003. *EVO #1: Endgame: Part 3*. Los Angeles: Top Cow Productions.

Thon, Jan-Noël 2014. "Subjectivity across Media: On Transmedial Strategies of Subjective Representation in Contemporary Feature Films, Graphic Novels, and Computer Games." In *Storyworlds across Media: Toward a Media-Conscious Narratology*, edited by Marie-Laure Ryan and Jan-Noël Thon, 67–102. Lincoln: University of Nebraska Press.

Tomb Raider. 1996. Developed by Core Design. Published by Eidos Interactive. MS-DOS.

Tomb Raider. 2013. Developed by Crystal Dynamics. Published by Square Enix. Windows.

Tomb Raider. 2018. Dir. Roar Uthaug. USA: Warner Bros. Pictures.

Tomb Raider II. 1997. Developed by Core Design. Published by Eidos Interactive. Windows.

Tomb Raider III: Adventures of Lara Croft. 1998. Developed by Core Design. Published by Eidos Interactive. Windows.

Tomb Raider IV: The Last Revelation. 1999. Developed by Core Design. Published by Eidos Interactive.

Tomb Raider V: Chronicles. 2000. Developed by Core Design. Published by Eidos Interactive. Windows.

Tomb Raider: The Angel of Darkness. 2003. Developed by Core Design. Published by Eidos Interactive. Windows.

Tomb Raider: Anniversary. 2007. Developed by Crystal Dynamics. Published by Eidos Interactive. Windows.

Tomb Raider: Curse of the Sword. 2001. Developed by Core Design. Published by Activision. Game Boy Color.

Tomb Raider: Legend. 2006. Developed by Crystal Dynamics. Published by Eidos Interactive. Windows.

Tomb Raider: The Prophecy. 2002. Developed and published by Ubisoft. Game Boy Advance.

Tomb Raider: Underworld. 2008. Developed by Crystal Dynamics. Published by Eidos Interactive. Windows.

Turner, Michael. 1997. *Tomb Raider/Witchblade*. Los Angeles: Top Cow Productions.

Turner, Michael. 1998. *Witchblade/Tomb Raider*. Los Angeles: Top Cow Productions.

Turner, Michael. 2000. *Resurrection of Taras: Part 1*. Los Angeles: Top Cow Productions.

Turner, Michael. 2002a. *Resurrection of Taras: Part 2*. Los Angeles: Top Cow Productions.

Turner, Michael. 2002b. *Resurrection of Taras: Part 3*. Los Angeles: Top Cow Productions.

Turner, Michael. 2002c. *Tomb Raider #25: Endgame: Part 1*. Los Angeles: Top Cow Productions.

15 Beyond immersion

Gin Tama and palimpsestuous reception

Susana Tosca

In "Blue and Red Ecstasy" (2011), episode 224 of the *Gin Tama* anime series (2006–2018), the protagonists get ahold of a Blu-Ray player with a disc stuck in it. When they accidentally play it, the disc shows a grainy sequence of a well and a ghostly female figure that climbs out of it, reminiscent of the horror film *Ring* (1998). They understand that the disc is cursed and begin to panic when the figure tries to get out of the television and into their living room, but she is prevented from doing so because she is carrying a *kotatsu*[1] that is too big for the television frame. After having discussed whether they should help her get out or not, the ghost, who is called Bluerayko, clarifies that she does not want to do them any harm. In fact, she is an angel, and she asks them if they can spare her one channel of their TV to spend the night.

Gin Tama is often described in terms of transgression and disruption (Jones 2013; Lee 2011; Pusztai 2015; Unser-Schutz 2015). This short sequence thematizes some of its most typical humorous mechanisms, juxtaposing modes (comic and horror), ontological realms (diegetic and nondiegetic from within the story), gender tropes (the men want to destroy the television, the woman wants to help), times (the modern Blu-Ray and the old-fashioned *kotatsu*), and even our cultural expectations about media formats (VHS and Blu-Ray). With its mix of genres and styles, its acute intertextuality, and its metalepses in the form of regular breaches of the fourth wall, the *Gin Tama* universe would seem a prime candidate for a low sense of immersion as audiences struggle to make sense of the many disparate elements. However, *Gin Tama* audiences report high levels of engagement and enthusiasm for a world they experience as consistent and engrossing. But can fragmentation and immersion really coexist?

The concept of immersion in relation to new media practices has been popularized specially through Janet Murray's definition as "the physical experience of being submerged in water [...,] the sensation of being surrounded by a completely other reality [...] that takes over all our attention" (1998, 98). This idea of a text claiming our absolute attention is of course not exclusive to audiovisual or digital works, and we can certainly recognize it in relation to other activities, such as being engrossed in a novel, or even a more performative experience, such as playing a musical instrument. This perspective implies that distractive elements pull us out of the immersion. Consequently, the concept of immersion is very much opposed to that of metalepsis, defined by Werner Wolf as "a usually intentional paradoxical transgression of, or confusion between, (onto)logically distinct (sub)worlds and/or levels that exist, or are referred to, within representations of possible worlds" (2005, 91). That is, when metalepsis appears, it destroys immersion (Wolf 2005, 103).[2]

This is why academic discourses around metalepsis in contemporary media, including my own, have concentrated on its effect as a disruptive trope from a textual perspective (Carrasco Yelmo and Tosca 2016). However, this chapter argues that the ideal of seamless immersion cannot explain our current transmedial reception practices, which are fragmented yet allow for intense engagement. Indeed, the *Gin Tama* reception experience is a prime example of the kind of heightened meta-interpretive activity that audiences perform in their encounters with transmedial texts (Tosca and Klastrup 2016). This activity, far from being alienating, is experienced as agglutinating by the fans, as the analysis will show.

In sum, this chapter wants to frame transmedial reception practices in a different way. What if instead of talking about breaches and disruptions, we thought of juxtapositions as additions? What if audiences were able to sum instead of subtract, unite instead of separate? In this chapter, I read *Gin Tama* as an example of a complex (trans)text where juxtapositions are exacerbated and therefore become extremely visible. The aesthetic analysis is here supplemented with an audience's reception perspective based on a qualitative empirical collection method. Briefly, I have monitored and selected fan commentary from sites such as *YouTube*, *Reddit*, *Crunchyroll*, *MangaKakalot* and have followed fan sites and social media tags like #gintama, #gintamamovie, #yorozuya. Moreover, as part of a research project about anime nostalgia, four *Gin Tama* fans were interviewed in 2017. Building on the analysis, I will finally propose the concept of *palimpsestuous reception* to describe the audience activity related to the interpretation and appropriation of such a text. I argue that this concept contributes to illuminating an interesting aspect of the aesthetic potential of transmedial reception in general.

Gin Tama's transgressions

Gin Tama, created by Hideaki Sorachi in 2003, is a typical example of a media mix (Steinberg 2012), as transmedial universes are known in Japan. At its core there is a long-running manga series (2003–) that has given birth to several other connected media instantiations. These include the abovementioned anime series as well as films, videogames, a live-action movie, music CDs, light novels, guidebooks, and all sorts of merchandise. The manga series is extremely popular, both in Japan and abroad through its English translation (Valdez 2018). The other *Gin Tama* media products have also enjoyed both critical and audience acclaim, with the probable exception of the videogames, which have been criticized as less innovative and merely exploitative of the other products' success.[3]

The story features a lazy samurai called Gintoki Sakata, who lives in an alternative version of Edo-period[4] Japan where aliens (here called Amanto) have conquered the earth. The shōgun government, controlled by the invaders, has banned samurais and their weapons. Gintoki survives by doing "odd jobs" for whomever cares to hire him and his associates, a young aspiring samurai called Shinpachi, and Kagura, a supernaturally strong alien girl. Together they form the Yorozuya,[5] a failing business where they often struggle to make ends meet. Their missions are both adventurous and prosaic, as they are hired to find lost pets, rescue kidnapped people, fight terrorists, recover stolen items, or protect eccentric individuals, all while avoiding their angry landlady. The story is organized in narrative arcs of uneven length, with a string of a few episodes continuing the same plot, but also with plenty of "loose" stand-alone episodes. The *Gin Tama* universe includes parodic versions of many historical figures, like the shōgunate police force of the Shinsengumi (with legendary swordsmen Kondō, Hijikata, or Okita), or the revolutionaries Katsura and Takasugi, who here fight both the aliens and the corrupt Bakufu government. Gintoki and his associates often get mixed up with both the shōgunate and its terrorist enemies in a complicated series of confrontations and unlikely alliances.

From its inception, creator Hideaki Sorachi has positioned the *Gin Tama* transmedial universe within the comic mode, with a steady mix of parody and satire, as well as scatological and surreal humor. Comedy is notoriously difficult to define, due to its wide range of forms and its shape-shifting nature. I find Roston's idea of identifying it as a "mode" compelling because it allows for a lot of flexibility and variation across media and within the same work, even though his focus is on literary texts (Roston 2011, 1–36). For Roston, the essence of the comic mode is the "deflating of human pretensions" (2011, 8), which is attained through three major strategies: superiority, incongruity, and relief, all of which are very active in *Gin Tama*. To begin with, its very title demolishes any pretension of it taking itself seriously. *Gin Tama* means "silver soul," but it sounds dangerously close to *kintama*, or "golden balls," a slang word for testicles.[6] This bawdy wordplay sets the mood for a transgressive story romp that has charmed others beyond the original male teenage target audience,[7] including a significant female following (Lee 2011, 173). Linguistic puns abound because the number of phonemes of Japanese is small, and so there is a large amount of homonyms that can be confused and tossed against each other for comic effect (Jones 2013, 65). In fact, "much of the humour arises from repeated incongruities through script opposition—the juxtaposition of two or more concepts which, when combined, are humorous in their contradiction" (Jones 2013, 63). Jones detects it very clearly in the way that *Gin Tama*'s female characters are portrayed. Women make fun of men and are superior to them in all confrontations. Even in comedy situations, women play the straight man role (*tsukkomi*) and men the idiot (*boke*), which is a subversion of typical gender roles. The strong women of *Gin Tama* deviate from the modest and polite speech expected of Japanese women and don instead "rough, aggressive, 'masculine' speech" (Jones 2013, 67).

An abundance of incongruities like these is consistent with classic approaches to comedy as "a divided and double experience" (Stott 2005, 9), for when situations are changed and subverted, they do not disappear from the stage. "Even though comedy often seems to be suspending, inverting, or abandoning dominant norms, these inversions are produced in relation to the cultural orthodoxies from which they must always begin" (Stott 2005, 8). As an illustration of this, Gintoki's lazy attitude and love of sweets is funny because it evokes our schemata of what a heroic samurai should be like (brave, hard-working, stoic). This simultaneity, the normal and the deviant appearing together in our mind, is key to laughter. Humorous texts are about multiplicity, and they create in the spectator "a continual awareness of the possibility of reading a scenario in two different ways" (Stott 2005, 9). In *Gin Tama*, the humorous duplicity operates on many different levels, from the linguistic puns and gender roles mentioned above to overarching genre tropes, well-known plot devices, historical interpretations, and visual forms. In particular, the titles of the different episodes act as a strong framing device, pointing to the absurdities and contradictions of everyday life, often disguised in the lapidary style of ancient proverbs that imbues them with a sense of truth and carnival at the same time[8]:

- "You Always Remember the Things That Matter the Least"
- "Life Moves On Like a Conveyor Belt"
- "Mom's Busy, Too, So Quit Complaining about What's for Dinner"
- "Stress Makes You Bald, but It's Stressful to Avoid Stress, So You End Up Stressed Out Anyway, So, in the End, There's Nothing You Can Do"
- "People Who Give Good First Impressions Usually Suck"
- "So in the Second Season of Prison Break, They've Already Broken Out of Prison, but the Name Works Once You Realize That Society Is a Prison"
- "Life and Video Games Are Full of Bugs"
- "People Almost Always Fight on Trips"

Previous academic consideration of *Gin Tama* has identified its comic aspect as its most central characteristic, paying attention to the disruptiveness of the series in various ways, be it aesthetic, historical, social, or in relation to media mix industry practices (Jones 2013; Lee 2011; Pusztai, 2015; Unser-Schutz 2015). Both scholars and audiences point to the abundant breaches of the fourth wall as the most salient characteristic of the *Gin Tama* universe. Its attachment to metalepsis, understood as the transgression of boundaries within the fictional world (Kukkonen 2011, 3), manifests itself in different ways according to each platform and its specific affordances. In the manga, characters refer to the length of panel sequences, to how scenes or other characters are drawn, to sound effects, or to how many pages something has been going on for. Once in a while, they become aware of being fictional characters appearing in a weekly magazine, of the identity of their author, and of the fact that there is a reader looking at them, only to slip back into the fiction immediately after. There are also many intertextual references, with allusions to media personalities of contemporary Japan who might also appear directly as characters, or mentions of other media texts, like *One Piece* (1997–), *Dragon Ball* (1984–1995), Hayao Miyazaki's films, or other popular culture products that the *Gin Tama* characters know and to which they sometimes compare themselves.

In the anime series, there is less aesthetic play with its form as an animated movie, but it establishes more allusions to intertextuality, with some interesting self-reflection about its own nature as an adaptation, as noted by Beáta Pusztai (2015, 141). The films (both animated and live action) have a tradition of addressing the spectator, especially at the beginning, as a sort of frame for the story. For instance, the second of the live action films, *Gintama 2: Okite wa yaburu tame ni koso aru* (2018), starts with the characters talking about how the first film did and the fact that neither film or main actor won any awards, before warning each other that the audience is listening in on their conversation. The videogames are less keen on metalepses, although there are breaches of the fourth wall in some of them. In general, they are much less disruptive, as if the videogame medium did not lend itself too well to this kind of play. The latest of the games, *Gintama Rumble* (2018), is a rather monotonous hack 'n' slash that combines fighting with the reproduction of some of the story arcs from the anime. It follows a heroic structure that is at odds with the parodic vibe of the rest of the transmedia universe, but it incorporates a feature called the "Pachinko Requirement Slot." This feature activates at certain points and randomly gives players an advantage (like having more attack power), but it can also be disadvantageous, for example pixelating the screen for a while so the player cannot see what she is doing. In this way, the absurd spirit of the *Gin Tama* universe shatters the purposefulness of the ludic form. But how does all this manifest in the actual reception by audiences? How disruptive is *Gin Tama*?

Experiencing *Gin Tama*: "The Monty Python of anime"[9]

Overwhelmingly, audiences praise the unique setting, the original characters, and the crazy stories, as becomes evident in the forum discussions, the *Gin Tama*-related hashtags, *Facebook* groups, *YouTube* commentary, and my interviews. As in other fandoms, many *Gin Tama* fans are articulate about what they like and why, and in this case, they are very aware of the different kinds of fragmentation that exist in *Gin Tama*. As an example, here is a fan trying to argue for why the anime is worth watching, coming up with reasons to counteract a dismissive commentary. I have highlighted the sections of the quote that I will elaborate on below[10]:

> The fact is, this anime is **more than just a comedy/parody.** Many people drop this show in the early episodes bec it's too slow. It's a character-driven comedy episodic that is also formulaic in the early episodes, but **it has an underlying plot that will be revealed once you know the characters.** The early episodes are build-up to their character relationships and setting introduction. So Gintama has also a plot. The comedy is just there to know more about the characters. Also Gintama has all types of humour: crude like toilet humour, **4th wall breaking,** parody, satire, also some of the jokes are hard to understand because they're too Japanese (like wordplay). or about Jap pop culture. They're **naturally funny especially if you understand the references.** The action of this show is one of the best I've seen in any shonen. About the genre.. that's one of the reasons people love it because it's a masterful mix of comedy, drama, action, etc. **It has every genre in anime you can find.** Mainly it's a samurai historical that's also a sci-fi set in feudal Japan.[11]

This comment acknowledges the hybrid, chaotic nature of the fictional universe but frames it as a source of pleasure. I would like to use the fan's words as a blueprint to note some of the most appreciated aesthetic traits of this universe, since it encapsulates the most common themes that appeared in my analysis of social media commentary and interviews and also points to the challenges to immersion I mentioned in the introduction. The first trait is the fact that "it is more than just a comedy/parody." Many in the *Gin Tama* audience explicitly note its capacity to turn everything upside down, its carnivalesque strength that not only gives space to the coarse and the forbidden (bodily functions or sexuality) but also makes fun of official structures and points to their inherent contradictions. Structure here refers both to the storytelling tropes typical of the Japanese media mix ("You will find it funnier if you are a regular anime watcher as it likes to make fun of it, especially the cliched shounen tropes"[12]), social conventions ("even if you expect a character to act a certain way they turn it 360 and surprise you. A main plus in my book are the female characters—all strong, badass, self-reliant heroines, and no of the damsel in distress"[13]), or political systems ("so the Japanese government is really controlled by aliens and you can really see how fucked up everything is, just like we cannot do anything without the EU or the NATO or Google and Amazon and Jesus Christ and his mother"[14]). Bakhtinian carnival is not just about empty laughs, as Stott points out: "[T]he inversions and suspensions permitted and legitimized by carnival represent substantive challenges to authority, therefore offering the possibility that comedy [...] may also be an expression of popular discontent" (Stott 2005, 34). This is not to say that carnival is a revolutionary progressive force that can effectuate real changes in society, but its inversions make the underlying system visible, exposing its contradictions and incoherencies, foregrounding "the tensions and desires that are elided parts of the identity of power itself" (Stott 2005, 37). *Gin Tama* audiences are aware of the absurd aspects of contemporary life, especially of their own powerless position. As social media commentary and my interviews with people in their twenties and thirties show, *Gin Tama* masterfully illustrates their own situation, trapped in a string of badly paid precarious jobs despite having completed secondary educations: "Each episode/series of episodes is just them doing random jobs, with no real lasting consequences. It's kind of like a slice of life in that way."[15] The fact that Gintoki and his friends are always facing failure and ridicule but that they get up after every fall, no matter how grotesque, is seen as a life lesson by these fans.

The second trait is the heavy intertextuality, "naturally funny especially if you understand the references." Audiences seem to enjoy the extraordinary effort required to decode the many intertextual jokes, and they often use this as a reason to dismiss criticism: The conclusion seems to be that the people who don't find *Gin Tama* funny just haven't understood the jokes. At the same time, newcomers to the universe are often encouraged to relax, as it can also be enjoyed without identifying all the references. Nonetheless, intertextual interpretation is a valued skill in the *Gin Tama* community, with people showing off to each other and sometimes collectively interpreting obscure references to current Japanese media personalities, for example. Fan subbers will also often annotate their work, explaining the references to a Western audience, and there are a few very extensive *Gin Tama* reference compilations.[16] Being skilled at intertextual interpretation is a source of pride and pleasure, and it is obvious that decoding references is not only about being able to *read* a text but also feels like a sort of *writing* in Barthes's terms, as Capozzi (1989, 418) proposes. Weaving an overarching text together, made of other texts from within and without the franchise, is very much like building a gigantic puzzle that becomes heavy with meaning. Picking another line from the initial fan quote in this section, "It has every genre in anime you can find." As Umberto Eco said of *Casablanca*, which for him is not only a movie, but "the movies" (Capozzi 1989, 420), *Gin Tama* would not only be a manga or an anime, but "the manga" or "the anime," its intertextual exuberance including many other works, tropes, and structures that are recognized and actualized in surprising ways. Inside the *Gin Tama* universe, intertextuality is sometimes made fun of, thematized as the proof that something is wrong with the characters. For example, the so-called "Monkey Hunter" arc parodies the *Monster Hunter* series of videogames, ridiculing all sorts of videogame conventions: about gameplay, about the way game characters talk and interact, and about how taking videogame tropes seriously is a sign of immaturity and social awkwardness in general.

Gin Tama audiences are thus teased. On the one hand, their knowledge of popular culture provides them with pleasurable interpretation of abundant intertextual connections. On the other, they are mocked precisely because they possess extensive transmedial repertoires. In a way, it is as if enjoying the heavy intertextuality was proof of a fail of character, since the expected "normal" reaction would be to be put off by it. Fans tend to be aware of this, and some interpret it in relation to their own lives, embracing Sorachi's playful teasing: "Gintoki is an adult and he reads *Jump* and all the characters are always going on about other manga and anime, teasing each other about being childish. This is like me and my friends. Actually, it is a bit scary that we can identify all these crazy parodies. It means we have spent too much time fleeing reality. At my age my mother already had a baby and I am fooling around reading manga made for young boys and dressing up for cosplay parties. But it is so much fun!"[17] There is both pride and shame in acknowledgements like this because reception is not just about texts, it is also about us. As Jane Torr (2007) has noted in relation to children's literature, intertextual pleasures are both related to recognizing other texts (a semiotic pleasure) and to relating the current text to our own lives (an autobiographical pleasure). *Gin Tama*, as this fan quote eloquently demonstrates, offers both. The subjective dimension of the reception process also affects the possibility of immersion, which arises as something contextual, and certainly not universal or absolute, but a process shaped by those who take part in it: the text and the audience.

The *Gin Tama* fans I have studied love to be directly interpellated, even if it is to be made fun of, and to be reminded that they are watching a carefully constructed fiction. They don't perceive the breaches of the fourth wall as alienating, but as incorporating. An illustration of this can be a short sequence from anime episode 271, "Arriving Late to a Reunion Makes It Hard to Enter," where Katsura is pointing out to Gintoki how special it is that they are getting together in a touching reunion and how he should be overcome with joy, and Gintoki's reply is: "Like hell I'd feel any of that. I've had enough of seeing your mugs in the openings and endings. You show up every episode, even though you're irrelevant. I'm sick of it. Nobody needs any more merch of you morons." As Gintoki is speaking, the image shows figurines and other merchandise made of Katsura. Some fans celebrate this moment as the "killing of the 4th wall,"[18] and clips like this one are circulated and celebrated on fan sites as pleasurable snippets that remind audiences of why they enjoy this universe so much. Perhaps paradoxically, the audiences I have investigated think that *Gin Tama*'s pointing to its own artificiality as an aesthetic device is more honest than the attempts at immersion of other well-known transmedial entertainment universes ("obeying the 4th wall is for the people with no kintama").[19] They are able to accommodate the regular change of rhythm of a story that makes you "cry of laughter in one moment and in the next second I'm crying my heart out,"[20] as it alternates between metalepses and traditional storytelling. In this way, ontological instability becomes normalized and expected.

The popularity of the male characters as attractive men is another prominent aspect of the *Gin Tama* experience in the fan community. Many female fans think that Gintoki, Hijikata, Okita, Katsura, Takasugi, and many others are a pleasure for the eye, and most fan fiction writing revolves around the different kinds of "ships," or relationships, that can be imagined and written about, as the actual *Gin Tama* universe avoids the depiction of romantic relationships involving the main characters, even though there are plenty of crushes and love stories for secondary characters. There is a sensuality to the manga drawing style (reproduced in the anime and the live-action movies, with their cast of attractive young actors) that again stands in contrast to the predominant comedic mode. Beautiful men and (to a lesser extent) women characters often become ugly and twisted in their confrontations and action scenes, their bodies made fun of as they eat like pigs, pick their noses, are shown defecating, or naked in ridiculous situations.

To conclude this section about the *Gin Tama* experience, I want to reflect on a last aspect mentioned in the fan comment at the beginning of the section: its insistence (twice) that "it has an underlying plot" and that the characters are consistent. That is, no matter how many breaches and transgressions occur at other levels, these fans clearly perceive a stable core that gives the series its emotional appeal beyond the laughs and the outrage. In a transmedial world context, we would speak of a recognizable sense of *worldness*, made of a well-established *mythos*, *topos*, and *ethos* (Klastrup and Tosca 2004) respected across the whole franchise. The topos of the alien-invaded feudal Edo is absurd but memorable, and it provides all sorts of contrasts (for example of modern technology versus ancient customs) that are the source of unique plots and turns of events. The mythos of traditional Japan (in history and in legend) is overwritten with a science-fiction narrative that directly connects to events and conflicts in our own contemporary reality. The ethos of old samurai stories is transformed into a tale of survival and banality, as the main characters offer a philosophy of life that is both laughable and commendable, at times heroic in their insistence of living according to their own principles.

If we look at the *Gin Tama* universe with an exclusively textual interest, we will no doubt be mesmerized by its instability and tempted to classify all the possible ways in which it is a fragmented object. In this section, I instead attempt to adopt an experiential focus based on actual audiences in order to unpack the perceived essential coherence of the aesthetic reception of *Gin Tama*, which fans are able to appropriate and connect to their own lives. Analyzing the audience's commentary, the semantic realm of *Gin Tama* appears to be comfortably installed in the carnivalesque, the wacky, the chaotic, the infantile, the random. Audiences apparently experience this as liberating. In contrast to other entertainment products, *Gin Tama* does not attempt to hide what it is. On the surface, it appears as a validation of the otaku life, an indulgent romp of internal jokes and low humor. However, audiences point out that for them, it also symbolizes an alternative to heroic tales and other fictions aimed at anesthetizing us, making us into cogs in the machine. The resistance to narrative immersion exploited across all the media instantiations of the *Gin Tama* universe is perceived as helpful by the fans in order to resist immersion within a social system that is both arbitrary and unfair. Narrative immersion can be a dangerous anesthetic. Like other works in the comedic mode, *Gin Tama* offers "an imaginative exploration of alternative social formulations, and a recognition of lack in the 'realist structurings of experience' that usually represent it. Through joking, the joker appears to gain privileged insight beyond the social construct where its meanings are neither exhaustive nor absolute, but are simply choices" (Stott 2005, 11).

The palimpsest as an alternative reception metaphor

A simple conclusion to be extracted from this reading of *Gin Tama* is that the reception activity of keeping track of formal transgressions and semantic disturbances actually makes for an engrossing experience. In other words, while the ontology of the fictional world is disturbed in many different ways, audiences seem to still be immersed while engaging with the *Gin Tama* texts. How is this even possible? To answer this question, we must ask ourselves if immersion is a quality of the object (the text) or something else. As introduced above, Murray's (1998) definition of immersion as being pleasurably submerged in a fiction, with all our senses engaged (and therefore shutting the world outside), is an idea with a long history.

In her book *Narrative as Virtual Reality* (2001), Marie Laure Ryan traces the appeal of the concept of immersion in Virtual Reality to a series of historical literary concepts all related to the idea of being caught up in a story. Immersion is suspect in postmodern eyes, perhaps because it is taken as a sign of uncritical surrendering to entertainment products. However, the idea of immersion is also present in more phenomenological approaches to reading, taking their departure in Coleridge's notion of the suspension of disbelief, Walton's theory of fiction as a game of make-believe, or the area of possible worlds studies, preoccupied with the imaginative effort of recreating a coherent fictional world. Even though all these perspectives varyingly take the reader into account as an active creative subject, I argue that they are still mainly focused on the fictional text itself as the source of the aesthetic illusion that the reader is making an effort to actualize. In this perspective, immersion is about a fiction coherent and interesting enough that it allows us to forget reality for a while as we engage with it: reading novels for hours and skipping meals, binging on TV series, or pulling all-nighters while exploring our favorite multiplayer gameworld.

However, what the analysis of *Gin Tama* demonstrates is that in the process of engaging with the multiple/fragmented text, audiences reach a kind of flow, understood as a state of concentration and absorption in a process (Csíkszentmihályi 1990). So instead of immersion, which is linked to a text, a product, we should instead find a way to describe this process. In a text like *Gin Tama*, the flow comes from actualizing all the disparate elements, from weaving them together in a *writerly* way, not despite the "interruptions" but because of them. This perspective is also useful to explain processes of transmedial reception, where the immersion perspective falls short because transmedial reception is always multiple by definition, even when we are only engaged with a single instantiation of a transmedial universe (Tosca and Klastrup 2019). While watching the *Gin Tama* action movie, we cannot keep the manga or the anime out of our consciousness, since it is constantly referring to them, calling them forth in our imagination. We cannot keep the world at bay either, since the characters are talking to us as spectators and reminding us that there are such things as film prizes and festivals, an industrial system of entertainment that produces the fiction with which we are engaging. Immersion in the sense described at the beginning of this chapter seems impossible.

So, let us assume for a moment that we do not care about the immersive quality of the fictional experience. Let us instead adopt Wolfgang Iser's view on the fictive imagination as "an operational mode of consciousness that makes inroads into existing versions of the world. In this way, the fictive becomes an act of boundary-crossing which, nonetheless, keeps in view what has been overstepped. As a result, the fictive simultaneously disrupts and doubles the referential world" (Iser 1993, xiv–xv). Indeed, connectivity not only occurs from text to text, but also between texts and other aspects of the real world about which audiences know, such as the media system in general, their everyday lives, or even autobiographical topics. If a consciousness of boundary-crossing is not detrimental to our aesthetic experience, other metaphors might heuristically be more helpful than that of being submerged in water and isolated from the world around us. What could express the juxtaposition of several simultaneous levels at the core of a transmedia reception experience?

It is here that I would propose the metaphor of the palimpsest, inspired by the work of Monica Kjellman-Chapin (2006) and Sarah Dillon (2007). A palimpsest is a writing material (for example paper or a scroll) that has been used more than once, and where the current text shows traces of the old writing. The word palimpsest is also sometimes applied to refer to writing in the margins, like the medieval marginalia of illuminated manuscripts. In palimpsests, then, several texts appear side by side, their boundaries clear but at the same time affecting each other. Kjellman-Chapin investigates the aesthetic strategies of collage, assemblage, and pastiche as a "family of palimpsestic modes" (2006, 97). They share the characteristic of allowing different materials or fragments to appear side by side to create a new work, even though they are different in their materiality and techniques. The palimpsest originates in the visual medium but can be expressed in many ways, and I also think that it can be applied to the textual medium, to make intertextuality more visible and inescapable. This is in line with

Dillon, who defines the palimpsest as "an involuted phenomenon where otherwise unrelated texts are involved and entangled, intricately interwoven, interrupting and inhabiting each other" (2007, 4). She proposes the adjective "palimpsestuous" (Dillon 2007, 4) as the result of that process.

I first came to think of a palimpsest in relation to *Gin Tama* while analyzing the audience's responses, as I organized codes and keywords in neat post-it pairs that always turned up together: feudal-modern, high tech-tradition, samurai-otaku... My double codes reminded me strongly of the paintings of Akira Yamaguchi, where Edo period officials sit inside planes or modern skyscrapers, tradition and modernity side by side, exposing each other's contradictions. Yamaguchi's focus is on juxtaposition, on sprawling scenes that give an impression of chaos and order at the same time. In *Gin Tama*, reception is always about multiplicity, about decoding several things at the same time, some in the foreground and others in the background, some intradiegetic and some extradiegetic. Like other transmedia universes, *Gin Tama* is a palimpsest of modes, texts, and media, probably more fragmented than many, which admittedly helps making the parts more visible. And if *Gin Tama* is a palimpsest, then we do not need to forget boundaries and shut the world out when interacting with it. Fiction, as Iser says, simultaneously disrupts and doubles the referential world. We can engage in highly intensive meta-interpretive activities and still be engrossed in a process of flow where unity and coherence are not at the level of the fictional world or the story itself, but at the level of the decoding experience.

The shadow of Bakhtin hovers over this chapter without my having engaged his work directly. Bakhtin pointed out that the perfect polyphonic genre (another form of multiplicity) was the novel, but I would now venture that transmedia universes such as *Gin Tama* are the perfect vehicle for hybridization, palimpsests where "many other texts merge, fuse, collide, intersect, speak to, and illuminate, one another—each with its own language and 'ideologue' " (Capozzi 1989, 413).

Notes

1 A low wooden table covered with a blanket and an attached heat source.

2 In later work, Wolf has admitted that certain kinds of works can include metalepses and still be immersive, namely "in cases where the text provides plausible (if physically impossible) explanations for the metalepsis in combination with a strong emotionality and possibly also specific generic frames" (2013, 127). One of his examples is *The Purple Rose of Cairo* (1985), a Woody Allen film in which a character comes out of the film screen and relates to flesh and blood characters. The metalepsis is thematized and becomes a part of the film's premise.

3 For a fan-made visual history of all the *Gintama* games, see BlaGeEvo 2018. Media and fan reviews often note how the games are derivative and do not bring a lot of new value to the franchise. See for example Husin 2018 for a review of the latest game, *Gintama Rumble*.

4 The Edo feudal period in Japan extended from 1603 to 1868. The government was based in the city of Edo (modern Tokyo) with the Tokugawa Shōgunate (also known as Bakufu). The emperor in Kyoto held no real power and was more of a symbolic and religious figure. This era is characterized by isolationist policies and a stable social order.

5 It can be translated as "the anything store."

6 These two near homonyms are written very differently, but sound very alike. "Silver soul" is written as 銀魂, and pronounced "gintama"; golden balls is pronounced "kintama" and written as 金玉.

7 Gin Tama belongs to the so-called shōnen genre, which caters to young men but is also read by other demographics. The serial magazine where it is published is tellingly called *Shūkan shōnen janpu* (Weekly Boys Jump), by Shueisha.

8 This device seems to be particularly appreciated by fans, since it is very extensively imitated in the fan fiction writing that can be found in sites such as *Archive of Our Own*. As one of the fans I talked to pointed out: "[I]t is just like my everyday banal life, and yet it is funnier. I am already laughing aloud when I see the titles."

9 Commentary from *Crunchyroll* forum, by user Felstalker on 9 June 2013: www.crunchyroll.com/forumtopic-819825/what-is-so-great-about-gintama (accessed 31 January 2020).

10 Due to the many mistakes in this passage, I refrain from using "[*sic*]" to indicate each individual mistake. I am citing the passage without any editorial corrections.

11 Commentary from *YouTube* discussion to the video "Top 7 Funny Dirty Jokes in Gintama," by user Hanameko (はなめこ), dated as "1 year ago" on 1 May 2019: www.youtube.com/watch?v=cb50TOXp-a4 (accessed 1 May 2019).

12 Commentary from Quora forum, by user Nihar Sawant on 5 June 2017: www.quora.com/Is-Gin-Tama-a-good-anime-series (accessed 31 January 2020).

13 Commentary from *Crunchyroll* forum, by user sally55510 on 9 June 2013: www.crunchyroll.com/forumtopic-819825/what-is-so-great-about-gintama (accessed 31 January 2020).

14 Quote from an interview with a 32-year-old male Spanish *Gin Tama* fan on 15 November 2017.

15 Commentary from *Reddit* thread, by user Speedy_Pineapple identified as "1 year ago" on 1 May 2019: www.reddit.com/r/anime/comments/6d7pj3/is_gintama_really_that_good/ (accessed 1 May 2019).

16 See, for instance, https://gintama.fandom.com/wiki/Parodies (accessed 31 January 2020), https://tvtropes.org/pmwiki/pmwiki.php/ShoutOut/Gintama (accessed 31 January 2020), and https://angry-gorilla.tumblr.com/post/116304934712/all-gintama-references-parodies (accessed 31 January 2020).

17 Quote from an interview with a 28-year-old female Spanish *Gin Tama* fan on 2 December 2017.

18 *Reddit* discussion dated as "1 year ago" on 1 May 2019 in: www.reddit.com/r/anime/comments/6r50bf/rip_4th_wall_gintama/ (accessed 1 May 2019).

19 *Reddit* discussion dated as "1 year ago" on 1 May 2019 in: www.reddit.com/r/anime/comments/6r50bf/rip_4th_wall_gintama/ (accessed 1 May 2019).

20 Commentary from *Crunchy Roll* forum www.crunchyroll.com/forumtopic-819825/what-is-so-great-about-gintama#44289301 (accessed 31 January 2020).

Works cited

Allen, Graham. 2000. *Intertextuality*. Abingdon: Routledge.

BlaGeEvo. 2018. *YouTube*, 24 November. www.youtube.com/watch?time_continue=34&v=BVjrV0pnbt8&feature=emb_logo (accessed 31 January 2020).

Capozzi, Rocco. 1989. "Palimpsests and Laughter: The Dialogical Pleasure of Unlimited Intertextuality in *The Name of the Rose*." *Italica* 66 (4): 412–428.

Carrasco Yelmo, Silviano, and Susana Tosca. 2016. "Meta-Literacy in Gameworlds." *Anàlisi: Quaderns de Comunicació i Cultura* 55: 31–47.

Csíkszentmihályi, Mihaly. 1990. *Flow: The Psychology of Optimal Experience*. New York: Harper Perennial.

Dillon, Sarah. 2007. *The Palimpsest: Literature, Criticism, Theory*. London: Continuum.

Gintama 2: Okite wa yaburu tame ni koso aru. 2018. Dir. Yuichi Fukuda. Japan: Warner Bros. Pictures.

Gintama Rumble. 2018. Developed by Tamsoft. Published by Bandai Namco. PlayStation 4.

Husin, Salehuddin. 2018. "Review: *Gintama Rumble* (PS4) Is a Wild Mash-Up of the Anime and *Dynasty Warriors*." *GameAxis*, 25 January. www.gameaxis.com/reviews/gintama-rumble-ps4/ (accessed 31 January 2020).

Iser, Wolfgang. 1993. *The Fictive and the Imaginary: Charting Literary Anthropology*. Baltimore: Johns Hopkins University Press.

Jones, Hattie. 2013. "Sex, Love, Comedy and Crime in Recent Boys' Anime and Manga." In *Manga Girl Seeks Herbivore Boy: Studying Japanese Gender at Cambridge*, Brigitte Steger and Angelika Koch, 23–81. Berlin: LIT Verlag.

Kjellman-Chapin, Monica. 2006. "Traces, Layers and Palimpsests: The Dialogics of Collage and Pastiche." *Konsthistorisk Tidskrift* 75 (2): 86–99.

Klastrup, Lisbeth, and Susana Tosca. 2004. "Transmedial Worlds—Rethinking Cyberworld Design." *CW '04: Proceedings of the 2004 International Conference on Cyberworlds*: 409–416. https://dl.acm.org/doi/10.1109/CW.2004.67 (accessed 31 January 2020).

Kukkonen, Karin. 2011. "Metalepsis in Popular Culture: An Introduction." In *Metalepsis in Popular Culture*, edited by Karin Kukkonen and Sonja Klimek, 1–21. Berlin: De Gruyter.

Lee, Rosa. 2011. "Romanticising Shinsengumi in Contemporary Japan." *New Voices* 4: 168–187.

Murray, Janet H. 1998. *Hamlet on the Holodeck: The Future of Narrative in Cyberspace*. Cambridge, MA: MIT Press.

The Purple Rose of Cairo. 1985. Dir. Woody Allen. USA: Orion Pictures.

Pusztai, Beáta. 2015. "Adapting the Medium: Dynamics of Intermedial Adaptation in Contemporary Japanese Popular Visual Culture." *Acta Universitatis Sapientiae, Film and Media Studies* 10: 141–152.

Ring. 1998. Dir. Hideo Nakata. Japan: Toho.

Roston, Murray. 2011. *The Comic Mode in English Literature: From the Middle Ages to Today*. London: Continuum.

Ryan, Marie-Laure. 2001. *Narrative as Virtual Reality: Immersion and Interactivity in Literature and Electronic Media*. Baltimore: Johns Hopkins University Press.

Steinberg, Mark. 2012. *Anime's Media Mix: Franchising Toys and Characters in Japan*. Minneapolis: University of Minnesota Press.

Stott, Andrew. 2005. *Comedy*. Abingdon: Routledge.

Torr, Jane. 2007. "The Pleasure of Recognition: Intertextuality in the Talk of Preschoolers during Shared Reading with Mothers and Teachers." *Early Years* 27 (1): 77–91.

Tosca, Susana, and Lisbeth Klastrup. 2016. "The Networked Reception of Transmedial Universes: An Experience-Centered Approach." *MedieKultur: Journal of Media and Communication Research* 32 (60): 107–122.

Tosca, Susana, and Lisbeth Klastrup. 2019. *Transmedial Worlds in Everyday Life: Networked Reception, Social Media and Fictional Worlds*. New York: Routledge.

Unser-Schutz, Giancarla. 2015. "What Text Can Tell Us about Male and Female Characters in Shōjo-and Shōnen-Manga." *East Asian Journal of Popular Culture* 1 (1): 133–153.

Valdez, Nick. 2018. "'Gintama' Manga Hits New Sales Record." *Comicbook.com*, 6 February. https://comicbook.com/anime/2018/02/07/gintama-manga-sales-record-55-million/ (accessed 31 January 2020).

Wolf, Werner. 2005. "Metalepsis as a Transgeneric and Transmedial Phenomenon: A Case Study of the Possibilities of 'Exporting' Narratological Concepts." In *Narratology beyond Literary Criticism: Mediality, Disciplinarity*, edited by Jan Christoph Meister, 83–107. Berlin: De Gruyter.

Wolf, Werner. 2013. "'Unnatural' Metalepsis and Immersion: Necessarily Incompatible?" In *A Poetics of Unnatural Narrative*, edited by Jan Alber, Henrik Skov Nielsen, and Brian Richardson, 94–141. Ohio: Ohio State University Press.

Index